LIVING IN TWO CULTURES

32.50

The views put forward in this volume, the selection of facts and the way in which they are interpreted are entirely the responsibility of the authors and do not necessarily reflect the opinion of Unesco.

Living in Two Cultures

**The socio-cultural situation
of migrant workers
and their families**

Gower

The Unesco Press

First published 1982

by the United Nations Educational, Scientific and Cultural Organization, 7 Place de Fontenoy, 75700 Paris, France

and Gower Publishing Company Limited,
Gower House, Croft Road, Aldershot, GU11 3HR, England

British Library Cataloguing in Publication Data

Living in two cultures.
1. Migrant labor
I. Unesco. *Division for the Study of Development*

305.5'6   HD5855

Gower ISBN 0-566-00459-3
Unesco ISBN 92-3-101869-8

Printed and bound in Great Britain by
Biddles Ltd, Guildford and King's Lynn

Contents

Epilogue. Living in two cultures: some sociological considerations
Dean Harper

Tables

Contributors

Sossie Andizian   Diploma in Advanced Studies (DEA), The Institute of Studies and Interethnic and Intercultural Research (CAFRI), University of Nice, France. Research Assistant at the National Centre for Scientific Research (CNRS), Paris.

Maurizio Catani   Doctorate (3rd cycle) in Sociology, René Descartes University, Paris V. Researcher at the National Centre for Scientific Research (CNRS), Paris.

Aaron Cicourel   Ph.D., Sociology, Cornell University, USA. Professor of Sociology, University of California.

Norbert Dittmar   Ph.D., Socio-linguistics, University of Konstanz, FRG. Professor of Linguistics, Department of German, Free University of Berlin, FRG.

Dean Harper   Ph.D., Sociology, Columbia University, USA. Professor of Sociology in the Department of Sociology and Associate Professor of Psychiatry in the Department of Psychiatry of the University of Rochester, USA.

Ayse Kudat

Ph.D., Anthropology, Princeton University, USA. Project Consultant, c/o DANIDA (Danish International Development Agency) Ministry of Transport and Communication, Nairobi, Kenya.

Mirjana Morokvasic

Doctorate (3rd cycle) in Sociology, René Descartes University, Paris V, Researcher at the National Centre for Scientific Research (CNRS), Paris.

Michel Oriol

Agrégé de Philosophie de l'Ecole Normale Supérieure de St. Cloud, France. Director of the Institute of Studies and Interethnic and Intercultural Research, (CAFRI), University of Nice, France.

Ronald G. Parris

Ph.D., Sociology, Yale University, USA. Programme Specialist, Division for the Study of Development, Unesco, Paris.

Jocelyne Streiff

Master's Degree in Sociology, University of Nice, France. Researcher at the National Centre for Scientific Research (CNRS), Paris.

Carolyn Swetland

Ph.D., Sociology, Columbia University, NY, USA. Director, Research Team, Ministry of Education, Norway.

Preface

As part of its social science programme on the appreciation and respect for cultural identity and within the theme of recognition of cultural pluralism and respect for the identity of minorities, Unesco organised a symposium at the University of Heidelberg (Federal Republic of Germany) from 23 to 27 May 1978. The purpose of this meeting was to evaluate for publication a number of research studies commissioned by the Secretariat during 1976-77 on the social and cultural problems of migrant workers and their families in Europe, especially as regards programmes for their education and training. The experts were also expected to offer recommendations, on the basis of the research results, for improving the situation of migrant workers.

The present volume contains those studies on migrant workers in Europe as selected for publication by the specialists who attended the symposium, and a study conducted during 1979-80 on the socio-cultural situation of migrants in the USA. These studies are intended to raise questions and point the way to useful areas of policy and further research and do not present a definitive ethnographic picture of the socio-cultural situation of migrant workers and their families. Critical evaluation of any of these contributions should therefore bear these modest objectives in mind.

The general theme of the book is the dilemmas faced by migrant workers in having to live in two cultures that are only marginally integrated. To the extent that these cultural models conflict or diverge, the migrant worker either loses himself between them or is forced to adapt by adopting one or the other. The migrant position is therefore one of 'continual strain between the old self and the new' — a condition of 'betwixt and between' in which these dilemmas are reflected in identity problems, alienation and tension. A basic ambivalence exists between the requirements of accommodating, if not assimilating the rules and laws of the country of employment, while at the same time trying to avert the discrimination that accompanies too great a demand on the status system of the dominant group (Cicourel, Chapter 1). The presence of migrants in the USA and elsewhere can, according to Cicourel, modify and threaten the stratification system of the country of employment, and it is the stratification practices directed against migrants in the various aspects of their everyday life that highlight this basic contradiction and pose serious problems in the areas of education, work and leisure both for the society of employment and for the migrants themselves. Cicourel focuses on the problem for the USA and indirectly discusses European conditions. Three other studies by Norbert Dittmar, formerly of the University of Heidelberg (Chapter 3), Maurizio Catani of the French National Centre for Scientific Research (CNRS) (Chapter 4), and Carolyn Swetland, former professor of Anthropology at the University of Panama (Chapter 2), make up Part I and focus particularly on the conditions, nature and effects of official language training programmes for migrant workers and their families in Europe. They also point to the various stratification practices, barriers and strategies that ensure the relative failures of the migrants, while maintaining a steady flow of cheap labour for the land and factories of Western Europe. The three case studies in Europe are followed by a joint commentary by these authors on the theoretical and methodological convergence and significance of their work.

The three studies in Part II, by Morokvasic, Kudat, and Andizian and Streiff (Chapters 7, 8 and 9), are concerned in a greater degree than those in Part I with the particular problems faced by female migrants and how the characteristics of the old culture facilitate or aggravate their adaptation to the requirements of the new in the face of the double burden of stratification in terms of their status both as migrants and as women. Not only do female migrants live in two cultures, but they are faced with the particular social and cultural burdens associated with their sex in their countries of origin and elaborated in varying if more subtle ways in their countries of employment. How then do female migrants transpose and reinterpret their traditional role in an immigration situation? Such basic issues are posed in a concise introduction (Chapter 6) to this part of the book by Michel Oriol of the University of Nice (France) who was commissioned by Unesco to coordinate a series of studies on female migrants in Europe of which the three presented here form a part. The introduction to this volume is written by Ronald G. Parris who examines and highlights some of the main issues raised by these authors. The epilogue is by Dean Harper of the University of Rochester, who also contributed to the editing of the studies.

On the whole, the fundamental questions of the studies, both in Part I and Part II are the same: How is everyday life in the countries of employment being managed by migrant workers and what are the particular problems of adaptation posed by having to live in or between two cultures; what are the daily stratificational practices and social controls that migrants encounter in the institutional areas of work, education, and leisure and how is the stratification system likely to be affected by their presence? These are questions that deserve the attention both of the general public and policy makers in the various countries of in-migration, the countries of origin, and above all, of the migrants themselves.

Ronald G. Parris
January 1981

General introduction
RONALD G. PARRIS

This introductory chapter is an attempt to summarise and highlight some of the main theoretical and substantive issues arising from the analyses which follow. Such an objective is complementary to the joint theoretical and methodological commentary in Part I presented by three research specialists on the European situation. This introduction starts with a review of how the migrant question in general has been approached within the context of Unesco's programmes.

Unesco's activities on migrant workers

The studies in this volume constitute part of the more recent activities of Unesco related to migrant workers. The interest of the Organisation in the general problems of migration goes back to the early phase of its social science programme. Although preoccupied by the problems related to postwar reconstruction, such as the 'tensions' project on the study of the psychological and sociological impediments to international understanding and cooperation, and the 'ways of life' series of studies on different countries, the Unesco Secretariat began as early as 1949 to give attention to the problems of the cultural assimilation of immigrants (see, e.g. Sauvy, 1957, Barrie, 1954 and 1958).

Within the context of increasing interest in questions of development, and a new international order, this concern with the problems of migration has been sustained; and given the present worldwide problem of migrants and refugees such interest is likely to continue. During the

1

early 1970s, the focus was on problems of cultural integration and training of young migrants, which were the subject of an international seminar in December 1972 organised by the German Commission for Unesco, with financial support from the Organisation. A series of studies on the social, cultural and educational conditions and needs of young migrant workers in several countries was also commissioned by the Youth Division in Unesco's Sector of Social Sciences and their Applications. These studies formed the basis of the consolidated report by de Montvalon (1976). Moreover, Unesco participated in the working parties of the committee of senior officials of the Council of Europe, which met in 1972 and 1973, with the aim of preparing an *ad hoc* conference in 1974 on the problems of the education of adult migrants and their children; it was also represented at the international colloquium on the children of migrant workers organised in March 1973 by the International Children's Centre, Paris.

The continuing importance the Organisation attaches to the education of migrant workers and their children was expressed in Resolutions 1.141 and 1.142 adopted by the General Conference at its seventeenth session (Paris, 1972). The first resolution (1.141) invited member states to take concrete measures to facilitate equality of access to education and of educational opportunity for foreign migrant workers and their children, and to improve their education. The second resolution (1.142) authorised the Director-General to seek extra-budgetary resources for assisting member states to take concrete measures to facilitate equality of education and opportunity for migrant workers and their children and to improve that education, their mother tongue being used in it as far as possible.

To explore these issues further, the Secretariat organised a consultative meeting of experts from 22 to 26 October 1973 at headquarters. Some six studies on the educational problems of migrant workers and their families in the Netherlands, France, Switzerland and the Federal Republic of Germany formed the basis of the discussion. Some of the proposals arising out of this meeting related to the need for increasing public awareness in countries of employment of the national cultures of immigrant groups; aiding the adaptation of the immigrant family to its new surroundings; educating and providing vocational training for both female and male adult workers and the schooling of the children in their native language and culture; arranging in the countries of origin for the reintegration of returning workers and their families.

Other activities undertaken since 1973 included the organisation by Unesco, in cooperation with the Swiss National Commission, of an international seminar in Geneva, Switzerland, from 26 to 30 April 1976, the purpose of which was to identify the problems encountered by migrants in adapting to the country of employment and in readapting on return to their country of origin, particularly as regards teaching the children of migrants their mother tongue and the language of the host country to the migrants themselves. The conclusions and recommendations of this seminar formed the basis of discussion at a meeting of experts on the planning and administration of education for migrant workers and their families, organised by Unesco from 13 to 17 December 1976 at headquarters. The principle that migration, originally viewed primarily as a labour problem, should be given recognition in its full political, demographic, social and cultural implications was endorsed, and it was recommended that states should implement an overall policy such that the choice of appropriate measures in the political, economic, legal and educational field might lead to the definition of a genuine charter for immigrants. The bases upon which such a charter could be established can be found in the principle of equality of treatment with the local inhabitants, but with the recognition of the validity of making particular distinctions where specific needs exist, the institutionalisation of close collaboration between countries and communities and associations concerned with migration, and the formation of the cultural identity of individuals and groups as a right.

During 1976-1977, the Social Sciences Sector (Division of Human Rights) carried out programmes related to questions on the cultural identity, education and social mobility of immigrants, by sponsoring a number of studies concerning the impact of migration on the social structures of selected countries of Europe. Of particular interest was the impact of such migration on ethnic group relations. In addition, studies were initiated by the population division on the patterns and consequences of emigration from rural areas of Africa, Asia and Latin America, and surveys were conducted on the mechanisms of adjustment, integration and assimilation in three capital cities in these countries. A symposium was also organised to evaluate trends in internal migration and related policy issues in developing countries.

The socio-cultural situation of migrant workers

The symposium at the University of Heidelberg (23 to 27 May 1978) on the socio-cultural aspects of programmes of education and training for migrant workers and their families thus formed part of the series of activities outlined above, which Unesco undertook to implement Resolution 1.142. The latter resolution was adopted by the General Conference at its seventeenth session in 1972, and called upon Unesco to launch a specific programme of action on behalf of foreign migrant workers and their children. The studies commissioned and discussed at the Heidelberg meeting as well as the research conducted on the socio-cultural situation of migrants in the USA fall, in terms of their

3

emphases, into two though not exclusive categories — one concerned with issues related to the education and language training programmes for migrant workers and their families; and the other dealing with the particular socio-cultural problems of female migrants in the countries of employment or residence. The basic question, however, in all the studies making up this volume is how are migrant workers and their families managing the social and cultural aspects of their everyday realities in the countries of employment, and what are the particular adaptive problems of their having to live in two cultures? Focus is on the daily stratificational practices and social controls that migrants encounter in the institutional areas of their work, education and leisure.

Living in or between two cultures

One general characteristic of the situation of migrant workers whether in the USA or Europe is what Cicourel describes as the condition of having to live in two cultures, with the resultant strain between the old self and the new, manifested in problems of identity, social ambivalence, alienation and rejection. The migrant worker is in what Swetland calls a 'no man's land, which is neither that of his country of origin nor that of his country of employment or residence' (Chapter 2). Catani finds what he calls a state of 'affective solitude' among female migrants in France correlated with the destructuring of the family group, an impact on the family structure of migrants not unlike that identifiable for a certain segment of the black population in the USA. In addition, the migrant worker is subjected, according to Catani, to work structures sufficiently paternalistic to confirm him in this situation. On the whole, his existence is organised around two poles: his family and fellow countrymen, in a cultural environment resembling that of the country of origin; and his work and public life, in a culture unfamiliar to him or her. This cultural dichotomy or divergence is seen as being most explicitly expressed in the gradual acquisition by the migrant of two autonomous language tools: his mother tongue which primarily serves him for private use with family and friends; and a specialised administrative language of the country of employment, which for the migrant is devoid of affective connotation and has essentially a passive and public function. The consequence of such institutionalised separation between a *language of power* and a *language of affect* is the tendency to impose on the foreign worker a division of his daily life into two disconnected universes: the universe of work and the cultural ghetto:

> Integrated with production, he is excluded in reality from social life: a worker but not a citizen . . ... Excluded, marginal, different, the foreign worker creates in return, by his mere presence — the sole affirmation of this difference — a

disturbing factor of the ideological comfort of the society of production.

In the case of the Federal Republic of Germany, Dittmar (Chapter 5) also describes a similar situation of alienation and isolation; of migrant workers being 'torn' from the security of family and friends in a rural area or small town, without the preparation to manage effectively the conditions of production or existence in large industrialised cities.

Whether for the USA, Norway, France or the Federal Republic of Germany, there is therefore general agreement that the cultural alienation, isolation and ambivalence that the migrant encounters in his everyday life in the country of employment forces him to live in two cultures and social universes that are generally disconnected and conflictual.

Whether or not this 'no man's land' of cultural hybridism leads the migrant to greater secularisation of his relations in which he is less dependent on others and more assimilated to indigenous social structures is finally answerable only after an empirical analysis of the range of his responses to the situation he actually confronts in the country of employment.

Structural factors in migration. On the whole, these studies reach for a general explanation of the situation of migrant workers in a theory of economic exploitation. Migrants sell their labour power abroad in order to provide for their subsistence and constitute a 'contingency buffer and reserve army for industry' because of the national and international effects of monopoly capitalism and the international division of labour (Dittmar, Chapter 5). The reproduction costs of the labour force in the capitalist system are viewed by Cicourel (Chapter 1) as a serious related issue. He compares the various costs borne by the countries that send temporary migrants with the costs of maintaining such workers in the countries of employment. For Swetland, the migrant labourer as a person has 'zero exchange value', though he is valued by capital for the surplus value his labour generates. The general recognition is that the reproduction costs of migrant labour are lower than those of indigenous workers, thus resulting in lower costs of social reproduction of the labour force as a whole and a higher overall rate of profit. Simultaneously, the migrant labourer, generally unorganised politically and of vulnerable legal status, is subjected to the full weight of the social controls of the legal and political state apparatus, functioning in the service of capital.

In this context, Catani (Chapter 4) clearly points out that such national and international economic and political factors, analytically outside the realm of education, contradict the stated official goals of training programmes for migrant workers and their families.

In short, while the studies in Part I do not spell out the causal factors behind the migratory flows and the socio-cultural conditions encountered by migrant workers and their families, they all take as a point of departure the basic international economic and political relationships generating these flows and largely responsible for the conditions of migrant workers in the western industrialised countries. This is clearly emphasised in the joint theoretical statement of three of the authors. One basic consideration is the uneven development among countries, regions and economic sectors, that tends to become structural and cumulative. A second basic set of factors has to do with the internal dynamics of the particular countries of migrant employment, including the search by capital for surplus value, differential productivity and levels of wages, as well as the structural unemployment in some sectors.

The contributions in this volume are not, however, aimed at a detailed analysis of the economic and political conditions of migrant exploitation, but more at the socio-cultural realities of his everyday life. Yet in each analysis, an explanation of the conditions of his everyday life is considered incomplete without recognition of the significant role that such economic and political relationships play in his socio-cultural experience, including the organisation of his education and training. The analysis by Catani confronts the intimate interrelationship of these factors and leads him to question most directly the functions and effects of the training programmes themselves. Their function, according to him, is to socialise the foreign migrant to the basic features of modernity and to an ethic of individualism at variance with the original system of symbolic references. Given the difficulty of influencing through training programmes the interrelated and complex situation in which the migrant finds himself, Catani concludes that one of the particular consequences of such programmes is to have him 'interiorise the individualisation of failure' and as such, these programmes are but a diversionary tactic.

A similar logic underlies Cicourel's insistence that a concern with the education and training of the migrant worker must be articulated with his labour or employment. It is for him insufficient just to study language or training programmes without any relation to the class stratification system of the country of employment. It is necessary to examine the effects of his presence on that system and the stratificational practices that are employed to keep him in a state of domination and cultural limbo.

In this respect, Cicourel points to the long-run effects of these stratificational practices not only on the migrant worker but on the stratificational system itself in the creation of a sub-stratum and the potential for political and social violence. The study of migrant workers for Cicourel therefore becomes 'the study of how different groups adjust to one another's presence under conditions when one group is dominant and stratificational differences exist within each group', and such a study 'becomes an essential part of our understanding of the social structure of societies or cultures'.

Racism

One persistent feature of the stratification systems of the countries studied is that of institutional discrimination against the migrant worker, as evident in racial or ethnic prejudice in immigration policies (Swetland, Chapter 2), indigenous attitudes (Dittmar, Chapter 5; Cicourel, Chapter 1); the daily practices on the job and in the classroom and in the general daily contacts between the migrant worker and the indigenous population.

It is therefore not accidental that the problems of migrant workers in the USA are examined within the general context of the problems of racial and ethnic minorities, of whom a large majority such as the American black and Indian population cannot be called migrants but are in fact indigenous and legal citizens. Yet the social situation of these indigenous minorities and the non-European immigrant population manifest similar characteristics that are ultimately attributable to institutional structures and practices that are racially and ethnically discriminating. A necessary question to be answered therefore is at what point and under which circumstances being a migrant becomes less important than being black, Indian or coloured, when one analyses the denial of access and equality of treatment in the institutional life of the country of employment or residence? For, as Cicourel points out, European immigrants to the USA by and large experienced greater institutional access and success than these indigenous racial and ethnic groups themselves, though within the European immigrant population in the USA internal differences are also observable. The differential official legal and social responses to the more recent wave of Cuban, Haitian and Asian immigrants (including those seeking refugee status) to the USA manifest at the very beginning of entry how such differences are established for later institutionalised outcomes of job and school success or failure. The same racial—ethnic prejudices that underlie the differential treatment of these various groups on entry to the USA are also evident when factors of racial and ethnic inferiority are later invoked to explain their failure and their problems. And as far as Europe is concerned, such differential responses and experiences among the immigrant groups are by no means absent.

Discrimination in the classroom or in the education and training of the migrant receives the greatest attention in Part I. One of the factors with which both Cicourel and Swetland are concerned is the reciprocal images or stereotypes with which the migrant and the native confront each other. Swetland provides a detailed account of the reciprocal images of Pakistanis and Norwegians. For Norwegians, Pakistanis are

7

'Pakkis' (analogous to 'nigger' in the USA), illiterate, speak a language that has no grammar and that is written in hieroglyphics. They also possess the typical and contradictory dichotomous attributes equally regarded by the indigenous population as bad but valid for racial and ethnic minorities or other groups finding themselves in similar marginal situations. For example, 'they bow to authority/they don't obey; they don't drink/they drink; they take our girls/they don't go out with girls'. For Pakistanis, Norwegians are drunk all the time, treat dogs better than humans and 'pretend equality but hide hierarchy in their dress' (Swetland, Chapter 2).

Such typical images, reflecting the conflictual social gap between the migrant and indigenous population, also enter the stratificational practices in the classroom. In the Swetland study, as for Cicourel, these practices revolve around the scheduling of classes, student assessment, teacher training, teacher—student relations and models of learning and teaching.

The result is domination and rejection of the migrant; such rejection itself requiring an 'apology of power' on the part of the teacher. Such structural and ideological domination in the classroom is maintained partly because the instability of the legal status and presence of migrant workers does not permit him to attack or threaten it. The result is the maintenance of the migrant as an abstraction, since he has found at most only an ambiguous place in the structural hierarchy. He is denied the 'possibility of becoming a person'; and not only are his needs ignored, but it is not even suspected that he or she has any personal plans:

> Functioning as an economic unit in a hierarchical structure that excludes him as an active cognitive unit, directed by foreigners (the natives) whose ethnolanguage remains foreign to him, and controlled by a power apparatus of persons to whom he has not delegated that power, the migrant has only two choices: go back home (a failure) or submit. His formal education consists in progressively being led to submission to a cognitive world into which he is told to enter but which refuses him when he makes attempts (Swetland, Chapter 2).

For Swetland, Catani, Dittmar and Cicourel, the refusal in training programmes to take into account the cognitive and institutional world of migrant and minority groups is one of the instruments, conscious or unconscious, of their process of submission and the failure of the programmes themselves. It is necessary to understand, as Swetland puts it, that the *cognitive world* and the *cognitive model* of migrant workers, while not necessarily convergent with those of the indigenous population, constitute an equally valid starting point for the organisation of his education and training.

Such issues are strikingly elaborated by Cicourel in his discussion of the education of migrant workers and racial and ethnic minorities in North America. The stratificational practices in American classrooms revolve around access or recruitment of the children of these groups and assessment of their intelligence, literacy and performance in tests. Such practices are exacerbated by inadequate textbook materials and the monopoly of textbook production, as well as the inadequate training and cultural biases of teachers involved in bilingual education. For Cicourel, it is therefore within the larger context of class and cultural differences that the failures and controversies surrounding such national policies as affirmative action and bilingual education in the USA should be assessed.

Class and racial and cultural features enter the very conceptions of literacy, knowledge and intelligence, and given the existence of only pretended objective measures of these, the result is that the children of migrant and minority groups 'become the victims of institutionalised procedures that preserve the status quo' (Cicourel, Chapter 1); the 'blatant and subtle forms of prejudice and discrimination in the school setting restricts the resources available' to them to deal with school tasks and homework; while the existence of cultural and language differences 'means that migrant children have more to learn'. The failure of the migrant in the classroom is therefore a continual self-fulfilling prophecy, generated from such general stratificational practices, particularly the indigenous cognitive models of intelligence, literacy and subtle notions of adequate performance. Consequently for these authors there is one starting point in the education and training of migrant workers and their families, and that is from their own social universe — from the theories of the migrants themselves, their explanations of their everyday social realities and the premises upon which they attempt to manage their material and social existence, adopting or rejecting new values and where necessary retaining or even stretching the old.

Female migrants

The problems posed in Part I concerning the education and training of migrant workers assume even more significance when female migrants are considered. The isolation and alienation identifiable in the general migrant population assume an added dimension, since to the economic and cultural alienation must be added the sexual, as the studies in Part II show. The female migrant finds herself not merely living in two cultures, but as put by Oriol in his introduction, she tends to be between two cultures — in a state of 'betwixt and between', bouncing back and forth against two cultural models and unable to restructure her personal values.

The studies in Part II of this volume are intended, therefore, to focus more particularly on female migrants, though in reality they provide an intimate continuity with the characteristics of the migrant situation presented in the first part, for sex differences do not necessarily alter or obscure the alienation the migrant experiences *qua* migrant, but as the studies in Part II show, may actually exacerbate or deepen the problems of cultural adaptation female migrants have to overcome. This is the logic for examining the particular effects of migration on the identity, status and cultural behaviour of female migrants, in their own right, both within the structure of the family and the wider society. The reproductive behaviour of the female migrant provides an important focus for such an examination, since it constitutes, together with her productive functions, the core elements of her experience in the country of employment or residence.

Adaptation of Yugoslav women

Morokvasic analyses the reproductive behaviour of Yugoslav women in France, the Federal Republic of Germany and Sweden, as it is affected by the migrant experience. Abortion as the major form of reproductive control generally practised by women in the society of origin is adopted also by Yugoslav migrants in each of these countries of employment, despite the fact that national policy is more favourable to birth control through the use of contraceptives, and abortion is either not fully legalised or is subjected to strict controls. Of the 258 women in the sample, some 146 or 50 per cent had abortions and at least one-third of them had more than three (Morokvasic, Chapter 7). In these three European countries, the proportion of Yugoslav women who had an abortion is highest in Sweden, though we find that Sweden has had the longest history of the sale of contraceptives and availability of information in the various languages of the migrants concerning contraceptive use and the participation of migrant women themselves (Yugoslav) in the system of birth control services. It is also the more striking, since more Yugoslav women in Sweden than in either France or the Federal Republic of Germany are reported to be knowledgeable of a wider range of contraceptives, and to have received, even before their departure, contraceptive information more from official channels than from friends. This finding probably suggests a state of transition from old practices to new forms, since Morokvasic also finds the largest proportion of contraceptive users among Yugoslav migrants to be in Sweden. Evidence for this transition state is also in terms of the fact that the highest proportion of Yugoslav women *rarely* having more than two abortions also occurs in Sweden compared with the frequency of abortions reported for them in France or the Federal Republic of Germany because the nature of the legislative support and services in

Sweden facilitates such acceptance. At the same time, however, the greater acceptance of contraceptive use does not negate the persistence of the major method of birth control typically adopted in the home country, particularly when this is not rejected outright by the reproductive norms in the countries of employment or residence. But even so, these old practices are themselves apparently undergoing change or re-interpretation. Morokvasic's analysis therefore provides an excellent example of the synthesis of two cultural models and the beginning of the re-interpretation of the old. Her analysis also suggests that the migrant experience is not always conflictual with the cultural forms of the home country and that in the case of the Yugoslav women, it may be compatible with or even support the cultural practices that obtained before migration, since given an already strong work ethic, the opportunity for work that migration brings actually reinforces their attitudes and behaviour in favour of birth control. The point is that the traditional pattern is not reversed because it is not incompatible with the range of birth control practices found in Europe, though the reproductive behaviour of female migrants from Yugoslavia is seen to correlate with some of the variations in reproductive practices in the different European countries of migrant employment. Another example of this phenomenon of convergence is that the greatest proportion of Yugoslav female migrants in Europe wanting no more than two children come from the northern region (Croatia, Nojvodina), where there is already an established pattern of low fertility, and these migrants are resident in the Federal Republic of Germany, where family planning legislation has been recently liberalised.

In short, from the evidence presented by Morokvasic, the reproductive adaptation problems of Yugoslav female migrants in Europe seem more related to the practical details of participating in the system of birth control services and are concerned more with access to information and communicative competence. But in a broader respect, these women may be *less* 'lost between two cultures' than female migrants from other national and cultural backgrounds, for the Yugoslav female migrant is still able to access the traditional cultural forms in the country of origin itself, in addition to the support from her own migrant community. For example, Morokvasic describes that even where relatively strong legal controls of abortion exist as in France and the Federal Republic of Germany, Yugoslav women find clandestine ways of getting around these laws, including 'going full circle' back to their country of origin for the purpose of having the abortion. This is an important adaptive response and underlines a dynamic process of cultural retention. It would appear that the 'problems' generated by adherence to the traditional reproductive patterns are problems for the Yugoslav women themselves, *only* if their behaviour is viewed from the cultural eyes or normative criteria of the countries of employment. And

11

when one considers that some 97 of the 116 women, estimated by Morokvasic as those in the sample not interested in additional children and so most likely to use contraceptives, actually do, this indicates a cultural adaptive process moving in the other direction. Despite the fact that a high proportion of Yugoslav women in Europe do have abortions and that not all those with estimated needs for planning their family actually use contraceptives, Morokvasic points to the fact that most of them say that the pill or some other contraceptive is the best method of birth control. To the extent that the use of contraceptives rather than the reliance on abortion is the accepted norm in France, the Federal Republic of Germany and Sweden, most Yugoslav women can be said to value the norm. The seeming contradiction in their reproductive behaviour rather reflects a particular dynamic stage in a cultural adaptive process towards this normative goal.

Adaptation of Turkish women

The situation of Turkish women in the Federal Republic of Germany, as described by Kudat (Chapter 8), reflects sharper discontinuities between the cultural past and the migrant experience. There is a marked disjunction in productive and reproductive roles: the reproductive role of the Turkish female migrant is viewed as being attenuated in favour of a greater economic one, resulting in alienation from her own family and shifts in the balance of power within the household, the loosening of affective maternal ties, the sharing of household membership with non-relatives as new attitudes evolve. Turkish women are, according to the author, ill-prepared for the 'multifaceted abruptness' of such breaks. We learn, however, that they come to adapt sufficiently by acquiring the skills and attitudes to survive in Europe. But even these skills and personal competences have little or no utility in the home country, for there are hardly any opportunities for exercising them or the structural and cultural support for sustaining the personal changes. The result is what the author calls a 'process of adaptation in the reverse direction' — an unlearning of the skills and behaviour suited for the country of employment in favour of a reactivation of the normative patterns of the country of origin. This 'forward and backward' process of change, however, does not result in absolute personal loss, for there remains the probability that some of the internalised values of the country of employment would be re-interpreted and find expression in new forms.

But the migrant experience and the subsequent changes remain only at the personal level. At the level of the society and the general condition of Turkish women, the situation remains the same, because the individual bourgeois aspirations of the migrants contradict the possibility of the development of the political and social consciousness to

12

translate the migrant experience into an effective movement to bring about societal change. On the whole, therefore, Kudat views the migrant experience as having a negative impact at the familial and societal levels, though at the personal level there is some 'loss in gains'.

Adaptation of Algerian women

In their study of Algerian women, Andizian and Streiff stress how the migrant experience could provide the context for recreating, transferring or re-interpreting the characteristic role patterns of the native culture. While there is no smooth transition from the traditional to the modern, the range of responses includes emulation, rejection and re-interpretation. The fundamental question is how does the migrant experience affect family relationships as far as the socialisation and the fundamental roles of women are concerned, including their role in group identity and its symbolic representations?

The particular relevant factors for the North African woman is that the possibility of outside work is inhibited by language problems, her obligations to children and resistance from her partner. The result is that the basic function of the female migrant remains within the household, that is a reproductive one, particularly in regard to her assumption of sole responsibility for the education of the children. Vigilance is required if the child's education is to be protected from the effects of the policy of assimilation, with its accompanying marginalisation and deculturation. The clash between or at least the coexistence of two different cultural models is therefore particularly acute for the young immigrant girl. Her behaviour must be seen therefore within the context of strategies employed to cope with the divergences of her cultural situation. But the response to her presence at school and at work remains distorted and paternalistic.

How then does she deal with job failure? These authors suggest that she seeks integration with her native milieu and opportunities to participate in the life of her migrant community. She is even able to work out a new behavioural pattern correlative with the changing definition of roles within the family.

We see therefore in these three analyses some of the various ways or strategies by which Yugoslav, Turkish and Algerian female migrants attempt to sustain or restructure their values in carrying out their productive and reproductive functions. Some of them bring certain social and cultural characteristics that permit them to do so more effectively than others. But such adaptive capacity *also* rests on the particular socio-cultural situation they find in the country of employment. While it is agreed that this area is generally a 'no-man's land' of cultural alienation and estrangement, their adaptive capacity in a particular country of employment is variously affected by the nature and range of the institutional support services available to them and the nature and range of the socio-cultural support available from their own migrant community to sustain them. These are the two major factors that determine in what manner and how effectively they are able to cope with the migrant experience, how they restructure their values and whether the kind of cultural response they adopt leads them along the road to cultural assimilation, integration, pluralism or isolation.

We learn too that even when they are able to develop the necessary skills and make the requisite personal changes for survival in the country of employment, the changes are not necessarily long-term, if the institutional and migrant community support is lacking on their return to the country of origin. This finding has significant policy implications both for the country of employment, for the country of origin and for the various migrant communities of workers in Europe and elsewhere. We learn from these studies another important fact: the female migrant worker, because of her own personal motivations and ambitions, her cultural orientation and unstable legal status, is not usually politically and socially conscious of the general situation of women and the changes she undergoes in the migrant experience are not the kind that could be translated into societal change and improvement in the condition and status of women.

The studies presented both in Parts I and II highlight the difficulties of these choices the migrant confronts and represent a useful contribution to an understanding of the migrant experience of living in two cultures. It is hoped that the publication of this volume, with the analytical and substantive issues it raises, will be a step forward in both the scientific consideration of the socio-cultural situation of migrant workers and the formulation of appropriate strategies of action at the national and international levels in their favour.

Bibliography

Barrie, W.D., *Italians and Germans in Australia*, F.W. Cheshire, Melbourne, 1954.

Barrie, W.D. (ed.), *Cultural Integration of Immigrants*, Unesco, 1958.

de Montvalon, R., *The Aspirations of Young Migrant Workers in Western Europe*, Unesco, 1976.

Sauvy, A., *Francais et émigrés*, Presses Universitaires de France, Paris, 1957.

PART I

1 Living in two cultures: the everyday world of migrant workers
AARON V. CICOUREL*

Introduction

The assimilation of immigrants is an old problem in the social sciences and there is a huge literature on the subject. In recent years there has been similar interest expressed in a problem that also has a long history. This second and related problem has been studied with a similar intensity. The problem is that of migrant workers. Migrant workers can refer to those who are foreigners and not permanent residents of the country in which they work, and migrants who are permanent residents and/or citizens. This chapter attempts to describe a conceptual framework that makes use of earlier work on immigrants and the problem of assimilation, while simultaneously addressing the problems of migrant workers, especially those working in western Europe. The kind of conceptual framework suggested below calls attention to the everyday experiences of migrant workers and their children in the host country, including the stratifying practices that affect changes in the status of children and adolescents.

* This chapter was written with the assistance of Fleur Baum and Harriett Romo. Many of the remarks on Mexican-Americans and Puerto Ricans have relied on unpublished papers by Harriett Romo. I am grateful to her for making these papers available to me. I wish to thank the following persons for their helpful remarks and suggestions on the first draft of the paper: Michael Cole, Troy Duster, Hugh Mehan, Harriett Romo, and Joachim Singlemann.

17

A number of American sociologists have written about European immigrants to the USA and Canada. These studies follow a similar theme: the idea of persons who live in two cultures and two societies. In *Varieties of Religious Experience*, James (1929) wrote about the conflict of culture in terms of the way a divided self emerges which leads to continual strain between the old self and the new. Park (1969) wrote extensively about the way the immigrant lived in and shared the cultural life and traditions of different groups. The difficulty such persons experienced, noted Park, was that they did not seem to be willing to break with the past, even if this were possible, and yet such persons invariably faced discriminatory practices even when embracing aspects of the new culture.

Park's work was heavily influenced by the teaching and writings of Georg Simmel (1950), the German-Jewish sociologist who wrote from personal experience about the 'stranger' who lived in two cultures that never completely interpenetrated or fused. For Simmel the emancipated Jew was typically a 'marginal' man. Park and Simmel's work influenced the book by Stonequist (1961) entitled *The Marginal Man* in which the same thesis is examined in more detail. But migrant workers are not 'marginal' to the host society even if they are treated in ways that make them feel they are not wanted. Migrant workers are an integral part of the stratification system of the host country. The blacks, Chicanos, and Puerto Ricans we shall be discussing in subsequent sections of the chapter are certainly *not* marginal to North American life. They occupy important economic, educational, political, and professional positions that are essential to all aspects of life in the USA.

Another important work is the book by Thomas and Znaniecki (1958) in which the migrant is described as a person who must leave a community which was the basis for his technological and social competence, personal identity and self-respect as exemplified in the language used, dress, social rituals, skills, knowledge, a sense of moral worth, sentimental ideals, and interests. These cultural elements from his former community now become the source of humiliation and contempt in the new community.

An historical example might also be appropriate here. In work on converted Sephardic Jews in Spain at the time of the Inquisition (Gilman, 1972), religious and ethnic differences within the same country resulted in persons converting from one religion to another but retaining the former identity. How a person retained a prior identity despite surface appearances of conformity to the converted religion is difficult to ascertain, but there is considerable evidence to argue that writers who were 'conversos' became preoccupied with the problem of identity in the literature they wrote.

In each of the above examples a persistent theme emerges over and over again: day-to-day encounters or interpersonal exchanges between migrant workers and their families with native members of the country of immigration become the key ingredient for understanding the impact or consequences of being persons perceived as strangers or outsiders or foreigners in a situation where 'normal' structural inequality is enacted on a daily basis. For some migrant workers and their families a considerable amount of acculturation may have taken place, but this integration into the host society is never complete and is always liable to become problematic in every day-to-day encounter because the members of the host society see them as different. The individual's identity and conception of self will always reflect an ambivalence and uncertainty that is a built-in feature of everyday existence.

Some consequences of living in two cultures. Park (1950) observed that one effect of mobility and migration was to secularise relations which were formerly sacred through a dual process of the secularisation of society and the individuation of the person. By leaving the intimacy of a prior cultural life and traditions that integrated the individual into a larger group and a sense of history, there was greater likelihood that in a very different cultural environment the migrant would alter or secularise previous relationships and rituals. The secularisation process is said to result in an individuation of the person by making his daily life less dependent on others, particularly those who form part of an extended kinship system.

The idea of a cultural hybrid for Park was a man or woman living and sharing the cultural life and traditions of two groups, but never quite willing to sever one of them, even if permitted or encouraged to do so. Yet there were also ties with his or her past not quite accepted by the 'host group' because of racial or ethnic prejudice. For Park these conditions reflected the plight of the bicultural immigrant. For Stonequist (1961) the idea of living in different social worlds was a reflection of the social maladjustment that was said to be characteristic of modern life. Social dislocation was viewed as inevitable because of cultural transitions and cultural conflicts.

A basic assumption of theoretical discussions of the stranger, the migrant, is that the process of migration and the collision of cultures leads to more heterogeneity and assimilation, but this dual existence produces identity problems that make it difficult for a person to sustain an integrated conception of self when one's culture and language are eroded.

The socio-cultural perspective that is fundamental to the above remarks draws our attention to forms of social organisation at the level of the family, community affairs, and contacts with larger social institutions and bureaucratic transactions. The extent to which we understand these forms of social organisation in both the country of origin and the country of immigration becomes a central issue in recommending further research and the formulation and implementation of policies.

The American experience as a possible model

The North American experience with waves of immigrants can be used to highlight similarities and differences with what has happened in Europe *vis-à-vis* migrant workers. Space does not permit a thorough discussion of rival interpretations of what has been called 'Americanisation'. Nor can we discuss the parallel phenomenon of Americanisation that occurred in Latin America. The idea that America was a place with a new stock produced by an amalgam of many different European strains was evident in the eighteenth century and there were many differences of opinion about the open policy notion that existed in the nineteenth century that all should be admitted under the assumption that all immigrants could be absorbed and would eventually contribute to an emerging national character.

The idea of the melting pot was not uniformly accepted, but the idea of preserving the valuable cultural qualities of each immigrant group has been expressed for some time. This idea of cultural pluralism and the notion of a melting pot conflicted with the view that Americans were basically a kind of British offspring to which new groups would have to assimilate. The ethnic and racial biases of immigration existed from the outset but the notion of a melting pot remains a cultural stereotype of sorts in various parts of American society.

Social scientists contributed to the melting pot notion until fairly recently, but careful research was seldom available for demonstrating what took place in practice. Many novels, plays, and musicals about the USA have attested to the mythology and the reality of daily living. But it took the turmoil of the civil rights movement and subsequent ethnic and racial movements to force social scientists and lay persons alike to face the reality of a society that remains a strange mixture of cultural, ethnic, racial, and religious differences that are cross-cut by socio-economic variations. There is a huge literature here that we shall only cite selectively (Mayo-Smith, 1904; Zangwill, 1909; Grant, 1912; Kallen, 1915; Grabo, 1919; Hansen, 1940; Handlin, 1951, 1959 and 1972; Jones, 1960, Higham, 1963; Zwingmann and Pfister-Ammende, 1973; and Greer, 1974).

Warner and Srole (1945) discuss the family organisation of ethnic groups that immigrated to the New England region of the USA. Their discussion could easily be used to describe the family organisation of migrant workers in Europe. The dominant role of the father is described in a context that includes references to ancestral traditions in the country of origin. The migration of married men who later brought

20

their families, and single men and women who planned to return to their country of origin, parallels in many ways the reports commissioned by Unesco on migrant workers in Europe. Warner and Srole note that wives who did not work became even more subordinate to their husbands because of being linguistically helpless and dependent on the husband for information on most of the aspects of life in the outside world.

The distinction made by Warner and Srole is between 'p¹' and 'p²' generations, or those (p^1) who arrived as mature 'crystallized personalities', and those who left their country of origin as 'immature, "unfinished" personalities'. The p^2 immigrant is viewed as someone who could more easily orient themselves socially to the host society, having entered the host country by 18 years of age or younger. They also suggest differences in the adjustment of children of p^1 and p^2 immigrants. These distinctions suggest ways in which we can identify potential problems among European workers and their families.

Recent descriptions of migrants

In a series of papers sponsored by Unesco on women migrants a number of common themes are identified having to do with the educational prospects, general social adjustment, and social mobility of women. The studies (Hoffman-Nowotny, 1978; Smith, 1978; Swetland, 1978; Kudat, 1978; Streiff, 1978; Oriol, 1978; Andizian and Streiff, 1978; Morokvasic, 1978; Buckland, 1978; Ley, 1978; and Catani, 1978) refer to Pakistanis in Norway, Greeks in Australia, Turks in Germany, Algerians in France, Yugoslavs in several countries, and different ethnic groups in Sweden.

Isolation, insecurity, and instability are perhaps the most obvious terms that should be used to describe the plight of migrant women, along with their alienation *vis-à-vis* economic, cultural, and sexual activities. Women migrants encounter different conditions across northern European countries as regards their ability and encouragement to find employment. If they have children they often must assume responsibility for guiding the children through the schools of the country of employment. Finding adequate instructors for teaching the foreign language is mentioned as a continual problem. Personnel such as social workers who can speak the language of the migrants are often in short supply.

Turkish women migrants (Kudat, 1978) pose special problems because they usually come from a cultural atmosphere where outside employment of low income or peasant women does not occur and the social restrictions placed on them are usually severe. A greater degree of adaptation is needed by Turkish women because of such cultural conditions at home and the striking contrast of life in Euro-

21

pean countries. Many of the married women will stay in the country of origin initially to keep costs down. We know little of the impact of such conditions other than to note that the women in question obviously must assume more responsibilities while probably experiencing a rise in material comfort because of the husband sending money home.

The Unesco reports contain observations about the consequences of having a mother-centred household and there are references to the organisation of black families in the USA. Some of the writers suggest that changes in family organisation probably can result from women assuming more responsibility at home when their husbands work abroad and then return. The question of whether the wife can hold on to this more 'emancipated' role when the husband returns remains empirically problematic. The extent to which there will be a social decline in the status of women or a more egalitarian family structure when migrant husbands return to their country of origin remains unclear. We are also unclear about the extent to which women achieve more egalitarian status in the country of immigration if they work or remain at home.

There now exists a large number of papers on migrant families. These papers provide us with general information about the problems that migrant workers and their families encounter or are likely to encounter in the foreign countries. Some of the papers describe the problems that children of migrant workers are likely to encounter in school settings. There is very little information, however, on the way older children and adolescents fare in the country of residence.

We have a large number of studies based primarily on demographic data and special studies of migrant labour processes. These studies and several surveys have provided us with documentation for our intuitive and impressionistic observations about the many problems faced by migrant workers and their families. Additional research has indicated that serious problems exist *vis-à-vis* bilingual aspects of the education of children of migrant workers and the possible effects these problems can have on future employment opportunities.

A report (Unesco, 1978) by a group of experts on migrant workers and their families notes a variety of discriminatory practices against migrants and spells out a veritable 'Bill of Rights' for such persons as regards their lives in the host country and the help they should receive in preparing to return to the home country. The report is thorough and nicely summarises the rights of workers, their families, workers' associations, and the education and schooling of adults and children. Included in the rights attributed to migrants is the right to compete in the labour market on a par with nationals, the right to preserve their language and cultural identities, and the right to participate in the society of the country of residence as an equal citizen. It would be difficult to disagree with the observations and recommendations. What is perhaps most ironical about the report is the fact that this 'Bill of Rights' for migrants is seldom if ever applied to minorities (who are also nationals) within many member states of the UN and its specialised agencies. In North and South America, the UK, Norway, Italy, Iran, Israel, Japan, to mention a few areas, we could make the same charges. The report, like so many others on file in different agencies of the UN system and countries with minority problems, is like a catalogue of stratifying practices by which we implement our beliefs on equality and inequality.

A paper prepared for the Intergovernmental Committee for European Migration by Eppink (1979) provides us with a useful overview of socio-psychological problems associated with the children of migrant workers in a context of cultural conflicts in the host and home country. The problems discussed by Eppink include how migration affects the parent—child relationship, the effects of an uncertain time commitment by the parent to remain in the country of employment, and the consequences of having a working mother. A number of other topics are discussed, including school and mental conflicts, the child's self-image and self-confidence, the effects of being in day-care centres, language development and personal identity.

Theoretical objectives

Recent studies, including those available from Unesco, outline a number of key issues affecting migrant workers and their families. These cover virtually all aspects of the problems faced by migrants as well as some of the problems faced by and remedies proposed by the countries of production or migrant employment. These papers, however, seldom provide details about the field conditions within which actual research was conducted. This chapter presents some of the theoretical and methodological issues that can be used to extend these important essays and research reports.

A general problem should be noted which cannot be addressed in this chapter. We need to ask about the role that migrant labour plays in a society, particularly capitalist societies of western Europe and South Africa. We need also to consider the costs of the renewal of the labour force as a serious issue — the costs that may be borne by the countries that send the temporary migrants, compared with the costs of maintaining such workers in the countries of employment. This broader stratification issue is discussed in a paper by Burawoy (1976).

In the pages that follow we shall selectively review studies of North American minorities and migrant workers and focus on problems associated with the education of the children of these workers. Our concern is with providing a broader framework for the analysis of the problems of migrant workers than is possible from demographic and survey materials while nevertheless relying on such materials as a point of departure for our own remarks. The larger framework we propose addresses the ways in which stratification systems must be examined if we are to understand the larger socio-cultural context within which migrant workers and their families must sustain an existence. We must understand the actual day-to-day experiences of migrants that structure and circumscribe their resources for dealing with the world. These experiences will be influenced by their projected stay in the country of employment and the possibility of remaining for a short period of time or becoming permanent residents and/or citizens.

A consequence of this stratification system is a set of stratifying practices reflected in the way teachers and classrooms are oriented and organised to receive all children, and particularly children who are less successful in the kinds of performance by which we assess intelligence and literacy. Our discussion will also include a reference to problems of the adequate training of teachers and how this training affects the stratifying practices associated with children who are less successful in school performance. These children are tracked early with little or no chance of moving out of their low status. The problems associated with the evaluation of students and the training of teachers, including how to deal with children with language differences, are linked to the stratifying practices of programmes of affirmative action as implemented in the USA, where such programmes are designed to increase the number of women and minorities in all aspects of the labour market and educational system. The official goal of the programme is for these groups to achieve parity in terms of income and status *vis-à-vis* the dominant group commensurate with their numbers in the total population. Affirmative action cannot be successful in practice even if such programmes seem to be satisfied legally so long as the stratification system in its daily practices sustains its normal prejudice and discrimination. One consequence of these stratifying practices is that methods of training teachers and the way that normal or routine teaching in the classroom occurs make it difficult to understand poor school performance. A related problem that will be discussed stems from the cultural and colour differences of migrant workers and their families and how these differences resemble the cultural milieu of blacks, Chicanos or Mexican-Americans, and Puerto Ricans compared to white Americans in the USA.

Bilingual education in the USA

Despite the existence of a multilingual society in the USA for many years (Kloss, 1977), there was no formal federal government funding or legislation promoting bilingual education until the Bilingual Education

Act was passed in 1967 and funded in 1968. A major problem was finding the size of the target group for whom special programmes were needed or desirable. There are some lessons to be learned in the US experience because the very notion of bilingual education needs clarification when we assume that one or more target populations exist for whom a second language is dominant rather than the language spoken by the majority group. The methods used for identifying those in need of bilingual education provide us with some insight into the general problem of testing for some level of competence, finding adequate teachers, and designing a curriculum that is realistically linked to the capabilities of those being taught.

The use of teachers to identify children in need of bilingual education proved ineffective. Most of the teachers involved had little knowledge of language learning, particularly second language learning. The key ingredient here was the fact that some children could function well in the classroom at a level which gave the appearance of a good command of American English. These children could follow instructions that were oriented to activities that did not include intellectual tasks. But when these students were observed in basic English reading groups they were found to be in communication situations which were beyond their comprehension. Many times these difficulties in following the language of instruction in the classroom were seen by teachers as a lack of motivation, retardation, or low intelligence because of the appearance of a good command of American English.

A similar finding in Sweden (Unesco, 1978) *vis-à-vis* Finnish children corresponds directly to the Chicano or Mexican-American or Puerto Rican cases in the USA: migrant students are often placed in remedial classes because of judgements by the teacher that their low performance in class is a result of mental retardation rather than due to cultural communication problems. The Unesco document on the education of migrant workers and their families also makes explicit reference to the identity problems of the children of migrant workers because of language and cultural differences.

The lesson to be learned here is that children of migrant workers will not give the appearance of a good command of the language of the country of residence initially, but then learn enough to appear to be fluent, yet not be able to use it adequately in an instructional setting. But having been placed in the instructional setting, the children may be judged as retarded instead of being weak in communicational resources. Establishing an adequate curriculum and finding appropriate teachers remains a difficult problem. We shall return to this issue below.

In addition to the teacher's judgements, in the USA extensive testing is also used to decide bilingual placement of the child. The tests are heavily oriented toward the child's knowledge of syntax.

The child's language needs can vary because of place of birth, how much time he or she has spent in the native country compared to the foreign country, previous educational experiences, and the socio-economic conditions of the parents. In the USA it has been very difficult to obtain accurate information on Puerto Ricans, Chicanos, and persons of Mexican birth. Census information is felt to underestimate the number of Hispanic minority people. Census counts do not permit us to infer the language(s) spoken and the degree of proficiency and literacy in the languages identified. The literacy that is identified, however, is usually low. Hence those persons who are planning bilingual programmes often lack adequate information about the target population they must serve.

A paper by Waggoner (1976) based on a July 1975 *Current Population Survey* and reported by the National Center for Education Statistics, generated estimates of persons with a limited use of American English as follows: the total size of the group is estimated to be from 15.2 million to 28.7 million and includes persons age four and older. This group is estimated to have from 3.6 million to 8.1 million children from age four to 18. This survey by the Bureau of the Census for the Bureau of Labor Statistics did not include regional concentration of language minority groups, but several findings are worth repeating.

The survey estimated that of the population of age four and older in July 1975, living in households, 13 per cent used languages other than American English. Spanish was the most often reported second language with Italian second. The Spanish speakers outnumbered the Italian speakers by nine to one. Of those who spoke no American English, 1.6 million or three-quarters were adults 26 years and older. There were estimated to be 8.2 million Spanish speakers. Adolescents between the ages of 14 and 18 who did not speak American English were likely not to be enrolled in school during 1974-1975, and these students were usually below the normal grade level for their age. The students who spoke a language other than American English were also more likely not to have completed high school than comparable groups who only spoke American English.

American congressional action stimulated school districts to pay more attention to students whose first language was not American English by offering funds for developing special language programmes. But not all school districts sought these funds despite having children who qualified for special programmes. In some cases special funds were diverted to other activities. There are several lessons to be learned from the North American experience.

The existence of funding for special programmes can lead to rather mixed results. In a few districts teachers developed special programmes that would enable children to take pride in their Hispanic origins while also encouraging the acquisition of Spanish language skills necessary to become convincingly bilingual. The bilingual programme was felt to be a way of promoting a better self-concept and more interest in school, thus lessening drop-outs and encouraging better academic achievement. The development of better American English skills, however, is the primary objective of federal legislation. The bilingual programmes are viewed as only transitional. Meanwhile, numerous problems emerged during the implementation of such programmes.

The cohort of students identified might include a broad range of persons deemed to be partially bilingual or in need of a special programme. Finding adequate teachers often proves to be a difficult task and making this judgement with explicit criteria in mind can be a sensitive issue. To qualify for special funds a school district must create a relevant group of potential students in need of the programme. Identifying these students depended on the particular director of the programme and the way teachers were included and then the way the teachers would help in identifying students. If the Office of Civil Rights cited a school district for inadequate academic programme offerings in bilingual education, the programme could be in jeopardy. A district could also be cited for initiating a programme but not having enough children who qualified.

A paper by Fishman (1977) covers a broad range of issues associated with bilingual education. The paper reviews an extensive literature but also reports that little data existed on classroom dynamics as would be revealed by ethnographic studies. Since Fishman's paper was written there have been several projects started and a few reports on findings are beginning to emerge. An important question is posed in Fishman's paper: can minority languages be 'saved' by bilingual education? Fishman states that even if such programmes were to operate at top efficiency, which is not the case, the school is not a reliable environment for language maintenance. The home and community are the places where language maintenance is likely to occur. Evidence from the USA, Ireland, Wales, Israel, Friesland, and other countries is cited by Fishman as places where language maintenance through bilingual education has not been successful.

A paper by Carrasco, Vera, and Cazden (in press) reports on the study of a bilingual Chicana student in a multi-grade/multi-ethnic classroom in San Diego, California (Mehan, 1979). There was a bilingual co-teacher in the classroom and speaking Castilian Spanish was always encouraged. But there was no bilingual education programme in the school. What is of interest about this case study is the way the student Veronica performs as a tutor for another student, Alberto. Veronica, at the time of the study, was repeating the first grade because of being 'weak' in English language skills. Veronica learns an English spelling lesson from the teacher and is supposed to teach it to Alberto, a younger student who is also Spanish dominant. The study by Carrasco,

Vera, and Cazden reveals what the child does when she is not being observed by the teacher. Detailed descriptions and some verbatim transcript material based on video tapes are presented in order to show how important it is to evaluate the child's behaviour when not being observed by the teacher. Veronica's communicative competence was seriously underestimated by the teacher. The lesson to be learned here is that teachers are amazed by video tapes of children considered to be 'slow' learners. The child's performance before the teacher does not constitute an adequate sample of the student's repertoire. The child placed in the role of tutor exhibits skills the teacher was unaware existed. These skills are not elicited successfully from the student by the teacher.

A paper by Cazden, Carrasco, and Maldonado-Guzman (1980) provides us with an important review of recent work on bicultural/bilingual education and the implications of this work for educational policy. The paper stresses the need to diagnose the classroom environments of bilingual education and the importance of developing bicultural environments which would reveal cultural patterns of language use.

These issues raise serious questions about what to do with children of migrant workers in Europe, especially *vis-à-vis* the policy of having the children learn the language of their parents' country of origin and the cultural patterns of that country. The delicate issue revolves around how long the children are likely to remain in the country of employment or residence and if there is a good chance that they might have to return to the country of origin at some point.

A difficult issue in bilingual education is that of identifying students in need of a special programme and students who have benefited from the programme and are now ready to join other students in regular classes. The screening process typically involves the use of several tests, especially those dealing with syntax, and others which are designed to assess oral skills. There are few instruments available or used for determining reading and writing skills in Spanish, English, or the student's home language, and all of the tests have received criticism. The tests are a problem because we have not been able to establish adequate criteria for evaluating normal language use or reading skills in any language, nor can we identify what makes some students more successful than others in reading. The problem we face is that there is a lack of basic research on reading comprehension in any language. Developing tests for bilingual programmes presupposes some kind of resolution to the problem of assessing oral and reading skills in one language. The identification of speakers with deficiencies is usually a function of the instruments used, but the deficiencies so identified are not in correspondence with students' day-to-day functioning in the classroom. As a result of using these testing materials, many of the students who are identified as proficient also suffer from being misclassified because they do not perform adequately in the classroom.

The American case can be instructive in formulating a general policy for educational programmes that would be different for children of migrant workers. Despite the efforts of various groups to develop tests that would identify general and specific problems in children with language and learning difficulties, we lack the basic research knowledge to implement the use of a series of tests in order to provide special educational opportunities for a particular group. The problem is quite general: we lack appropriate testing materials and find it difficult to identify adequate personnel.

Puerto Rican migrants

The *United States Census Current Population Report for March, 1978*, using a sample survey, estimated the number of persons of Puerto Rican origin in the USA at 1.8 million. The main concentration of this group is in New York State, close to one million, and the others are distributed throughout the mainland, particularly in New Jersey, Illinois, California, Pennsylvania, Florida, Connecticut, and Ohio. There are believed to be 3.1 million Puerto Ricans in Puerto Rico. A few words about the mainland group are in order because they resemble European migrants in a few respects because of bilingual issues, minority status, and their frequent trips back to the island Commonwealth. But Puerto Ricans differ from migrants in Europe because the latter group remain foreigners (except for those with permits to stay), while Puerto Ricans are citizens of the USA. But even the children of migrants in Europe can sometimes be deported to their parents' country of origin once they reach a certain age.

We can begin by noting that Puerto Ricans residing in the US mainland have less formal education than whites, blacks, and other Hispanic groups. The differences in educational achievement are considerable despite improvements with the younger group of persons of Puerto Rican background born on the mainland. These educational differences exist despite the fact that the island economic conditions, school curricula, legislation, and language policies have been dominated by the mainland USA because of the political association with it.

The Puerto Rican situation is unique because Puerto Ricans have been made US citizens over the objection of their one elected group. The US economy and governmental aid and military institutions dominate virtually every aspect of the island's activities. According to Singelmann (personal communication), the US government is currently reassessing the tax incentive programme for manufacturing enterprises in Puerto Rico. If the incentives are eliminated then the government could propose increased welfare payments to make removal of the tax programme more acceptable to Puerto Rico. The current official unemployment rate is supposed to be over 20 per cent and further unemployment could make it a virtual welfare state. Singelmann suggests that industry and government groups might be thinking of using Puerto Ricans as a 'reserve labor force' that could be brought to the mainland when there is a strong economic trend, and returned to the island during economic recessions. There are different views on the island about the benefits and drawbacks of attaining statehood and full citizenship. A key issue, and one that is also reflected in the case of European migrants, is the extent to which Puerto Ricans are able to maintain their cultural identity and language after long periods of residence on the mainland. This problem is viewed with alarm by some groups on the island opposed to statehood because they fear that there will be a gradual and perhaps marked Americanisation of their heritage.

One reflection of the Americanisation policy can be found in the way language instruction has changed over the years of American control of the island. There have been a number of changes, including the practice of instruction in one language (Spanish) through element-ary school, then English in the middle or junior high school, and English and Spanish in senior high school. Spanish prevails today, but English is a required second language and the one that can lead to increased monetary return in the labour market. These conditions parallel the European scene when there are attempts to preserve the culture and language of migrant workers while simultaneously promot-ing the language and culture of the country of employment for success in the labour market.

An interesting comparative element between Puerto Rican and European migrant workers and their children can be found in the case of language instruction. Puerto Ricans brought up or born on the main-land have returned to the island not being able to speak or read Spanish adequately. Special bilingual classes had to be set up to accommodate these children. A familiar problem here is finding teachers on the island as well as the mainland who could handle this situation.

On the East coast of the US mainland the problem of new migrants from Puerto Rico assumed serious proportions for school districts and these problems have continued because of the large numbers of new students that come and then return. The population turnover was and continues to be a serious problem in planning for students and in obtaining special funds for new programmes that would help school districts prepare to teach English to non-English speakers. Some attempts to resolve existing problems included the development of materials for teaching science and giving occupational training, as well as opening up the traditional curriculum to these students. Tests and other measures were developed in order to compare Puerto Rican with mainland students. Different school districts tried different prog-rammes, including special classes for part of the day, but few have been willing or able to implement full bilingual programmes. Early studies (Morrison, 1958; Hernandez, 1976) revealed serious problems stemming from the lack of previous school experience and proper age-grade placement of Puerto Rican students in US schools. Considerable up-grading and down-grading and retention in the same class were practised with detrimental effects.

The practice of retaining students in the same class or grade level created several problems. Differences in physiological and emotional development with other students in the same grade level seem to have prevented the Puerto Rican students from performing better than they did. They were often bored and depressed by their situation, and associated with these conditions were more discipline problems, truancy, and other problems, including dropping out of school. Being delayed in school created problems for these students as they became young adults when they found they did not have adequate skills for better jobs.

At the lower levels of school, in grades three to six, many of the students could not understand much of what was said in class, and they had little opportunity to speak English, or to ask questions. Newly arrived students were silent, seldom participated in the class, and were indifferent for months and in some cases years of schooling. Teachers and students were seldom able to understand each other. Students often felt the teachers were different from island teachers, not interested in them, and lacked affection or kindness. Students who were more successful were found to be learning English from an older sibling, relative, or friend. The Morrison study found that students who were born on the island but residing for several years in New York City, improved their performance in reading and arithmetic for four years, but this performance decreased after the fourth year. These changes were attributed to not having learned enough basic concepts and knowledge at specific developmental stages in order to catch up with the other students who were native speakers of English. Some of the students, even as many as 30 per cent, surpassed non-Puerto Rican students in reading and arithmetic computation. But test results show that there is an overall failure to educate Puerto Rican children at levels comparable to the majority group.

The slow progress made by the students in improving their school performance is said to have left the parents with little or no confidence in the educational system and to view the school as a sort of 'enemy' that has led their children to becoming disinterested in school and showing poor performance. Many of the consequences of poor school performance are described (Margolis, 1975; Lucas, 1974; Hernandez, 1976) as leading to discouragement and humiliation among students, and difficulties with their confidence in themselves and the community.

A recent paper by López (1978) addresses the extent to which bilingualism has any lasting effects on the educational, occupational, and income achievements of Chicanos. Additional interests of the paper are the extent to which language and discrimination contribute to the large socio-economic gap between Chicanos and Anglos. The study is based on a 1973 survey of 1,129 Chicano households in the Los Angeles area, but the author restricts his analysis to Chicano men between 25-44 years of age raised in the USA.

Some of the results reported by López include the finding that home/school bilingualism and external factors must be examined to understand the important differences in education and occupational achievement between Chicanos raised in Spanish versus those raised in English. The author states that home/school bilingualism does not have lasting effects on occupational achievement despite the fact that bilingualism negatively affects educational achievement. Middle-class children are reported to be able to overcome the disadvantages of bilingualism, but for lower income groups, for whom language and ethnic solidarity (speaking Spanish and identifying with the Chicano community) are important for counteracting the discrimination resulting from Chicano ethnicity, the negative effect of bilingualism on educational achievement will persist. Hence the key element here may not be bilingualism, but one's social class and the stratifying practices associated with a person's interaction with others.

The study by López does not report findings on the way Chicano ethnicity is conveyed by bilingual speech styles both within the group and the larger society. Nor does his survey provide direct evidence for the way an ethnic job network among Chicanos exists and is revealed in day-to-day practices. By using correlational data based on his survey, López infers a number of possible consequences of the effects of home/school bilingualism. For example, a negative correlation (−.23) between home/school bilingualism and education means a 'depressing' effect on educational attainment, but a positive balancing effect is supposed to occur because home/school bilingualism is reported as positively correlated (.08) with income. The idea is that if there are negative aspects associated with home/school bilingualism, then depending on the correlations generated by the survey data, the author infers that schooling was hindered as well as early occupational achievement because of correlations of −.23 and .01, respectively. If there are positive correlations between bilingualism and later income level achieved, then it becomes possible to infer that no serious long-run effects or consequences occur. But the refinement of the survey data due to the use of path analysis obscures how respondents reacted to the questionnaire. Actual questions used in the survey are not reported.

External sources of information or speculation become relevant for asking: what could be 'softening' or 'blunting' the effects of bilingualism *vis-à-vis* occupation and income despite the negative impact home/school bilingualism has on education? The author then suggests that the quality of the education received by finishing or not finishing high school is probably affected by bilingualism. This suggestion is followed by the finding that those Chicanos whose families used English at home attain an educational level close to the national average for the USA.

References to information external to the survey are also invoked to point out that while home/school bilingualism has a dampening effect on level of schooling attained, it can help in finding a job because it makes it easier to communicate with other Spanish-speaking Chicanos about job information and because of casual personal contacts that are mediated by a knowledge of Spanish. We can also imagine situations where knowing something of two languages can be an advantage in the wider labour force. There is also a reference here to 'preliminary field investigation' as a source of information about how mutual aid is given among Chicanos, but no details are provided. The idea that knowing Spanish serves as a stigma to outsiders but solidarity for one Chicano to another, is an important observation but is not covered by the survey data reported in the paper.

The general point we wish to make is that López's paper provides us with a good example of how survey research can make use of limited information about the daily lives of a sample of a population by invoking impressionistic and plausible intuitive observations about what is likely to happen in everyday settings. As in other surveys, the one by López is not detailed enough to tell us about what constitutes some kind of fluency in Spanish or English, or the lack thereof. We do not have independent information about the school and occupational settings, nor about the job network and how knowledge of Spanish facilitates access to it while also creating or reaffirming solidarity within the group. Actual field research would be necessary to clarify the survey findings and the speculations and intuitive explanations used to embellish them. Field research would also help us understand the ways in which future surveys could be designed to obtain information about how bilingual problems affected daily experiences. López's use of his and others' own impressionistic information and intuition or personal experiences were central to the way he interpreted his survey findings, but the nature and status of such impressions and experiences as data remain obscure. This problem is also characteristic of studies of European migrant workers and their families.

In 1978 an evaluation was made of the impact of the first five years of the US Federal Title VII Spanish/English Bilingual Education Program. The report noted that some school districts retained students in the special programme despite their ability to function in American

English in regular classrooms. Many of the students were found to have a better level of functioning in American English than was deemed appropriate according to federal guidelines. There have been numerous controversies generated by this evaluation because there was no controlled definition of ability to function in English. Most of the conclusions were derived from surveys of programme directors far removed from the classroom. The first and fifth year programmes were grouped together, and programme goals of Spanish language maintenance were not considered.

A general issue that is continually debated in the USA is what should be the goals and elements of a bilingual programme? For some professionals bilingual education is a way of helping Spanish-speaking and other minority students become proficient enough in American English to join classes where only English is spoken. The time period often mentioned is two to three years. But for others, a transition goal is not enough. This second view argues that Hispanic students, for example, would need more than a transitional programme if they are to maintain and develop their own cultural traditions and strengthen their linguistic skills while allowing them the opportunity to improve their American English language skills. Encouraging a stronger self-concept so that there is the possibility of better achievement and more years devoted to study are all identified as central to a strong bilingual programme.

The controversy in the USA over bilingual education has become very complicated because the Supreme Court has entered the arena (Lau *vs* Nichols, January 1974) and ruled in favour of transitional bilingual programmes and 'opening up' the curriculum to non-English speakers. In the case of Chinese-speaking children in San Francisco the parents claimed that their children needed special help in American English in order to avoid the possibility of their children becoming drop-outs and unemployed youths with no skills.

Considerable controversy now exists over the interpretation of federal standards and guidelines for special programmes because of ambiguities in the court decision and a task force report that did not clarify the decision but which supported bilingual programmes, yet was never published in the Federal Register. Thus while some school districts are being cited for non-compliance with the court decision, others are saying the programme requirements are ambiguous because the task force report was not officially published.

The task force establishes what appear to be specific student identification guidelines (monolingual speaker of a language other than English, or a 'bilingual') but leaves it up to each district to decide how to interpret the guidelines. This in turn depends on the motivation of directors and teachers to pursue the matter. As noted above, the financial inducement may be as much of a hindrance to pursuing the guidelines as an aid to their development. There is so little basic research on the issue that school districts and their specialists and teachers cannot avail themselves of descriptive and analytical materials and procedures for creating some notion of 'adequate compliance'.

Meanwhile, those groups that oppose special programmes for bilingual education feel that the school should be involved in a minimal way and that it is up to the family and community to push such special programmes. There are many tacit overtones about the opposition to bilingual programmes. Some of them seem to be based on costs and the fact that creating the necessary expertise may be foolish because the need will not continue indefinitely nor even for a long enough time to warrant the cost. Other critics may be operating from a perspective of 'super' patriotism or prejudice in the sense of opposing special programmes for people who are not native Americans and who do not on their own learn to adapt to language and cultural customs associated with the use of American English. Court cases are being heard at present in Texas because of school districts refusing to provide free educational services to students of parents without documented residential status.

One way to resolve the bilingual issue in the USA would be to link it explicitly to another programme, namely a growing federal concern with the lack of foreign language teaching in the USA. Instead of bilingual programmes for minority students, several languages would be taught in the schools early on.

Teaching and the school setting

American teachers are seldom trained to deal with the multi-cultural backgrounds or languages of immigrant and minority children. Curricula are set up in a standardised way in each state to ensure some kind of uniformity, but there are differences across and within states. The training of teachers varies considerably *vis-à-vis* their exposure to language acquisition studies, child development research, and human information processing and problem-solving abilities. This variation in training also applies to their knowledge of racial and ethnic differences among different groups, the significance of social organisation, cultural beliefs, and the nature of language use and social interaction in daily life.

In such fundamental issues as reading comprehension and the acquisition of language skills there is often an enormous discrepancy between what is taught to future teachers and available to present teachers, and what is being taught and reported in research in major universities and centres of research on these topics. We are only now beginning to learn about the wide differences that exist in the way our students are able to learn new information by listening or reading. It is only recently that we are beginning to understand differences between successful and less successful learners among the dominant members of a society. We know very little about the way we should help less successful students from different ethnic or racial backgrounds learn from written and spoken materials. A key issue is what Bransford, Stein, Shelton and Owings (undated) call 'the learning to learn problem'. Research on the processes whereby new representations of knowledge are acquired is still in its infancy (Bransford, Nitsch and Franks, 1977; Brown, 1979; Neisser, 1976) and seldom if ever reaches teachers and those learning to be teachers.

Some specific issues have to do with how a child's working or short-term memory can be affected by inefficiency in decoding materials (Perfetti and Lesgold, 1978), but it is not clear how we should test for such problems or how we can increase decoding speed. We know little about the relation between spoken and written language or how a child acquires the ability to decode visual materials and render a spoken or written account of these materials. We need to know more about the way particular types of language experiences can affect differences between successful and less successful learners. These are basic issues in education that are especially important for understanding minority children and the children of migrant workers. But our point is that such information is seldom available to teachers and prospective teachers because of the organisation of colleges and universities and the dissemination of knowledge in western societies. The schools are seldom equipped to deal with children who have problems and there does not exist the financial support or motivation by school personnel for changing this, nor would it be easy to alter the structure of schools of education despite changes in professional educational research over the past ten years in America. There is no reason to believe that teachers in Europe or the UK are any better trained to deal with children with learning problems.

We are beginning to realise that children with limited types of language experience may have difficulty learning from materials that are not compatible with the way they have been learning before entering school. Hence the way textbooks are written becomes an important focus of attention for our understanding of such children. Yet there is little if any interaction between those who write textbooks and those who are doing the basic research on reading comprehension and language development. There are current efforts being made by the American Social Science Research Council Committee on Cognitive Research to correct this curious imbalance. Teachers are not in touch with the writers of texts, and because textbooks are a multimillion dollar industry in the USA, it is difficult to influence their preparation of books by insisting on more attention to recent basic research. In the case of textbooks for Hispanic groups there is often confusion because of differences in the Spanish spoken.

Another important issue has to do with the fact that reading activities in a classroom often differ from the way such activities are assessed in a laboratory. Only recently have researchers into reading comprehension and language competence started to examine these differences. The way language and reading are taught in the classroom and the way tests are given there to assess students is in contrast to what takes place in a laboratory. Teachers are usually unaware of the theoretical and methodological grounds for the assessment of reading and language skills in the laboratory and how they contrast with what the writers of textbooks assume when they prepare texts and reading and language tests.

We wish to stress that the assessment of children's and young adults' linguistic abilities and reading comprehension are not merely technical educational issues that European countries of migrant employment can readily delegate to their respective educational establishments. In the USA this delegation is an integral part of the way minority students are evaluated and the consequences have not proved adequate. Intervention in the educational system is a delicate matter both professionally and politically because there are many obvious vested interests. The pressures to intervene are growing in a large state like California where the concern with bilingual education and affirmative action creates pressures for the higher education establishment. Yet higher education in California, a system as large as in most countries in Europe, is not authorised or prepared to intervene in local education. In Europe a regional type of intervention would be necessary in order to break the hold that state and provincial officials have over education. But the key factor is recognising that we do not know much about the basic issues of language use, literacy, and their measures.

We do not have an adequate way of describing and measuring successful comprehension. We do not know the best way to identify what the reader needs to bring to an assigned text in order to satisfy the notion of 'successful comprehension'. We do not know what kinds of knowledge and skills readers need to be successful. We are still not clear how reading is different from taking a reading test: nor can we be clear what it is that a reading test is testing *vis-à-vis* a person's knowledge and experiences. We need to explore the instruction necessary for children to understand what is expected in a reading test. Specifying some of these details here is necessary if the general point is to be clear: *understanding the problem of minority students in America and the children of migrant workers in Europe requires basic research knowledge about educational issues that include all persons exposed to an educational system.* These problems are exacerbated in the case of minority students and the children of migrant workers, but we need basic research knowledge if we are to understand the circumstances that produce less successful students regardless of their origin and personal problems. The relevance of different cultural backgrounds, family organisation, and peer influences cannot be examined carefully if we do not understand learning as specific and general processes. When we seek to sustain social, cultural, and national identities and language use from the migrant's country of origin while simultaneously encouraging the learning of a new language in a different cultural context, we presuppose knowledge that is simply not available or if available not easily accessible for those faced with immediate policy decisions.

The reference to the discrepancy between what university researchers do and teach, what textbook writers assume they are conveying by their books and reading tests, and what teachers presume is adequate classroom performance, is all part of a larger institutional context that includes the way teachers' socio-cultural and educational backgrounds are formed, the way teachers are trained and supervised, the way they are kept abreast of new developments in their field, the way they assess students in the classroom, the way classroom materials are assigned and used, and the way standardised tests used for assessments carry serious consequences for the children. We cannot pretend to understand why minority students and the children of migrant workers are less successful than majority or indigenous students unless we examine these stratifying processes. But these issues occur in a socio-cultural context that is itself not a passive ingredient in the way the educational system works.

Teachers and administrators, aids or helpers in the classroom, and the majority group or children of the country of production (or employment) all function in a context of existing and changing prejudices and forms of discrimination against minority and migrant worker children. These patterns of prejudice and discrimination are embedded in everyday encounters that can be blatant or quite subtle and yet in all cases can be perceived as rejection and can hurt those afflicted. These patterns are not confined to the school; they occur wherever the minority children or the children of migrant workers encounter the majority groups or host population. *We wish to stress that the blatant and subtle forms of prejudice and discrimination in the school setting restrict the resources available to the child in order to deal with school tasks, hence making school work more difficult. The cultural and language differences mean migrant children have more to learn.* We know very little about the resulting literacy that emerges. If and when these children return to their country of origin, they are at a disadvantage compared to the children who did not accompany migrant parents. Hence these children often have difficulty becoming part of either society.

The concern with literacy is often defined by narrow linguistic and learning tasks that purport to address how to speak, read, and write a language. We can acknowledge that experiences and other forms of knowledge play important roles in assessing literacy, but the measures and tests we use seldom clarify the kinds of subtle yet basic knowledge structures that we acquire, seemingly effortlessly, by day-to-day living in an environment that we can identify with as natives. When we are dealing with native speakers the cultural experiences and knowledge are taken for granted in making up reading assignments and devising tests, yet as noted above, we still know very little about the reading or learning process and what is involved in successful and less successful reading and academic achievement among natives.

When we must face the problems of minority children and the children of migrant workers we tend to modify existing reading materials, tests, and conceptions of literacy as if they were obvious and readily applicable. Here the work of cross-cultural psychological research on intelligence can teach us something about the importance of not assuming a narrow conception of literacy based on forms of reasoning inherited from the Greeks as the backbone of what is meant by clear or logical reasoning. Recent work by the Laboratory of Comparative Human Cognition (Cole and Riel, undated) summarises the key issues.

Culture and intelligence

The issue of school performance of minority group children and children of migrant workers can be addressed in a more general way by calling attention to a long-standing view about the role of standard intelligence tests in orienting government policies to provide additional resources to national minority groups and the performances of third world groups on these tests. Throughout this century there have been discussions about the importance of racial and cultural theories of intelligence (Cole and Riel, undated). This line of work specifically addresses the inability of current theories to explain the relationship between culture and intelligence. One part of the paper is devoted to showing how difficult it is to reach agreement about what is meant by the terms intelligence and culture, much less the way culturally organised experience influences the development of clearly defined problem-solving skills.

We lack clear evidence about the principles that govern what must be done to be successful in the tasks selected as defining intelligence, yet there is now an internationally organised testing business dedicated to reporting correlations between the products of cognitive activity necessary for carrying out specific intellectual tasks, and the products that an individual generates as a consequence of the activities. We are still left with considerable doubt about the psychological processes that generate the performances that have been correlated (Cole and Riel, undated). Levels of performance can be the result of different factors and it is not clear that we can develop a testing device that will produce higher correlations between an IQ score and school success (Cole and Riel, undated; Cole, Sharp, and Lave, 1976).

In reviewing a vast literature on the relationship between culture and intelligence, the Laboratory of Comparative Human Cognition group notes that we have as yet not seriously addressed what is meant by the prior life experiences that can affect performance on different tasks used by cognitive psychologists. A serious difficulty that is central to this chapter is the point raised by the Laboratory of Human Cognition group: we cannot ensure that individuals have been given an equal opportunity to learn, and we know that individuals and groups have had differential practical experiences on tasks used on standard IQ tests. Moreover, research strongly implicates frequency of exposure to tasks as a strong determinant of the qualitative as well as quantitative aspects of performance. In more familiar terms, ignorance masquerades as stupidity. Present testing procedures and research on problem solving emphasise the extreme difficulty, if not the theoretical impossibility, of creating a culture-free intellectual task. A long tradition in cognitive psychology insists that we cannot easily infer the processes necessary for problem solving from the products of problem solving. If culture influences the way we reason and make inferences, then we cannot assume that the products of standardised intelligence tests give us some kind of direct access to higher and lower levels of ability.

In our discussion of minority groups in America and migrant workers and their families, we must keep in mind the fact that differences in culture and prior experiences are considered to be relevant factors for observing differences in school performance and testing activities using standardised tests. In the case of blacks in America, claims have been made by a few academics that genetic factors are the cause of lower IQ scores despite exposure to western schooling. Studies among African natives who have little or no western schooling reveal low performance on standardised tests, although schooling produces very marked improvements (Cole, Sharp, and Lave, 1976). But schooling alone is not enough to explain these differences. We do not hear genetic arguments made about the western-schooled children of Finland, Turkey, Spain, Mexico, Italy, Greece, and Portugal who remain in their country of origin. But we find persistent reports of the lack of achievement of these children when low-income families have migrated to European and North American countries. When there is a combination of higher income and western education we seldom if ever hear of deficits in learning ability and low IQ scores.

An important point underscored in the work of Cole and his colleagues is that cross-cultural psychologists have not been successful in sampling the everyday behaviour that is supposed to be associated with the assessment of intellectual abilities. The requirement of standardisation makes it difficult to recognise cultural differences especially when the issue of equal opportunity to learn cannot be satisfied. Cole and his associates have followed work by Russian psychologists, especially Vygotsky, in emphasising that the child's environment is socially organised and hence an integral part of the changing knowledge base needed for adequate development. The child is exposed to adults who regulate their social interaction and orient the child to adult patterns of behaviour. For the minority child and children of migrant workers the environment is seldom stable and they are often exposed to different adults who regulate and guide the child's behaviour and social interaction in a cultural context that changes outside the home. Unless we examine the socially organised contexts in which development and schooling occur, we cannot assess the problems of minority children and those of migrant workers, nor can we develop meaningful policies and programmes of intervention. We are reminded of Park's (1950) remarks here. The migrant family can organise practices that are dysfunctional in school, but they are probably realistic given the social constraints of the home.

The work on cross-cultural studies of cognition and intelligence provides us with an important lesson: cultural and class differences are integral aspects of conceptions of literacy despite claims by some researchers that culture-free, objective tests have been used. Cultural or folk conceptions of what is knowledge and intelligence are built-in features of assessment procedures. Yet we pretend that we possess objective measures of language skills, reading comprehension and intelligence. These measures become reified and distorted conceptions of literacy instead of being viewed as weak and crude attempts to understand very complex processes. The children of minority groups and migrant workers become the victims of institutionalised procedures that preserve the status quo while having a serious impact on the lives of many. Minority groups and migrant workers highlight what is amiss about western societies and their systems of inequality. Measures based on so-called objective tests incorporate notions of intelligence, cognitive processes, language skills, and socio-cultural knowledge that are derived from conceptions favourable to the majority group or indigenous population. We create a self-fulfilling prophecy of failure and degradation for those affected while seeking an objective solution to the problem.

We assume it is easy for a group or country to be able to step back, and with the detachment we attribute to scientific research, examine its routine practices of discrimination and use of so-called objective tests and measures in order to identify, develop, and implement corrective practices for a way of life that is so integrally a part of the host society's or group's way of life. We can all agree that every migrant worker and his or her child should be guaranteed the right to sustain their cultural, social, or national identity and language. We find that people pay lip service to the legality of such ideals, as well as affirmative action programmes, civil rights, and perhaps bilingual school curricula. The 'lip service' also covers cultural ambivalence where the policies are either political compromises or are undermined at local levels by those who are supposed to carry them out. If we want to enforce and implement such ideals we need to change patterns of daily living, of speaking, of interaction, of reasoning, and of expressing emotions. These changes are strongly resisted because they are contrary to the way we actually live.

What appear to be contradictions between ideals and practices in western democracies are different aspects of normal living. Our research and intervention is not likely to make or effect big changes in these daily practices. We need to ask if our essays and research on different aspects of a group's or society's activities can provide sufficient knowledge with which to cushion the impact of the consequences of normal contradictions and resistance to change. Can we recognise the constraints of our knowledge about group life and individual differences in order to make low-level changes that can be cumulative and lead to a gradual realisation of idealistic goals?

What sorts of changes at local school levels could have long-term effects? These local changes, however, presume that we can expect to recruit teachers with diverse ethnic and cultural backgrounds, who are better trained. We would also need more elaborate attempts to monitor and intervene in the instruction of children at an early age. Changing teacher education programmes is quite difficult, and even when we can train teachers differently they must adjust to a more conservative school district. A commitment to reorganise teacher training programmes, and efforts to achieve a better articulation between those engaged in basic research on learning skills, those who write textbooks and those who devise tests, must be linked to what is practised by teachers in pre-school and school programmes. Improving the skills of all children at an early age will result in more competition in schools and an improvement in general school performance. Many middle-income level families would probably react because their children would encounter more difficulty in achieving access to college-oriented courses. These families often influence their children's educational career although the children cannot meet the required normal levels of achievement.

The suggested changes in teacher training and more direct contacts between those doing basic research, teachers, and writers of texts and tests, and more direct intervention in the lives of children with poor school performance, are attempts to change society from the 'inside' in recognition that more general and drastic political changes from the top down would encounter serious opposition. The possibility of such changes remains doubtful.

In the USA we are facing a confrontation with respect to affirmative action programmes in higher education because of a statistical argument that can be used effectively to show that current affirmative action programmes are failing despite concerted efforts by governmental agencies and the use of threats and various sanctions. These programmes cannot be implemented unless there are systematic changes in the educational system. Nor can we expect to eliminate the discrimination and prejudice that are a normal part of the American way of life. But we can seek to create conditions which attempt to give minority groups a better chance to compete successfully. This competition will probably generate other tensions but it should help blunt the self-fulfilling prophecy that now seems to be built into existing conditions of inequality that are normal activities throughout the USA and Europe.

Perspectives attributed to migrant families

Some researchers (Rosen, 1973) have argued that foreign workers have shown that they develop high educational aspirations for their children in a way that is similar to immigrants. These families can become sources of important changes in the careers of their children so long as formal and informal policies of the country of residence do not block these efforts. Hence we need to know more about the initial and subsequent contacts between the families of migrant workers and the school systems in the country of residence that accept their children. For example, we can expect migrant parents to perceive the educational setting as a place where they must face language obstacles. The parents' conception of what they will encounter based on what others have told them, or based on some preliminary contacts, will influence the extent to which parents create expectations about the school setting, including ways of talking that enable school personnel to intimidate the parents or to create an atmosphere where the parents are not sure of their rights or what they can do about specific and general problems they perceive. It is at the everyday level of contact with the schools that we must direct some of our research energy in order to learn more about the obstacles that are perceived and encountered by the families of migrant workers. This school contact is part of a larger concern to be presented below in terms of language use and the nature of social interaction in different social settings that the migrant families must negotiate each day or week.

By observing migrant families in the school setting we can learn something about the way the bureaucratic organisation in the country of residence perceives migrants and the kind of official and subtle reactions and treatments that can be expected and practised. We need to know the extent to which the bureaucracy defines the ground rules within which migrant parents will be permitted to express themselves and learn about their children and the educational setting. To what extent do cultural patterns of the migrants' country of origin influence their behaviour in the country of residence? The migrants may bring beliefs and expectations that set the tone of the encounters even if the educational officials (teachers and administrators) are sensitive and sympathetic to the problems of migrant workers. For example, do teachers and administrators permit and encourage the parent to speak informally, in a narrative form that enables the parent to be expressive? Or do teachers and/or administrators create conditions wherein the parent feels intimidated and then withdraws or becomes hostile and angry?

There has been some recent research on a few of the issues discussed above but the kinds of data obtained and analysed vary considerably. In their work on immigrants in Western Europe, Castles and Kosack (1973) note that the educational opportunities offered to minority and immigrant groups are extremely restricted. Immigrant workers rarely receive vocational training and this means that they will encounter considerable difficulties in being promoted beyond a semi-skilled level. These authors state that the children of immigrant workers face educational difficulties that are the result of being placed in a strange setting of different teachers and students. These children are unlikely to reach the same level of achievement as those of the majority group. Castles and Kosack note that it is not in the interest of the dominant group to create and follow policies that would lead the migrants and their children into better circumstances because such action would deprive the country of employment of an adequate supply of cheap, unskilled labour. Similar remarks have been made about Mexican migrant workers in the USA who were recruited for a short period but who then settled in the country of employment and brought their families.

The children of migrant workers are often recipients of what have been called 'compensatory instructional programmes' in the USA. These programmes include special provisions for children who are bilingual and encounter difficulties in normal classrooms. Labov (1968) has argued that compensatory educational programmes organised for minority and immigrant children are often inadequate because they are derived from deficient models that assume that a rich educational environment is lacking in the homes of these children. A stereotypic perspective assumed by such programmes is that the parents of minority and immigrant children do not value education highly, do not encourage their children to succeed in school, and spend little time helping their children with school work or with learning new cultural ideas. We lack adequate studies of the nature of the school environment from the perspective of migrant parents. These perspectives need to be contrasted with the views of teachers and administrators and students of the country of residence.

44

School conditions

A sensitive issue that is cited over and over again in the American case has to do with school districts that are lax in the way they deal with minority students with language and cultural problems. Such districts are viewed as not having sufficiently trained professional personnel, especially teachers, to handle the problems that the minority students can have. In developing a policy or a set of guidelines that could be of help to countries with large contingents of migrant workers, it would be important to stress the necessity of examining the general orientations of their educational personnel and the day-to-day practices and views held by professional educators and teachers who are involved with the children of migrant workers. We need studies of the different views that exist within educational circles in order to deal with the problem of educating the children of migrant workers realistically. It is all too easy to assume that the educational establishment will have appropriate personnel and will deal with the matter in a competent manner.

The American experience is not likely to be different from that in European countries in the broad sense, nor even in the particulars of actual achievement, drop-out rates, lowered self-esteem, frustration and under-achievement in the classroom, withdrawal from school life, discipline problems, and the like.

The evaluation of the experience of children of migrant workers in European schools requires information on the distribution of such children in particular schools. It is important to know the extent to which these children interact with each other and how much contact they have with other children. The familiar problem here is the benefit, on the one hand, of having indigenous children with whom a child can communicate, while on the other hand, being relatively isolated. We do not know if this child will become more strongly motivated to pursue the study of the language of the country of residence. Sustained contact with the children of other migrant families can result in a stronger sense of group identity, but we do not know if it can also lead to higher drop-out rates, frustration and under-achievement in the classroom, discipline problems, and withdrawal from school life.

Our evaluation of the problem requires observation of actual classrooms and interviews with teachers and administrators in order to establish a first-hand source of information about day-to-day experiences. These observations and interviews would also necessitate additional interviews with students and parents in order to understand how indigenous students and migrant worker children perceive each other, and how their respective parents view their children's involvement with host or migrant children.

In assessing the performance of Mexican-American and Puerto Rican children in the USA, special attention has been given to the extent to which these persons repeated different grades. Repeating grades creates social problems of adjustment, while the practice of promoting the child who does not do well in school has been associated with serious intellectual and then discipline problems. In each case careful observation in classroom settings is necessary if we are to understand the consequences of poor school performance on the children of migrant workers. The child who is reading below grade level in the fourth, eighth, and twelfth grades, common among Puerto Rican and Mexican-Americans in the USA, poses problems for the kind of future employment that can be available. Low reading ability in the early grades is not likely to change by later grades and we must be able to intervene early in the school career if we are to assess the extent to which remedial work will have an important impact on the child's achievement.

What appears to be a simple problem of tabulating drop-outs for Puerto Rican and Mexican-American adolescents is not so simple when we examine the conditions under which such information is obtained and then forwarded to some official agency as 'fact'. The administrative staff of a school reviews attendance forms to infer a lack of attendance or truancy. Follow-up information on these youths is not always available and a stereotyped interpretation of such cases as having 'moved on' and hence not worth pursuing is common. The stereotype attributes irresponsibility to Puerto Rican and Mexican-American adolescents and a feeling that such cases are not worth the trouble. Similar stereotypes exist for the adolescent children of migrant workers in other parts of the world.

Students who take the trouble to report leaving school because of moving to another district, or dropping out of day school to enrol in adult continuing education courses at night, may be leaving for reasons similar to those who are having difficulties with their studies or because of feeling frustrated about the teaching setting, but in each case we seldom know if the students actually continue their education. The communication between the student and a counsellor or administrative official is under-utilised as a source of information about the student's problems and as a source of information about how the school personnel relate to the students. Available statistical information (cf. Romo, undated) reveals that students are reported as leaving primarily for 'lack of attendance and habitual truancy', but virtually never for academic failure. The statistical information, however, tells us nothing about the students' perception of the problem; nor are we told anything about the relationship between student, teacher, other students, and administrative personnel.

A neglected area of research is the parental perception of the school setting and their influence over the child's continuance in school. Except for Rosen's (1973) study, we do not know the extent to which parents (one or both) view the school experience as essential or as a luxury: nor the extent to which parents prefer their children to leave school as soon as possible to begin working. The nature of school-parent interaction and the kinds of information that are communicated from school to home and vice versa, is never addressed ethnographically in studies of migrant workers and their families. Considerable effort may be needed in order to stimulate the parents' interest and even more effort to keep the parents informed when subtle if not more open discrimination exists in the country of residence towards migrant workers and their families. The extent to which school officials establish relations with parents needs to be studied, as well as the nature of these contacts.

Learning about the parents of school children is necessary if we are to assess the child's motivation to enter and continue an educational programme. A basic policy issue here is the extent to which the children of migrant workers will be encouraged to compete with indigenous children for educational rewards. To what extent will encouragement include competition for higher education as well as for entry into programmes which train adolescents for skilled jobs that would place them in competition with the adolescent children of the host country?

The level of detail needed for understanding the school environment and its impact on migrant children and their parents can be outlined as follows:

1 Who assumes responsibility for dealing with the school? Is the responsibility arranged unilaterally by the husband? By the wife?

2 What language factors influence parental contact with the school? Do parents begin to delegate their responsibility to children who speak the host language better? What sorts of interaction exchanges occur in the family *vis-à-vis* these issues?

3 What channels of communication exist for the parents to contact school authorities? Do parents discuss such issues as the kind of schooling their children should receive and for how long?

4 What awareness do parents have of their children's school activities? Can and do they help with the homework?

5 How are the problems of special school clothing (if relevant) handled? Do meals become a problem for the child at school?

6 Do the parents become involved in contacting school officials about their child's academic performance in class? Are they aware of the child's achievement level? How does their knowledge and participation compare with that of the native parents of comparable socio-economic level?

7 Are there school activities attended by the parents that include and exclude the children? Do migrant workers and/or their spouses attend such activities? Are there volunteer activities where parents are encouraged to become contributors to the classroom?

8 Do parents remove their children from school for special trips back to the country of origin? If so, what are the consequences of such trips for the children?

9 Are the parents aware of classroom activities? Do they ever visit the school and the child's classroom?

Schooling and the labour market

The larger policy issue of removing barriers so that children of migrant workers can compete with those of the country of residence can have profound consequences for the overall stratification system of that society. The kind of labour needed is often unskilled but we need to know what demand exists for semi-skilled and skilled positions. If the country of employment is successful in raising the educational and vocational skills of even 25 per cent of the children of migrant children, then the number of such children who can compete with native children can pose problems *vis-à-vis* increased unemployment by native workers. If wage differentials are permitted openly if not covertly, then industrial practices can exacerbate the problem of unemployment for the latter, while increasing the potential for conflict between the two groups. The problem we must address is the consequences of being successful in socialising the children of migrant workers to the educational and occupational levels of the country of employment.

Although it is seldom possible for migrant workers to remain in the country of employment long enough for the children to enter the labour market, displace natives, and also remain in the country after the parents have retired, the necessity of a long-range policy is evident if migrant workers remain for more than one generation. As migrant workers and their families become permanent residents the question of their legal rights will become more and more of an issue, particularly in the way their children are affected. If the country of residence is successful in socialising the children to more education than their migrant parents, with even moderate success in competing with indigenous children, then important changes in the social stratification of the country of employment can occur.

The preceding paragraphs have alluded to the general problem of migrant workers remaining for long periods; they and their grown children begin to assume tacit if not demand explicit rights regarding health, retirement, and housing. Hence we are talking about large-scale and permanent changes that are likely from having migrant workers resident in the country of employment for long periods. The American experience under these conditions would become even more relevant to an understanding of the European setting. If the job stability of employment demanded by the country of employment depends on individual workers, then there can be serious changes in the way migrant workers and their families can be treated *vis-à-vis* housing, health care delivery, education, vacation and retirement benefits, and the like. But if stability of employment means periodic replacement of migrant workers, then few concessions have to be made and there is not likely to be much social mobility. The society, therefore, becomes dependent on migrant workers and perhaps more antagonistic or conflicting with them as workers if they remain longer and longer in the country and if the children of these workers begin to achieve some level of success in competing with members of the country of residence.

When the children of migrant workers cannot succeed in competition with natives, the problems will be of a different sort but no less serious. The country of residence can expect adolescents of migrant workers who are more knowledgeable about the host society, and have a greater proficiency in the use of the native language, to want more than their parents, to demand more, and to be prime candidates for more illicit types of activities if they are unable to compete successfully in the job market.

An idealised solution is not likely to be a viable alternative because it is unlikely that the indigenous population will spend extra time and exhibit great interest in migrant workers and their families, even under the best economic conditions. There is no indication that Europe is any better at accepting migrants of different ethnic or racial background than the Americans have been. The problems of European migrants and their families, therefore, become world problems in the sense that we find similar circumstances wherever we look.

Cultural identity and the educational success of migrant workers

At a 1978 meeting sponsored by Unesco on migrant workers a number of experts met to affirm the right of these workers and their families to maintain their own language and cultural, social and national identity. By emphasising the importance for the workers of finding solutions to social isolation, the difficulties of meeting the challenge of a new environment, and their lack of knowledge about the language and way of life in the host country, these experts recognised that pressures will emerge to push the migrants towards assimilation while experiencing prejudice, rejection, and discrimination. In this section we wish to stress the peculiar contradictions that exist because of the simultaneous conditions of maintaining an identity and language consistent with the country of origin, fighting pressures for assimilation, and living with a problematic set of circumstances regarding the social structure of the country of residence — for example, being sufficiently successful so that the natives become threatened by a group on which they have also become dependent.

We wish to draw a parallel between the migrant workers of Europe and Puerto Ricans, Mexicans, and Mexican-Americans or Chicanos of the USA. The parallel is not unlike that between migrants to North America and South America, and immigration to Australia. In the case of Puerto Ricans and Mexicans and Chicanos concern has been expressed to preserve a language and identity consistent with the country of origin. With other immigrant groups researchers stress the ability of these migrants' children to assimilate the language and customs of the new country, and even the parents, depending on their age at the time of immigration, will also achieve considerable assimilation. The studies by Lloyd Warner (1945) and his associates provide us with relevant data here.

The recent Unesco reports expressing concern with maintaining the cultural heritage of migrant workers in Europe has also existed as a serious issue in the USA where there has been preoccupation with developing and sustaining one's cultural heritage and language and civil rights by legal means. An integral aspect of this concern with cultural identity and civil rights are the affirmative action programmes that have become a national concern in both public and private sectors, and especially in educational circles.

Opponents of bilingual and affirmative action programmes in the USA have often taken the position that 'everyone' should speak American English and that everyone should be treated the same regarding admission to educational programmes and employment practices. The existence of tacit or covert practices of discrimination, argue the opponents of bilingual and affirmative action programmes, does not justify a 'reverse discrimination' of allowing minorities to move ahead of better or even equally qualified members of the 'majority' *vis-à-vis* educational admission and jobs. The insistence on quotas and time schedules by minority group members has only intensified the efforts of opponents to block such ideas by their own legal measures.

The opponents of bilingual and affirmative action programmes in the USA point out that the children of Asian and European immigrants have shown remarkable success in education and occupational pursuits despite prejudice and discrimination and having to deal with a home language that was different from American English. Opponents of affirmative action ask why no one has been able to come up with a clear explanation for differences between Puerto Ricans, blacks, and Chicanos, and Asian and European immigrant children with respect to school success, and scores on standard intelligence and achievement tests. Some researchers have attributed this differential to genetic differences, while others would specify cultural differences and the lack of environmental resources. But we cannot find adequate support for the genetic view. Some researchers might want to argue that discrimination against European immigrants has never been strong.

There is a curious paradox here. The children of immigrants from Europe to the USA are viewed as success stories, while the Puerto Ricans, blacks, and Mexican-Americans are viewed as educational failures. In Europe perhaps many of the children of migrant workers can be viewed as failures, and this group covers a wide spectrum of cultural differences. We are talking about Lapps, Finns, Greeks, Spaniards, Moroccans, Yugoslavs, Italians, Portuguese, Turkish, Algerians, Tunisians, West Indians, and Black Africans. In a country like Italy genetic differences are invoked in northern Italy to explain the performance of southern Italian children of migrant workers. Swedes can join Americans: the former can find 'retarded' children among the Finnish, while the latter can find them among Puerto Rican and Mexican-American children based on school performance. In rejecting the genetic argument we are not saying that cultural and environmental perspectives are without problems. We are, however, arguing that explicit and subtle prejudice and discrimination can be a more powerful force when employed by a dominant group that perceives the minority group as sustaining cultural identities and languages that are viewed as alien and foreign to the majority's way of life. The very conditions which have been proposed as necessary for the integrity, stability and continuity of an ethnic or cultural identity among minorities and migrant workers and their families, seem to be important sources of subtle discrimination and prejudice by the dominant majority. But in the USA even when low-income minority groups like Puerto Ricans and Mexican-Americans avoid living in groups that perpetuate the cultural orientation of their country of origin, and become assimilated, monolingual, and American English speaking, the prejudice and discrimination against them does not vanish or diminish dramatically.

The affirmative action programmes currently in force in the USA do not address directly the social organisation of American society *vis-à-vis* the education of minorities and the extent to which the cultural context of the family discourages and does not support academic success, especially when the family perceives the educational system as a hostile entity that is not likely to further the chances of increased economic support from its younger members. One perspective here is that there are strong economic demands coming from the family and the peer group to enter the labour market in order to participate in highly valued and needed material consumption. This perspective argues that young minority members are not motivated to think of educational success because of difficult school experiences. In other words, why put up with a frustrating and unsuccessful educational experience that is also viewed as a burden that leads to delayed monetary or material gratification for one's efforts?

The minority child in the USA enters a school system and a labour market that contain conditions of prejudice and subtle discrimination. We could suggest that the legal and public pressure approach to civil rights and affirmative action and bilingual education has made white Americans more sensitive to the necessity of becoming subtle, clever, and innovative as far as exercising any negative views or prejudice or discrimination against minorities. This more subtle approach to dealing with minorities occurs at a time when the latter groups are quite vocal in their demands for more involvement in the rewards of the society. The push for more realisation and protection of minority rights and rapid compliance with some kind of scheduled affirmative action programme and bilingual education could be viewed as helping opponents develop a justification for claiming reverse discrimination while simultaneously practising subtle forms themselves. But what about those whites who support affirmative action, better educational opportunities, better occupational positions, and protected civil rights for minorities?

Whites who support affirmative action, civil rights, and bilingual programmes must face the fact that existing data do not reveal much chance of changing current conditions; affirmative action programmes are not succeeding. Questions arise about the 'pool' of available minorities given existing educational practices. Some people have started to ask that Asian minorities and even women should not be included in future evaluations of affirmative action because these latter groups are making considerably more progress than are blacks, Puerto Ricans, and Chicanos. This would decrease the 'pool'.

Some demographers in the USA are predicting higher fertility for minorities than for the majority and hence increased minority enrolments in higher education for the remainder of the twentieth century. But there is no clear consensus here. These demographic projections may be accurate with regard to fertility, but their relevance for education is not clear because of the daily practices of social organisation and social interaction at school and work. If the social organisation of the schools continues to produce differentials in educational success among minorities and the majority groups, then there is not likely to be that much change over the next decade unless this social organisation changes. These changes cannot be accomplished only by laws; they require changes in daily practices.

Can we change the cultural views about minority groups that exist within the dominant majority? Can we change school systems, train new teachers differently and re-train current teachers, counsellors, and testers that now populate school districts? It is unlikely that we can make that many changes in these groups and institutions over the next decade. Such changes run against powerful interests and beliefs that the trouble is not to be found in the educational system, but in the alleged laziness, incompetence, indifference, and inferior nature of minorities who do not succeed. But even among those who believe the educational system needs to be changed (including conservative interests), there remains the belief on the part of many Americans that minorities who do not succeed cannot succeed, at least not with their own resources.

The same conservative and liberal groups surely exist in Europe as they exist in America. The migrant worker of Europe is subject to very similar kinds of subtle prejudice and discrimination when trying to compete for jobs with native workers. In the school system the same kinds of views about the inability of the children of migrant workers to compete will prevail. Such views can be found in different parts of Europe.

A familiar question must be asked about minorities in America who do not succeed and migrant workers and their families in Europe who experience difficulties in school and in adjusting to the country of employment. Is it possible for minorities in America to sustain their language and social, cultural, and national identity, and for migrant workers and their families in Europe to do the same, while simultaneously acquiring the 'host' language, and the knowledge of social organisation and cultural beliefs and practices of the American scene or host country? What constraints do individuals and groups encounter here because of competing resources that must be used to deal with the two forms of life? Is this an appropriate way to pose the problem? The argument is that there are not the same constraints for Polish-Americans, Greek-Americans, Lebanese-Americans, and Chinese-Americans who seek to sustain ethnic ties while simultaneously demonstrating native American characteristics and competing successfully in school and in the labour market. We believe that the constraints are different and the basis of this difference is to be found in forms of social organisation and the cultural factors that keep the minority groups and migrant workers oriented to their home country. What do we have to know about the everyday life of these groups in order to demonstrate that significant differences exist in their social organisation and cultural beliefs and practices, and that these differences result in serious discrepancies in the ability of one group to compete successfully in school and in the labour market?

But what of those Puerto Ricans, blacks and Chicanos who have succeeded? Can we find comparable migrant workers and particularly younger members of their families who have succeeded? But in Europe and in the USA we are not equating success in school and in the labour market with an integration of these persons with members of the dominant society; nor is such integration implied with the others mentioned above as successful immigrant groups. We really know very little about those members of minority groups who can be called 'successful' in both the world of the dominant group and a minority group. We know little about the educational systems of the USA and Europe. We can only be speculative about the organisational or institutional constraints and practices that could account for poor performances in the classroom and in testing situations among minorities and the children of migrant workers considered 'unsuccessful'.

Concluding remarks and recommendations

A tacit and sometimes explicit thesis running throughout this chapter has been the idea that the economic conditions which lead to the use of migrant workers is a reflection of a system of social stratification that defines undesirable but necessary work conditions. The economic necessity of importing workers leads to serious social consequences that go considerably beyond the economic conditions cited. The social consequences refer to altering the stratification system by creating a new lower stratum. The economic demands can be satisfied with positive results for the economy. The social organisation of the society can be altered in ways that generate new conflicts and antagonisms. Housing, schools, recreational areas, and public transportation are affected fairly quickly. Interpersonal contacts are affected, including stereotypes about the migrants. As migrants and their families remain longer in a country there are increasing strains on social services and all aspects of community life.

A difficult dilemma invariably emerges with migrants. They are expected to assimilate enough in order to know the country of employment sufficiently well so that they can obey laws and customs and communicate adequately *vis-à-vis* their work, leisure, and routine daily activities. But migrants are not expected to make demands that begin to encroach upon the dominant group's status superiority. A little social mobility can be perceived as threatening. With more assimilation and acculturation the migrants are likely to demand more rights and this can intensify the discrimination by the dominant group. The story is an old one and is well known to the reader.

The attempt to teach language skills, educate and socialise migrant workers and their families has led to the identification of a number of different problems for all age groups. One central issue, however, emerges and persists: the school systems and governmental agencies of the country of migrant employment seldom make the needed distinction between the language skills necessary for getting along in the everyday life of a specific country, and the linguistic skills necessary for competing successfully in the school system. The language skills necessary for adapting to everyday community settings and low-skilled or semi-skilled employment are not the same as the skills needed for competing in a labour market that will enable migrant workers and especially their children to become socially mobile. Success with linguistic and cognitive skills in school is perceived by industry and governmental agencies as necessary for better jobs. Without these skills migrant workers and their children will remain stagnant in the labour market.

The case of blacks in North America has been a stark lesson. Black youths in the USA are exceptionally proficient in an oral tradition that exists in what is called the 'inner city or black ghetto'. These black children can reveal oral language skills that are equivalent if not superior to middle-income white children. But when these children are in school the white students routinely out-perform the black students from the 'inner city' on formal linguistic skills and reading comprehension.

If we want to develop a language programme that recognises the black experience we need to create learning conditions that will make use of the cultural circumstances of successful language use as claimed by Au and Jordan (in press) for Hawaiian children. But what is more important is the distinction between the language skills needed to 'get along' in German by the wives of Turkish factory workers, and the formal linguistic skills needed by their nine-year-old daughter enrolled in the German educational system. The courses developed for adults to 'get along' in everyday community and work settings are likely to be less rigorous than those the daughter must learn in her school. The Turkish factory worker who wants to improve his social standing through a better job will need formal linguistic skills.

The point we are trying to make is that the articulation of educational and labour institutions remains the key issue in all systems of social stratification. We cannot keep language skills and formal educational skills separate in the labour market because they have serious consequences for employment and social mobility and reveal important ways that stratifying practices operate in all countries.

The idea that migrant workers are 'guest workers' who presumably will remain in the host country for only a short period of time can be a convenient myth for not addressing problems which have been endemic to the USA since the country was founded. Even without a fair level of European prosperity, there will be a migrant worker problem. The longer such workers and their families remain in the country of employment (including those who have attained permanent resident status), the more difficult will be the relationships between the indigenous group and the migrant groups. As the children of migrant workers grow older their progress in school will help determine the extent to which they will compete with native workers for different kinds of employment.

The more acculturated the children and adolescents of migrant workers become, the greater the likelihood of dating and intermarriage between the minority and majority groups. The stratification system is always affected. Two general forms of contact and relationships between dominant and minority groups will be day-to-day contact necessary for daily living, and contacts that are perceived by the host group as challenging existing stratificational practices. We need more information about both kinds of contacts. The present literature and research is not adequate for an understanding of what has and will happen with migrant workers.

We need studies that can combine elements of a survey and extended interviews with forms of participant observation and quasi-field experiments. These would include sending migrants of different ages and gender to everyday settings in communities of the country of employment in order to assess the stratifying practices and discrimination that exist. Native observers would follow in the case of trying to rent an apartment, or be unobtrusively present when routine or more complex bank or purchasing or leisure activities are involved.

The quasi-field experiment is an important methodology for obtaining first-hand information about conditions in the country of migrant employment. But these studies also require selected ethnographic projects that can point to problems of migrants and their families as encountered in everyday life. If we are to explore the remarks suggested earlier about classroom and testing environments in which children of migrant workers are tested and evaluated, we need ethnographic studies that can sample the actual stratifying practices of the classroom and testing exercises. We need a cognitive—linguistic ethnography that enables us to assess school and testing performance as they are affected by socio-cultural forms of organisation. Unless we can implement such studies it will not be possible to assess the age at which school performance begins to become a source of information for classifying the children of migrant workers as less successful than native children.

Ethnographic studies are required for an understanding of the daily round of activities that parents and children pursue. (For school studies see Mehan, 1977; 1979; Hymes, in press.) Such activities become the basis for assessing the nature of migrant—native interpersonal relations and provide us with a baseline from which to conduct quasi-experimental research. The combination of ethnographic and quasi-experimental research enables us to clarify policy issues and plans for possible intervention studies that could guide us in attempting to make socio-cultural changes. Such changes are difficult to realise. But there is little point in seeking such changes unless we have an adequate data base with which to formulate policy issues. At present we have accumulated considerable demographic and survey data and impressionistic accounts to convince many people of several problem areas and the kinds of difficulties migrants face as well as those faced by the country of migrant employment. But these sources of information are not sufficiently contextualised to permit us to know what sorts of reaction we could expect from the indigenous population if we were to recommend specific policy changes and programmes.

Policies and programmes that are designed to help migrants will surely affect the indigenous population, but we cannot assess the consequences unless we know something about the stratifying practices that exist in the socio-cultural contexts within which migrants are contracted for work and how local authorities perceive their arrival and plan for their presence. We have noted above that the larger social stratificational system of the country of immigration will always be altered by the presence of migrant workers. We have neglected studying the stratifying practices of the country of residence for too long by relying on demographic and survey data that are necessary for an overall picture, but which do not provide sufficient information with which to assess daily life conditions. The demographic and survey data can give us a general picture of school success, social mobility, and changes in material life style. But these data cannot tell us much about the processes and mechanisms in everyday life that create choice points: Decision conditions that are embedded in interpersonal encounters and are subtle in the way they are resolved: the systematic yet tacit ways in which discrimination is practised; and the way subtle obstacles are placed in the way of migrants.

The blatant and subtle aspects of 'migrant—host' country encounters have perhaps been captured best by fictional and cinematic accounts. The study of these experiences and stratifying activities is difficult but feasible. A particularly vivid way to capture the blatant and subtle aspects of discrimination and the indifference that generates feelings of rejection in migrant workers and their families can be found in the socialisation experiences of children and adolescents. Children are often exposed to more blatant aspects of 'host' culture rejection by other children. These stratifying encounters will be re-told to other children and to the parents. The burden of the re-telling will often fall on the mothers.

Children can be rather direct in the way they ridicule another child's language use, dress, eating habits, food consumption, hair style and the like. Daily social relationships are affected by the way groups play during class breaks, after school, and in the way that parties are organised and guests invited. The impact of adult stratifying practices is always felt by children. We are referring to conditions that are obvious, difficult to know about by using demographic and survey data, but which must be studied in natural settings.

The impact of adult stratifying practices as employed by the country of migrant employment becomes more explicit and obvious as children enter adolescence and begin to wonder about the utility of identifying with their parents. The child's concern can be with escaping from reactions they perceive are meted out to their parents by members of the majority group. The dual culture notion becomes relevant here because of the identity problems that adolescents are supposed to have normally in western societies that prolong childhood by creating adolescence. The issue is now that of toying with or choosing between two possible identities and trying to 'pass' by simulating native or indigenous stratifying practices, including some that appear to punish their migrant parents, or adopting a hybrid identity marked by language, dress, and patterns of behaviour that may be viewed negatively by the 'host' country and home country natives.

The concern with school proficiency must not ignore what the adolescent student must be able to do when he or she leaves school and must face a difficult employment situation. By difficult we do not simply mean one in which there are few jobs, not a trivial problem in itself. We refer instead to the more delicate, subtle discrimination in hiring practices whereby a person's qualifications are not honoured in a clear and open way because of appearances and the fact that a negative social stigma is often attributed to migrant workers and their families, especially when these persons move into settings in the country of employment where they are felt not to 'belong'. Subtle discrimination within the school setting is a serious problem. When it also extends to the work environment and by necessity to social spheres of life in the country of employment, the problem can become tense and volatile.

The relationships between adolescents of migrant workers and those of the 'host' society become an important way to learn about possible patterns of assimilation and acculturation. The daily round of activities of adolescents, their use of their native language, their knowledge and use of the language, become windows to an understanding of the changes that we can expect and that do occur among migrant workers and their families.

We need studies, therefore, of how these adolescents enter the labour force, at what age, and the way they are advised to seek employment. Do they rely on a network based on the migrant community? This is a common pattern in all countries where there is a critical mass of migrants. The availability of this network facilitates obtaining employment, but it does not ensure that the adolescent's capabilities will be assessed adequately so that better jobs will be possible. Unless we can trace the way these young adults find their way into the labour force and understand their perception of what is available and what obstacles are likely to be encountered, we will not be able to assess the extent to which generational changes are occurring, or the extent to which normal stratifying practices prevail.

An important area we must learn about to understand the adjustment of young adults from the migrant community revolves around their interpersonal relations with other young adults, including those from the country of residence and especially relationships with persons viewed as potential sexual or marital partners. These relationships are part of a larger leisure-time set of activities in which we can expect young adults to be more active than their parents in seeking to penetrate the social settings of the country of residence. In order to understand leisure activities and interpersonal contacts, we need to know about the way leisure activities occur outside the home after school. Contacts between adolescents of migrant workers and those indigenous to the country of production or employment will form the basis for how each group perceives the other. The extent to which individuals or groups will seek more or less contact will depend on the way encounters occur or are avoided. These encounters provide the adolescent with the experience and knowledge base for planning or avoiding future contacts.

We need to know how adolescents and young adults of migrant workers assess the stratifying responses of the indigenous adolescents and young adults. What sorts of stereotypes does each group employ when speaking about the other group? What is the nature of their interpersonal contacts? What experiences do migrant adolescents and young adults have when trying to date or strike up a friendship with their counterparts in the host society? When migrant adolescents and young adults create their own groups, do they ostracise those who seek out and frequent with members of the host society? And the obverse? How do indigenous adolescents and young adults react when they have and tell each other about the advances or their contacts with migrant adolescents and young adults? Do they tend to ostracise those who associate with migrants? There are many such examples, but little in the way of systematic study. Again, the North American case illustrates the point because there are many anecdotes and impressionistic data on the matter, but there is little in the way of careful ethnographic and observational research. There are novels and cinematic portrayals of these problems, and various journalistic accounts, and in the USA these issues have been subjected to popular cultural discussion and portrayal for many years. The lack of carefully gathered information continues.

Our central recommendations, therefore, have been made by reference to the lack of adequate studies about the nature of 'migrant—host' contacts, their stratifying practices, and their perceptions of each other. We need to know about these contacts and the kinds of stereotypes that are employed and learned if we are to understand the equally serious long-range implications of having migrant workers in the countries of employment for long periods of time. The problem then becomes more like the immigration problems that have occurred in North and South America, Australia, New Zealand, to mention some key areas. We have generated too many general reports about the nature of the problem while ignoring the larger consequences for the social stratification of the societies involved.

This chapter has repeatedly stated that we must examine the problems of migrant workers in the larger context of the social stratificational systems of the countries of employment. We must understand the nature of stratifying practices that normally exist in these countries and how these practices are altered or sustained when migrant workers and natives encounter each other. Stratifying practices include the socially sanctioned ways a society has developed to assess the competence of its members in social, school, and occupational settings. Hence the way children are tested for placement in a school, a reading group, a higher grade level, movement into higher levels of education, all become exemplars of these stratifying practices. In the social realm this means the way dress and general appearances are planned and evaluated, and the way ethnic, religious, and skin colour differences are assessed and hence stratified by members of the host society and members of migrant communities.

Another area we must address is the kind of communicative competence displayed by persons in everyday life, including their ability to use language in ways that are recognised as 'native' and which convey the subtleties of the new culture. All these conditions enable people to stratify others in daily life and become central ingredients for understanding the way a person's relative success in the labour market, marriage market, or interpersonal market is accomplished. Hence any concern with migrant workers and their families must address these stratifying practices within the larger context of the host society, how they operate, and with what consequences for their daily living in the host society.

Many readers will ask if the conclusion of this report simply means that we must first know the host society before we can develop and implement policies about migrant workers. Such a suggestion would be viewed as unworkable. Our central point is that any study of migrant workers and their families, and the development and implementation of policies, can only make sense within a context of research on the interaction of the two groups while simultaneously paying attention to the general stratifying practices that are an integral part of any society or group. We must know about the way members of the host country react to, and their ways of dealing with migrant workers if we are to address what is called the 'migrant worker problem'. In so doing, we shall, of course, learn more about the country of immigration as well. In addition, we must know something about the country of origin of the migrant workers if we are to understand the impact of living in the host country when this latter group continually returns to the country of origin. What stories or accounts about comparisons of the two countries are produced?

The study of migrant workers, therefore, is the study of how different groups adjust to one another's presence under conditions where one group is dominant and stratificational differences exist within each group. The study of migrant workers thus becomes an essential part of our understanding of the social structure of societies or cultures. Present research and essays on this topic tend to neglect the necessity of approaching the problem with general theoretical principles and a methodology that can address the day-to-day issues that migrant workers and their families must face and resolve while living in the host country and returning to the country of origin. We have tried to suggest a general theoretical framework which addresses basic issues in social stratification, stressing the necessity of studies that examine the routine stratifying practices that exist in school, at work, at home, and during leisure activities in the country of employment.

Bibliography

Andizian, S. and Streiff, J., 'The Changing of Women's Traditional Roles in the Migrant Situation', Unesco SS-78/Conf. 801/12, 15 March 1978.

Au, K.H. and Jordan, C., 'Teaching Reading to Hawaiian Children: Finding a Culturally Appropriate Solution' in H. Treuba, G.P. Guthrie and K.H. Au (eds), *Studies in Classroom Ethnography*, Newbury House, Rowley, Mass., in press.

Bransford, J.D., Nitsch, K.E. and Franks, J.J., 'Schooling and the facilitation of knowing' in R.C. Anderson, R.J. Spiro, and W.E. Montague (eds), *Schooling and the Acquisition of Knowledge*, Lawrence Erlbaum Associates, Hillsdale, N.J., 1977.

Bransford, J.D., Stein, B.S., Shelton, T.S. and Owings, R.A., 'Cognition and Adaptation: The Importance of Learning to Learn', Manuscript, undated.

Brown, A.L., 'Theories of memory and the problems of development: activity, growth, and knowledge' in L.S. Cermak and F.I.M. Craik (eds), *Levels of processing in human memory*, Lawrence Erlbaum and Associates, Hillsdale, N.J., 1979.

Buckland, D., 'Isolation of Immigrant Women in Australian Society', Unesco SS-78/Conf. 801/14, 12 January 1978.

Burawoy, M., 'The Functions and Reproduction of Migrant Labor: Comparative Material from Southern Africa and the United States', *American Journal of Sociology*, vol. 81, no. 5, 1976.

Carrasco, R.L., Vera, A. and Cazden, C.B., 'Aspects of Bilingual Students' Communicative Competence in the Classroom' in R. Duran (ed.), *Latino Language and Communicative Behavior. Discourse Processes: Advances in Research and Theory*, vol. 4, Norwood, N.J., Ablex, in press.

Castles, S. and Kosack, G., *Immigrant Workers and Class Structure in Western Europe*, Oxford University Press, London, 1975.

Catani, M., 'I am Nothing or Changing One's Country Means Changing One's Flag', Unesco SS-78/Conf. 801/15, 17 April 1978.

Cazden, C.B., Carrasco, R.L., Maldonado-Guzman, A.A. and Erickson, F., 'The Contribution of Ethnographic Research to Bicultural/ Bilingual Education', to appear in *Current Issues in Bilingual Education*, Georgetown University Round Table on Language and Linguistics, in press.

Cole, M., Sharp, D.W. and Lave, J., 'The Cognitive Consequences of Education: Some Empirical Evidence of Theoretical Misgivings', *The Urban Review*, vol. 9, no. 4, 1976.

Cole, M. and Riel, M., 'Intelligence as Cultural Practice', Laboratory of Human Cognition, March 1980 (unpublished).

Eppink, A., 'Socio-Psychological Problems of Migrants' Children and Cultural Conflicts', Intergovernmental Committee for European Migration (ICEM), fourth seminar on the adaptation and integration of permanent immigrants, Geneva 8-11 May 1979 (MC/SAI/-IV/3).

Falchi, G., 'Education of Migrant Children, Including Guidance and Language Training', ICEM, fourth seminar on the adaptation and integration of permanent immigrants, Geneva 8-11 May 1979 (MC/SAI/IV/2).

Fishman, J.A., 'The Social Science Perspective' in *Bilingual Education: Current Perspectives*, vol. I, Center for Applied Linguistics, 1977.

Gilman, S., *The Spain of Fernando de Rojas: The Intellectual and Social Landscape of 'La Celestina'*, Princeton University Press, Princeton, 1972.

Grabo, C., 'Americanizing the Immigrants', *The Dial*, vol. LXVI, 1919.

Grant, P., 'American Ideals and Race Mixture', *North American Review*, vol. CXCV, 1912.

Greer, C. (ed.), *Divided Society: The Ethnic Experience in America*, Basic Books, New York, 1974.

Handlin, O., *Boston's Immigrants*, New York, Atheneum, 1972.

Handlin, O., *Immigration as a Factor in American History*, Prentice-Hall, Englewood Cliffs, N.J., 1959.

Handlin, O., *Uprooted*, Little, Brown and Co., Boston, 1951.

Hansen, M., *Immigrant in American History*, Harper and Row, New York, 1940.

Hernandez, J., *Social Factors in Educational Attainment Among Puerto Rican Students in US Metropolitan Areas in 1970*, New York, Aspira, 1976.

Higham, J., *Strangers in the Land*, Atheneum, New York, 1963.

Hoffman-Nowotny, H.-J., 'Sociological Aspects of the Situation of Migrant Women', Unesco, SS-78/Conf. 801/11, 15 February 1978.

Hymes, D., 'Ethnographic Monitoring' in H.T. Treuba, G.P. Guthrie, and K.H. Au (eds), *Studies in Classroom Ethnography*, Newbury House, Rowley, Mass., in press.

James, W., *Varieties of Religious Experience*, The Modern Library, New York, 1929.

Jones, M., *American Immigration*, University of Chicago Press, Chicago, 1960.

Kallen, H., 'Democracy Versus the Melting-Pot', *The Nation*, 1915.

Kloss, H., *The American Bilingual Tradition*, Newbury House, Rowley, Mass., 1977.

Kudat, A., 'Personal, Familial and Societal Impacts of Turkish Women's Immigration to Europe', Unesco, SS-78/Conf. 801/12, 1978.

Labov, W., 'The Logic of Non-Standard English' in G. Alastis (ed.), *Linguistics and Language Study*, Georgetown University Press, Washington, D.C., 1969.

Ley, K., 'Change of Status of Women Immigrants in Switzerland', Unesco, SS-78/Conf. 801/9, 15 March 1978.

López, D.E., 'The Social Consequences of Chicano Home/School Bilingualism', *American Journal of Sociology*, no. 83, p. 1491, 1978.

Lucas, I., 'Puertorriqueños En Chicago: El Problems Educativo Del Dropout', *The Rican: Journal of Contemporary Puerto Rican Thought*, vol. I, no. IV, May 1974.

Margolis, R.J., 'The Losers: A Report on Puerto Ricans and the Public Schools' in *The Puerto Rican Experience: Puerto Ricans and Educational Opportunity*, Arno Press, New York, 1975.

Mayo-Smith, R., *Emigration and Immigration: A Study in Social Science*, New York, Johnson Reprints 1904.

Mehan, H., *Learning Lessons: Social Organization in the Classroom*, Harvard University Press, Cambridge, Mass., 1979.

Mehan, H., 'Ethnography' in *Bilingual Education: Current Perspectives*, vol. I, Center for Applied Linguistics, 1977.

Morokvasic, M., 'Limitation of Births Among Yugoslavian Women Migrants in France, Germany and Sweden', Unesco, SS-78/Conf. 801/10, 15 March 1978.

Morrison, J.C., *The Puerto Rican Study 1953-1957: A Report on the Education and Adjustment of Puerto Rican Pupils in the Public Schools of the City of New York*, Board of Education, New York, 1958.

Neisser, U., *Cognition and Reality*, W.H. Freeman, San Francisco, 1976.

Oriol, M., 'Research on a "Lost Generation". The Problem of Educating Women Migrants in Industrialized Countries', Unesco, SS-78/Conf. 801/7, 15 March 1978.

Park, R., *Race and Culture*, Free Press, Glencoe, 1950.

Park, R. and Miller, H., *Old World Traits Transplanted*, Arno Press, New York, 1969.

Perfetti, C.A. and Lesgold, A.M., 'Coding and Comprehension in skilled reading' in P. Carpenter and M. Just (eds), *Cognitive Processes in Comprehension*, Lawrence Erlbaum Associates, Hillsdale, N.J., 1978.

Romo, H., 'The Puerto Rican Spanish-Speaking Population', unpublished, undated.

Romo, H., 'Working Paper: Problems in Bilingual Education in the US', unpublished, undated.

Rosen, B., 'Social Change, Migration and Family Interaction in Brazil', *American Sociological Review*, no. 38, pp. 198-212, 1973.

Simmel, G., 'The Stranger' in K. Wolfe (ed.), *The Sociology of Georg Simmel*, Free Press, Glencoe, 1950.

Smith, H., 'Living Conditions of Female Migrants in Sweden', Unesco, SS-78/Conf. 801/6, 7 April 1978.

Stonequist, E., *The Marginal Man: a study in personality and culture conflict*, Russell & Russell, New York, 1961.

Streiff, J., 'The Programs of Formation on Female Migrants with Aspects on Social Conditions and Development in France', Unesco, SS-78/Conf. 801/6, 7 April 1978.

Swetland, C., 'The Ghetto of the Soul — Socio-Cultural effects of programs of formation on migrant workers and their families in Norway', Unesco, SS-78/Conf. 801/6, 7 April 1978.

Thomas, W.I. and Znaniecki, F., *The Polish Peasant in Europe and America*, Dover Publications, New York, 1958.

Unesco, Meeting of Experts on the role of migrant workers' associations in the education and training of migrant workers and their families. Unesco, ED-78/Conf. 630/Col. 8. 1978.

US Bureau of the Census, Current Population Reports, Series p-20, no. 328 'Persons of Spanish Origin in the US', March 1978 (Advance Report), US Government Printing Office, Washington, DC, 1978.

Waggoner, D., 'National Center for Education Statistics. Geographic, Nativity, and Age Distribution of Language Minorities in the United States, Spring 1976, Bulletin 78B-5.

Warner, W. Lloyd and Srole, L., *The Social Systems of American Ethnic Groups*, Yankee City series vol. III, New Haven, Yale University Press, 1945.

Zangwill, I., *The Melting Pot*, Arno, New York, 1909.

Zwingmann, C. and Pfister-Ammende, M., *Uprooting and After . . .* , Springer-Verlag, New York, 1973.

Glossary of abbreviations for chapter 2

AOF	Educational branch of the Confederation of Trade Unions (Norway)
AS	Conservative Party Evening School (Norway)
ASx	Anglo-Saxon
C1	Code 1
C2	Code 2
C3	Code 3
C4	Code 4
CO	Classroom observation
Fr	French, France
FU	Friundervisning (largest adult education institution) (Norway)
FW	Foreign worker
LO	Confederation of Trade Unions (Norway)
LU	Lahnda/Urdu
N	Norwegian, Norway
NAF	Employers' Union (Norway)
P	Pakistani, Pakistan
R-L/L-R	Right-Left/Left-Right script
SLF	Special language formation
SOV	Subject-object-verb construction
Sp	Spanish
SU	State Office for Foreigners
T	Turkish, Turk, Turkey
TS	Teachers' Seminar

2 The ghetto of the soul: socio-cultural factors of language training programmes for migrant workers in Norway*

CAROLYN SWETLAND

Introduction

Pakistanis define their Norwegian language needs as follows:

I. To be able to go to the grocery store and say what I want to buy.

B. After two years, perhaps I could get into a trade school and learn a profession.

H. So as not to have any problem anywhere — hospital, office, shop, changing my job.

N. To have a better life in Norway we *must* learn Norwegian. I do want a better life in Norway, so I'm learning Norwegian (AS session no. 4, 25.4.77).

None of these needs is met in the planning or in the institutional supports, or in the methods of Norwegian language training courses for migrant workers as they exist in Norway today. In this chapter we shall attempt to explain why, focusing on three facets of language learning as experienced by migrant workers:

---

* This chapter was written with the assistance of Saeed Anjum, Ali Abbas Asim, Nirmal Brahmadoorna, Even Hovdhaugen, Aud Korbøl, Sunil Loona, Berit Løfsnaes, Manuel Machado, Lars H. Rydell, Ayako Tsuda and Hasan Yildirim.

1 linguistic;

2 pedagogic;

3 comparative ethno-linguistic.

While an understanding of linguistic aspects is necessary in order to teach Norwegian to migrant workers, neither a knowledge of these aspects, nor of pedagogical ones, can solve the problem without a comprehension of the dominant role played by ethno-linguistic aspects.

As regards linguistic terms, there is much that remains to be discussed in matters of predicting the transfer of elements of morphology and syntax and in understanding the progression in undirected language learning. Yet when we realise that a sizeable number of migrant workers cannot read or write in their own language and that an even larger number have completed only 3-5 years of schooling in the country of origin, we realise that grammar cannot be explained to them in grammatical terminology and that semantic aspects often remain either grossly generalised or unperceived.

Illiterate and semi-literate persons are often assumed to be either 'stupid' or 'unteachable'; however, this rather naive assumption does not take into account the fact that many illiterates speak a number of languages fluently (West Africa is only one example). To say that 'they grew up with them' is not the answer; many have learned them as adults. What can be said, however, from a comparative ethno-linguistic point of view is that the *cognitive worlds* as well as the *cognitive models of learning* of a Bambara-speaking African who also speaks Peul, Wolof and Soussous, are mutually comprehensible.

This is *not* the case with a migrant worker from Africa, India, Pakistan or Turkey in Western Europe (we exclude here citizens of these countries who have completed higher education since, in so doing, they have been forced into an apprehension of the occidental cognitive world and models of learning). Since the majority of the natives of the country of production or employment — administrators and teachers included — are unaware that alternative cognitive worlds exist and are equally valid, the impasse remains.

This chapter points to some linguistic aspects of the existing system, criticises pedagogical aspects, raises some contrasting ethno-linguistic considerations and draws some conclusions. Until the dimension of ethno-linguistic aspects of cognitive worlds of alterity is fully grasped, the migrant worker will continue to remain what he now is: the inhabitant of a no-man's land which is neither that of his country of origin, nor that of his country of work and residence.

Present foreign population

General description. The total foreign population in Norway (70,927) represents only 1.8 per cent of the total population and is composed in its majority (77.4 per cent) of other Scandinavians (24,960), North and Eastern Europeans (17,110) and North Americans (10,897). Less than one-quarter (22.6 per cent) come from Southern Europe, Latin America and the Caribbean, Asia and Africa combined. This group, which may properly be referred to as 'migrant', represents only 0.4 per cent of the total population of Norway.

Although a halt on immigration went into effect at the beginning of 1975, there were a number of dispensations, so that in effect it was not a halt, but rather an instrument for restrictions. Roughly three-quarters of the populations that are properly 'migrant' are to be found in the Oslo area, and the migrant population in Norway is approximately 80 per cent Moslem.

A reflection on the above figures reveals that this immigration policy results in a 'keep Norway white' migratory policy. It must also be noted that a work permit is not required of citizens of the other Scandinavian countries and that the English language is commonly spoken and understood by Norwegians. The disadvantages facing the 'migrant' population, therefore, already exist in several aspects of the particularities of the Norwegian situation before the migrant ever arrives.

Pakistani populations. As the Pakistani population represents by far the most numerically important group among migrants (5,177), we have chosen this population as the basis for our study. Pakistanis first came to Norway in 1968, the majority of them from rural areas of the Punjab, chiefly the district of Gujerat and the majority with little education. Up to the late 1960s emigration was not actively encouraged in Pakistan. It was difficult for an ordinary person to obtain a passport because there were only four passport offices: Lahore, Karachi, Peshawar and Quetta. Also, the procedure for securing a passport was complicated. Only first class *gazetted officers*[1] could guarantee. In the late 1960s, however, the government greatly simplified the procedure. Lower-rank government officials were given gazetted classifications and Class II officers, such as accountants, for example, could stand as guarantor on the passport form. Thus the situation changed in 1968 with the opening of new passport offices and the relaxation of rules for issuing passports.

---

1 *Gazetted officer:* a colonial term used to designate British officers of all kinds (Army, Administration, Civil Service, etc.) in the colonies, as opposed to natives, who were called 'non-gazetted' officers. In 1935, with the first election and first constitution, a fight was made for natives to be given 'gazetted officers' posts. The term continues in use after independence.

Private agents in Europe providing labour to the European migrant labour market discovered the situation in Pakistan and at the same time expanded their activities in Norway, giving rise to a sudden influx of Pakistani labour to Norway. This culminated in the startling sight, in the summer of 1971, of hundreds of Pakistanis sleeping outside on peaceful Karl Johans Street in the middle of Oslo; many of these came from Germany and Denmark, where thousands of Pakistanis were waiting to find work somewhere in Europe. The Red Cross immediately set up emergency headquarters and the government tightened the entry regulations.

The newly tightened regulations turned out not to be tight enough. The hoped-for solution was found in the English test. Before a Pakistani could enter Norway, in addition to everything else, he was required to go through an interview in the Norwegian Consular office in Karachi (manned by a Pakistani) to prove that he could speak English. To de-discriminate this new rule, it was stated that all migrants would, thereafter, have to be able to speak a European language. This took care of the Yugoslavs and the Turks. (Turkey is often classified as an Asian country in Norwegian statistics, but linguistically it is regarded as European.) The new regulation, however, was never applied to the Chinese from Hong Kong who work in Norway's Chinese restaurants and who cannot speak a word of anything other than Cantonese.

Though the government may have been concerned about this new labour force, the employers were generally pleased. The Pakistani was presented as a person who did not drink and remained happy. Here was a person who did not like to go on leave, liked to work overtime, was always available for whatever shift, worked properly with higher than average production, was prepared to wash dishes, sweep floors and never complained. He became, in fact, so popular with many employers that some work-offer letters were sent out to the younger brothers, sons, cousins or friends of the Pakistani worker already working in Norway.

The Pakistani government also appeared to be pleased with the new emigrants. The Minister of Wages (Religious Property) and Minorities began to talk about Pakistanis working abroad and suggested that their problems be dealt with in his Ministry. He complimented them for their efforts to send money home which greatly helped the government in alleviating the problem of shortage of foreign exchange.

In February 1975 the government of Norway stopped immigration. On 15 October 1976 a visa requirement for Pakistanis was proposed, discussed internally among the concerned ministries, adopted and put into effect in exactly three months; this was done in spite of the fact that the government had claimed it would not establish such a policy.

Languages: the four codes

We have chosen to base our analysis of the formal aspects of language learning on four ethno-linguistic codes.

We call code 1 the original ethno-linguistic code of a given foreign worker. In Norway, this is usually not the national language of the foreign worker's country of origin. In the many cases where it is not, we must assume that he has already passed through one language-learning process before he entered Norway. Thus, he can already be considered bilingual.

We call code 2 the portion of the ethno-linguistic code of the country of production or employment (in this case Norwegian) that the foreign worker himself acquires outside formal institutions of language teaching. We place this code as number 2 since its acquisition begins even before he attends any formal language training course (in the event the migrant decides to attend a course). It begins immediately on arrival or even before.

We call code 3 the portion of the ethno-linguistic code (in this case Norwegian) that is formally taught by the existing institutions.

We call code 4 the optimal code of the country (in this case Norway).

Code 1: the mother-tongue — Lahnda/Urdu

Pakistan is a multilingual society. Many languages are spoken in most areas and passive knowledge of different dialects is widespread. Monolingual persons are hard to find.

The original ethno-linguistic code of the majority of Pakistanis residing in Norway is Lahnda. Instead of Lahnda, some linguists use the term Siraiki, which is also the term now most frequently used in Pakistan. Siraiki covers South and North Lahnda, while Lahnda is the term still commonly used for the northern dialects. Since the differences between the various Lahnda dialects are small, we find it inconvenient and misleading to use two separate terms here. We shall therefore use the term Lahnda for all these dialects.

The national language of Pakistan is Urdu. It is the main, and to a great extent the only, language of official communication in mass media and education. Although Urdu is rarely their mother-tongue most adult Pakistanis know the language. The Pakistanis in Norway read newspapers, magazines and books in Urdu and listen to the ten-minute weekly local broadcast in Urdu. To some extent they also use it as a spoken language, mostly with a certain stylistic effect. It is used on more formal occasions (talking in assemblies, teaching) and in private conversations to mark distance, formality, or unfriendliness. Since most Pakistanis in Norway have learned Urdu as a second language both at school and also in the society where it is widely used, their main acquaintance with language learning and methods of language teaching is linked with their acquisition of Urdu.

Urdu and Lahnda are closely related languages, a point which has some consequences for our project. First, Pakistanis are accustomed to a great variety of closely related dialects within their own linguistic society. In many respects this variation resembles the linguistic situation in Norway. The variation which they find in the Norwegian linguistic community and the strong degree of interference between the codes within it is not an unfamiliar phenomenon to Pakistanis and is not as unusual as most Norwegians are inclined to think.

A large number of English loan words are incorporated into the Urdu vocabulary. A high percentage of these are administrative and institutional terms (e.g., school, office, district administrator) incorporated into the vocabulary under British colonialisation and maintained in use ever since.

As the dominant ruling group language, English is a status symbol language for the majority of Pakistanis. A Pakistani who speaks English well is looked upon as having higher status than one who does not. The fact that English is considered a status symbol language, besides being a language of universal use, leads to a learning situation which has no parallel. Norwegian is a vehicular language for Pakistanis, its relevance (and status) being related only to the fact of working in Norway, usually for an undetermined period of time. As a vehicular language, the motivation for mastering it is highly variable. They would much prefer to learn English and a number of them do so. They have informally asked for English schools in which all the subjects would be taught in English.

This feeling is reinforced by the knowledge that English is spoken fluently by all educated Norwegians, and passably well by most others. Norwegians like to show their proficiency in the English language and all teachers of Norwegian for foreigners speak English and use it as a helping language. The student who does not understand English is generally considered as hopelessly stupid.

Code 2: Norwegian learned outside formal institutions

In several respects code 2 has a unique position among the four codes we have chosen to describe and its description raises several problems not found elsewhere. Since code 1 and code 4 are normal and fully developed linguistic systems, a linguistic description of them can partly be based on the linguistic intuition of the speakers of these codes. Code 3 is a sub-code of code 4 and can be described on the basis of code 4.

On the other hand, code 2 is not a sub-code of any of the other codes; therefore a linguistic description of it presents several problems that are typical in the description of interlanguages. It has no native speakers and accordingly there is no linguistic intuition on which the description can be based. Code 2 is neither formulated nor controlled by the speakers of code 1, but code 1 is obviously a factor of importance in code 2. Code 3 does not affect code 2 except through possible influences picked up from other migrants who have attended formal courses. We have no possible way of measuring this at the present stage of our study.

The Norwegian spoken must be assumed to have been learned from Norwegians (and to a lesser and non-measurable extent from other migrants) with whom the speaker has come in contact on the job, in administrative offices, shops, restaurants, transport vehicles, neighbourhood, possibly boy or girl friends. Which version(s) of code 4 any given speaker has been exposed to (presumably various) and which version(s) he has been most influenced by, we have no way of measuring.

Pidgins, interlanguages and code 2, all have several traits in common. They show great variability, significant vacillation in all components of grammar, simplified morphology and syntax and have no native speakers. To justify the label, we would have to prove first that code 2 is also used by Norwegians in communication with Pakistanis. There are some indications that Norwegians to some extent modify their spoken language when speaking with Pakistanis, but we have no data that would show such modifications or show the degree to which this language approximates code 2. In Norwegian literature there seems to be a rather sterotypic form of Norwegian used to characterise foreigners, a stereotype that in some respects significantly resembles code 2; this point will not be further elaborated here since the material is meagre and we have no proof that this language has any influence whatsoever on the formation of code 2. It is further worth noting that the morphology and vocabulary of code 2 is completely Norwegian-English with no elements from code 1.

Code 2 is used by migrants of all nationalities in conversing with one another when they have no other language in common, and by the majority of migrant workers (the majority having never attended formal courses) in speaking to Norwegians. On the other hand, to our knowledge it is never, or rarely, used by Norwegians when speaking to migrants.

Code 3: Norwegian learned in formal institutions

Although Norwegian as a foreign language has been taught for several centuries in Norway, language teachers have never been given organised training at any level. The teaching of Norwegian as a foreign language has never been included in the curriculum of the teacher training colleges or the universities. Accordingly, neither the teachers nor the people who plan and organise language teaching have any relevant preparation; they have to rely on material and methods developed elsewhere, on their own common sense and on their own background knowledge, which may not always be adequate or appropriate. The educational background of the teachers is generally considered as being satisfactory or, sometimes, a few weekend seminars are regarded as sufficient to qualify them. There are no courses specifically designed for migrant workers; they have to attend the courses for foreigners along with NATO officers, diplomats, American, German, Dutch, British, and Japanese businessmen, housewives, students and others.

Code 4: Norwegian as used

From a linguistic point of view it is far from easy to define exactly what is meant by the term Norwegian and in several respects the linguistic situation in Norway is quite unique. There are many geographical and social dialects but they are generally mutually comprehensible to a degree that is far from common in most other linguistic communities.

The most peculiar aspect of the linguistic situation in Norway is that there is no standard language, either written or spoken. There are two official written languages (Bokmål and Nynorsk) both of which show a remarkable degree of variation both in orthography and morphology. Apart from this there are several written variants, which are not officially recognised and which are not allowed to be used either in schools or in the administration. One of these variants, Riksmål, is widely used in newspapers, theatres and by a significant number of authors.

Riksmål, which is spoken by rather few people, mostly as a home dialect, corresponds closely to some dialects of the West End of Oslo, Nynorsk is based on the rural dialects and spoken Nynorsk is generally more or less influenced by the speaker's local dialect. Bokmål, which today is the most widely used language in Norway, corresponds rather closely (at least in the more conservative variant of it) to the spoken language of the educated middle class in Eastern Norway. Some linguists call this variant of spoken Bokmål, Standard Eastern Norwegian, but it is still much less homogeneous than standard prestige dialects in most other countries and the pronunciation is, in most cases, clearly influenced by the speaker's local dialect. The variation is not limited to pronunciation, but concerns also morphology and vocabulary.

Officially, Bokmål and Nynorsk are given equal status and are expected to have a balanced distribution in radio, television, and all official documents and forms. All schoolbooks should be in both the languages. In practice, however, Bokmål is quite dominant in radio, television and newspapers (besides Riksmål) and, at least in the Oslo area, most documents, forms and schoolbooks are available only in Bokmål.

There exist two official variants of both Bokmål and Nynorsk. As already mentioned, both languages are characterised by a strong degree of variation. This means that for many words there exist two officially accepted spellings and in many cases one can freely choose between masculine and feminine gender, between two different past forms of verbs, and the like, but for use in the schools and in some other cases, there exists a more restricted variant with less optional choice (Laereboknormalen) of both languages. As for the spoken language, there is no standard in Norwegian schools. On the contrary, the teachers, at least in principle, are expected to learn the local dialect and to adjust their spoken language to the language of their pupils. But since the local dialects in the Oslo area have a very low prestige, the teachers there mainly use some variant of Standard Eastern Norwegian.

The differences between the different written Norwegian languages are small (e.g. much smaller than the differences between some of the geographical dialects) and the geographical and social dialects in the Oslo area are also quite similar. This means that all variants of the Norwegian language that migrants confront differ only in minor details that have little influence on mutual understanding as far as Norwegians are concerned.

The dialects spoken by the working class in and around Oslo differ both from Bokmål and Nynorsk (and very much from Riksmål) but most closely correspond to the 'radical' variant of Bokmål. However, these dialects (as well as the radical variant of Bokmål) differ considerably from Standard Eastern Norwegian, especially in morphology, i.e. the use of feminine gender, the use of the -a past and certain pronouns.

Language education: policies and practices

Policy recommendations

The following quotations, taken from Ministry of Home Affairs and Labour (1976) can be read as a statement of government policy:

> The mother-tongue and the needs of the participants must be decisive in the choice of the teaching programmes, methods and teaching materials . . . *Goals for the teaching of Norwegian and orientation into the society.* The teaching of Norwegian to immigrants has as its task the exercising of a limited central vocabulary, expressions and grammatical structures, and to give a good pronunciation so they can

grasp and understand everyday language, express themselves verbally in simple language situations in work and free time, read and understand simple written information and, to a certain degree, express themselves in writing.

Orientation concerning Norwegian society is given equal importance.

In addition, teaching shall to the greatest possible extent inform the migrants about Norwegian society. Orientation in the society shall provide the migrant with knowledge of conditions and rules that have direct meaning for his or her own situation in Norway. At the same time, he/she should be given an insight into the way of life of Norwegians, our administrative organs and orientation or the conditions of nature, of settling, business and cultural life.

State subsidy

Since 1 January 1975 the state subsidises the cost of Norwegian language teaching for migrant workers and their adult family members for up to 240 hours. Previously (from 1970 onwards) the state subsidised Norwegian language instruction only for workers and not adult family members. Under the then existing arrangements, the worker was required to pay for the course first and, if he attended 75 per cent of the time, he could then apply for a refund. The problems of shift work and obligatory overtime were not taken into consideration in devising this arrangement.

The definition of who is entitled to these 240 hours of free language tuition is vague:

The subsidy arrangement is aimed primarily at persons who remain in our country for at least one year and for whom language and orientation in the society are essential if they are to be able to orient themselves and manage things in a satisfactory manner in work and in the society outside.

Other groups who have need for such tuition can participate in the same way, when this does not lead to appreciably higher costs (Ministry of Home Affairs and Labour, 1976, p. 52).

Foreign students fall outside this arrangement because it is assumed that they are provided for at the universities and high schools.

In practice, subsidies are granted for attendance in these courses to almost any non-Norwegian; American, British, Dutch, German and French persons also attend these courses. This in itself would be of little importance for us were it not for the fact that the funds allocated for this purpose are presumed to be used for *migrant workers* and are so listed under a separate new item in the national budget, under adult education. After having informed the Parliament what the costs for this education had been in 1975 and 1976, the White Paper continues:

> On the basis of these costs, 240 hours for each immigrant will, in other words, cost Kr. 2,304 ($460). It will therefore cost at least Kr. 4,500,000 ($900,000) to give for example 2000 immigrants yearly instruction in groups (Ministry of Home Affairs and Labour, 1976, p. 53).

It is clearly stated here that the funds are intended for immigrants, but the number of persons who are *not immigrants* and who benefit from this provision for language instruction is not known.

Administration

So far as the administration of language instruction is concerned, the Ministry of Church and Education (1975) has given its directives. On the local level, the school boards are responsible for the administration and professional attention, as well as for running expenses, which are reimbursed by the state. On the regional level, the school directors are responsible for coordination at their district level. Centrally, the Ministry of Church and Education is responsible for administration and financing. However, some of the directors of the teaching institutions indicate that they have no contact with the Ministry.

Teaching institutions

As stated earlier there are no classes in Norwegian (with rare exceptions) that are specifically organised for migrants. However, classes in Norwegian are held for foreigners, which migrant workers can also attend. As will be shown, 50 per cent of the students attending these classes are Anglo-Saxons. The institutional justification for not organising classes for migrants is that there are so few migrants and so many different nationalities; the administrative difficulties of planning courses especially for them would be too great. It may be noted, however, that a high percentage of migrant worker population is in the Oslo/Akerhus/Oslo fjord area.

The teaching of the Norwegian language to adult foreigners takes place mainly within two institutions: Friundervisning (FU), which has indirect connections with the University, and the educational branch of the Confederation of Trade Unions (AOF). A third, the evening school of the Conservative Party (AS), started courses for Pakistanis in the autumn of 1976. Our comments concern these three institutions and our class observations cover these three institutions within the Oslo area. A few other classes exist here and there but are numerically irrelevant; therefore they are not included in the following description.

Friundervisning (FU). FU has the majority of the students who are learning Norwegian. Our analysis of the distribution of students enrolled in Oslo institutions during the first three months of 1977 indicates that 81 per cent of these were enrolled in FU and 19 per cent in AOF. Classes in Norwegian for non-Norwegians at FU have been held since the Second World War.

The courses in Norwegian for foreigners constitute a part of the general list of courses offered. In addition to the general catalogue where all courses are listed, FU stencilled a single sheet entitled 'Norwegian for Foreigners', with information on how and where to enrol, in the following languages in this order: Norwegian, English, German, French, Spanish. The courses were also announced in the Norwegian press and the course programmes were sent to some factories.

Information obtained from applicants at registration is minimal. This year, for the first time, FU recorded, though incompletely, the following facts at registration: name, address, birth-date, nationality, profession, previous schooling. In addition, applicants were sometimes asked to indicate other languages they knew.

FU holds an examination (against payment of Kr. 50 = $10, fee) at the end of the third level (180 hours), though anyone may take it without having attended FU classes. A certificate is issued to the successful candidates stating: '. . . has passed the examination in Norwegian for foreigners. The candidate has been tested in both oral and written skills'. To pass the examination the candidate must show that he can understand and speak Norwegian within a frame of approx. 1400 frequent words and master the basic grammatical structures (FU files).

In addition to the oral part of approximately five minutes, the examination consists of: dictation; grammar; reading; comprehension; two written portions: one called 'Vacation tips', where the candidate is asked to write a 100-word dialogue between Mr Hansen and Mrs Jensen who are both on vacation in Mallorca and given certain Norwegian words and expressions to use; and where the candidate is asked to write a 150-word description of the Jensen family day, the various activities of which are shown in pictures. The judges for the examination are the present and previous section leaders themselves.

The results for 1974, 1975 and Spring 1976 were as shown in Table 2.1. Of the five non-Anglo-Saxons who have passed in these two and a half years, two were Spanish-speaking, two Slavs and one unknown. No Pakistani who has taken this examination has ever passed.

Table 2.1

FU Norwegian language examination results, 1974, 1975 and Spring 1976

	Took exam	Of which:		Passed	Of which	
		Anglo-Saxon	Non-Anglo-Saxon		Anglo-Saxon	Non-Anglo-Saxon
1974	21	19	2	9	8	1
1975	21	11	10	12	10	2
Spring 1976	23	n.a.	n.a.	8	6	2
Total	65			29	24	5

Educational branch of the Confederation of Trade Unions (AOF).
Courses in Norwegian for non-Norwegians were begun by AOF in the
Autumn of 1965. As with FU, Norwegian language courses for non-
Norwegians are listed in the general course programme. No separate
sheet on these courses is published. The courses are announced in the
Norwegian press, through the State Information Service. The general
programme of all courses is sent to leaders of group study or elected
union representatives at various factories.

Asked if the pupils were registered by nationality, the director
replied: 'We don't discriminate here in AOF. All are welcome'. We
discovered later, during observation, that the teacher records nationality and date of birth. We do not know what happens to this
information.

There is considerable rivalry between these two institutions — FU
and AOF — and there is no cooperation in planning, preparation,
methods, back-up or evaluation. Some students attend courses in both
places at the same time. Both institutions are aware of this, but how
many this might be they do not know as they do not normally contact
one another.

The same situation of non-cooperation exists at the national level
both within each institution and between them. Neither FU nor AOF
directors in Oslo had any idea whatsoever of what was being done
within their institution at the national level, when asked this question
by a team member:

> We in Oslo know very little about what takes place on a
> nation-wide basis. However, since FU in Oslo has existed
> longest and because I know many outside Oslo personally,

the Oslo branch functions as an advice-giving office for many all over Norway. They ring me and ask for advice; but there is nothing systematic. FU Int. 8.6.77.

The Conservative Party evening school (AS). This institution is unique as far as the teaching of Norwegian to migrants is concerned. The evening school was established in 1962 as a part of the Conservative Party's Information Organisation. The planning of courses for migrants was begun in May and the courses began in the Autumn of 1976.

A group of Pakistanis contacted the Conservative Party and, among other things, mentioned that language teaching was poor and that none of the existing facilities was adequate. The Party then contacted the evening school and the Pakistanis themselves participated in the planning phase.

This is the only programme for adult migrants where the two-teacher system is used: a Norwegian teacher and a Pakistani teacher. The idea came from the director himself, who had previously been a teacher in Karasjok (Sami area in the North) where two teachers in a class were used, instead of removing the Samis from regular classes for auxiliary courses. This began in the autumn of 1976 with three classes and 45 pupils. The possibility of organising courses for other nationalities has also been discussed, but no initiatives have been taken.

The school has no contact with the university. The only other evening school at a national level with which they have any contact is Stavanger (oil), but there has been no cooperation between them.

As it is the only institution with courses for migrants, AS advertises them as such. Whereas both FU and AOF (correctly) call their courses 'Norwegian for foreigners' in its announcement AS call them 'Norwegian courses for immigrants'. The announcement, a one-page photocopied sheet, is written in both Norwegian and Urdu.

In the Spring session of 1977, two courses were offered in Norwegian first level (60 hours), one each in second, third and fourth level, as well as 'Norwegian for women'. The last two were dropped as a result of too small a turn-out.

Courses at the place of work

Courses are also organised at the places of work. Of all the foreigners enrolled in Norwegian language courses in the Oslo area during the first three months of 1977, only 8.5 per cent of them were enrolled in courses at the place of work. Most foreign workers went to FU and not, as one might suppose, to AOF (trade unions). FU had courses, among other places, at Elkem-Spigerverket, Standard Telefon og Kabelfabrikk, Kvaerner Brug, among the three largest plants in the Oslo area. AOF had courses at Nylands Verksted (shipbuilding and oil platforms)

80

a Chinese restaurant, the Post Office, the university restaurant and a few other places including the opera house (autumn session 1976). In addition, FU has courses for translators, for women at the Office for Foreign Workers and for the Norwegian Refugee Council.

Interviews with the directors of FU, AOF and AS indicated that there have been some difficulties in setting up courses at work places: some employers have reacted negatively to such courses or have set them up on a non-work day, such as Saturday, which requires workers to return just for the course. But they also indicated that some employers in larger organisations have developed their own language courses and have sought help from one or other of the directors.

The Committee for Immigrant Education, Adult Education Council, which includes one representative each from the Employers' Union (NAF) and the Confederation of Trade Unions (LO) urged that Norwegian language teaching should take place at the place of work within working hours and without loss of pay. The Ministry of Church and Education supported this, but the Ministry of Home Affairs did not. They asked the two main unions — those of the employers (NAF) and of the workers (LO) — to take up this question and together make a concrete proposal to the Ministry.

Characteristics of workers enrolled in language classes

Information on the characteristics of workers enrolled in the classes during the first three months of 1977 was obtained from FU, AOF and places of work. Some of this information is shown in Tables 2.2, 2.3, 2.4 and 2.5. A total of 1,157 students had enrolled during this time — 972 in FU courses and 185 in AOF courses. Of these, 52 per cent dropped out of the FU courses and 45 per cent from the AOF courses. Thus, Tables 2.2 and 2.3 are based on 466 students in FU (48 per cent of 972) and 102 students in AOF.

As can be seen in Table 2.2, a majority of immigrant workers in FU came from countries using a Latin alphabet whereas the relation was reversed for AOF classes. FU courses enrolled relatively more students, housewives and skilled workers than did AOF, which correspondingly enrolled relatively more unskilled workers. Table 2.3 indicates that a larger percentage of enrollees were men in both classes, and were in the young adult (i.e. 20 to 30) age group. The largest percentage of workers came from Asia, with that tendency being more pronounced in AOF classes, and the next largest percentage comes from the USA and the UK.

Table 2.4 shows characteristics of the 98 immigrants who were enrolled in classes at their place of work. (These 98 were also included in Tables 2.2 and 2.3.) Relative to all courses, those held at the place of work enrolled a larger percentage of immigrants from Asian and

Table 2.2

Distribution of workers in two institutions by language and by occupation

	FU	AOF
Language group		
Latin alphabet	61%	41%
Non-Latin alphabet	39	59
	(466)	(102)
Occupation		
Skilled	46%	25%
Unskilled	22	69
Student	18	3
Housewife	14	3
	(466)	(102)

Middle Eastern countries.

Table 2.5 shows the drop-out rate for three schools. FU had the highest drop-out rate and AS classes the lowest. Little information was available on the characteristics of the drop-outs, but what there is indicates that the drop-outs are mainly immigrants from Pakistan and the Mediterranean area.

Textbooks and other back-up material

One textbook alone dominates the field. Another is less widely used — mainly by AOF. In a few courses the teachers prepare their own materials and a few other textbooks are infrequently used.

Though the teaching of Norwegian to the indigenous (Samish and Finnish) minorities has existed for over a century, its effect on the production of textbooks has been negligible. Norwegian was taught as though it was the students' mother-tongue.

Interestingly enough, one small group of refugees from Eastern Europe (Hungarians in 1956-57) provoked the writing of a textbook — John Gaasland's *Laerebok i norsk for Ungarere* (Oslo, 1957) — and a Hungarian-Norwegian/Norwegian-Hungarian pocket dictionary was also quickly produced, which has no parallel in the history of the teaching of Norwegian as a foreign language. Similarly the arrival of another small group of East European refugees (Czechoslovakians in 1968-69), almost none of whom understood English and many of whom attended

Table 2.3

Distribution of workers in two institutions by sex, age and area of emigration

	FU	AOF
Sex		
Male	57.8%	60.6%
Female	40.8	31.7
Unknown	1.4	7.7
	(466)	(102)
Age		
Under 20	13.0%	5.0%
20-30	55.0	40.1
30-40	21.6	15.1
Over 40	8.6	7.0
Unknown	1.8	32.8
	(466)	(102)
Area of emigration		
US, UK	25.3%	24.3%
Western Europe	15.7	11.2
Eastern Europe	6.7	6.5
Scandinavia	3.6	1.2
Asia	31.9	46.7
Middle East	7.4	7.1
Africa	5.6	5.0
Central America	4.4	4.2
	(466)	(102)

Norwegian courses at the university, stimulated another immediate response: the realisation that English as an auxiliary language did not work and that new textbooks had to be written.

The first of these non-English audience textbooks to appear, though rarely used now, was *Norsk for utlendinger* by Harry Persson. It was soon replaced by *Snakker du norsk?* by Inger Helene Arnestad and

Table 2.4

Table 2.4

Characteristics of workers enrolled in language courses at place of work

Area of emigration		Course level	
US, UK	7.7%	Level 1 (60 hr)	55.0%
Western Europe	7.7	Level 2 (120 hr)	11.2
Eastern Europe	3.3	Level 3 (180 hr)	20.4
Asia	51.6	Other or higher levels	13.4
Middle East	26.4		
Central America	3.3		(98)
	(98)		

Table 2.5

Drop-out rate for three institutions during Autumn 1976 and Spring 1977

	Autumn 1976	Spring 1977
FU	52.2%	48.0%
AOF	45.0	61.5
AS	22.5	n.a.

Anne Hvenekilde (1971), which soon became the standard text in the field and which is used more than all the other textbooks together. It is used in all FU classes for the first three levels (180 hours). It is also recommended for use in the 7-9th grades for migrant school children, at all the university classes and in most courses in Norwegian given abroad at non-Norwegian universities.

The two authors, both teaching Norwegian to foreigners at the University of Oslo, have also published two other books: *Laereveiledning til Snakker du norsk?* (Teacher's guide to do you speak Norwegian?) and *Pa'n igjen!* (At it again!). The latter, published in 1975, is more advanced, consisting mainly of excerpts from newspapers and is used at the fourth level (240 hours) and other more advanced courses. In practice the two authors dominate this field and hold an almost complete monopoly. To a large extent, code 3 is formed by these authors. We could even say that code 3 is formulated by two Norwegian university women and is therefore to a certain degree influenced by their social, cultural and geographical background.

The book has been reprinted several times with revision only of details. Cassettes have been made (marketed by the publisher of the book) which cost Kr. 420 ($84) for the first 24 lessons, Kr. 210 ($42) for the next 10, or Kr. 630 ($126) for the entire series, equivalent to 180 hours, course work. The book itself is priced at Kr. 44 ($8.50). The migrants, under the state subsidy arrangement in effect since January 1975 receive free material worth up to Kr. 50 ($10), i.e. equivalent to 180 hours' free text material, but not 240.

In this book grammatical structures are introduced, but without any explanations. As an example, in the first lesson of the book *all* the following constructions appear, without comment: a simple statement (S-V-P); interrogative, requiring inversion (V-S-P); negation (S-V-Neg-P); two models of negative interrogation involving two different word orders (IP-Av-S-MV).

The book is an excellent example of ethno- and socio-centrism, culturally unreadable for a migrant unfamiliar with Norwegian life. For such migrants, the nomenclature and male—female roles presented are incomprehensible (no equivalents in their culture) and kinship terminology is lacking (no equivalents in Western Europe for their kinship system), although correct usage of these variants is necessary in the most elementary communication. The examples used of foods, beverages (including much drinking of alcoholic beverages), geography, transport (much boat vocabulary), dogs (dearly loved by Norwegians), are all Norwegian models unknown and unused by the migrant. Occupations, objects possessed (boat, house) are, in the main, examples drawn from upper middle-class life, whereas migrants, in the main, are dishwashers.

Classrooms

With the exception of the few courses held at the place of work, all teaching takes place in formal classrooms. Both FU and AOF have their own classrooms in the centre of Oslo (many migrants live far out in the suburbs) and in addition they also use classrooms in regular school buildings in the evenings.

Teachers

With the beginning of Norwegian language courses for foreigners at the university, teachers were recruited, to a large extent, from the university milieu. They had almost no pedagogical training, had low status and to some extent were rather isolated even at the university. To teach Norwegian to foreigners was considered an easy job, almost beyond the dignity of an academician and it is significant that even today only one of the teachers has tenure at the university, all the others (8-10) being low paid assistant teachers appointed for one year only. Many of the teachers teaching today at both FU and AOF are university students working for a degree. Thus, there is large turnover.

Two nation-wide seminars (attendance was voluntary) have been held for teachers and administrators of Norwegian language for foreigners (not specifically migrants) in the Spring respectively of 1976 and 1977. The attendance was somewhat over 50 at the first, but around 100 at the second. Some speakers were invited, but the work consisted largely of group discussions.

Exchanges in the classroom

The classroom is the place where all codes meet. Code 4 of the teachers, code 3 of the textbooks, codes 1 and 2 of the students are brought together in one place and are often used at the same time. Although the classroom situation in many respects is an artificial one, it is nevertheless important for the study of the relationship and mutual influence between the codes. We start by describing the position of the four codes in the classroom.

Code 1 (or C1) has in theory no place in the classroom at all, but in practice it is used everywhere, although to variable degrees. When a class is homogeneous concerning language background or language knowledge, C1 is widely used between the students. A typical example was the class at AS where all communication between the students both in the classroom and during the pauses was in C1. In that case, one of the two teachers had C1 as his mother-tongue and used it frequently when teaching. More than 50 per cent of the oral communication in that class was in C1.

At FU and AOF the situation was quite different. The classes were less homogeneous and there were usually only groups of two or three persons who had the same C1. English, French and Spanish were often used in communication between the students, although these languages were not always their mother-tongue. The teachers used Norwegian with English as an auxiliary language. The attitudes towards the use of C1 were very different in the classes. At AS the students were free to use C1 and only in a few cases did the Norwegian teacher ask them explicitly to use Norwegian. When they were unable to answer in Norwegian, they were free to answer in C1 and also to ask the teachers questions in that code. At FU the use of C1 was generally prohibited and the students using it were reproached by the teacher. The prohibition was not always accepted by the students and the teacher was also more lenient towards those who spoke English and French than towards those who spoke Urdu/Lahnda or Turkish.

At AS, code 2 was used only in conversation with the teachers and when students were asked to use Norwegian. One of the teachers also used it when talking Norwegian. At FU and AOF it was used by the students not only in communication with the teacher, but also to some

written and read from right to left, like Arabic; they made no attempt to emphasise this difference from Norwegian.

Some comparative ethno-linguistic considerations

In the previous section, we discussed government policies concerning language training of migrant workers; we also presented some observations on how those policies are carried out in practice. This section raises some additional considerations that relate to the teaching of Norwegian to immigrants.

Reciprocal images

Norwegian image of Pakistanis
— Called *Pakkis*, a derogatory term equivalent to *nigger* in the USA, used also by Norwegians in the country who have never seen, met, nor had anything to do with a Pakistani.
— *Pakistani* assimilated to the term *foreign worker*, so that foreign worker is instantly interpreted to mean Pakistani.
— Jokes: many derogatory ones circulate regularly among Norwegians stereotyping Pakistanis, no stereotype jokes about other nationalities.
— *They're Moslems*! Comment used to explain away everything Pakistanis do or do not do. This comment not made about other Moslem groups, e.g. Moroccans and Turks.
— They bow to authority/They don't obey (bad both ways).
— They don't drink/They drink (bad both ways).
— They take our girls/They don't go out with girls (bad both ways).
— They don't eat pork/They eat pork (bad both ways).
— They pray 5 times a day/They don't pray and besides they're not Christians (bad both ways).
— They're illiterate (synonymous with 'stupid') and therefore can't learn anything anyway.
— Their language has no grammar. It is written in *hieroglyphics* (latter comment made in all seriousness by one of the leaders of Norwegian language courses for foreigners to one of our Norwegian team members).
— Plus the usual ones such as: they take our jobs, don't pay taxes, use up our social security, etc.

Pakistani image of Norwegians
— They treat dogs better than humans.
— They discriminate against us.
— They close their houses and their whole society to us.

- Unfriendly.
- Drunk all the time.
- Insult our women.
- In defence against Norwegian jokes about Pakistanis, Pakistanis invent jokes of their own about Norwegians. Example:

> Three Norwegians meet: 'There are too many foreigners in this country. It's getting too crowded. You can't even find a place in the forest to be alone any more', and decide to go somewhere to find peace and quiet. They choose the Himalayas as a sure spot. One year passes.
> 1st N: 'It's nice and quiet here'. Another year passes.
> 2nd N: '*Ja*'. Another year passes.
> 3rd N: 'You guys talk too much', and he left.

- They pretend equality, but hide hierarchy in their dress.

> Everybody wears the same dress, Norwegian uniform: blue jeans. Blue jeans is the dress of labourers but some jeans-people have much money. Our dress is much better than Norwegian, because you can tell!

> .AS session, 27.4.77

'We take off clothes to work, but they put them on!'

> Ibid.

- They even had to import their King.

> *Q*: Who is more powerful, the Queen of England or the King of Norway?
> *Several*: The Queen of England!
> *R.*: They only have a King because the King is borrowed from Denmark. (Laughter.)

> Ibid.

- Our jobs are limited.

> 'After having listed the jobs they could aspire to in Pakistan, they were asked what jobs could they get in Norway if they could speak good Norwegian. The following were agreed upon: post-office, bank clerk, office, warehouse man, secretary and controller of cleaning workers (further described as driving around in a car from place to place where your people were cleaning).
> I: Couldn't be police chief even if you could speak good Norwegian!

> Ibid., 25.4.77

- Who you have to obey in Norway.

> After agreeing upon the categories of persons it is necessary to

obey in Pakistan, they were asked:

Q: Do you have to obey the same people in Norway?

Several: The police! (Laughter.)

Q: The administration?

Several: Yes.

Q: Elders? (must be obeyed in Pakistan).

X.: What type of order?

H.: If they advise us we respect them, but we don't have to obey them.

Ibid., 27.4.77

— Asked to name the things they were able to say in Norwegian to Norwegians about Pakistan, they named:

Vegetables — many — cheap. Buy meat cheap. Don't eat pork. Don't drink beer (some do). People go to the Mosque. Baths, toilets, loudspeaker in Mosque. People read the Koran. Zoo open all year.

Ibid., 13.4.77

— Asked to name the things they would like to be able to tell Norwegians about Pakistan, but cannot because of the language:

Why we live together (collective life).
Marriage ceremonies and its festivities.
Villages.
50,000 people work in the new steel industry.
Pakistan has a turbine dam, as big as Aswan.
Pakistan is a big country — also snow — don't go skiing.
The reasons for arranged marriages.
Who father's elder brother is.
Why we (boys) won't undress naked in front of other boys in gym.
The bus carried school children 20 miles for only 5 øre.
What the two colours of the Pakistani flag — green and white — represent.

Ibid.

Some side comments in Panjabi during this:

N.: Do you think they can explain about their celebrations? (Laughter.) If they can't, it isn't necessary that we should be able to explain about ours.

S.: J., what do you think?

J. (ironically): I am obedient, kind and good. (Everybody laughs.) I want to please people and you don't understand. (More laughter.)

Ibid.

Defensive reactions

In addition to the usual ones of withdrawal, isolation, formation of own communities, limitation of life to work—sleep—eat—work—repeat cycle:

— The *Ola Nordmann* (John Doe) Pakistani also exists (*'I'm* not like *other* Pakistanis'), the colonial houseboy only geographically removed from his colonial antecedents, continuing the colonial-counterpart tactics for, he hopes, upward mobility.
— Referring even the most irrelevant things back to the homeland: the project leader, who conducted the AS sessions, had written her first name on the board the first evening. The group was discussing easily remembered/forgotten words, when suddenly:

> I.: Carolyn? (Pause.)
> S.: He asked if your name is Carolyn.
> C.: Yes, my name's Carolyn — like it's written there.
> Several: Carolyn.
> I. (loudly): CAROLYN!
> C. (somewhat confused): Hello everybody!
> I.: There are clothes named Carolyn.
> C. (not understanding the connection): Hum?
> I. (slowly and carefully): There is a shirt with the name 'Carolyn'.
> C.: repeats this statement, stalling for time.
> I.: *Ja.* 'Carolyn'.
> C. (finally understanding): That I've never seen. Here in Norway? or in Pakistan?
> I.: In Pakistan. Shirt named 'Carolyn' in Pakistan.
>
> AS session, 13.4.77

— In reference to the homeland, many grown men, when asked what they miss most in Norway, reply: 'Birds. The singing of birds'.

Some semantic aspects of communication

We mention below only some of the relevant points found in our material. We also proceed from the social point of view and accept the statement of Buyssens (1968): 'It is necessary to define language as a means of acting upon the auditor, not as a means of expression' (page 76). We consider of relevance here H. Delacroix's statement that communication cannot take place other than on the basis of common experience.

Word categories. A word test was administered to the AS group. Ninety-eight Norwegian words, which they had used, were given to them and we found the following results: 89 per cent of the nouns were remembered, compared with only 19 per cent of the verbs. We coded the nouns into four classes: *vécu* in Pakistan; *vécu* in Norway; not *vécu* in Norway; neutral. This gave us the following: of the words *vécu* in either Pakistan or Norway, 51.4 per cent were remembered, of the neutral nouns 34.3 per cent were remembered, whereas of those not *vécu* in Norway, only 14.3 per cent were remembered. We had coded the verbs into five categories: past participle having adjectival functions; movement of body and things; state of being or doing; uncertainty; communication. This codification gave us one result of particular interest: all the verbs in the past participle having an adjectival function were remembered. Between 60 and 66 per cent remembered the verbs of other categories.

Synonyms and near-synonyms are little used and quickly forgotten. When one word had been used to describe an object or action, it was subsequently used almost exclusively to cover everything that might possibly be included under the first-learned description; for example, in the AS group five different verbs had been learned describing five different ways of walking: *trasket, ruslet, sjanglet, snublet, vi listet oss*, but they were all immediately forgotten and replaced by the verb to go (*å gå*).

Some ethno-linguistic transfer impossibilities

The word 'yes'. We will take only one example here, from the AS sessions. The group had discussed the topic 'who do you have to obey in Pakistan?', then the question was asked, in Panjabi: 'In your opinion, are they the same people we have to obey here, or some other people?' The first speaker answered: *Aahoo jee*! In this answer he was using the expression in its meaning of 'Yes sir', though it is more polite and more positive. However, it must be noted that *aahoo jee* in other situations can mean: 'I know the hidden meaning of the sentence', or 'I am aware of your conversation, but for my own interest or for the sake of diplomacy I do not want to contradict you', or 'I know you are talking without any logic, there is no reason in what you are saying, even though I am accepting you for the sake of interpersonal relations'.

While the Norwegian word *ja* (yes) can be used to express affirmation, negation, doubt and a variety of other meanings according to intonation and situation, it is rarely possible for a migrant to use *ja* to express anything other than yes. Had this question been asked in Norwegian (assuming rapport and a wish to respond truthfully), the possibilities would be only three: *ja* (yes), *nei* (no), *kanskje* (maybe) none of which might have been what he wished to say. Thus, it is impossible to transfer the diverse meanings of the 'yes' in Panjabi to the 'yes' in Norwegian.

Kinship terms. For all cultures possessing extended kinship terminology (to which all ethno-linguistic groups in Pakistan belong), translation of the significance of these relationships to another language not possessing them is, of course, impossible. The poverty of kinship terminology in Norwegian (as in most European dominating ethno-linguistic groups) is a permanent and, for a migrant, a sometimes dangerous barrier. Cases of this are too numerous to list, as for example the migrant who knew the word *bror* (brother) in Norwegian but replied, each time he was asked who lived in his flat with him: *far* (father) when, in fact, his elder brother also lived there. Knowing that the Norwegian language does not mark this differentiation, he simply assumed, logically, that he could not mention him, there being no word for *older* brother.

Extension of kinship terminology. The extension of kinship terms to non-kin causes even more serious problems. If it is impossible to translate kinship terminology, then any attempt at translation of this terminology to non-kin is doomed before one begins, although all ethno-linguistic groups possessing extended kinship terminology apply it extensively and with extreme precision to non-kin. The examples of the serious troubles this causes the migrant coming from such a culture are endless. They often blacklist him with the police and sometimes land him in jail. The many cases of Pakistanis (and others) insisting to the police that 'he is my *bror* or my *onkel*' where no blood relationship exists all lead to various degrees of disaster. The police, on the basis of their evidence (correct from a Norwegian classificatory system), call him a liar and he insists he is not.

However, another related factor is of relevance to the barriers of communication. A speaker coming from such an ethno-linguistic background has no corresponding terms in Norwegian to call Norwegians by, nor does he have any relationship structure to guide him in a society where no such structure exists. Since the application of extended kinship terminology to non-kin implies that one knows, even before one has met a person, in which relationship one stands to him, initial barriers of social intercourse are non-existent. Finding himself in a culture lacking this and with no clues being given him, he is helpless. He vacillates from neutrality (yes/no answers) assumed to be a relatively safe procedure, to colonial-style submissiveness (*takk* = thank you, but even here he has no way even to say *Takk, Sir*, a formulation that does not exist in Norwegian). Or he invents his own linguistic phrases for friendliness, which often build more barriers than they break, e.g. a Pakistani who speaks Norwegian fairly well always greeted one of our female Norwegian observers with: *Hei, det er der du er!* (Hi, it is there you are!). While the Norwegian language possesses various terms of greeting, expressing various degrees of formality (e.g. *god dag* = formal good day, *morn* = informal hello, *hei* = very informal hello) but having no clues as to kinship terminology reference, he has no way to distinguish these correctly either, often using them incorrectly and provoking disconcerting results.

Nomenclature and address. All proper names in Lahnda/Urdu mean something. They may distinguish occupational caste (persons bearing low-caste names often change them), or they may have special meanings such as 'the man who protects himself', or they may be one of many religious names. Family names do not exist. An individual's name has a very particular meaning for him. The migrant from such a culture searches in vain for meaning in Norwegian names. One Norwegian teacher, attempting to supply this in class explained that the name *Hansen* meant son of Hans and that this was why so many persons are named *Hansen* in Norway. Many Norwegian family names attach to geographical areas and farms are given a name. Even were this to be explained to migrants, their lack of knowledge of both geographical areas and the relative status attributed to them leaves the terms as meaningless as before.

Other name complications connected with address arise. It is common in Norway to call a man by his last name (*Hello Hansen*); however if a Pakistani were to go into a tobacco shop and say 'Hansen, please give me a pack of cigarettes', *Hansen* would not be pleased. One calls men by their last names in Norway, but one does not address women that way. Another complication is that migrants can quickly learn to say *Fru Hansen* (Mrs Hansen), but when it comes to a younger woman, problems arise (cf. above, *Hei, det er der du er!*). He must finally settle for calling her by her first name if he has met her several times before, but this causes him troubles also, as the use of first names often implies greater intimacy; otherwise an extended kinship term is used. More often than not, he settles for calling her nothing at all (considered safe), but this is not correct either. None of these problems was clarified in the classes.

Invention

Finding necessary words lacking in the new language, migrants may invent what they need. For example, though migrants (as indicated in one language class) knew that there was no sex differentiation in Norwegian terms for occupational statuses, they invented *sjef* to indicate a male boss, and reserved *sjefen* for a female boss. Although they were content with this lack of sex differentiation in some cases (existing in Norwegian for some occupations, but not for others), it was not allowed to exist in an important part of their life such as relating to the boss at work.

The function of a sentence

Buyssens (1968) defines language from the social point of view:

> Since the primordial function of language is to influence the entourage, it is necessary to define language as a means of acting upon the auditor, not as a means of expression.

We find his analysis of the functions of a sentence of particular relevance here:

> Every sentence fulfils one of the four following functions: 1) inform the auditor [listener], 2) question him, 3) give him an order, 4) use him as witness to a desire. No other possibility exists (Buyssens, 1968, p. 77).

While he is also questioned and informed, a migrant worker is, above all, ordered. Since he is far less often asked to express himself in terms of either function 1 or 4 above, his linguistic incompetence is strongly evident in these two areas; it is considerably less developed and not correlated with his competence in vocabulary and grammar.

Almost every one of the 25 job interviews bears witness to this. Asked a direct question requiring a direct answer without descriptions or explanations, he answers promptly; asked to inform (function 1 above) he begins coherently and with a competence more or less commensurate with his vocabulary and grammar, and then quickly the whole linguistic apparatus he has at his command begins to go to pieces. He stumbles, repeats, stumbles and stops. Example:

> Question: What kind of papers do you need to be able to work?
> Answer: *Her for å finne noe ondentlig jobb, må ha noen — ondentlig brev — eller — at jeg har gått på yr- yr- yr- yrke-skole, som diplomat fra yrkeskole, så det blir veldig litt å fa-finne jobb.* (Here to find any decent job, must have some — decent letter — or — that I have gone to tr- tr- tr- trade school, as diploma (wrong word in Norwegian) from trade school, so it is very little to get—find job.)

The zero exchange value of migrant workers

Man's structural steps in the midst of irrational things have been based on exchange value (Claude Lévi-Strauss, 1969). For what is given, something is received. And for what is received, something is given at all levels of human relationships. Although the exchange relation if often complex, hierarchically arranged, and not directly or immediately perceivable, the human being has constructed his web of social and economic relations upon it.

The zero exchange value of migrant workers as a mobile group is evident in a number of ways in the classroom. For example, there is an apology of power expressed by the teacher. The act of rejection of the migrant attending the very courses presumed to teach him the new language requires apologies. There are many. A classic one is: as time is short and classes mixed and the migrant does not understand, efforts must be directed to the best students (the Anglo-Saxons and English-speakers)!

> After class, the teacher took hold of me. She said that she had a fast tempo and would help only those who understood most.
>
> CO 17.2.77

> The teacher corrected no one except the best.
>
> CO 17.2.77

> It is clear that some 'receive permission' more than others. R. (Amer.) doesn't have to answer with whole sentences, he uses gestures and charms. G. (Pak.) is corrected and the teacher is irritated that he does not understand.
>
> CO 2.2.77

> M. (Turk) continues to be broken off and stopped with his relevant questions outside the text.
>
> CO 9.3.77

> M. asked in Norwegian, the teacher didn't understand so M. went over to English. The teacher answered, irritatedly: 'I don't understand English, you must speak Norwegian'. M. answered that she had said it in Norwegian, but that it was the teacher who had not understood. The class sat absolutely silent and listened.
>
> CO 31.1.77

> The teacher asked M. (Sp.) if she understands English. She shook her head, no. However, the teacher continues to explain words to her often in English. She shakes her head and gives up.
>
> CO 2.3.77

The time or the place of the class is sometimes altered. This is said in Norwegian (or English). Those who do not understand take the consequences.

> The teacher excused herself to me after class. Said it had been a poor session. Class should have begun 15 minutes

earlier this time. She had written it on the blackboard and said it several times, but few came on time. She was very irritated and said she hadn't been able to get through what she had planned.

CO 4.2.77

The termination of the course suffers the same fate.

The teacher didn't say that the next meeting was the last.
CO 17.2.77
(In all the courses we observed, we found students waiting outside the door who did not know that the class had terminated.)

Another common one is: courses exist, why don't they come? This results in schedules suitable for the institutions and teachers, but often not for the migrants. The timetable of the course at the place of work that we observed was set according to available rooms, after other factory courses had been scheduled. This gave the following results (among others) when the course was set at 13.00 hours:

M. (Sp.) told me that most work the 6-12 shift (= wait 1 hour before the 2-hour course begins, an 11-hour day from leaving home to arriving back again) and some work the 15-21 shift (= come 2 hours before work begins to attend course). Some work overtime.

CO 8.3.77

S. (Pak. woman) comes with her little daughter to class. She works from 16-21.45 (= comes with her child 3 hours before her cleaning shift begins, attends class 2 hours, waits 1 hour, cleans for 6 hours, goes home again).

CO 22.2.77

No assessment having been made of the students' knowledge of Norwegian before this work-place course started, it was discovered later that some knew some Norwegian and some did not and that the group therefore had to be divided into 1 and 2 level classes, on the basis of their knowledge of Norwegian (though some of the more advanced wished to stay behind, so as to help their countrymen who knew neither Norwegian nor English). This division was made in the fifth week of a 15-week course.

The group is now divided. At 11.30 nobody had come. Ten minutes later E. (Sp.) came then left again, to get the others I think. Anyway Mrs M. (Pak.) and Mrs T. (Turk) came. We changed rooms. We began all over again on page 1 in the book.

CO 22.3.77

(Note: later all dropped.)

How this course was announced and began:

> I asked M. (Sp.) how he came to know about the course. He said his section boss had told him and signed him in. No notice about the course has been posted.
>
> CO 2.3.77

> At 13.00 when the course should have begun (1st day), the leader, the teacher and I were still upstairs in the leader's office, the door to the room where the course is to be held being locked. When we finally came down 15 minutes late, 2 Pak. students were standing around in the hall and 2 more came in later (= 4). There are 14 enrolled. The leader said such things as: 'Maybe they've forgotten', 'maybe they've lost the way', etc. and sent 1 Pak. to the canteen to fetch some. He came back after a while with 1 more. The actual period lasted 1 hour (not 2 as scheduled) as it started ½ hour late and the teacher stopped ½ hour early.
>
> CO 22.2.77

> When I asked the section leader (a month later) why so many didn't come or hadn't come at all, he said that the reasons were that many were on vacation or on sick-leave. It could also be because *they had to work*. I asked if the course was planned outside working hours, he answered no (cf. above).
>
> CO 22.3.77

The Third World migrant is perceived by teachers as having zero exchange value; this perception is shared by the authorities and by Norwegians in general. Thus, we can understand the nature of the language training programme as it has evolved for the Asian, African and Latin American migrant worker in Norway — a programme that, for the most part, has been a failure.

Untouchable domination

The concomitant to the holding of power is its maintenance. Migrants, as a result of their legal situation and the resultant instability of their presence, can rarely afford themselves the indulgence of attacking this domination — both structural and ideological. For example, at one class, three Pakistani students spoke, in Norwegian, to their teacher.

> There's discrimination here in this country! Only Norwegians can misuse social security money and they do! Foreigners are watched, they have to work all the time, they're sworn at if they are absent from work, despised if they accept social security! But Norwegians! They often go to the social security, they're on sick leave for months on end.

The teacher tried to shade this picture, but one migrant stopped her.

> You don't understand anything! It's the bosses who decide. They're Norwegians! Preferentially treated Norwegians! They exploit foreigners! The doctors are Norwegians too and they favour Norwegians!

It is the non-migrants and the handful of migrants without family responsibilities who represent a threat. Our observers, although accepted, were most often handled with polite caution, since they might criticise and, by so doing, undermine the power over migrants that the teacher alone in his or her classroom holds.

> She wouldn't introduce me as someone who was going to try and find out how Norwegian could be learned faster. She introduced me as X.Y. who has come to see the methods.
> CO 31.1.77 (Norwegian observer).

> Before class began, it came out that neither M. nor C. have understood that I am Norwegian. The teacher told me later that several have asked her if they will be as good at Norwegian as I some day.
> CO 9.3.77

> The teacher was nervous about us as observers. Asked: What were we going to do? Would we break in?, etc.
> CO 22.2.77

The teachers have no time to talk with the students.

> The teacher springs up after class. She has only 15 minutes to the next class and she must change classrooms.
> CO 31.1.77 (Note: this is typical for most).

The teacher has no time for those who do not understand and, sometimes, no time for anybody.

> She didn't give the students time to answer. When they didn't understand, she became impatient and went over to talking herself.
> CO 9.2.77

A questionnaire given at the teachers' seminar, filled in by 66, was particularly indicative. As the questionnaire did not follow the unwritten rules about what one asks in such questionnaires, it caused considerable shock. That questions of any type can be and are posed to migrants is assumed to be natural and necessary. The reverse, however — often the same kinds of question posed to teachers — is frequently regarded as an invasion of a private domain, a threat to the teacher's dominion.

100

Written in large scrawl: 'THE WHOLE QUESTIONNAIRE IS USELESS! It presumes that the participants at this seminar are idiots.' 'IS THIS A PSYCHOLOGICAL TEST OF US? In that case, it ought to be said!' Along the page asking a number of questions (8-15) about the mother-tongue in general and Urdu in particular: 'TENDENTIOUS! The questions presume that one believes in the meaningfulness of language (knowledge?)'. The only question answered on this page: Which language do the Pakistanis here in Norway have as mother-tongue? was answered incorrectly (Urdu). Four questions, including: Is Norwegian language learning set up in such a way that it aims at keeping foreign workers in low-status jobs?, were all marked: 'SCANDALOUS QUESTIONS!'

> TS, no. 1 (5 years' experience teaching adult foreigners).

'What is supposed to be the function of this questionnaire?' To the choice of texts: 'Nonsense'. To the questions regarding mother-tongue and Urdu: 'Dear God, how you underestimate us!' (None of these questions were answered, including the one regarding the mother-tongue of most Pakistanis in Norway — which no one answered correctly.)

> TS, no. 16 (5 years' experience as leader).

One indicated their willingness to have a home country teacher, along with a Norwegian, but only *as assistant*.

> TS, no. 13 (4 years' experience teaching both school-age and adult foreigners).

Superiority of the school as established value and rejection of all other models of learning

The justification of any teaching institution involved in the training of migrant workers and their children must be based on a preliminary categorisation and systematisation of the status attributed to the means and instruments of learning used in the country of origin and in the country of production or employment. Only then would it be possible to develop appropriate methodological supports and a relation between teacher and taught on the learning level.

Historically, the means and instruments of learning in Pakistan and India have been largely non-institutional. Almost the only form which existed prior to British colonialisation was religious education, consisting in knowing the Koran for the Moslems and the Sanskrit verses for the Hindus. Traditionally, Moslem religious education has always been very well organised. In Pakistan, the mosques frequently provide the location for classes on the Koran and lectures on literacy and religious topics.

It was the British who first institutionalised education in a Western way. The educational institutions and curricula introduced by the colonialists reflected a desire to bring the presumed benefits of Christianity and Western civilisation to a small segment of the population in the sub-continent. The education policy of the British argued for an education that would ' . . . form a class of persons, Indian in blood and colour, but English in taste, in opinions, in moral and in intellect' (Thomas Macaulay). In line with this policy, only a small class of people was allowed access to these institutions.

The elitist groups that gained political control of Pakistan and India after the British departed in 1947, have been both unable and reluctant to change the basic colonial nature of the educational institutions in these countries.

The institutional/non-institutional modes of learning do not, obviously, represent a 'better' and a 'worse' type, but they necessarily require different cognitive strategies and logical processes. One who learns through careful observation and progressive participation learns through a *logic of a type of circular tendency* (not to be confused with circular logic). This basically implies that all the elements of learning are encompassed within the act of work, i.e. within the lived experience of the worker. It is the *continuous act of learning itself that becomes interiorised* for him, not any institution or 'course', since no scholastic or literary preparation is a necessary prerequisite.

The relational model of learning in the Western countries, on the other hand, where the means and instruments of learning are largely institutionalised, is based on a *logic of a linear tendency*, which implies that the learner must go through many years of institutionalised literary and scholastic preparation before he can step into the act of work. For him, it is *the institution itself that becomes interiorised*, as this progressive passage through institutional courses is the necessary prerequisite.

The institutionalised learning strategy of the Western type is essentially deductive logic, proceeding from abstract principles to details. The Asian motor mechanic, for example, in contrast, proceeds from details to principles. His learning consists of a vast number of complex perceptions and observations which are then combined with vast amounts of data stored in memory, a synthesis of which then forms his principles and plan of action.

Needless to say, the cognitive strategies employed by both the Asian and Norwegian motor mechanic are equally logical and reasonable. In fact, under certain conditions, the cognitive strategy of the Asian may be superior, for when external conditions change forcing alterations in the act of work (e.g. the appearance of a new car model with a different engine, construction), the Asian motor mechanic simply has to add the new dimension to his overall perception and continue working toward the solution. The Norwegian motor mechanic, on the other hand, may be forced to abandon his original plan. He must apply a new set of principles, work out a new plan and presumably consult a new book before he can make the first tactical response to the changed conditions.

Of the children of migrant workers attending SLF classes in Oslo, the following has been said:

> Several teachers have asked why immigrant pupils read and solve arithmetic problems mechanically. That is to say, while doing mathematics, they either ask their teacher, 'You do one for me and I'll do the rest', or they copy down the answer.
>
> Referat, Teachers' Meeting 79/76, 13.12.76
>
> The Norwegian school is based upon principles of self-motivation and individualised learning. It looks like our pupils (immigrant children) cannot understand, take seriously, or respect this form of learning.
>
> Ibid.

A teacher teaching Norwegian to foreign students at the University of Oslo has this to say of students from developing countries, especially Asian students:

> Everyone is more or less 'blank' when they start at Level I, but unavoidably there is soon a *big gap between the 'good' and 'less good' students* at this level . . .

She presumably is not familiar with the widely differing results of IQ tests designed by Anglo-Saxons and administered to Anglo-Saxons and non-Anglo-Saxons alike, and those of IQ tests (the 'Bitch 100' in the USA, for example) designed by non-Anglo-Saxons and administered to Anglo-Saxons and non-Anglo-Saxons alike. She continues:

> The reason for this is primarily the different background of the students. The difference in very many cases is between students from industrialised and developing countries, the background and *previous abilities* of the students from developing countries. Some of them behave in such a manner that it is difficult to imagine that they have an education equivalent to that required to be admitted to the University. Many students, especially from developing countries, *look upon being able to go to the University as something 'great'* and they also get many advantages from it . . .
>
> 5.1.77 (our italics).

103

This teacher then goes on to suggest that all elementary education in Norwegian should take place in an institution other than the university and that all students wanting to study at the university first take an entrance examination in Norwegian. In this way, she hopes one will be able to filter out the students who 'just go to a course' in Norwegian from those who 'actually study it'. Ironically enough, she is also referring to a group of students who come from multilingual societies and who have already mastered at least three languages.

First the relational model of learning of Norwegian is imposed upon migrants and then failure of both the training programmes as well as the model of learning are rationalised away by such statements as:

- they have a poor school background
- the school system in their country is not sufficiently developed
- they have poor resources, they are culturally deprived, etc.

One of the teachers teaching immigrant children says the following:

> Pupils from foreign cultures can be difficult to integrate. Pupils must have knowledge of the important elements of *our* culture. . . Islam has some of the Greek conceptual thinking but not enough. Pupils should, for example, have knowledge of the elements of Christianity, Roman Law and Greek thinking.
>
> Referat, Teachers' Meeting 25/76, 5.4.76.

It is quite common for Norwegian teachers to call the Latin alphabet *vart* (our) alphabet.

To explore the comparable Norwegian/Pakistani tenacity of semantic classification (a word *is* what it stands for and therefore cannot be switched), we used the well known Piaget model (can the sun be called the moon and vice versa? why not?) and asked two groups — the Norwegian teachers and directors of Norwegian language learning at the seminar; and the AS group of Pakistani students — if a donkey could be called a horse and vice versa, selecting a model very close to Pakistani culture and relatively so to Norwegian. To the Norwegian group, the question was phrased: 'If the Norwegian government adopted that, from 1978 on, all horses shall be called donkeys and all donkeys shall be called horses, would you follow the new regulation?'

To the AS Pakistani group, the question was first stated simply: 'Can a donkey be called a horse and a horse a donkey?' 'No'. 'Why not?' then developed through various levels such as: 'If everybody in your village did . . . ', 'If everybody you know did . . . ', 'If everybody did . . . ', 'If the whole world did . . . ', to 'If the boss said you had to . . . ' (invoking the stereotype of Pakistanis as submissive to authority). Answer: 'He's only one person! *I* have a head!' — then further to 'If the Prime Minister of Norway said you had to . . . '

Answer: 'He's only one man too. He can't decide that without the Parliament' — to 'If the Norwegian Parliament . . . ' etc., same question as presented at the seminar to the Norwegian teachers. Answer: 'If the Norwegian Parliament has nothing better to do than think about changing the name of horses and donkeys, they can't be doing much for the Norwegian people!'

AS session, 17.4.77.

Results: with two exceptions, 1 Norwegian, 1 Pakistani, both women said they would if they were told by the government that this was a law and must be obeyed (the Norwegian teacher qualifying her answer by saying, 'but only in class'). Both Norwegians and Pakistanis continued to hold fast — not different from the answers that Piaget got. There is no difference between Norwegians and Pakistanis in the *irreversibility of a semantic classification*. We stress this as it is illustrative of our claim that comparative ethno-linguistics and the corresponding recognition of cognitive worlds of alterity are central to a successful programme of language training of migrants.

With the exception of the few students in the AS classes, the language formation programmes for adult migrants that are provided in Norway, take place inside classrooms, based on the formal model and with the cognitive strategies of Western relational models of learning and, important to note, *with Norwegian semantic classification models of words as the only valid ones*. The migrant has two choices: bend, or not attend.

Explicit equality. Equality denied by the act of refusal of alterity formulations are needed to confirm its explicitness. Symbolic terminology may be employed.

Officially, the students are called *deltagere* (participators) (Cf. whole report).

An assertion of equal job opportunities is made:

The word *arbeid* (work) was illustrated by:
— I work in an office.
— I work at a school.
— I work in a factory.

CO 31.1.77

(Few migrants work at any of these places).

A slide was used that was supposed to show a *hybel* (small, rented room). The *hybel* had the following furniture: 2 armchairs, a desk with steel desk lamp, door mat, carpet, drawing room table, guitar.

CO 4.2.77

The teacher explained carefully various kinds of sports (all Norwegian), then asked different people what kind of sports they engaged in.

S. (Pak.): No time, job, school.   CO 24.1.77

During the pause, Y. (Pak.) found the picture that showed 'At the restaurant'. Asked what I wanted to have, 'Irish coffee?' 'What?', I asked. 'Coffee without sugar and milk', he answered and added 'whipped cream cake'. That comes to Kr. 20.50 ($4.10). I remarked that was expensive. He laughed.

                                                     CO 22.2.77

The blackboard eraser doesn't erase. It needs to be wet. The teacher has tried it, says it needs some water on it, he doesn't know where the water is. M. (Sp.) says he can do it and jumps up from the back of the room where he is sitting. The teacher, having sat down at his desk again, says he can do it himself. M. goes out, comes back with wet eraser.

                                                     CO 22.2.77

Implicit hierarchisation. Concomitant with the preservation of the myth of equality, there exists a hierarchisation that has no parallel in Norwegian life. The Norwegian teacher when talking with another Norwegian (cf. many of our class observation notes made by the Norwegian observers) assumes the role into which Norwegian hierarchy places him. Confronted with a migrant, presumably unfamiliar with Norwegian hierarchical structure, the teacher then places himself into the higher spheres of upper or upper middle class hierarchy and deals with the migrant from that lofty level. These two worlds do not meet, nor is there any comprehension — real, imagined, or attempted — from the teacher of this, the migrants' 'other' world, from the mythical level to which he has fictitiously raised himself. Examples:

Teacher: 'In the book it says that many go to the city because there are jobs there, but it is difficult to find a place to live'. The same day the radio reported that 300 foreign workers in Oslo were out of work.

                                                     CO 30.3.77

Teacher: 'Why do people move away?' C. answered that it was because there weren't enough jobs. The teacher added that many thought it was more interesting to live in town.
                                                     CO 30.3.77

When A. (Pak.) was telling about the factory that had to close down, it was absolutely silent in the classroom and all listened with much attention.

CO 30.3.77

Teacher: 'The house is empty. What does that mean?'
M. (Turk): 'Available'.

CO 30.3.77

S. (Pak.) continues to be provoking, asks the teacher questions and makes comments: 'How long a work day do *you* have?' '*You* don't understand how it is with *us*', etc., etc.

CO 23.3.77

To the question, 'What are you going to do Easter vacation?', S. (Pak.) answers something I could not hear.
Teacher: '*Jasa* (So!) you're going out in the sun to sun yourself'.
S: 'Yes, in the garden'.
Teacher: 'Do you have a garden in front of your house?'
S: 'No. Frogner Park'.

CO 30.3.77

H. (Pak.) asks what do *fra* (from) and *mot* (towards) mean. All are interested and the Pak. teacher explains. He uses as example the subway *fra* and *mot* centre (of town). None had known what *mot sentrum* (toward the centre) meant.

CO 14.2.77, a Level 2 class.

(Note: this is the only way in which the direction of the subway is marked, *fra* and *mot sentrum*.)

In answer to Question no. 20 at the teachers' seminar: 'What percentage of foreign workers do you think complete the 240 gratis hours of Norwegian language learning?', 24 did not answer, six said *over 50 per cent*, seven said from 20 to 30 per cent, 16 answered from 0 to 10 per cent. To Question no. 21: 'What per cent do you think have completed the 1st Level (60 hours)?' *nobody answered 0*, 11 answered from 50 to 75 per cent and 31 did not answer at all.

Teacher: 'Did you manage to do anything else yesterday except read?'
M. (Turk): 'Two hours in shop'.
Teacher: 'Did you sell much?'
M.: 'No, I wash'.
Teacher: 'Oh yes, you washed there'.
A. (Pak.): 'We don't sell, we wash'.
S. (Pak.): 'I got yesterday extra work'.
Teacher: 'So you managed to do quite a lot extra'.
S.: 'I'm often made to do extra work at the job'.

CO 23.3.77

Zero exchange denies the *other* the possibility of becoming a *person*. If he has no place in structural hierarchy he cannot exist. He remains an abstraction, transparent, not there. His education then becomes the education of an abstraction. The failure to perceive this is basic to the failure of most of the courses under FU and AOF, whereas this was *not* the case with the AS courses.

> N. (Pak.) came a little late the first day, chose the seat front R side nearest the teacher, obviously eager to learn. On L side were more students, especially a very talkative one. Teacher immediately turned his chair around directly facing them. Result: conducted whole period with his back to N., directing everything he said to L side.
>
> CO 22.2.77

> Overhead pictures are projected in such a position that they can be seen by only half of the class.
>
> CO 2.2.77

> There is a picture of a dog in the textbook. The teacher asks: 'What should one do to get a dog to come to you?' Nobody answers. Teacher whistles. Nobody understands why the teacher has suddenly whistled, they just sit there looking puzzled. The teacher asks further what one shall do to get a dog to sit nicely, answers his own question: 'Sit!' and 'Give your paw!'
>
> CO 2.3.77

> There is a picture of a cat in the book. S. (Sp.) asks if the word *pus* (pussy) can be used. The teacher says yes and if she wants to call a cat, she shall say: 'Pzzzzz, pzzzzzekat'.
>
> CO 2.3.77

> S. (Pak.): It's difficult to learn Norwegian.
> Teacher: Yes, it would be difficult for me to learn *Pakistansk* too.
>
> CO 23.3.77 (teacher with 5 years' experience with adult migrants).
>
> No language named 'Pakistani' exists.

> The teacher is discussing different customs. She asks if there are big differences between customs in Pakistan and in Norway.
> M. (Pak.): Yes, women in Pakistan wear veils, old men wear caps or wrap cloth around their heads.
> Teacher: Yes, that is called a *turban*.

CO 30.3.77

(Unthinkable, for example, for a Norwegian teacher to tell a Christian NATO officer that what old men in his country wear is called a Jewish prayer cap. Not knowing, the initiative would be left to him. Though this teacher has had many years' experience teaching adult migrants, including both Pakistanis and Indians, she has apparently not been interested enough yet to discover that a turban is a Sikh religious symbol and has, of course, nothing to do with Moslems (Pakistanis).

The class is discussing the word *viktig* (important).
H.: 'Is *ma* (must) the same as *viktig*?'
N.: 'Coca Cola is viktig'. He gets a lecture from the teacher on nourishing foods.

CO 14.2.77

(Coca Cola is consumed to excess in Norway.)

Reinforcement of insecurity

A migrant arrives in the new country in what we will call a state of equilibrium. He is young, the country is new, the faces are new, the smell and sound and touch are new, the cafes and cinemas are new, the language is new — it is all an exciting adventure to know and explore. Rapidly, however, the doors close, the police appear. The circle closes in. Courses appear to 'form' and 'assimilate' him, if not 'integrate' him. In these courses in Norway, the last back turns on him, the last door closes. He fits no longer within the cognitive circumference of the world behind; that of the world he is in holds him outside. Non-existent in both, he inhabits a third — a world that has no structure, no signs. From his classroom experiences, he concludes he is a failure, constitutionally inept.

M. (Pak.) asked where I come from. I answered Norway and explained why I was there. He then asked if I was there to *kontrollere* (check on). I asked what he thought I would be checking. He shrugged his shoulders and said: 'Everything'. I said maybe he thought I came from the Police, but I didn't, I wasn't there to check on people.

CO 30.3.77

The teacher hopped over the Pakistani woman and directed himself only to the Spanish corner. They speak better Norwegian.

CO 17.2.77

When I go around the class, H. (Pak.) calls me and tells me he is 'illiterate' and therefore will need a lot of help. He can read and write Urdu, but has never learned English or the Latin alphabet.

CO 2.2.77 (Asian observer).

Met G. (Pak.) out in the hall before class began. He sat alone. I greeted him and he made a sign that I should sit beside him. Showed me a list of words he had written in Norwegian and Urdu in his notebook. Among others: frying pan, flour, almonds, tomatoes, chicken, pork, lamb meat, paprika, eggplant, spinach, onion, cupboard, politics, polite, to fight, to like, factory, sweater, small change. I asked if he was going to continue. He didn't understand, didn't know that the course was finishing the next day.

CO 17.2.77

Talked with M. (Turk) before class began. He was now much more uncertain if he would be able to come into vocational school. He has read the whole textbook now, but doesn't talk any better.

CO 23.3.77

Some who never answered in class or answered incorrectly and seemed not to understand amazed me with their ability to talk to me when we were alone. Big variation between their oral ability with me and with the teacher.

CO 7.2.77 (Norwegian observer).

One of the team members, of the same nationality and on very good terms of friendship with some of the Pakistani students, arrived at his home one evening late for a meeting with them and found a note signed:

'The countryless king, the beggar, the brainless intellectual, the servant.' His comment: 'They are discriminated for their ambitions. They desire to advance, it is cut, desire, cut, desire, cut. The cycle repeats.'

Team member note 12.5.77

The road to submission

Functioning as an economic unit in a hierarchical structure that excludes him as an active cognitive unit, directed by foreigners (the natives) whose ethno-language remains foreign to him and controlled by a power apparatus of persons to whom he has not delegated that power, the migrant has only two choices: go back home (a failure) or submit.

His formal education consists in progressively being led to submission to a cognitive world into which he is told to enter, but which refuses him when he makes attempts. The teacher, in the refusal of the migrant's cognitive world, is a major — though unconscious — instrument in this process.

Teacher: What does one ask a possible employer?
E. (A-Sx.): How much will I be paid?
M. (Pak.): *Undskyld, jeg vil gjerne ha jobb* (Excuse me, I so much want job).

CO 9.3.77

(No comments from teacher.)

G. (Pak.) answers wrong again. He heard the word *bo* (live) and answered, resigned, 'Oslo 1'.
Teacher: The question was: where did your father live?
He understands nothing and answers again, 'Oslo 1'.

CO 4.2.77

Teacher: What does *a bli oppsagt* (be dismissed from a job) mean?
M. (Pak.): Not to be able to do anything afterwards.

CO 30.3.77

G. (Pak.) gets guilt feelings. He makes mistakes, errors, sinks the class.

CO 4.2.77

The teacher is explaining the word *motsatt* (opposite).
N. (Pak.) says that it is the same word in Urdu (*mutzaad*) and it has the same meaning.
Teacher: I don't know if I should believe you.

CO 16.3.77

(N. was correct; it is the same.)

M. (Pak.) knows quite a lot of Norwegian. He is the one who proposes many such expressions as: employer, employee, vacation, free day, etc. The teacher cuts him off constantly.

CO 9.3.77

After the class, the teacher draws me into a room. Wants to know what I think of G. (Pak.). In her opinion, he is hopeless and must take Level I over again. I answer vaguely, saying she must decide.

CO 16.2.77

G. is now repeating Level I over again with her, but he doesn't understand anything she says.

111

(This student had been ignored and put down by the teacher during the whole Level I course.)

Our conclusion is reflected by what Christine Josse (1976) has so clearly stated in 'Technostructures of Inequality': 'From genocide to progressive assimilation, one and the same strategy: domination'.

The one notable exception to the traditional pattern we observed and have described above was the AS classes. Requested by Pakistanis themselves who said they were learning nothing in the FU and AOF courses, planned by an administrator with previous experience in North Norway in the ethno-linguistic problems Sami students face (subordinated structurally, ideologically and linguistically) and using the two-teacher system (one Norwegian, one Pakistani), these classes avoided the impasse of the refusal of alterity of a cognitive world at variance with the dominating one. It is only to be regretted that these classes are few in number, that the importance of this model of learning goes largely unperceived and that the domination of the two monopoly institutions continues to be 'untouchable'.

While waiting, the migrant remains where we found him when we started this report:

— Oslo, Copenhagen, Stockholm, Paris — the group word?
— Airport.

The ghetto of the soul has no epicentre.

Appendix: methods of research

Composition of research team

Considering an inter-disciplinary approach to be fundamental in constituting the research team, we selected specialists who were not only competent in their own respective fields, but also had experience with and keen interest in the problems of migrant workers.

Another criterion in the selection of the team members was to mix university academics with non-academics, as we consider it paramount in all matters having to do with foreign workers (as well as in a number of other fields) to break the long-established university intellectual monopoly on 'correct thinking' and let some fresh air in.

The team consisted of the following nine members:

Saeed Anjum (Pakistani), bilingual teacher, Oslo Community School System; Ministry of Social Affairs, project leader for the planning of free time activities for Pakistani youth.

Ali Abbas Asim (Pakistani), psychologist, Professor of Psychology, Government College, Punjab University, Lahore, Pakistan, on leave of absence in 1977; returned to resume position in Pakistan in 1978.

Even Hovdhaugen (Norwegian), linguist, Professor, Linguistic Institute, University of Oslo, Blindern.

Aud Korbøl (Norwegian), sociologist, Institute for Social Research, Research Director; representative of the Ministry of Church and Education to the Immigration Council.

Sunil Loona (Indian), psychologist, Oslo Community School System, Psychology Office.

Berit Løfsnaes (Norwegian), social worker, Ministry of Social Affairs, Counsellor on migrant workers.

Manuel Machado (Portuguese), ethno-psychologist, former student at l'Ecole des Hautes Etudes, Paris, three years under Otto Klineberg.

Carolyn Swetland (naturalised Norwegian), project leader; social anthropologist, formerly Professor of Anthropology and author of a number of ethnological films, Administrative Director and General Secretary, Foreign Workers Association, Norway; presently member of Ministry of Church and Education, Adult Education Division, Committee on Education of Migrants; Ministry of Church and Education, research project leader in Norwegian language teaching for migrants, 1978.

Ayako Tsuda (Japanese), sociologist, assistant teacher of sociology, University of Oslo, Blindern; worker Oslo Community Youth Clubs.

Classroom observation

Classes in FU, AS and AOF were observed each session for the period of their duration — three months. These classes varied from beginning (Level 1) to advanced (Level 5). Each class was observed by two different observers, one Norwegian and one non-Norwegian, who attended the class on alternate observation days. The method of study was that of participant observation.

Job interviews

Thirty-three interviews with unemployed migrants were collected at the Foreigners' Employment Office. Of these, eleven were made with Pakistanis. The questionnaire used for the interview was prepared in such a way as to reveal vocabulary and linguistic ability learned outside formal institutions, in areas having to do with work, the place of work, work comrades, the labour organisation, relationship with bosses, the worker's own evaluation of his previous jobs, and his job expectancies before he came to Norway. Such questions as: 'When you don't agree with the boss, what do you do?', 'What is LO?', 'What is marked on your payslip?' (did he understand his payslip?), 'What machine do you work at?/tell me about it/describe it to me', were asked. The questions were not necessarily phrased in that way by the interviewer. He posed them as best as he could in each situation to solicit descriptive talk on each topic. Additional information concerning duration of work and stay in Norway, age, sex, previous schooling, attendance at formal language course and nationality was also secured for each interviewee.

Comparative ethno-linguistic sessions

Five informal group discussions were held with the AS class that had been observed earlier; these began immediately at the end of the course and lasted three weeks. Almost all the original students attended. These sessions were conducted by the social anthropologist. Among the topics discussed were the language course, life in Norway, family life among Pakistani immigrants, and the like. These sessions were a source of additional data on language learning.

Interviews with directors and section leaders

At various times we interviewed the directors and teachers of the language courses. In addition, a number of interviews, as well as informal talks, were held with various other persons in the Ministry of Church and Education, and with various teachers and individuals engaged in this field.

Data analysis

Tabular analysis was made of the data on all the students enrolled in both FU and AOF courses in Oslo during the first three months of 1977. The data had been gathered from the FU and AOF files.

All of the Unesco Guide references were either previously known or have been consulted by, at least, the project leader. We do not consider it necessary to repeat that list here.

Bibliography

Buyssens, Eric, 'Le langage et la logique' in Martinet, André, *Le langage*, Encyclopédie de la Pléiade, Editions Gallimard, 1968.

Chanin, Teodor, *Peasants and Peasant Societies*, Penguin Ed., Middlesex, England, 1971.

Council of Europe, Strasbourg, France: all material 1975-77 (mimeo., restricted circulation) on *The Teaching of Modern Languages to Migrant Workers* (various experimental programmes, e.g. in Turkey, Italy, etc.); *Education of Migrant Workers' Children* (organisation of special classes for 1977-78) and reports on current experiments in special classes; *Social and Economic Repercussions on Migrant Workers of Economic Recessions and Crises* (all reports); *Clandestine Immigration* (all reports).

Deip, Didrik Arup, *Norsk språkhistorie*, Oslo, 1931.

Dittmar, Norbert, *Sociolinguistics: A Critical Survey of Theory and Application*, Edward Arnold, London, 1976.

Dumont, Louis, *Homo Aequalis, Genèse et épanouissement de l'ideologie économique*, Bibliothèque des Sciences Humaines, Gallimard, Paris, 1977.

Dumont, Louis, *Homo Hierarchicus*, Paladin, London, 1972 (English edition).

First Pan-European Conference of Migrant Workers, report, Wageningen, The Netherlands, November 22-24, 1974.

Hartman, Jean, *Industrien i Norge*, Tapir Forlag, Trondheim, 1971.

Heidelberger Forschungsprojekt, various publications on *Pidgin-Deutsch Spanischer und Italienischer arbeiter*, 1975-77.

Hoëm, Anton, '*Skolen og heimen*', in Homme, Lina R., *Nordisk nykolonialisme*, Det Norske Samlaget, Oslo, 1969.

International NGO Conference Report on *Discrimination Against Migrant Workers in Europe*, Palais des Nations, Geneva, 16-19 September 1975.

Josse, Christine, 'Technostructures of Inequality' in Cahiers de l'I.E.D., Geneva, *Les modes de Transmission du didactique à l'extrascolaire*, Presses Universitaires de France, Paris, 1976.

Leach, E.R., (ed.), *Aspects of Caste in South-India, Ceylon and Northwest Pakistan*, Cambridge University Press, Cambridge, 1971.

Lévi-Strauss, Claude, *The Elementary Structures of Kinship*, Beacon Press, Boston, 1969.

Lévi-Strauss, Claude, *The Savage Mind*, The University of Chicago Press, 1966.

Lieberman, Sima, *The Industrialisation of Norway 1800-1920*, Universitets forlaget, Oslo, 1970.

Mahkubul, Haq, 'The Strategy of Economic Planning: The Case of

Pakistan', *Pakistani News Digest*, 15 June 1970.
Ministry of Church and Education (Kirke — og undervisningsdeparte-mentel, Rundskriv) F-77/75, 18 March 1975.
Ministry of Home Affairs and Labour, *On the Immigration Stop and Work with Immigration Questions*, White Paper no. 107, to the Parliament, 21 May 1976 (unofficial translation).

Naes, Olav, *Norsk grammatikk*, Oslo, 1972.

Otnes, Per, *Den samiske nasjon*, Pax Forlag, A.S., Oslo, 1970.

Parin, P. et al., *Les Blancs pensent trop* (13 interviews with Les Dogon), Bibliothèque Scientifique, Collection *Science de l'homme*, Payot, Paris, 1966.

Shackle, C., *The Siraiki Language of Central Pakistan: A Reference Grammar*, School of Oriental and African Studies, University of London, London, 1976.
Smirnov, U.A., *The Lahndi Language*, Languages of Asia and Africa Series, NAUKA Publishing House, Central Dept. of Oriental Literature, Moscow, 1975 (English edition).

Wadnim, Johan A., 'Den Samiske stat', in *Dyade*, no. 2, 1976.
WFTU, Econ. and Social Dept., *Migrant Workers and Their Problems*, 1976.

Periodicals

Dawn, Pakistani weekly for readers abroad, 1976 issues.
Historisk statistisk, Statistisk Sentralbyrå, Oslo, 1968.
Journal of Contemporary Asia, vol. 4, no. 4, 1975.
Pakistani Adab (literature), Jan-Dec, 1976.

Acknowledgements

The team wishes to express its appreciation to the following for their cooperation:
First and foremost, to the many migrants both in and out of classrooms whose eagerness to talk — in whatever language they could — when we were eager to listen is the basis of the veracity of this report; to the many Norwegians not directly involved, but whose interest in migrants led them to give long days and evenings to this project; to the section leaders of the three language formation institutions, Friundervisning, AOF and Aftenskolen for having opened their doors and files to us; to the teachers who permitted us to sit in their classrooms and observe; to the Labour Office and, under it, the foreign workers' employment bureau for having allowed us to interview job-seekers there and having put an office at our disposal; to the many persons at many levels of various ministries, departments, offices, schools who helped in the many ways they could; to Marta Aarseth, Institute for Social Research, for having done the bookkeeping job; and to the Ministry of Home Affairs and Labour for having granted funds which made this research possible.
Any errors that may have crept into the text are the sole responsibility of the team.

116

3 The unguided learning of German by Spanish and Italian workers
NORBERT DITTMAR*

Introduction

The present report summarises a study devoted to the learning of German by immigrant workers in the Federal Republic of Germany (FRG) and to their knowledge of that language. It is a socio-linguistic study of a relatively small sample of immigrant workers from two countries — Italy and Spain. The social conditions under which Italian and Spanish workers learn German are certainly not sufficiently different from those of other nationalities to prohibit us from drawing conclusions valid for all foreign workers in the FRG on the basis of our research with Spanish and Italian workers.

Our study is based on a single investigation. It is an inventory of the knowledge of the German language by 48 workers under dissimilar individual conditions, staying for different periods of time in the FRG and placed in quite varied learning contexts. Although the present investigation does not follow foreign workers over a period of time, and thus cannot detail the chronology of language learning, it does approximate such a developmental study because immigrant workers are observed at various stages of learning.

* This chapter was written with assistance from Angelika Becker, Margit Gutmann, Wolfgang Klein, Bert-Olaf Rieck, Gunter Senft, Ingeborg Senft, Wolfram Steckner and Elisabeth Thielicke. The study is a collective work by the members of the Heidelberger Forschungsprojekt 'Pidgin-Deutsch'. We wish to thank the Institute of Germanic Studies of the University of Heidelberg and the various institutions in Heidelberg and its environs for their assistance and support. The views put forward in this document, the selection of facts and the way in which they are interpreted are entirely the responsibility of the authors and do not necessarily reflect the opinion of Unesco.

It should be noted that second language learning in the form of appropriate instruction has virtually been non-existent heretofore in the FRG. Between six and ten per cent of the individuals questioned during the investigations stated that they had attended courses in German (see Federal Ministry of Labour, 1974; Mehrländer, 1974). This means that the great majority of foreigners living and working in the FRG have not attended and are not attending courses in German, but have to learn German through their interaction with the German population.

The learning process resulting from such a situation is called 'unguided' because it does not comprise any interventions in the form of language courses. The example of children who, placed in a foreign linguistic environment, learn relatively quickly the language of the country, provided they have contacts with native children, shows that the process of unguided learning can indeed be very effective. The fact that it does not function as well in the case of foreign workers cannot be attributed merely to biological differences between children and adults, for the notion that the learning faculty diminishes with age is not uncontested – save in the field of articulation. Their difficulties in learning the language of the country of immigration must above all be attributed to the fact that the conditions of learning they encounter are entirely different from an optimal 'language immersion' (see Dumas, Selinker, Swain, 1973).

It is no exaggeration to state that the language of immigrant workers in industrialised societies reflects the restricted conditions under which it is learned (see Richards, 1972; Bickerton, 1975, showing the develop-ment of pidgin and creole speech in colonial societies). The formation of a variety of German as a second language among immigrant workers in the FRG, with a structure having many formal similarities to pidgin jargons, could have been avoided only if the immigrants had received language training (that would have given them a basic knowledge of German) just before, or at least immediately following, their arrival in the country. In contrast to this desirable situation, the two million salaried foreigners already living in the FRG for several years have acquired a certain knowledge of German and have all already gone beyond the initial phase of learning, which is also the most active. Their command of the second language has, in most cases, reached a certain degree of stability. It has 'fossilised' after a number of years at a more or less advanced level, with practically no chance of ever attaining, through a process of unguided learning, full command over the target language. It is these immigrant workers who are at the core of the Heidelberg pidgin German research project, which proceeds from the hypothesis that in order to plan efficient language instruction intended for immigrant workers, it is necessary first to have knowledge of the deficient systems for acquiring language without guidance, with a view to their subsequent use for language-instruction purposes.

The present chapter is organised as follows: the second section deals with the unguided learning of a second language, as distinguished from guided learning. The third section describes the sample studied and the techniques employed for obtaining the linguistic and social data. In the fourth section we set forth, by use of the grammar of varieties (Klein, 1974), the results of the linguistic study of 48 varieties of language of Italian and Spanish workers (for details see Heidelberger Forschungsprojekt 'Pidgin-Deutsch' (HPD), 1976 and 1978; and Dittmar and Rieck, 1977). The fifth section then establishes the relations between the linguistic and social data. In the sixth section we state several conclusions concerning the institutionalisation of language courses.

Unguided language learning and the language of foreign workers

The importance of unguided language learning

Despite considerable efforts, the language instruction intended for foreign workers in the FRG has thus far been ineffectual. One of the many reasons for its failure is the fact that there exist no language courses adapted to the specific language problems of foreign workers. Scientific efforts should aim at remedying this state of affairs. This chapter examines this point in some detail.

In our opinion, well founded language instruction is not conceivable without prior study of the unguided learning of a second language (hereinafter shortened to 'language learning') by foreign workers, that is, what they learn through their daily contact with Germans in their social context. The study of unguided language learning is essential for three reasons:

1 Foreign workers already acquire through their contacts with Germans linguistic knowledge of rather unequal quality. Language instruction should take this into account: guided language learning should in such cases complement the unguided learning. This has positive and negative aspects: on the one hand, certain knowledge already acquired has no further need to be transmitted; on the other hand, certain phenomena have been incorrectly learned; language instruction must then attempt to correct them.

2 What foreign workers learn without guidance gives us important indications regarding the nature of their *communication* needs. It is highly unlikely that they learn through their social contacts very many things that they do not require in order to communicate. This obviously does not mean that

they have no need for all that they do not learn. Hence the study of unguided language learning does not set the instruction goals, but helps to do so. This contribution is the more important as we have very few criteria for determining pedagogical objectives.

3 Independently of the problem peculiar to foreign workers, the bases for the teaching of foreign languages must be considered as quite inadequate despite innumerable studies on the subject. Such instruction is based more on practical experiments and on unverified ideas born of other disciplines (such as the psychology of learning, pedagogy, contrastive linguistics) than on reliable scientific research on the manner in which foreign languages are learned, the factors that determine this process, and how it could be influenced.

General conditions concerning the study of language teaching

Anyone studying a language reaches his ideal objective when his linguistic behaviour is indistinguishable from those whose mother-tongue it is; in that respect he has a certain latitude, for the language of natives reveals, as is well known, differences of social origin. The linguistic behaviour of the language learner must be situated within this space of relative freedom. Very few reach this ideal objective, although it is not ideal in the sense of being inaccessible. In practice, the idea is to approach it as closely as possible. Hence language learning can be understood as a process during which a learner acquires a certain repertory of behaviour. This is an oriented process; it leads from a certain initial stage towards a certain target behaviour, though deviations from the 'straight line' are occasionally evident. The progression of this process may be quite variable, and depends on a number of factors. The task of the study of language learning consists in identifying factors, determining their influence on the language-learning process and describing in detail the unfolding of this process.

The process of language learning can be influenced to a certain degree. The influence may be direct, and bear on the direction and speed of development. It may also be indirect, in the sense of an action on the factors participating in the determination of language learning, for example, by exercise of the auditory faculty and of memorisation, by stimulating motivation, etc. We call language instruction these two types of influence which in practice are generally found together. Several conditions must be fulfilled in order for them to be effective. In particular the following conditions must be met:

1 The above-mentioned task of the study of language learning must be defined more precisely; as long as the respective

influence of the various factors is not known, nor how they may foster or hinder learning of the target behaviour, language teaching will remain an art that some people possess perfectly because of their experience and talent. But it cannot be said that the methods rest on sound scientific bases.

2 From bases determined in this manner, methods must be devised to permit optimal intervention.

3 The target behaviour must be described precisely. In this field, the current results of research are quite insufficient.

4 All this must be applied to actual cases; that is, instruction units must be conceived and the educational material developed.

These conditions are logically interlinked: thus the fourth point also implies the second and third; the second point in turn implies the first; that is, in order to give optimal form to interventions, one must know the regularities of the process in which one aims to intervene. Hence the first condition takes precedence from the standpoint of research. This is now discussed.

Analysis of language learning

After studying a foreign language for a period of time, most people become capable of making statements which resemble to a greater or lesser degree those of the target language. Another formulation of the same fact would be to say that one speaks a particular *variety* of target language. This is because, as a general rule, a target language is not homogeneous but consists of a certain number of dialectal, social or situational varieties that speakers of the language appreciate quite diversely. The current 'language status' of the one learning the language also constitutes such a variety. Most native speakers consider it bizarre or deficient; but that is a matter of appreciation by the speakers. The language used by the novice is a variety characteristic of a transitional stage. The language learner first acquires it and later abandons it for another variety that, as a general rule, is nearer the target language. The process of language learning as a whole can therefore be conceived as a passage through a series of different varieties possessing among themselves certain similarities and directed towards a given variety, the *target variety*. As a general rule, the latter is never attained, but the process stops somewhere before. Between the 'final variety' attained by the language learner and the target variety (i.e. what in principle he was supposed to attain, or sought to attain), there always exist differences.

The form of these varieties and the manner in which they are traversed depend on a great many factors, such as the duration of learning, the intensity of social contacts, the mother-tongue, all the specific individual conditions peculiar to the learner, and, in guided language learning, the type of instruction. Hence from the extra-linguistic standpoint an entire set of well defined factors corresponds to the different varieties. Let us suppose, to illustrate this, that three of these factors exist (in reality they are naturally much more numerous):

1 motivation, comprising three degrees of intensity: m_1 = strong, m_2 = average, m_3 = weak;

2 the duration of learning: t_1 = 6 months, t_2 = 12 months, t_3 = 18 months, t_4 = 24 months;

3 the mother-tongue of the one learning the language, e.g. l_1 = Spanish, l_2 = French.

Hence what we will have is a total of $3 \times 4 \times 2 = 24$ combinations of possible factors, for example (m_1, t_4, l_2) = a strongly motivated Frenchman having studied for 2 years. To these combinations of factors, 24 varieties of spoken language correspond, not necessarily all different; it is possible that after 2 years a strongly motivated Spaniard may speak as well as a Frenchman of average motivation after 2 years.

All these varieties are naturally closely interrelated: identical in some respects, different in others. In principle, there are various possibilities for describing these similarities and dissimilarities. The process that we devised and used for these purposes is the *grammar of varieties* (see Klein, 1974). This is a relatively accurate process well suited to the analysis of large quantities of data.

The grammar of varieties

The two central concepts of the grammar of varieties are the *space of varieties* and the *probabilist* grammar. A space of varieties is an *ordered* set of varieties that one wishes to study. The 24 varieties mentioned above are an example of such a space of varieties (with 3 dimensions, corresponding to the 3 different factors). For practical requirements here, the spaces of varieties are represented in linear fashion; this linearity is obtained quite simply by numbering the 24 varieties from V_1 to V_{24}. Obviously, this order does not correspond to an order in time.

The second concept is that of 'probabilist grammar'. Different types of such a grammar exist. In our study we use a grammar formulated in an explicit manner — an extra-contextual grammar. We attach to each rule a probability that determines the likelihood that it will be applied. However, the probabilist grammar will not be discussed here. The results of the linguistic study are understandable without a detailed knowledge of these technical developments. (Details of the probabilist grammar can be found in Klein, 1974; Dittmar and Riecke, 1977; and HPD, 1977.)

The grammar of varieties makes it possible, at least in the grammatical field, to describe with precision both the language development during learning and the manner in which this development depends on certain factors constituting the space of varieties. Were such study actually realised, one would naturally be obliged, before collecting and analysing the data, to formulate a hypothesis concerning the pertinent factors for language development; that is, one would have to determine an appropriate space of varieties.

For determining such a space of varieties two things are important. First, the factors considered important and thought to be observable must be identified. Second, such factors must be operationalised. In order to systematise this to some degree, we adopted a viewpoint somewhat different from the usual one. Language learning depends, among other things, on two sorts of factors: individual conditions; and statements of the target variety that serve as the basis for developing a particular variety of learning in terms of the given individual conditions. Hence these two factors can be divided into two distinct groups: the factors corresponding to the individual conditions of the subjects, which will be called 'bias factors'; and the factors which as a whole constitute the context of learning, which will be called 'contextual factors'.

Age, interest, social origin, mother-tongue, educational level and, contingently, knowledge of other foreign languages are part of the first group. The list is obviously not complete. The factors belonging to the context of learning are essentially the nature, duration and intensity of the statements of the target language, plus the manner in which these are presented, e.g. in natural situations, as in the case of unguided language learning; in the form of more or less elaborately simulated actual conditions, for example, by playing roles; in mediatised fashion, that is, by no longer presenting statements in the foreign language, but descriptions of them, e.g. in the form of grammatical rules. Naturally, this mediatised presentation never occurs alone. Also part of the contextual factor are certain imponderables, such as 'the teacher's commitment', 'the attractiveness of the linguistic material presented', 'social pressure', and the like, all of which can play an important role. But these are very difficult to operationalise.

The above outline represents the theoretical framework for our research, which is limited to the study of unguided learning and of the factors affecting it. It appears from our research that there is a relation between some of the hypothesised factors and the actual development of learning. This will form the material of the following two sections.

Collection and preparation of data in the Heidelberg study

This section presents the methods that were used to select the informants, to collect the linguistic and social data, and to prepare the data for analysis.

The sample

We started with the limitation that the recordings to be studied must not exceed 100 hours. An average duration of two hours per interview resulted in a sample of 48 respondents. This sample was represented in equal parts by Italians and Spaniards, two-thirds of whom were men and one-third women; this corresponded, more or less, to the proportion of women among foreign workers as a whole (see Federal Ministry of Labour, 1973, p. 27). The length of residence in Germany constituted an additional criterion for determining the sample: 12 informants had been in the FRG for less than 2.7 years; 12 between 2.8 and 4.3 years; 12 between 4.4 and 7.0, and 12 for more than 7.0 years.

Table 3.1 shows the composition of the sample, according to nationality, sex, and length of residence.

Table 3.1

Heidelberg project sample

Length of residence		Italians		Spaniards		Total
		Men	Women	Men	Women	
< 2.7	years	4	2	4	2	12
2.8-4.3	years	4	2	4	2	12
4.4-7.0	years	4	2	4	2	12
> 7.0	years	4	2	4	2	12
Total		16	8	16	8	
			24		24	48

Collection of data

For collecting data, we used two complementary techniques: interviews and participant observation. The interview technique provides the following advantages: possibility of determining in advance the population of persons to be interviewed; possibility of interviewing a great many individuals in a short space of time; ease of recording interviews on magnetic tape; speed in obtaining data on the social situation of those interviewed.

124

We based our study of the learning of German by foreign workers on the linguistic data gathered through interviews. A detailed report on the results of the participant observation is given in our book *Language and Communication of Immigrant Workers* (HPD, 1975a, pp. 60-111).

The socio-linguistic interview was used on the one hand to gather social data which should help to explain the linguistic properties of statements, and on the other hand, to obtain good quality recordings of conversations as natural as possible. This means that the interview must be conducted as an informal conversation, in the guise of 'continuous interviews'.

Interviews with foreign informants

The guiding line should enable investigators to direct the conversation to a subject of major interest to foreign workers, such as, for example, their origin, their individual and social situation in their country of origin; their move to the FRG; the situation at their place of work; housing and family; leisure pursuits; accidents and illnesses; and their intentions regarding return to the country of origin (see also HPD, 1975a, p. 54). In general, an interview took from two to four hours. It was conducted by two or three collaborators of the research group, one of whom attempted to orient the conversation as naturally as possible towards the subjects chosen. Immediately following the interview, a situation report was prepared in which the observations considered important for conducting the interview were noted, dealing with communication and interactive behaviour.

Interviews with German workers of the Heidelberg area

In addition to the interviews with Italian and Spanish workers, we also gathered linguistic data from the German workers of Heidelberg. The purpose was to determine the variety of language used by German workers of the same social class as the foreign workers in communicating with the latter in everyday situations. This variety of language is to be considered as the 'target variety' towards which the various pidgin varieties converge and hence can be linked to the linguistic varieties of the foreign workers.

The following are the criteria which guided our selection of German informants: employment at Heidelberg enterprises employing many foreign workers; apportionment by sex and age corresponding to that of the foreign workers; and use in speech of the Heidelberg dialect.

The interviews were conducted in dialect. In addition to the goals pursued in our interviews with foreign workers, i.e. collecting linguistic and social data on the speakers, we wished to obtain information regarding problems of communication and the learning of German by foreign workers, as viewed by their German colleagues.

Preparation of data

Following the interview, one of the investigators listened to his recording and prepared a listening report in which he noted the social data concerning the informants (age, length of residence, contact situation, etc.). At the same time, he selected passages that were to be transcribed phonetically. Per interview, there is a total of 15 minutes of transcribed text.

The learning of grammatical and semantic aspects of German

This section sums up the most important results of the linguistic study of the varieties of learning of foreign workers. Description of the syntactic aspects plays a predominant role here. A later sub-section testifies to the increasing importance that we attribute to the semantic aspects. On the other hand, we make do with samplings for phonology and morphology, but that obviously does not mean we attach less importance to these fields. Our presentation is informal. A detailed report on the technical aspects of our descriptions is to be found in Klein (1974) and HPD (1975a; 1976a, chapters 3 and 4).

Characteristics of foreign workers

At the outset, it can be said that the languages of the foreign workers are even less homogeneous than the 'German' or 'French' of native speakers. It is true that these languages are divided into numerous dialects and sociolects. But each of these varieties is a full-fledged language from the functional standpoint.

The German language varieties of foreign workers, on the other hand, are characterised by their status as a second language and by the process of their learning. At the extreme, they can be broken down into as many varieties as there are subjects, because each subject, depending on the influences of his mother-tongue, of the context of learning and of his individual efforts, has a very reduced repertory or a complex set of words and grammatical rules.

The varieties of language learning represent a spectrum of greater or lesser linguistic deviations from the target variety. But given that the subjects frequently have in common their origin, mother-tongue, milieu and social contacts, the hypothesis of our study appears rather plausible, that in their relations with the natives and among themselves foreign workers develop specific forms of linguistic communication ('norms') which make it possible to describe the levels of command of a second language peculiar to a given group. Hence we employ here the term *varieties of learning* to designate the various states of linguistic knowledge peculiar to given groups of subjects learning a second language. These varieties are defined by their deviation from the language of native speakers at the various linguistic levels.

As adult speakers, the foreign workers are already in full possession of their mother-tongue. They have not only learned the rules of grammar, but their language also serves them as an' individual, cultural and social means of orientation. The unconscious resort to the mother-tongue during the unguided learning of German is all the more understandable in that familiarity with the second language is very limited. The influence of the mother-tongue on the varieties of learning lessens in proportion as deviation from the target language diminishes.

Although little is known of the manner in which one learns a foreign language, it can be assumed that an adult learns a second language differently from a child. It appears that in a sufficiently stimulating environment that fosters integration, children quickly overcome the stages of agrammaticality and inacceptability in acquiring a second language and completely assimilate the target language; this is very rarely the case with adults. Adults can certainly attain the same goal as a child. But owing to the fact that with adults learning is much more susceptible to slowing down, stagnation and regression than with children, we can conclude that the context of learning is of paramount significance. To the extent that the optimisation of the learning process does not automatically and mechanically occur, the degree of command of the second language depends on the *nature of the context of learning*, i.e. on the frequency and intensity of communication with natives; on the properly formed character of the statements the subject hears; on correction of the incorrect statements produced by the subject; and on the contributions by natives during communication which favour learning, by arousing in the subject a personal interest in regular improvement of his second language learning.

Although social conditions are certainly different in each particular case, sociological studies (see Borris and Mehrländer, 1974) as well as our own observations in the fields of 'work' and 'leisure' contacts (HPD, 1975a, chapters 4 and 5) reveal that good contacts during leisure hours are clearly the exception and not the rule. Contacts at work are characterised by overt or latent tensions between German and foreign workers; the sort of work (e.g. assembly line production, as opposed to hotel work); and the work environment.

The result is that necessary communication during work between the ethnic groups occurs, but that most often it does not occur in 'freer' situations (during work breaks or time off). Thus one of the factors fostering learning of a second language generally does not exist:

personal contacts linked to a willingness to correct errors explicitly.

The aim of communication between Germans and foreigners during work is indeed that of achieving mutual comprehension. The fact that German should be the vehicle for such communication is the result of the existing majority relationship. As neither of the two groups understands the language of the other in communicating, the minority must conform to the majority. Words and expressions required for the immediate performance of actions are learned in rudimentary fashion. There is no time, during work contacts, for grammatical instruction or for correcting linguistic errors. Hence a mode of communication must be found spontaneously, i.e. without any major preparations. The solution to this problem appears to consist in normative simplifications of German. The foreigner is obliged to resort to such simplifications, because he has no precise knowledge of the words, or the grammatical rules. To facilitate matters for him, the Germans often reduce their statements to the mere informative level. This means that a German who wishes to address the following question to a foreigner with only limited linguistic knowledge: *'Um wieviel Uhr ist gestern Ihr Unfall an der Maschine passiert?'* (At what time yesterday did you have the accident with the machine?') will choose the following simplified formulation: *'Wieviel Uhr Unfall Maschine gestern?'* ('What time accident machine yesterday?'). The simplified sentence contains the basic semantic information: TIME − YESTERDAY − ACCIDENT. The significant core of the sentence is the question concerning the time of a happening. The quantifier *wieviel* marks the interrogation; *Maschine* is an additional place indicator.

Thus the Germans simplify the problems of communication of the foreigners. It is, above all, an economic mode of communication; hence, progress in the learning of German depends on the form in which statements in the foreign language are presented to the foreigner. A work pidgin, internalised by dint of routines, only cements a given level of linguistic knowledge. This does not mean that there are not, in addition, plenty of Germans who use complete and acceptable sentences, thus offering foreigners improved opportunities for learning. Linguistic simplifications by Germans, also often referred to as their register for foreigners, represent only one of the reasons why most foreign workers never reach a level of more than rudimentary knowledge of the second language.

The phenomenon which is characterised by ultimate cessation of the learning process at a certain level of linguistic knowledge is referred to as fossilisation. It is assumed that linguistic competence in the second language no longer develops among subjects from the moment it suffices to meet their communication requirements. As the contacts of foreign workers with Germans are limited in most cases to working hours, the learning of the second language runs the risk of becoming fossilised very easily when the knowledge acquired suffices for correct performance of assigned tasks. Moreover, numerous workers show no interest in improving the bases of their knowledge of German, for they intend to return soon to their country of origin.

The aspects dealt with thus far clearly show that socio-economic factors more than any others strongly influence the contact with natives and hence conditions learning by foreigners. We shall deal later with other sociological causes explaining the great diversity in the varieties of learning. In what follows, we shall ask which linguistic properties of the varieties of learning necessitate special explanations and how such varieties can be described.

Introductory remarks on the description of varieties of learning

Our description stresses syntax and semantics. We slanted our study towards these fields, and especially towards syntax, in the belief that such a study was of fundamental importance to the formulation of language instruction. From the linguistic viewpoint, phonology and morphology are obviously of equal importance. But for establishing and maintaining basic comprehension, the syntactic and semantic aspects appear to us to take precedence.

For methodological reasons, we separate the levels of syntactic, semantic, morphological and phonological description. In reality, these levels are obviously mutually interdependent, according to the learning variety level. Anyone with only a few words at his command will tend to over-generalise. Subjects in the opposite situation are more prone to differentiated use. The smaller their repertory, i.e. the shorter their statements and the fewer differentiating constituents they comprise, the less they will be able to apply syntactic, semantic and morphological rules. This principle is especially important for our quantitative analyses. If a subject's statement consists on the average of only two or three constituents, he can choose between only two or three positions for placing his words. Hence restrictions at a given level are accompanied by restrictions at another. It follows from the interdependence of the different levels that we must also subject the quantitative distributions obtained from the learning varieties to a qualitative linguistic interpretation.

The starting point of our study was an inventory of the elementary syntactic constituents of the learning varieties of 48 Spanish and Italian workers. The studies on word order and semantic, phonological and morphological aspects relate to it in various ways. First, the corpus of 100 sentences per informant, used as the basis for syntactic analysis, is also the starting corpus for the other descriptions. We have made use of additional occurrences solely in the case of prepositions and phonology.

The results of the description of the elementary syntagmatic structure of learning varieties were used to classify the 48 Spanish and Italian subjects in terms of their syntactic level. Such a classification is useful in that it makes possible a precise determination of the respective deviations of the subjects from the target variety and serves as a basis for classifying subjects into groups having relatively similar linguistic properties. The hierarchical classifying of subjects was done as follows: one assigns to each subject a syntactic 'profile' which consists of a characteristic value summarising the values relative to the expression of a few syntactic rules particularly important to the development of learning (see below).

On the basis of this hierarchical classification of subjects according to their level, we have formed groups of subjects whose levels have common properties. For our analysis, we use an initial division into four groups (I to IV) of twelve speakers each and a second into eight groups (1 to 8) of six speakers each. Group I (or 1) then corresponds to the lowest linguistic level; group IV (or 8) to the highest level, i.e. the one nearest the target variety. It is obvious that division into eight groups permits more differentiated observations than division into four groups. However, the division depends on the quantitative data and the possibility of interpreting them. The division into groups appears to us relevant for two reasons: on the one hand, the learning conditions among numerous subjects are similar. Hence these conditions can be considered as specific to a given group. And, on the other hand, in language teaching one also works with groups defined by a level of comparable knowledge. That is why the observations concerning group aspects seem to us particularly useful for the practice of instruction.

Inventory of the syntactic constituents of the sentence

We shall present briefly the analysis of the syntagmatic structure to which the varieties of German of 48 immigrant Spaniards and Italians and those of a reference group of Germans were subjected.

The recorded discourse of the subject was first transcribed by means of a system developed in the Heidelberg research project. Then, in succession, a body of 100 sentences was extracted, i.e. verbal units having a complete meaning, from informants' discourse of varying length. These sentences were subjected to syntactic analysis by use of the grammar of varieties presented earlier. This grammar, specially developed for the requirements of the present study, contains approximately 100 rules. It is a syntagmatic component comprising extra-contextual rules patterned after the standard model of the transformational generative grammar (Chomsky, 1965). By analysing the 100 sentences of a given informant with this grammar, one obtains a set of 100 probability values which indicate, in respect of said informant's variety, the relative frequencies of the application of rules.

The aggregate probabilities associated with the rules of the variety of a given informant can be considered as his syntactic 'profile'. Complete analysis of the 48 varieties hence provides us with 48 syntactic profiles that we can compare point by point. For such a comparison of the command of syntactic rules to be fruitful, it is essential to classify informants according to their degree of syntactic development. In principle, it is possible to establish for each rule a classification of the informants. But such an approach does not enable us to evaluate clearly the aggregate syntactic knowledge of the subject. For that reason, we developed a process (which is not described here) that attributes to each of the 48 informants a characteristic syntactic value, also known as the syntactic index. It consists of the probability values of eight syntactic rules. These rules are those which reflect most clearly the different development stages of the informants and which, in addition, can be considered as especially important for German syntax. (The formal procedure for reducing the complex matrix of data to eight rules differentiating development is described in detail in HPD, 1976, pp. 144-149.) These eight rules describe the following syntactic phenomena of the sentence:

1 Presence *vs* absence of the subject
2 Presence *vs* absence of the verb
3 Complexity and differentiation of the verb group
4 Complexity of the complements of the verb in the predication framework
5 Degree of pronominalisation
6 Nature and complexity of the nominal predicates
7 Expression of the determinant in the nominal syntagma
8 Expression of the adverbial syntagmas.

We could observe that a strong correlation exists between these rules. This is corroborated by the fact that these rules are apparently learned in a specific order in the course of second language acquisition, which means, for example, that to a certain stage of the learning of the German verb group there corresponds a certain stage of pronominalisation and of the expression of adverbial constituents.

Hence the first important finding of our study is that *unguided learning of the syntactic properties of the second language is not done in a completely idiosyncratic manner*. It appears that certain syntactic properties of a language have a strong influence on the way it is learned. This means, for the teaching of German to immigrant workers having already reached a certain level of unguided learning, that one must not expect appreciable differences in the learning of certain syntactic phenomena at a given level of linguistic knowledge. The relation between a given stage of learning and a certain pattern of present and absent syntactic constituents, shared by all subjects, also justified the division already mentioned of subjects into groups; these constitute the basis for the report of our results.

The syntactic properties of German are learned in the following order by Spanish and Italian workers: at first, the sentences consist either of a noun by itself, or a noun accompanied by a simple determinant. In general, these nouns have the function of designating, naming or determining the place and time. At most, a few invariable verb forms are found. Sentences are very short, morphology non-existent.

The subjects at a slightly higher level then begin to form sentences consisting of a verb and a subject. A few pronominalisations are found. One begins to detect the first rudiments of a formation of prepositional syntagmas and a temporal determination of the verb, despite a practically non-existent verbal morphology. A limited number of nouns are accompanied by attributive adjectives and complements. The only few examples of subordinate clauses are adverbial syntagmas.

The next phase, characteristic of group III, consists essentially in extension of the elements learned in the second phase. Pronominalisation, though limited to subjects, is better exploited. Differentiation of the nominal group by more frequent use of articles, quantifiers, attributive adjectives and complements progresses, as does the temporal and modal specification of verbs. The use of subordinate clauses, however, is still limited to adverbial clauses, but these are more differentiated functionally. The third level of learning is distinguished from those preceding it by a broader knowledge of rules. But the number of rules learned for expressing in a differentiated manner certain syntactico-semantic aspects — as for example temporal indications, or specification of the function of an adverbial expression by a preposition — is limited: one or two, or at any rate very few. The consequence of this is that a given rule has astonishingly high values. We limit ourselves here to noting this fact, but we shall speak of it in detail, from the semantic standpoint, later on.

In comparison with the learning levels dealt with up to now, the level of the most advanced foreigners is much more complex and differentiated. This stage of rather complete assimilation of German syntax is characterised by the following:

1 The application of rules essentially obeys the syntactic and semantic conditions of German. (The means for specifying the tense and mood of verbs are adequate; the form in which adverbial syntagmas are expressed clearly indicates their function; etc.)

2 An economic use of the pronominal system makes it possible to avoid overloading the sentence with heavy nominal groups.

3 The rules governing morphology of the cases and verbal morphology (especially as concerns the finite and impersonal forms of verbs), although they are still not used correctly, are nevertheless used in a differentiated manner. This helps especially to ensure understanding.

4 Aside from the differentiated use of adverbial clauses, the appearance is noted of nominal and attributive clauses. Hence the number of subordinate clauses per sentence has considerably increased.

5 The varieties of the most advanced subjects are, on the whole, strongly marked by characteristics of the local dialect.

Hence even though the use of a few particular rules does not completely coincide with that of the target language, the subjects in group IV nevertheless exhibit a distinct tendency to adopt the local variety of the native speakers. We have been able to demonstrate this phenomenon in describing acquisition of the rules of German syntax that progresses from an elementary to a differentiated level, i.e. in the direction of increasing syntactic complexity. We now intend to complete this report by analysing a few aspects of the surface structure of verbal expressions of the immigrant workers (word order, phonology, morphology) and by explaining the significance of the rules for a learning subject.

The order of syntactic constituents in the sentence

Let us consider the order of the syntactic constituents according to the various learning levels. We shall first deal with the position of the verb.

The importance of order in the learning of German syntax. The inventory of the syntactic constituents expressed or unexpressed in the varieties of learning is, in our opinion, more important than their linear order in the sentence. Indeed, on the one hand the number of possible positions in a given sentence increases or decreases according to the number of constituents; additionally, the position of constituents does not seem to be particularly pertinent for meaning. Missing constituents are more prejudicial to the understanding of a sentence than ill-placed constituents. Hence the positional analysis will constitute above all a 'correction factor' in relation to the analysis of the inventory of constituents, in which it could not be taken into consideration. From the linguistic standpoint, word order is based on arbitrary conventions, as the following Italian, Spanish and German examples clearly show:

1 *Abbiamo mangiato* pane, formaggio e frutta.

2 *Hemos comido* pan, queso y fruta.

3 Wir *haben* Brot, Käse und Früchte *gegessen*.

As concerns the order of constituents, the three sentences differ solely by the fact that the finite verb *haben* and the participle *gegessen* (which we shall also designate, with Helbig and Buscha, 1972, pp. 473-517, as 'the grammatical part of the predicate') occupy different positions in the German sentence from those in the Italian and Spanish sentences. Whereas in the Romance languages, the two verb elements follow each other immediately, in the affirmative German sentence the finite verb occupies the second position and the corresponding participle the last. Doubtless this fact has no influence on the meaning of the sentence, for although sentence 4 is considered as unacceptable, any German would understand it:

4 Wir *haben gegessen* Brot, Käse und Früchte.

Examples 5, 6 and 7 show that in the two Romance languages the elements of the verb group proper occupy the same position in the main and subordinate clauses, whereas such is not the case in German.

5 Il libro *introduce* a la grammatica tedesca, perché gli stranieri *devono studiare* il tedesco.

6 El libro *introduce* a la gramática alemana; porque los extranjeros *deben aprender* el alemán.

7 Das Buch *führt* in die deutsche Grammatik *ein*, weil die Ausländer Deutsch *lernen müssen*.

Here again it is the position of the verb that must be noted and not that of the other constituents of the sentence. Contrary to Italian and Spanish, in German a distinction must be made, in respect of the verb position, between main and subordinate clauses, finite verb and grammatical part of the predicate, root of the verb and separable particle. Examples 3 and 7 make it possible to outline the rules for the position of the verb in affirmative (but not in interrogative and imperative) sentences and in subordinate clauses as follows:

(a) In the main clause, the finite verb occupies the second position; the grammatical part of the predicate (impersonal verb form) and the separable particle (e.g. the separable prefix *ein* — in *einführen*) the final position.

(b) In the subordinate clause, the finite verb occupies the final position; the grammatical part of the predicate the penultimate position.

(c) The separable particle can be dissociated from the finite verb only in the main clause.

The examples quoted justify the prediction that, as concerns the learning of word order in German, it is especially the position of the verb that will pose problems for speakers of Italian and Spanish. Indeed, in Spanish and Italian, the finite verb occupies the first, second or third position in the main clause — the second position appears to be the most usual — immediately followed, where applicable, by the grammatical part of the predicate. This is also the case in respect of subordinate clauses. Hence the German rules outlined can give rise to difficulties of learning because, by applying the rules of Spanish or Italian to sentence 7, the following unacceptable sequence is obtained:

8 Das Buch *einführt* in die deutsche Grammatik, weil die Ausländer müssen lernen Deutsch.

Although word order is not, as we have seen, pertinent from the linguistic standpoint in respect of meaning, it is a carrier of social significance, especially when it obeys a norm. Apparently the components of discourse, such as phonetics and word order, are the object of social attention, for the good reason that they are surface-structure phenomena expressed unconsciously and subject to strong normalisation by the linguistic community. They are external signs of social identity which, independently of understanding of the meaning of a statement, are the object of a social evaluation. Hence, in the following study, we shall assume, even though we cannot prove it empirically, that failure by the foreign subjects to observe the rules of the word order contributes in part to characterising socially their various linguistic varieties.

Fields studied and processes of description. Our study of the order of constituents of the sentence is based on the same sample of 100 sentences for each of the 48 foreign informants and the 6 German informants from the Heidelberg area, already used earlier for analysing the syntagmatic structure. Positional analysis of the constituents was accomplished with the help of a computer. Comparison of the foreign subjects with each other and of the foreigners with the German speakers is based on classification of the foreign subjects according to their syntactic index, already described. The purpose of the positional analysis is to associate with each sentence spoken by the foreign subjects the linear sequence of its syntactic constituents, to determine the regularities of these sequences on the one hand in terms of properties of the language of the learning subjects and on the other hand in terms of deviations from the rules of position in relation to the local German dialect, and to relate the results of this analysis to those of the syntagmatic structure of the varieties of learning.

Although we have made a positional analysis of all the constituents, we shall present here only the results concerning the position of the verb (i.e. of the finite verb, of the grammatical part of the predicate and of the separable particle). The description of the position of the verb is based on a corpus consisting of 2,548 sentences meeting the following criteria: the position of the verb was studied only in affirmative clauses (main and subordinate), there not being enough examples of interrogative and imperative clauses; the corpus contains only sentences which, in addition to the verb, have at least a subject.

Results — position of the finite verb in the main clause. Table 3.2 indicates the position of the verb among 48 subjects, i.e. 8 groups of 6 speakers each, and compares these results with those of Heidelberg

Table 3.2

Position of verb in relation to total affirmative sentences comprising both subject and verb among eight groups of foreigners and a group of German speakers from Heidelberg (HD)

Groups*	Percentage of sentences containing a subject and a verb in relation to total affirmatives	First position (%)	Second position (%)	Third position (%)	Other positions (%)
1	21	—	63	34	3
2	26	3	57	30	12
3	41	3	50	36	11
4	42	3	67	23	6
5	46	7	54	29	10
6	56	4	67	20	8
7	76	5	79	15	2
8	90	8	85	6	1
HD	99	6	92	1	—

* Each group comprises 6 speakers.

Germans. Except for rare occasions, the verb most often occupies the second position in the sentence. To explain this phenomenon, we can adduce the following reasons:

1 In the two Romance languages concerned, the verb frequently occupies the second position. This favours adoption of the rule for positioning the verb in the main clause in German.

2 The verb most frequently occupies the second position in the sentences heard by foreign subjects in the course of their verbal contacts with Germans.

136

3 Most of the subjects in the two upper groups have an explicit knowledge of the rule concerned.

4 It is more or less by chance that the subjects in the two lowest groups place the verb in the second position. The fact that their sentences frequently have no more than three constituents creates as it were a sort of structural pressure to place the verb in the second position.

The value for the group of speakers from Heidelberg in Table 3.2 indicates that the verb almost mandatorily occupies the second position. This value is appreciably higher than that observed for the most advanced group of foreign speakers, indicating the deviation in comparison with the target variety.

Table 3.2 shows that in 6 per cent of the cases the German speakers use the first position. After examining the Heidelberg speakers' data, we reached the conclusion that the initial position of the verb is a stylistic device grammatically acceptable in oral narration. Certain speakers are quite prone to use it. We must therefore include the finite verb at the beginning of the sentence among the positions acceptable to native German speakers; this is in addition to the second position of the verb. From the viewpoint of the target language, all the other positions are therefore to be considered as unacceptable.

The relatively high percentage of verbs in the third position, found in groups 1 to 5, can, with some plausibility, be attributed to the influence of the speaker's mother-tongue. The verb is rather frequently placed in the third position in statements by the foreign subjects; that is in conformity with the possibilities in Italian and Spanish, in which the subject and the verb can be preceded by an adverbial expression.

At the lowest levels, in most instances, the following constituents are the ones which, placed with the subject before the verb, result in the latter being found in the third position: circumstantial subordinate clause followed by the subject; circumstantial complements of place, time and manner occupying either the first or the second position; the particle *do* (*da, dann* [there] in standard German), which, although an adverb of time, quite often in the Palatine dialect has the ritual function of introducing discourse.

Less frequently, an object, in addition to the subject, precedes the verb. In all the cases mentioned, the foreign subjects do not know the rule of German requiring that one of the two constituents of the verb preceding the verb must be placed after it.

What would appear to characterise the levels of learning in respect of placing the verb in the sentence (second or third position) is the influence of the mother-tongue. On the other hand, in certain instances, the position of the verb is probably due, particularly at the lower levels of learning, to strategies of learning. The advanced subjects have to a large extent adopted the norms of the target variety; this is evident especially in the exploitation of the acceptable initial position.

Results — the place of the grammatical part of the predicate (impersonal forms of the verb) and of the separable particle in the main clause. The finite verb constitutes, with the impersonal forms of a verb or a separable particle, the verbal framework. (For example, *da habe ich gerade Ärger gehabt*/I have just had troubles.) Different constituents can be placed outside this framework, that is, after the impersonal form of the verb or after the separable particle. In the case of subordinate or comparative clauses (*er hat in die Menge geschrien wie ein Wahnsinninger*/he shouted in the crowd like a madman), this construction is perfectly grammatical; in the case of circumstantial complements (*Ali hat den Deutschunterricht aufgegeben in dieser chaotischen Grosstadt*/Ali gave up the German courses in this chaotic big city), it is considered acceptable; it is not considered acceptable in the case of an object (*Pedro hat seinen Kollegen empfohlen das Buch*/Pedro recommended the book to a colleague). Hence, one observes certain variations in respect of the impersonal forms and of the separable particle. The transfer of a circumstantial complement beyond the impersonal form of the verb or separable particle is rather frequent because it is typical of the spoken language.

The linguistic material of the present study is apportioned rather unequally in the sample, because the complex verbal structures are essentially found among the foreign speakers who are rather advanced in their learning of German: the upper half of the sample alone contains 88 per cent of the occurrences of such structures (modal verb + infinitive, auxiliary + participle); this amounts to approximately 20 occurrences per informant. The other half totals only 12 per cent, scarcely three occurrences per informant. That is why our observations can claim only a restricted validity. It follows also that this rule of position is learned relatively late in the course of acquiring German.

Table 3.3 first gives the position of the impersonal forms without taking into consideration the length of the sentence. We distinguish three main positions, one of which, the penultimate, is subdivided according to the nature of the element that follows: a subordinate clause *vs* another constituent. The last row clearly shows the marked increase in occurrences among advanced speakers. The values for groups 1 and 2 are too low to permit a comparison with the other groups. The number of occurrences is rather low in the case of groups 3 and 4, but the upper groups provide sufficient data.

The rows are arranged in decreasing order of acceptability of the position of the impersonal form. But we must stress that the rule governing the position of the impersonal form cannot be considered as mandatory in German, seeing that it allows of certain variations. The

Table 3.3

Position of grammatical part of the predicate (impersonal forms of the verb) in the main clause among eight groups of foreigners and the speakers from Heidelberg

Position	Group								
	1	2	3	4	5	6	7	8	HD
Final	*	*	57%	55%	56%	62%	66%	77%	76%
Penultimate followed by subordinate clause	*	*	0	0	2	5	2	9	14
Penultimate followed by another constituent	*	*	29	39	33	28	22	11	9
Other positions	*	*	14	6	9	6	10	3	1
Total number of occurrences	—	—	21	62	54	86	125	222	191

* Not calculated for lack of enough occurrences

occurrences in rows 1 and 2 are altogether acceptable. Comparative study of the percentages reveals an increasingly marked tendency to place the impersonal form in the final position; likewise, the positions of limited acceptability decrease. The very deviant positions (final column) are relatively rare among the groups.

The separable particle obeys the same position rule as the impersonal verb form. It can be separated only from a finite verb form; that is, it remains linked to the impersonal form. Inasmuch as we have only a few infrequent occurrences of separable particles, we shall present only a few informal remarks. Apparently what is involved here is a grammatical phenomenon of German that is learned relatively late. 28 out of 60 occurrences (in 4,314 sentences) are divided among 45 speakers, which gives an average of 0.8 occurrences per sentence. Other research will have to be done to determine the reasons for such a low occurrence. Only in the upper third of the foreign speakers does one find examples of the correct formation of the verbal framework consisting of a finite verb and the separable particle.

The sentences requiring separation of the verb and particle, and placing of the latter in the final position, are apparently difficult for foreigners to express. That is why the subjects at the lower levels appear to avoid this sort of construction. They perhaps have a tendency to choose verbs without a separable particle for the beginning positions of the sentence. On the other hand, the verbs in the final position are more frequently separable. We assume that the compulsory separation of particle and verb constitutes an additional learning difficulty; foreigners try to avoid the second position, morphological marking and separable particle whenever they use a verb. The more frequent use of composite verbs in the final position seems to indicate that they are not understood as consisting of a verbal base and a prefix, the two elements being able to perform different grammatical functions, but as lexical units having a specific non-decomposable meaning.

Results — the position of the verb in subordinate clauses. Learning of the verb position in subordinate clauses occurs relatively late. Our analysis shows that 46 per cent of the occurrences of subordinate clauses are found in group 8; groups 2 to 6 inclusive total only about 4 per cent of such occurrences. In the first group, there is no occurrence of a subordinate clause comprising, at the same time, a subject and a verb.

The following comments summarise our findings about the verb place in a subordinate sentence:

1 Only group 8, comprising the most advanced subjects, provides an acceptable number of rather complex predicates (combinations of a finite verb and an impersonal verb form) and of different types of subordinate clauses. In addition, this group differs from the others by the use of subordinate clauses in which the verb is correctly placed in the second or penultimate position. This would seem to indicate the adoption, by the subjects of group 8, of the position rules peculiar to the local dialect.

2 The lower learning levels are characterised by a relatively high percentage of morphologically unmarked verb forms and by an appreciable number of unacceptable occurrences of verbs in the second position. Once again, this phenomenon may be attributable to the influence of the speaker's mother-tongue.

3 The higher the learning level, the greater the number of verbs in the final position, thus indicating the gradual adoption of the norms of the target variety by foreign speakers.

This concludes the study of the order of constituents in the varieties of learning, and we now embark on the more detailed study of the syntactic and semantic functions of certain types of lexical units.

A few lexical and semantic aspects of the varieties of learning

The number of modal verbs and prepositions used by the foreign speakers were studied in considerable detail. Our starting point was the preceding analysis of the syntagmatic structure, the results of which were summarised. This discussion, unlike the previous section, is based on a division of the subjects into four groups (I-IV) of twelve speakers each.

The learning of modal verbs. The over-generalisation of a certain form or a certain rule of the target language during unguided second language learning is a well known phenomenon (e.g. Richards, 1973). As an example, we studied the learning of modal verbs whose morphologically marked forms (generally finite forms) are frequently used in combination with impersonal verb forms. A rule of rewriting of the syntactic component corresponds to the occurrences of the 'modal verb + impersonal verb form' syntagmas. Table 3.4 indicates the frequencies of use of this rule among the foreign speakers.

Table 3.4

Absolute and relative frequencies of lexical expressions
of the rule for modal verbs

| Modal verbs | Group | | | | | |
	I	II	III	IV	Total	%
Können	1	3	6	19	29	2
Wollen	3	9	12	26	50	3
Müssen	–	13	75	19	107	55
Sollen	–	–	1	5	6	26
Mögen	–	–	–	3	3	15
Total	4	25	94	72	195	
%	1	13	48	39		100

We were unable to take the German speakers into account, for at the time of preparation of the present study we had not yet completed analysis of the data from that group. This does not entail any disadvantages for our analysis, since we consider that the speakers in group IV at all events most nearly approach the target variety.

Table 3.4 reveals a relatively high value for group III, one considerably exceeding that of group IV. This is the more astonishing as a wider and more differentiated use of modal verbs by the speakers in group IV was rather to be expected, owing to the fact that they are already very near the local target variety. In addition, the increasing values for groups I and II would seem to indicate that application of this rule continually increases from group I to group II. That is why the decrease of 11 per cent between group III and group IV requires explanation. In order to explain the discrepancy of group III, it appears desirable to examine first the lexical expressions of the rule for modal verbs. The modal verbs found in 195 sentences from our corpus are the following: *können, wollen, müssen, sollen* and *mögen.*

Table 3.4 shows that the most used modal verbs are *müssen, wollen* and *können; mögen* and *sollen* are learned very late and *müssen* alone provides more than 50 per cent of the examples of application of a rule. What is most surprising, however, is the fact that group III, with its 75 occurrences, reveals a very high use of the verb *müssen*. For group IV, *müssen, wollen* and *können* are used approximately in the same proportions. The high value for *müssen* in group III can possibly be explained either by particular themes or by specific learning strategies. In the latter case, the meaning of *müssen* is broader than that normally accepted in standard German.

Study of the interviews with the subjects in group III shows that the cause of the frequent use of the verb *müssen* seems ascribable to uses or particular verbal strategies rather than to specific themes. *Muss* is apparently used as a substitute for the morphological marking of the verb tense. Therefore, its function is over-generalised in the sense that it covers not only the meaning of *müssen* in German, i.e. the obligation to do something, but also the aspectual and temporal system of the verb.

The interview with Tomás A., a Spanish worker, illustrates this interpretation. In the course of conversation, the interviewer realised that Tomas A. was using the construction *muss + impersonal verb form* even when it was not necessary in German. Hence, when the informant used such a construction, the interviewer immediately reacted, saying that he did not understand the sentence and asking the informant to explain it to him in Spanish. These requests were taken as an attempt to overcome difficulties of comprehension. For example, Tomas A. said 'ich *muss gesehen*' (I must seen), or 'yo lo he visto' (I saw him).

Linguistic and sociological arguments can provide a preliminary explanation for the over-generalised use of *müssen*. From the linguistic viewpoint, *muss* functions as an over-generalised element and as a hidden error. The use of *muss* is over-generalised because it covers a broader field of grammatical and syntactic meanings than in the German dialect. And often the construction contains a hidden error, in that it is well formed on the surface, but incorrect in respect of its deeper semantic structure, that is, its interpretation. The speaker inserts *muss* merely to obtain a superficially acceptable construction. But the latter is contextually and semantically unsuitable. The selection of *muss* as an appropriate formal expression of this strategy of learning may be explained by the fact that the forms of the first and third persons singular of *müssen* are identical (*muss*).

From the sociological viewpoint, the over-generalised use of *müssen* has three interesting aspects. First, it is probably the modal verb that the foreign workers hear most frequently in daily communication, especially during their work. But although its selection as a substitute for the aspectual and modal system of the verb would appear to be socially motivated, its significance is primarily linguistic, seeing that the specific meaning of *müssen*, i.e. the expression of an obligation, is unconsciously over-generalised. Hence the sense of *müssen* has been only partially understood. Second, the insertion of *muss* before the verb permits avoiding the use of morphologically unmarked verb forms (infinitive) which are considered as socially negative characteristics of the use of German by foreign workers. The use of *muss* has then the function of increasing the social prestige of foreign workers by 'improving' their linguistic behaviour.

Finally, exaggerated use of the construction *muss + impersonal verb form* would appear to be characteristic of a particular group of speakers, namely, those who have already acquired enough knowledge of German (even if it leaves something to be desired from the normative standpoint) to be able to meet everyday communication requirements. Such speakers have lived for some four to six years in the FRG and are between 20 and 30 years of age. Their contact with Germans, their way of life and the nature of their employment all seem to indicate that they are becoming adapted socially. But this conclusion is to be considered with as much caution as the observation that the over-generalised use of *müssen* is more often encountered among men than among women. At all events, additional data will have to be collected and described before the preceding ideas and remarks can be verified.

Prepositions — purpose and method of the analysis. Prepositions will be studied from the viewpoint of their syntactic and semantic functions. We shall study this class of lexical units because it constitutes, with word order and inflection, one of the essential means for expressing and clarifying existing relations between the various syntactic units in the sentence. Hence prepositions are of great importance to the understanding of a statement and to successful communication (see Barkowski, Harnisch and Kumm, 1976, p. 65).

The purpose of our analysis is to examine the various uses of prepositions in the different varieties of learning. Our starting point is the prepositions present and lacking in our corpus, and a syntactic and semantic description of these lexical elements. We shall attempt, as in the preceding analyses, to determine the lines of development of the prepositional system by resorting to a comparison of the groups of foreigners among themselves and with the German speakers from the Heidelberg area.

The present detailed study was carried out on only 24 foreign speakers (12 Italians and 12 Spaniards) and on 6 German speakers. The linguistic material is more abundant than that of the 100 sentences per informant used for the syntactic analysis. We have used all the transcriptions, representing an average of 1,000 words of text per subject. Hence we have taken that figure as the reference base for the absolute frequencies resulting from the quantitative analysis. This broadening of the data base was necessary in the perspective of a detailed study of infrequent elements. As the unit of analysis is the prepositional group and not necessarily the sentence, we can also include in our study fragments of sentences comprising prepositional syntagmas, prepositional syntagmas obtained in reply to a question, etc., i.e. constructions that were excluded from the syntactic analysis.

Starting with a division of informants into four groups based on the syntactic index, we selected from each of these groups three Italian and three Spanish speakers. Identification of the prepositional syntagmas was done on the basis of reconstruction, in the target language, of certain syntactic constituents. This means that we have coded as 'prepositional syntagma' all the constituents in which a preposition is used *and* those of constituents whose context indicates that a preposition is required to make them acceptable.

In our syntactic description, we have differentiated prepositional syntagmas according to their syntactic function in the sentence (see Helbig and Buscha, 1974, p. 67): prepositional syntagmas functioning as attributive adjectives, i.e. dominated by a nominal syntagma (for example, *die Betten von Haus*/the beds of the house); other prepositional syntagmas, i.e. dominated by a verbal syntagma (for example, *komme nach Köln*/am coming to Cologne).

For the semantic description, especially important for the analysis of the use of prepositions, we have divided prepositional syntagmas into the following categories: place, non-directional (*arbeite im Büro*/work in the office); place, directional (*kommt zu mir*/comes to my house); temporal (*fertig im April*/ready in April); personal/non-personal incidence (*schwer für mich*/difficult for me); modal (*auf Deutsch sagen*/ to say [it] in German); final (*eine halbe Stunde für die Mittagspause*/a half-hour for the noon break); and others (comparative, causal, partitive, etc.).

With each occurrence of a preposition in the learning varieties, the corresponding semantically correct preposition of the target variety has been associated. This was done to recognise possible extensions or restrictions of meaning of prepositions in the learning varieties.

Results — ratios between expressed and unexpressed prepositions. Table 3.5 presents these results. The total number of occurrences of prepositional syntagmas increases from group I to group III, thereafter decreasing. The German speakers' value is lower still than that of group IV. The use of prepositional syntagmas seems to play an important role in the intermediate stages of learning. At the upper levels, prepositional syntagmas are apparently replaced by other syntactic structures.

The proportion of prepositions expressed markedly increases from group I to group IV. Reduction of the number of prepositional syntagmas lacking prepositions continues more or less regularly up to group IV, with only 6 per cent of prepositions unexpressed.

Table 3.5

Per cent of expressed and unexpressed prepositions

	Group				
	I	II	III	IV	Heidelberg
Expressed	51	71	83	94	100
Unexpressed	49	29	17	6	0
Total number	282	346	413	321	250

Types of prepositions. As can be seen in Table 3.6, the number of different prepositions clearly increases with the level of learning. Group I uses an average of three different prepositions, group II five, group III eight, group IV eleven, and the group of German speakers twelve. All the groups, including the group of German speakers, frequently use the prepositions *in, bei* and *mit.* They comprise 91 per cent of the occurrences in group I; *in* is the most frequent preposition, followed by *bei* with 27 per cent and *mit* with 10 per cent. The acquiring of prepositions other than the three most frequently encountered apparently occurs more or less at random at this stage of learning and seems to depend on the individual learning situation.

Table 3.6

Relative frequency of use of expressed prepositions
(figures are percentages)

	Group				
Prepositions	I	II	III	IV	Heidelberg
in	54	43	31	28	22
bei	27	14	20	17	14
mit	10	11	16	10	18
others	9	32	33	14	46

A more marked differentiation appears from group II onward. At the intermediate learning levels, the three prepositions mentioned constitute approximately two-thirds of the total occurrences. The corresponding value for group I, 55 per cent, is almost identical to that of the German speakers.

Syntactic function of the prepositional syntagma. The prepositional syntagmas in the aggregate can be divided according to their syntactic function into two classes: those which are part of the verb group (er ist *vor drei Tagen aus München gekommen*/he came from Munich three days ago); and those which are part of a nominal group (ein Kollege *von mir*/a colleague of mine).

As used by the Italian and Spanish workers *and* also by the German workers, about 90 per cent of the prepositional syntagmas are part of the verb group; 10 per cent are part of the nominal group. No significant difference is noted between German and foreign speakers as regards the distribution between the two classes.

Semantic function of prepositional syntagmas. Our analysis was based on the categorisation into the seven semantic classes described above.

Table 3.7 shows that among all the foreign speakers, by far the most frequent function is 'place, non-directional'. The high frequency for group I can be explained by the fact that the low level speakers chiefly transmit concrete information referring especially to places (country of origin, host country, place of work, etc.). This hypothesis is supported by the large number of constructions of the type preposition + proper noun, which are almost twice as frequent in group I as in group IV.

Table 3.7

Relative frequencies of prepositional syntagmas according to semantic function among four groups of foreign speakers and a group of German speakers from Heidelberg

Semantic functions	Group				
	I	II	III	IV	HD
Place, non-directional	56	35	33	30	26
Place, directional	15	13	19	18	19
Personal/non-personal incidence	19	24	20	22	29
Temporal	6	12	8	15	6
Modal	4	9	10	7	13
Final	1	1	4	4	–
Other	–	2	3	3	2
Unclassifiable	–	4	4	1	–

The semantic category of second importance is that of personal/non-personal incidence. By this concept is meant the use of a preposition serving to designate the personal — or, less frequently, the non-personal — aspect of a happening or situation (e.g. *spricht mit mir*/speaks with me). Usage in this category occurs nearly equally among the four groups of foreign speakers. These figures apparently reflect the necessity felt by the speakers, during communication, to define their own rules and viewpoints relative to the happenings and situations expressed.

146

Directional prepositions of place occupy the third rank in all the groups. Their use is closely linked to that of verbs of motion. Even in group I, where few verbs are encountered, the majority of the prepositions of this type accompany a verb.

The occurrences of temporal prepositional syntagmas increase from the lowest to the highest level of foreign workers, thereafter decreasing, with the group of German speakers, to the value in group I. The possibility of expressing temporal indications without resorting to prepositions, a tactic very frequently used by the German speakers, is either not yet used, or is less used, by the groups of foreign speakers.

Table 3.7 indicates, from left to right, a distinct differentiation of the semantic functions of the prepositions used. Among the lower learning levels, a small number of different prepositions serve to express a small number of frequently used semantic functions. These prepositions then undergo a considerable extension of their meaning.

Prepositional syntagmas introduced by *bei* expressing personal incidence are encountered almost without exception with *verba dicendi*, such as *sprechen* (to speak), *sagen* (to say), *rufen* (to call), *fragen* (to ask); they frequently replace in such instances a direct complement or indirect object. This applies to such verbs as *kosten* (to cost), *interessieren* (to interest). *Bei* is also used with adverbs and adjectives in the sense of the preposition *für* of standard German.

It is interesting to note that *bei* is the only preposition whose use differs between the Italians and Spaniards. Eighty-two per cent of the occurrences of this proposition were by Spaniards. On the other hand, the semantic functions expressed by *bei* was the same for both nationalities, namely, place/non-directional, place/directional, personal/non-personal incidence. But their quantitative distribution is different. Among the Italians, the few occurrences of *bei* are equally divided among the three functions, whereas among the Spaniards 50 per cent of the occurrences come under the personal incidence category. Among the Spaniards, this function is almost always expressed with the use of *bei*; among the Italians, where the same frequency is found, the preposition *mit* is more often found. The preponderance of the use of *bei* among the Spaniards is still unexplained for the time being. It may involve a phenomenon of interference, a problem which remains to be studied in detail.

Social conditioning of the unguided learning of a second language by immigrant workers

The aim of this section is to identify the social factors governing the learning process in German. We shall first define a frame of reference enabling us to study the connection between the social and the linguistic situation. Within this framework, we shall thereafter summarise the results of our sociological analysis. The degree of correlation between the diverse factors and the linguistic data will serve as a criterion for determining which factors foster or, conversely, hinder the learning of a second language.

The context for learning German

As a general rule the learning conditions of immigrant workers are unsatisfactory. The national and international effects of the capitalist economic system and the division of labour at the international level resulting from it compel immigrant workers to sell their labour potential abroad in order to provide for their subsistence. Serving as a contingency buffer and reserve army for industry, they work at ill-paid, unpleasant and to a large extent mechanical jobs (see Geiselberger, 1972, chapters 2 and 3; and Nikolinakos, 1972, chapter IV). The corollary to economic exploitation is social discrimination. This situation has the following consequences: immigrant workers are torn from a rural-area or small-town professional and social structure to face, without preparation, the conditions of production and existence prevailing in large cities and industry. It follows that they are torn from social conditions offering security (family, friends), without being able to find anything to replace them in the country of immigration. They meet with the massive prejudices of the German population, doubtless explained by the difference in socialisation, cultural background, and the fact that a large proportion of the German population does not clearly understand the reasons for the hiring of immigrants, or the policy followed in this regard by capital, and views the immigrant workers as competitors in the labour market, wage lowerers, and the like. It also follows that they find themselves incorporated in productive processes that are largely standardised and hence poor in communicativity.

These factors lead to loss of self-assurance, separation and isolation (see Borris, 1973, chapter VIII); rather frequently also, the immigrant reacts to this situation by consciously returning to his national group in the host country. Social isolation entails isolation from the standpoints of language and communication. It is obvious that such conditions are very unfavourable to the unguided learning of German.

Correlation between linguistic factors and social factors in the learning of German by Spanish and Italian workers

Method. To determine the connection between linguistic and social factors, we proceeded as follows (a detailed presentation is to be found in HPD, 1976, chapter 6, pp. 283-351).

Using the data provided by exploratory interviews, participant observation and related sociological techniques, we selected the social variables describing the individual conditions of the workers on the date of immigration, and their social context in the FRG. For each of the 48 workers examined, we correlated the variables with the subject's 'syntactic profile' level, i.e. his rank on the speakers' scale in terms of the syntactic index. The link between syntactic level and social factors was measured by use of the correlation ratio η and the correlation coefficient γ (see Benninghaus, 1974, pp. 230-256). We shall present the variables in decreasing order of their importance for unguided second language learning, as revealed by our investigation.

Results — leisure-time contacts with Germans. This variable presents the greatest correlation with the syntactic level ($\eta = 0.64$). The speakers with many contacts are found at the top of the syntactic scale; those with few contacts are part of the most feeble group.

What ensures a high level of learning is living with a German partner. In reality, only a minority of the immigrant workers enjoys such a situation. Among 60 per cent of those interviewed, contacts are limited to the strict minimum: exchanged greetings with neighbours, the few spoken words required for making purchases, and the like. Found in this group are all those housed in company lodgings and who live in a sort of ghetto.

Generally speaking: (a) none of the subjects questioned maintains contacts with German colleagues during his free time; (b) aside from the immigrant workers living with a German partner, the subjects seek satisfaction of their needs for contact within the circle of relatives and friends of the same nationality; (c) male immigrant workers know hardly any situations enabling them to establish contact with Germans, and this is even more the case with female workers.

Results — age of immigration. This variable is second in importance ($\eta = 0.57$; $\gamma = 0.56$). It involves an inverse relation: the greater the age of the immigrant, the lower the level of language learning. The average age of immigration to the FRG of the ten speakers with the highest syntactic indexes was 20. On the other hand, the speakers who arrived at the age of 40 or more are part of the least advanced group. Those who were between 25 and 35 years of age on arrival form a relatively compact group in the middle. It therefore appears that the conditions of learning are particularly favourable when the foreign subject arrives young in the FRG (up to age 23 approximately), and particularly unfavourable when he arrives at age 40 or more. Naturally, those who arrived young are more open to contacts and more capable or more desirous of adapting, whereas older individuals are rather disoriented and tend to withdraw.

Results — contacts with Germans at the place of work. Given the few possibilities of contacts with Germans during leisure hours, the place of work still offers the best opportunities for communication with natives. The correlation between the level of learning and this variable is $\eta = 0.53$. It appears that the importance of contacts at the place of work depends in each case on the following factors:

1 Type of activity: the greater the obligation to collaborate at the place of work, the greater the communication; jobs involving different sequences (e.g. handcrafts, the use of several machines, jobs requiring a prior agreement (e.g. construction work, site assignments) and service activities (e.g. chauffeur, hairdresser, cook's helper) all foster communication.

2 Type of employment: the requisite condition for contacts is that the immigrant worker finds himself solely among German colleagues; quite often, noise, accelerated cadence, prohibition of conversation, piece work, isolation in space of the work position, etc. prohibit any oral communication.

3 Worker's position in the enterprise: foremen are usually obliged to communicate more often, e.g. to break in newcomers, check work done; company interpreters, i.e. bilingual immigrant workers, serving as intermediaries between foremen or supervisors and immigrant workers with limited knowledge of the language, must also communicate more.

Results — professional qualification acquired in the country of origin. This variable and the following one (length of school attendance) take into account, in learning of the language, the initial situation at the time of emigration. This variable presents a low correlation to the level of learning. In the cases studied, $\eta = 0.42$. Three-quarters of the subjects questioned were workers 'with initiation' or 'untrained'. Those considered as untrained are the immigrants who had worked as peasants, day labourers, housewives. To the 'with initiation' group of workers belong those who, in their country of origin, most often in small businesses, had had the benefit of a period of initiation or apprenticeship. No difference in the learning of syntax was found between the two groups. On the other hand, the syntactic level is distinctly higher among skilled workers.

Results — length of school attendance. The correlation with the syntactic index was: $\gamma = 0.33$ and $\eta = 0.35$. The speakers without primary school training are part of the least advanced group. Those who went beyond primary school are in most cases found to be better learners.

The syntactic level increases with the length of school attendance, the correlation being approximately linear.

Results — length of residence. No correlation was found between the length of residence and the linguistic level attained. The rise in the syntactic level was not at all proportionate to the length of residence; instead, after a certain time, the syntactic level that is linked to other factors becomes set, or 'petrifies,' at a certain stage. The following observation is interesting: the subjects having resided for less than two-and-one-half years have a lower syntactic scale score than subjects in a comparable or even less favourable social situation, but who have lived for a longer period of time in the FRG. The low syntactic level of the former would seem to relate to the shortness of their residence. This manifestly means that during the first two or three years, *all* the subjects make progress in syntax. Following this stage of elaboration, they stabilise at a particular level, which depends on such factors as 'contacts', and the like. The speakers having favourable learning conditions achieve more during this period than those having unfavourable conditions. Once the syntactic level stabilises, it appears that it cannot be dynamised unless certain social factors change.

Conclusions and recommendations

In this section, we summarise a few practical conclusions reached in the light of our socio-linguistic research. These conclusions define the conditions that must be fulfilled if the language instruction of immigrant workers is to be effective. They are both socio-political and linguistic; socio-political in that the successful teaching of a language depends on a social and political framework that juridically fosters the learning of a foreign language and positively influences approaches to learning; linguistic in that the subjects' unguided linguistic level must be amply known in order for judicious and effective instruction to be formulated.

Conditions for transforming the context of learning

In the introduction, we mentioned that learning a second language without guidance did not mean that the resulting command of the learned language was *ipso facto* inferior. On the contrary, all the experiments conducted with subjects optimally 'immersed' in a second language indicate that language learning acquired through frequent and intensive contacts is better and faster than that acquired by the use of manuals. Since good relations between immigrant workers and Germans are the exception and perturbed relations the rule, one cannot leave the solution of this situation up to the individual; it must be improved by means of a guided intervention. Instruction in German can, in this situation of perturbed contact, perform such a role, since it offers at a formal level, the means (grammatical rules of German) and, from the standpoint of content, the verbal strategies, whereby the social and intercultural impediments to direct communication between German and foreign workers can be eliminated (see also Berkowski, Harnisch and Kumm, 1976b).

In this perspective, the institutionalised teaching of German, dispensed at all levels, constitutes a necessary, though not a sufficient condition for transforming the social situation of foreign workers. However, the reality that we observe in this regard in the FRG must not be lost sight of: the right to instruction in the language does not exist, and at the *Länder* level, there is no compulsory and uniform legislation permitting the regular offering of courses. Only institutions such as the Goethe Institute and the popular universities contribute to such instruction, but what they offer differs regionally and, in the aggregate, amounts to very little. The central institution in this field, specially founded by the West German government and concerned with teaching German to immigrant workers (the Sprachverband Deutsch für ausländische Arbeitnehmer e.V.) stated that, so far, it has instructed 10,000 individuals in German. This corresponds to less than one per cent of the total population of foreign workers living in Germany at present. Little has changed since publication of the Federal Ministry of Labour report (1973, p. 31) indicating that more than 70 per cent of the foreign workers acquired their knowledge of the language at their place of work, whereas only 6 per cent of them have had courses of instruction.

The language-training policy practised in Sweden is diametrically opposed to this situation: since 1973, Sweden has had a law providing that immigrant workers have the right to follow courses in Swedish for 240 hours during their paid work time. It appears that at least 70 per cent of the immigrant workers currently living in Sweden have taken language courses. As opposed to this, judging by the figures that we were furnished, in the entire FRG, at most 10 per cent of all foreign workers have taken language courses.

The reality, which we have frequently seen reflected in the course of our three years of investigation, shows that foreign workers with practically no command of the second language (they constitute the great majority of our sample): (a) are able to make themselves understood by only a very small number of interlocutors; (b) do not possess, in the foreign language, the ability to make long, coherent statements that can be understood by anyone; (c) can express themselves on only extraordinarily limited subjects; (d) do not possess the verbal techniques of argumentation (for asserting their rights), of making contact (for articulating private needs), of expressing feelings (to communicate pain, interest and joy — but also dissatisfaction), such techniques being necessary for mastering the social and individual situation.

With respect to point (d) above, no one will require that instruction in German 'impose on the migrant adults undergoing training a rhetorical and normative language that would be foreign to their daily social environment' (Unesco 1977, Recommendation 16, p. 21), but it is clear that with a greatly restricted grammatical and lexical repertory it is very difficult to argue, make contacts, swear, or tell jokes. But that is precisely what everyday communication consists of. Our linguistic analyses have sufficiently shown that what is lacking is the elementary linguistic tool for truly living communication — such communication being the condition not only for establishing contact with someone, but for maintaining it. Development of such verbal practices will not be possible until the microcosm of basic morphological, lexical, syntactic and semantic rules, which we have been able to study only in part, has been mastered.

Consequently, practices like those in Sweden should be instituted in the FRG. A programme should provide for an approximately equivalent number of hours of instruction, legally guaranteed, and available, without exception, to all foreign workers during their paid work time. That such instruction should be given during paid work time has been shown by numerous analyses: individual motivation to follow courses of instruction during free time is too poor; furthermore, the work load precludes long-term participation in such courses. One of the most difficult problems of language teaching to immigrant workers, who seldom have been living for less than five years and frequently for more than ten years in the FRG, is that it has to correct deep-rooted errors, semantic blurrings, fossilised over-generalisations and structures of learning. The effectiveness of instruction in the language will be doomed to failure so long as special concepts have not been developed for overcoming fossilisation and rooted erroneous routines. As these constitute the negative phenomena attending unguided foreign language learning the instruction reserved for immigrant workers must be started as early as possible.[1]

It is clear that, for immigrant workers, the right to German language instruction is only one element in a series of measures capable of improving, materially and in the long term, their social and communicative conditions. Hence in the final analysis an improvement in the learning situation implies improvement in the social and juridical status of foreigners living in the FRG. Any such improvement (see also on this subject Allbrecht, 1976) should, at least in its practical implementation,

1 The Unesco congress of 1977 on the language of foreign workers recommends that the governments concerned have research done 'aimed at discovering . . . the means of motivating migrants to go beyond the minimal level of use of the second language, so as to avoid "fossilisation" of said language' (Unesco, 1977).

meet the following requirements:

1 Right to naturalization after an uninterrupted residence of three years in the FRG

2 Echeloned guarantees relative to the legal aspect of residence

3 Right to participate in political life, particularly at the level of municipal and federal electoral legislation

4 Equality of German and foreign workers in the labor market

5 Right to courses of instruction in German during paid work-time

6 Right to bilingual education for the children of foreign workers (Dittmar, 1978, p. 21).

Conditions for an appropriate conception of the teaching of German to foreign workers

In this report, we have repeatedly stressed that the success of German instruction dispensed to immigrant workers depended, to a large extent, on our knowledge of the factors conditioning unguided second language learning. On the one hand, there are few true beginners and, on the other, there are foreign workers who have acquired an incorrect knowledge of various fragments of German. It is in relation to this background that the results of the present study are pertinent.

Account must be taken of the following factors which, although they relate to Spanish and Italian workers, also apply to other groups of foreigners:

1 Unguided second language learning tends to copy the local variety of the dialectal environment.

2 Many important grammatical rules of German are lacking in the varieties of learning as compared with the target variety.

3 Numerous rules are badly learned, i.e. they are not used in the normal manner and in part give rise to confusion.

4 The foreign workers' varieties of German have the characteristics of the mother-tongue, particularly at the phonological level and apparently also at the syntactic level.

5 Among what is rapidly learned, one finds: simple substantives, without complement (designations, proper nouns), simple verbs (very rarely compound verbs, copulas, modal and auxiliary verbs), simple adverbial expressions (of place and time, often without preposition), simple deictic forms

such as *dies* (this) or *das* (that), numerals, a form of negation, a form of intensification (usually *viel* [much] and adverbial syntagmas).

6 Slowly learned are: all the morphology, a differentiated level of the systems of mood and tense, the pronominal system, conventions relative to the position of words in main or subordinate clauses consisting of complex predicates, nominal and attributive sentences, pronominal adverbs and such lexical units as *ja, nun, doch,* etc. of the spoken language.

This incomplete list provides only approximate guidelines, but helps us to make certain decisions in formulating an appropriate instruction of German.

Dialect vs standard language. The varieties of the most advanced subjects reveal quite distinct dialectal influences. As we are obliged to take account of the primary contacts of the individuals concerned, a set place must be reserved for the dialect in teaching the language.

The part that the dialect should occupy in teaching of the language is determined by assessing the importance of the standard language. One important argument is that only the standard language is written. Moreover, if we consider the fact that workers must pay careful attention to choosing which variety of language to learn, for reasons (a) of mobility (change in the place of work and hence in the dialectal space); (b) of understanding at the national level (one need only think of dialects as dissimilar as Bavarian, Swiss German, or Low German) and (c) of the frequent stigmatisation of what is called 'immigrant workers' language' (dialectal influences being likely to intensify such discriminations), the debate should conclude in favour of the standard language as the variety to use in instruction. However, we cannot approve such a decision of principle if the dialectal varieties learned by the subjects are not merely accepted as *bona fide* expressions, but taught on the same basis as the rules and expressions of the standard language. Hence the goal to attain would be passive command of the dialect, since it is clear that the dialect predominates where the immigrants work.

Priorities of learning. Two particular phenomena mark the unguided learning of a second language by immigrant workers: deficiencies in the systems of learning; and the unacceptable or incorrect use of certain linguistic constituents. Given these flaws, measures of elaboration and of elimination must be adopted for the instruction.

The two especially striking characteristics of the varieties of learning, i.e. deficiencies and mistaken uses, imply the necessity for priority insistence in teaching on the learning of basic syntactic and semantic rules. This is further justified at an empirical level: morphology is learned only late (see Huber, 1977); manifestly, it is only of moderate importance for direct communication. The phonology of certain varieties of learning is greatly deformed in part, but as a rule the phonic constituents of the words in general use can be articulated intelligibly. Only secondary importance should be attached to the position of words, for elements that have not been learned cannot be incorrectly placed. Hence particular stress should be placed on enlarging the lexicon and on the repertory of syntactic and semantic rules. We can summarise the viewpoints just enunciated by stating that intelligibility takes precedence over grammatical correctness. Once the former is practically assured, the latter can be stressed.

Measures of elaboration. By this is meant all the measures that, in the instruction, aim at filling in and completing the subject's deficient structures. Analysis of the inventory of lexical elements found in the varieties of learning will determine in what field and to what extent these must be completed. For subjects whose level is very low, virtually all the modal verbs will have to be introduced. The same does not apply to numerals. Likewise, the inventory of prepositions governing the semantic function of adverbial complements will have to be considerably enriched. For the closed classes, it is easy to establish diagnoses; on the other hand, for the open classes, we depend, for determining the extent of the lexicon, on criteria bearing on the content.

In the field of syntax, our research provides a relatively clear picture of the measures of elaboration to be adopted in terms of each level of learning. By way of example, we shall mention a few points concerning the following syntactic constituents: the verb, the nominal syntagma, and the adverbial syntagma.

The verb. Verbs should be introduced before copulas. The unguided learning process shows quite clearly that the copula performs no significative function. Among the forms of the past, formation of the perfect with *have* should be taught before the preterite. The subjunctive, which can be rather easily replaced by the use of adverbs, should be introduced still later. With respect to word order, it is advisable to introduce the modal verbs and the auxiliaries as early as possible, because the inability to express tense and mood satisfactorily leads to the anteposition of temporal and modal adverbs and thus to more frequent placing of the non-marked verb in the final position; the ambiguity of such sentences can be partially dispelled by the use of modal verbs and auxiliaries, the final position of the verb favouring such a measure.

Nominal syntagmas. One must begin with substantives alone and complete them thereafter; this is where articles and quantifiers play an important role. Numerals can be neglected, as most have been learned, even by subjects whose level is low. Pronouns should be introduced after simple nominal syntagmas.

Adverbial syntagmas. Adverbial syntagmas of time and place should be dealt with before those performing a different semantic function. By enlarging the prepositional system, one can obtain a more differentiated use of adverbial syntagmas. Finally, enlarging the spectrum of adverbs of place, time and manner should precede the introduction of pronominal adverbs.

Moreover, as has doubtless been understood, the measures of elaboration start concretely with what has already been learned, incorporate it productively into the instruction and develop it proportionately to the deviation from the basic dialectal or standard variety.

Measures of elimination. These are all the measures adopted in the instruction for correcting errors — whether over-generalisations, or semantic blurrings or transfers — due to improperly learned rules and meanings, and for replacing them within the limits of customary utilisation norms. Such errors are in a causal relation with the deficient learning system; that is why elaboration and elimination measures are correlated. We have already shown that a speaker who knows only one preposition, e.g. *bei*, will use it for totally different semantic purposes, whereas German uses other prepositions. By using *bei* not only in its semantic function of place/non-directional but also for personal incidence (e.g. *ich spreche bei dir* instead of *zu dir*), the subject neutralises the existing dilemma between verbal means he does not possess and the exigencies of differentiation required in communication. The result, in the guise of a structural constraint, is semantic blurring stemming from a deficient system of learning. If we consider the cases of the modal verb *müssen*, which may express aspects of tense and mood of the verb and simultaneously perform the pleasing function of making sentences more acceptable, we observe that what this involves is fundamental verbal strategies on the part of the subjects: *for a field of semantically distinct functions, the subject chooses, from a limited repertory of the language, the element which, under the unfavourable conditions of semantic blurring, still offers an optimum of comprehension, acceptability and compatibility with the syntactic and semantic properties of a language.*

In language teaching, one must correct this strategy, which is certainly economical, by providing the means for a greater differentiation of the over-generalised element. As these strategies have been absorbed in the course of daily living, they can be effectively corrected only by making the subject conscious of their functioning. For courses given to foreign workers, as opposed to the preparation of German instruction for others, a catalogue of elimination measures is sufficiently important to determine success.

Contrastivity. Reference to the subject's mother-tongue plays a significant role, particularly with respect to phonetic correction, but it can also be used for vocabulary and syntax. In teaching, the mother-tongue can be used to produce conscious awareness, through contrast, of the priorities of German; and to explain points that have not been understood.

When dealing with Spanish workers, it is certainly pertinent to teach the word *Kollege* before *Freund*, as the Spanish word *colega* resembles the German word. On the other hand, the combinations of consonants possible in German as compared to Spanish must be explained circumstantially. Beyond the phonological field, it is certainly difficult to reduce errors of learning to contrastive aspects of the languages involved. The concept of 'contrastivity' encompasses not only the mother-tongues but also the varieties of learning, as is clear from this report.

Concluding remarks

As conditions for an appropriate conception of the teaching of German to foreign workers, we have dealt with linguistic aspects related to our research. We believe that grammatical rules must occupy a central position in the teaching of German. Determining *how* that is to be done is more a matter of didactics. For foreign workers, the instruction will be given in quasi-game form using visual extra-linguistic material (see Barkowski, Harnisch and Kumm, 1976b). But this does not alter the fact that the curricula should be based on a linguistic progression whose background consists of an analysis of the varieties of learning.

In conclusion, the linguistic progression should be integrated in a pertinent framework for content. At the core of this concept should be found: the 'presentation and elimination of the cultural and identity conflict' of the foreign workers, which results from the tension between initial socialisation in their societies of origin and subsequent socialisation in the countries of employment; the teaching of German as an obligation toward the 'goals and methods of worker training'. In other words: 'it should instil awareness of the interests of workers and of the necessity for solidarity; it should work from experiences in concrete living, should not communicate abstract knowledge, but emphasise learning linked to real people and things' (Barkowski, Harnisch and Kumm, 1977, p. 2 ff.).

Bibliography

Albrecht, G. (ed.), *Das Düsseldorfer Reformprogramm zum Ausländerrecht*. Presented by the committee for the reform of foreigners' rights from the 'Diakonisches Werk' of the Rheinland Protestant Church, Bonn, 1976.

Augustin, V. and Liebe-Harkort, K., *Feridun, Ein Lesebuch und Sprachprogramm nicht nur für Türken*, Abado-Verlag, München, 1977.

Barkowski, H., Harnisch, U. and Kumm, S., 'Sprachhandlungstheorie und Deutsch für ausländische Arbeiter', *Linguistische Berichte*, no. 45, pp 42-54, 1976a.

Barkowski, H., Harnisch, U. and Kumm, S., *Handbuch für den Deutschunterricht mit ausländischen Arbeitern*. In the series 'Lernen mit Ausländern. Modelle und Perspektiven', Scriptor, Kronberg/Ts, 1980.

Benninghaus, H., *Deskriptive Statistik*, B.G. Teubner, Stuttgart, 1974.

Bickerton, D., *Dynamics of a Creole System*, Cambridge University Press, London, New York, 1975.

Borris, M., *Ausländische Arbeiter in einer Grosstadt. Eine empirische Untersuchung am Beispiel Frankfurt*, Fischer, Frankfurt am Main, 1973.

Chomsky, N., *Aspects of the Theory of Syntax*, MIT Press, Cambridge Mass., 1965.

Corder, S.P., *Introducing Applied Linguistics*, Penguin, Harmondsworth, 1973.

Demetz and Puente, *Deutsch — Ihre neue Sprache*, Hueber, München, 1973.

Dittmar, N., *Sociolinguistics. A Critical Survey of Theory and Application*, Edward Arnold, London, 1976.

Dittmar, N., 'Die soziale und rechtliche Diskriminierung von Arbeitsimmigranten in der BRD. Zur Einschätzung von Möglichkeiten ihrer Aufhebung'. Kühlwein, W. and Radden, G. (eds), *Sprache und Kultur: Studien zur Diglossie, Gastarbeiterproblematik und kulturellen Integration*, Gunter Narr, Tübingen, 1978, pp 123-160.

Dittmar, N. and Rieck, B.O., 'Datenerhebung und Datenauswertung im Heidelberger Forschungsprojekt "Pidgin-Deutsch ausländischer Arbeiter" ' in Bielefeld, U., Ernest, Hess-Lüttich, W.B. and Lundt, A. (eds), *Soziolinguistik und Empirie, Beiträge zum Berliner Symposium 'Corpusgewinnung und Corpusauswertung', 15-18 January 1976.* Frankfurt, 1977, pp 59-96.

Dumas, G., Selinker, L. and Swain, M., 'L'apprentissage du français langue seconde en classe d'immersion dans un milieu torontois', *Travaux de Recherches sur le Bilingualisme*, no. 1, The Ontario Institute for Studies in Education, Toronto, 1973.

Federal Minister for Labour and Social Order, 'Proposals from the Länder Commission for the development of a comprehensive policy conception regarding the employment of foreigners' (IIa, 5-24, 200/22 Bonn), *Journal G*, pp.23-40, 1977.

Federal Ministry of Labour, Presseinformationen no. 51/77 (August 4 1977), Nürnberg.

Federal Ministry of Labour, *Ausländische Arbeitnehmer: Beschaftigung, Anwerbung, Vermittlung, Erfahrungsbericht* 1972/73, Nürnberg, 1974.

Federal Ministry of Labour, *Repräsentativuntersuchung 1972 über die Beschäftigung ausländischer Arbeitnehmer im Bundesgebiet und ihre Familien- und Wohnverhältnisse*, Nürnberg, 1973.

Geiselberger, S. (ed.), *Schwarzbuch: Ausländische Arbeiter*, Fischer, Frankfurt am Main, 1972.

Heidelberger Forschungsprojekt 'Pidgin-Deutsch', *Sprache und Kommunikation ausländischer Arbeiter. Analysen, Berichte, Materialien*, Scriptor, Kronberg/Ts, 1975a.

Heidelberger Forschungsprojekt 'Pidgin-Deutsch' 'Zur Sprache ausländischer Arbeiter: Syntaktische Analysen und Aspekte des kommunikativen Verhaltens', *Zeitschrift für Literaturwissenschaft und Linguistik*, vol. 5, no. 18, pp. 78-121, 1975b.

Heidelberger Forschungsprojekt 'Pidgin-Deutsch', 'The Acquisition of German Syntax by Foreign Migrant Workers', Sankoff, David, (ed.) *Linguistic Variation. Models and Methods*, Academic Press, New York, 1978, pp. 1-22.

Helbig, G. and Buscha, J., *Deutsche Grammatik. Ein Handbuch für den Ausländer unterricht*, Leipzig VEB, 1972.

Huber, H., *Morphologische und semantische Beschreibung des Verbsystems im Deutsch ausländischer Arbeitnehmer. Exemplarische Untersuchungen anhand einiger ausgewählter Sprecher*. Admission dissertation for the academic examination for the teaching profession at grammar schools, Saarland University, 1977.

Klein, W., *Variation in der Sprache. Ein Verfahren zu ihrer Beschreibung*. Scriptor, Kronberg/Ts, 1974.

Klein, W., 'Maschinelle Analyse des Sprachwandels', in Eisenberg, P., (ed.) *Computerlinguistik*, Berlin, 1976.

Klein, W. and Dittmar, N., *Developing Grammars. The Acquisition of German Syntax by Foreign Workers*. Springer, Berlin-Heidelberg-New York, 1979.

Mehrländer, U., *Soziale Aspekte der Ausländerbeschäftigung*, Schwann, Bonn-Bad Godesberg, 1974.

Swedish Ministry of Education, 'Swedish Policy in respect of Immigration and the Training of Immigrants in Sweden', Swedish National Committee to Unesco (ed.), *The Literacy Requirements of Migrants, Final Report and Recommendations*, Stockholm, 1977, pp 30-48.

Nikolinakos, M., *Politische Ökonomie der Gastarbeiterfrage: Migration und Kapitalismus*. Reinbeck bei Hamburg, 1973.

Richards, J.C., 'Social Factors, Interlanguage and Language Learning'. *Language Learning* 22, 1972.

Richards, J.C., 'Error Analysis and Second Language Learning Strategies'. Oller, J.W. and Richards, J.C., *Focus on the Learner. Pragmatic Perspectives for the Language Teacher*, Newbury House, Rowley, Mass., 1973, pp 114-135.

Rieck, B.O., *Die Interlingua spanischer Arbeitsimmigranten*. Magister Dissertation, German Seminar, Heidelberg University, 1974.

Schumann, J.H., *The Pidginization Process. A Model for Second Language Acquisition*. Newbury House, Rowley, Mass., 1978.

Unesco, *The Literacy Requirements of Migrants*, Swedish National Committee for Unesco, Final Report and Recommendations, Hasseludden, Stockholm, 1977.

4 Changing one's country means changing one's flag
MAURIZIO CATANI

Introduction

This chapter concerns a training programme (1974-1975) for women cleaners employed in a private school run by nuns in the Paris area. Let us emphasise that the aim of the study, over and beyond an analysis of the effects of a training programme, is to determine the significance that a 'foreign presence' takes on in the country of production and residence.

The methodology employed is ethnographic; however, the great difficulty encountered with that approach is well known: the material for observation is abundant and, since the reader must be familiar with the data in order to appreciate the analyses, the publication is always voluminous. Thus we have had to resign ourselves to eliminating almost entirely 'the foreigner's testimony' and to presenting only our results. However, we shall return to that aspect of the problem in our conclusions. Similarly, part of the general statement on methodology had to be sacrificed. Details and an account of the practical teaching situation will be found in Allain-Dupré et al.(1977).

The research team

The research team consisted of Maurizio Catani, a sociologist of Italian nationality, and an immigrant; Marie-Claude Muñoz, a psychologist of Spanish origin, the daughter of immigrants; and Anne Verger, group

163

leader,[1] who had been active in the labour movement.

The team was made up according to a 'research-action' model. Maurizio Catani was responsible for drawing up the methodological principles and the training of instructors among whom was Anne Verger. He also took part in the educational follow-up of the training course analysed below and of other programmes of the same type between 1974 and 1976. During the same period, Marie-Claude Muñoz closely followed other programmes which were, however, in an identical institutional setting and had relatively closely related theoretical aims.

Although they professed no uniform doctrine (and did not succeed in overcoming all points of disagreement), the three members of the team, who have known each other for some years, were able to provide a study based on at least a common perception of the questions, even if the solutions proposed were not the same and the analyses were not always as searching or subtle as the research team would have wished. The final drafting, of which only a part is being published here, was undertaken by Maurizio Catani.

From the available statistical data, it is impossible to indicate in sufficient detail *what* proportion of women is employed in *which* 'services' within each migratory flow. We can therefore only note, at the common-sense level, that most of the cleaning women employed today by various organisations were previously housemaids if they were of Latin origin (Spain, in decline; Portugal, situation perhaps stable, even before immigration to France was halted; Italy, distinctly falling off), whereas when they are in Yugoslavia, they do not go through this stage of domestic work. In this sector of activity, the number of North African women is very limited.

Courses for cleaning women

In the training course observed (1974-1975), we were concerned with the particular careers of Guilhermina, a Portuguese woman who has been in France since 1962; Francisca, from the Cape Verde Islands who has been in France since 1965; Cecilia, of Portuguese origin, who migrated to France in 1970; Mrs B.S. from Morocco, who has been in France since 1959 and who joined the group late; and Albert, a Portuguese national, who left the course after two weeks.

Reference population and cycle observed in 1974-75. We shall discuss with a certain monographic — and not statistical — exactness women

---

1 There is some variation in the use of 'group leader' and 'teacher'. The latter term should be used more generally, in view of its social function. However, it has not always been easy, when analysing the training procedures, to distinguish and hierarchise the two functions which, from the viewpoint of the methodology applied, should alternate according to circumstances.

cleaners employed in private schools in the Paris area, where we had the opportunity of meeting, in the course of several cycles of language training, some one hundred foreign women (reference population). We shall also allude occasionally to other groups, composed of some thirty women cleaners, employed by service enterprises, whose training conditions were in all respects similar (control population) because even though the employing and training organisation may have been different, the methodology was the same.

Two-thirds of the service personnel in the schools concerned are foreigners; Spanish and Portuguese cleaning women in turn make up two-thirds of all the foreign personnel, thus forming the principal population of the courses. The remaining third of the foreign women (men being limited to only a very few individuals) consisted of a few North Africans, Italians and Poles. These last were relatively elderly women who had emigrated before World War II or immediately following it.

At the end of the courses and the test interviews, it was found that, in relation to the reference population, the foreign women who attended the French courses could be divided into sub-groups: those who planned to take advantage of the training to seek other work, better paid and more highly regarded, and those who did not plan to change employers and who considered the training received as an end in itself and not an opportunity for social mobility.

Not all the individuals in the first group achieved their wish to leave. It is significant, however, that at least two of them (Cecilia and Tina) did so, and a third, two years later, should be able to specify both where she expects to find a new job and the way she hopes to secure it.[1] It must be added, however, that the *decision* to leave was not a result of the training, for that possibility had been envisaged earlier, though the training may have reinforced it.

Those individuals in the second group belonged to two different categories: those who were too old, too tired or too alone to have the desire or ability to leave the reassuring and familiar environment of the school establishment where they work; and those who, in the same schools, have special positions as cooks, concierges, etc., offering them a few advantages — financial, legal, material and frequently all three together — which seemed to them to counterbalance the hazards of further job seeking. It seems that the variable of age, which was both implicitly affirmed during the discussions and explicitly noted in several groups, is more important than that of marital status. In the decision to resign after training (3 occurrences) (case A), we have:

Francisca — unmarried, two children
Tina — unmarried, no child

1 In 1977, Francisca has not yet left, but her talk on the subject is far from unreal: she knows how to get domestic work at a hotel, and as her son Alex can now manage for himself, she may well go ahead with her plan. She is also asking for additional training, technical this time.

Cecilia — married, one child.

Among the others (case B), there are also both married and unmarried women.

In reality, there are two categories of cleaning women, whose expectations differ. We make this observation straight away, applying it to the 100 women whom we met over a two-year period thinking that the detailed analysis of the women which follows shows that the conclusions go beyond their particular cases and apply in a general way to the population under reference.

Future of the reference population. We place in case A only the three women about whom we have detailed indications, but even among the population classified in B we heard women say that they wanted to change jobs. Two years after training, they are still working at the same place. In this sector of activity as a whole, the situation appears likely to remain unchanged until retirement. It involves a long-lasting career in which the very low qualification required, added to personal history, results in this type of work being accepted as the only real possibility.

From this standpoint, it is not certain that differences of age or of migratory flows weigh more heavily in the balance than the personal characteristics common to this population. Thus, though a ,certain number of Polish women cleaners are so marginalised that their employment in a suburban school in all likelihood constitutes the last chance of steady work before sub-proletarianisation, it is also true that certain Italian or Spanish women, younger, less worn out and generally more highly considered because belonging to migratory flows with standards closer to those of the French, plan to stay permanently in their present jobs, the same as the Poles.

The common characteristic of these women is affective solitude, the de-structuring of the family group when they are married, and a relationship of subjection to a paternalist structure which, by relying on favouritism and reciprocal gratitude, confirms them in a situation where the brutally modern demands of productivity and speed are not so stressed as to eliminate any personal relationship with their employers.

Lastly, so long as the schools are administered by nuns (for when the administration is handed over to laymen the work-pace and the interpersonal relations appear to change), it is the hierarchical relationship — degraded into paternalism — that maintains a superficial cohesion and encourages staying put rather than looking elsewhere for work.

If such is the general situation of the reference population, it will be seen that the questions are the same in the group observed. Even the unique case of Cecilia, who is young, gets on well with her husband, has already worked in a factory and says that she prefers that type of work, breaks down because of the way she regards her own relationship to work itself, her employment being considered of secondary importance as compared with that of her husband.

Ethnography

Our analysis is based on some 500 typewritten pages of study material consisting of transcribed recordings of training sessions of the group observed, post-training discussions, and travel notes; transcriptions of sessions with the population under reference; observation of the structures and operation of the training body; participation in, and evaluation of the training of teachers, both in the observed group and the control population. We also have data available concerning the countries of origin, but have not systematically used them; stress has been laid on the new country of residence and production.

The training agency

Here we shall describe only a single body, namely the one which administered not only the course observed but most of those given for the reference population.[1] We do not feel that, apart from superficial differences among the employing enterprises, the situation among the various training agencies fundamentally varies. The questions brought to light are of a general nature, whatever the institutional system sponsoring the training agency and whatever in turn the socio-political options of the teachers.

The training agency (hereinafter designated as TA) is an association governed by the Law of 1901. In reality, it does not administer a training fund but confines itself to submitting a series of 'proposals' to its silent partners.

Information is to be found in the TA publications defining it legally and — as regards principles — in an altogether different manner; however, it was quite apparent, at the level of daily tactics, that the TA had no means of making its declarations of intent correspond to the realities of its quest for contracts. Constantly required to prove its existence, paring prices, obliged not to encroach on the ill-defined field of the 'political' prerogatives of the heads of the establishments that send their staff there, frequently reduced to nothing but a relay-station between its silent partners and other training agencies capable of providing training that it is unable to launch itself, the TA is constantly on the defensive. The contributing employers view it as simply another component in the complex administrative red tape to which

1 The law of 16 July 1971 defines the basis for the institution and development of 'Continuous (or life-long) Training'. People employed by a firm are entitled, on certain conditions, to training, without loss of pay, during working hours. Employers are required to set aside 1 per cent of the total wages budget for such training activities and to allow 2 per cent of the wage-earners to be undergoing training at one time. Many firms arrange for their funds to be administered by specialised bodies.

they are subjected. The TA members realise, without putting it in writing of course, that they lack any true autonomy.

The training courses for foreigners are the lengthiest and, considering the salary scales, the most costly in the salary/price ratio. The consequence is that the training courses hardest to have approved and to organise are those for foreigners.

General considerations concerning application of the law on continuous training. In small and medium-sized enterprises, it is actually impossible to provide training for the percentages of those entitled to it in the case of foreigners, the more so when, as in our case, the problem involves service personnel who, in part, are trained on the job. The situation is as follows: the school where the courses are given cannot refuse to enrol all their foreign women employees; that would upset 'social peace' (there are few individual drop-outs in such cases). Hence this school largely exceeds the legal framework, which allows for the training — at one and the same time — of only 2 per cent of the staff. The other school, which sends one or two individuals to round out the group, perhaps makes a 'selection' more in conformity with the law, for it releases fewer foreign personnel than the first school. However it must take account of travel time, which occasionally results in the loss of an entire afternoon of work for only two hours of courses. Thus the problem of the gap *vis-à-vis* the law is one relating to the number of training hours paid for in comparison with the total sum set aside from salaries for the purpose.

It is here that a *reductio ad absurdum* provides proof of one of the most common defects with which the law is charged: the impossibility of combining within a single legal category the continuous training of national and foreign workers, when the latter are seeking basic language training (French courses). Indeed, learning the language of the country of residence and production is an entirely different matter from learning to perfect some skill or to acquire another.

In reality, the law is inapplicable because 120-160 hours of language training is not enough for actual mastery in reading and writing everyday language. Moreover, once acquired, such mastery constitutes only a preparation for improving one's qualifications which could only be possible two years later, if the law were to be strictly applied. But the law is also a dead letter because the other staff members do not request training courses — at least not in sufficient numbers — whereupon internal tolerances are established, supported by the compensatory financial mechanisms mentioned above, which may eventually work to the advantage of the migrants, though at the same time leaving them exposed to the criticisms of their native colleagues. In fact in the eyes of many natives, migrants 'consume' too much training.

It can be said that the permanent staff and teachers of the TA operate in what we would call an imaginary circuit, symbolised by the 'lack of time' constantly invoked, in which the only happy moments — for there are some — are precisely those spent with the trainees. Cases here vary, since each individual reacts differently towards his groups, but it is certain that in this institutional vacuum the groups are what help their group leaders to survive. If there is any 'intervention', it is from the group towards the leader rather than vice versa, and it is of a therapeutic nature: a therapy of support, offered by the simple good-heartedness of these foreign workers who, countless times each week, provide a break in the unending circle of declaration of intent and the reality of unfulfilment. We feel that a certain number of individuals within the TA are aware of this situation and manage as best they can to cope with it. Others are submerged by it.

Attitude of employers towards training. Employers have a very mixed attitude towards the training and its potential effects. Three main lines can be discerned. The first is pure and simple rejection of the training because it disorganises work and may even run the risk of inciting the foreign women to leave the firm. Second, certain employers are prompted to request *ad hoc* training focused solely on the practical training of women cleaners.[1] Last, certain employers consider training as a work of charity, related to the fact — 'sad' or 'unacceptable' to them — of illiteracy (often confused with merely not knowing French, for frequently these employers have no idea whether the individual concerned can read and write her native language).

In all three cases, the following basic question is not broached: should training be given in speaking, reading and writing French? This leads to the following institutional questions: under what conditions of place and paid time? And, only finally, the methodological questions: according to which principles and didactic techniques?

It goes without saying that the first question is implicit in the others as well, but it does not appear to be reflected upon, at least not by the training organisation or its instructors, nor by the persons being trained. In this context, the immigrant is a pure abstraction; her needs are totally ignored *and* it is not even suspected that she has any personal plans.

Personnel involved in training. We should point out that the only women cleaners affected by the law on continuous training are

---

1 The demands expressed are the following: training on the school premises, with no outside workers brought in to complete the group numerically; frequent presence of a member of the management; a technological programme. The latter requirement partakes of the nature of an extremely significant paradox; these women cleaners should be told how to use detergents and the few — scarce — electrical machines, and especially how to clean 'thoroughly' in the 'French' way. This was not done, fortunately.

salaried employees inserted in the structures of collective negotiation where the law can be applied (although procedures depend on the good will of the firm's management, especially when there is only an autonomous union not affiliated to one of the three major national federations, for in such a case the autonomy most frequently amounts to endorsement of the management's decisions).[1] The type itself of the structure concerned — firms with more than ten salaried employees — bars the 'small fry' from training, though numerically they constitute a very large component in this type of work, for housemaids together with cleaning women form the essential component of the general category: 'service personnel'. This points up both the inadequacy and the abstractness of juridico-administrative separations. Nothing is then left for the majority of such women except evening courses organised by voluntary instructors (see Arondo, 1974).

The training cycle

Deficient use of test results, or the institutional abstraction. The group in training should have been homogenised by the use of tests so as to lead to the organisation implied by the methodology adopted by the TA (cf. Allain-Dupré et al., 1977). In reality, though the tests were given to the three Portuguese-speaking women, they were not given when it came to integrating the Moroccan woman, one month after the training programme had started.

Furthermore, the tests confirmed that Guilhermina belonged in the initial-training stage (spoken language and preparation for reading the written language), whereas Cecilia and Francisca belonged in the following stage (writing and reading the language), or even in finer sub-divisions. For reasons of economic profitability, they were all lumped together in a single group, to which Mrs B.S. was added. Thus no account was taken of either methodological criteria or the criteria which the foreigners might themselves have expressed in terms of their personal plans.

Differences in ethnic origin, age, experience and length of residence were all overlooked, only one criterion being considered as pertinent: the fact of being foreign and a woman cleaner. Even language knowledge was secondary, in that it was necessary at all costs in the final analysis, to justify the existence of the TA, the latter attempting to create a demand, whereas the women were not sensitive to the offer, *as it was presented*. Indeed, the offer was vague as to its procedures, its

---

1 Admittedly over-simplifying, the *Confédération Générale du Travail* (CGT) may be said to come close to the Marxist lines of thought supported by the French Communist Party; the *Confédération Française de Travailleurs* (CFDT) which, way back, was Catholic in origin, nowadays supports a form of Socialism often leaning towards self-management; while *Force Ouvrière* (FO) seeks to remain a-political.

purposes, and its results from the standpoint of a professional career.

The training is based on criteria pertinent only in terms of the country of production and of residence, but if one wishes to grasp what it can represent in relation to the plan of the individuals being trained, one must turn to their experience.

We stress that this restoration of the importance of the 'foreign slant' in our analysis is a reply to the questions relative to the effects of training on families and relevant groups (cf. Unesco, 1977).

Analysis of the teaching methodology[1]

The linguistic universe of the foreign worker.[2] The language space bears the mark of conflicts and of individual and social differences. The way in which each of the members of a community uses the language is determined by the role assigned to him or imposed on him in that community. The use of language — speech[3] — is the reflection of individual and collective relationships.

The social space thus far allotted to foreign workers by the society of production places them in a marginal linguistic universe; conversely, the linguistic exclusion of which they are victims tends to reinforce their cultural and social marginality. The literacy course is born of a contradiction between this implicit though real exclusion suffered by foreigners and the explicit ideological project of assimilation currently being developed by the institutional spokesmen of the society of production.

It was in the context of the temporary instability of this situation that our attempt at a reconsideration of the conventional 'teacher' and 'pupil' relations through school language was formulated. As soon as he arrives in the country of production, the foreign worker is plunged into an unfamiliar linguistic universe. His first material problem is that of survival: he must eat, drink, sleep and — work. A reception structure organised by the workers from his own country generally enables him to provide for his immediate subsistence and, if he has no contract, to begin to look for work.

Hence, from the beginning, a foreign worker finds his existence organised around two poles: on the one hand, the workers' centre, the family, etc., where he finds his fellow countrymen and speaks his native language and where he is immersed in a cultural environment resemb-

---

1 This section consists of extracts from *La parole de l'autre* (Allain-Dupré et al., 1977).

2 We consider that any group of foreigners is indicative of the migratory situation in general, once the researcher has maintained a sufficiently long relationship with it. There is no other rule in ethnography, nor in sociology, than the length of the observation period.

3 We use the Saussurian dichtomony 'langue-parole'.

ling that of his own country, and, on the other hand, the pole of his work and of public life where a language unfamiliar to him is spoken: French. Usually, he is helped by his fellow countrymen in his initial contacts with the administration, his employer and the police. Later on, he learns to get by on his own.

His linguistic exchanges, limited to the rare contacts he has with the workers and foremen in his firm, with merchants, officials, etc. then enable him to acquire a basic French made up of a number of key words, stereotyped syntagmas, set phrases. Most of this apprenticeship is a passive process: he receives orders, he is asked for information, he looks at advertising, television, motion pictures, etc., but he is never asked to express himself, nor really to converse.[1]

After a few months' stay, the foreign worker finds himself possessed of two autonomous language tools whose use is entirely separate. On the one hand, his mother-tongue no longer serves him except for private use: it is the language of home, of friendship, of family. French, on the other hand, is only of public, essentially passive, use to him. It is a specialised language, administrative, totally devoid of any affective connotation.

The separation thus instituted between a *language of power and a language of affect* tends to impose on the foreign worker a division of his daily life into two disconnected universes: the universe of work and the cultural ghetto. Integrated with production, he is excluded in reality from social life: a worker but not a citizen, he is comparable, from that standpoint, to the freed slave of ancient Rome. Excluded, marginal, different, the foreign worker creates in return, by his mere presence — the sole affirmation of this difference — a disturbing factor in the ideological comfort of the society of production. Furthermore, rejected from social life, he takes relatively little part in the 'great consumer effort', because in most cases he dreams of returning to his own country.[2]

Definition of publics. There is no school public typical of foreigners. Neither is there any typical request made by the foreign worker of the school institution.

The individual and collective past of foreigners, their nationality, their length of residence in France, their possible degree of school

1 The relative quality of the French he thus acquires is a direct function of the situation made for him. Excluded from daily familiar verbal communication, he can acquire the public language only passively. This circumstance must be viewed as the reproduction today of a classic pattern of linguistic domination. In it, the mother-tongue, which is the language of affect, is depreciated in that it permits no movement within the locus of the distribution of power and money.

2 Hence the society of production is caught between a social practice of exclusion and the economic and ideological necessity of assimilation. This paragraph is made up of extracts from Allain-Dupré et al. (1977).

attendance, the location and nature of their work and, of course, the training policy of their firms are factors that predetermine the setting up of a school course. Though the conventional presentation of the various training cycles theoretically comprises four levels, ordered in accordance with a criterion of scholastic progression (language learning), it is found in practice that the publics catered for by each of these cycles differ greatly in terms of their level of progress.[1]

The image of school or the stereotyped request. We have already stressed the fact that expectations from the school are traditional in type, simply because the image which the foreigners have gained of it, in one way or another, is that of a practice essentially based on the vertical teacher-student relationship. This ritual also ensures the group's defence and even a certain cohesion: not only is it not tactically advisable to confront it directly as if it were altogether negative, but it must be regarded as a powerful factor for change. It is through comparison that practices may be altered.

The foreigners want to read and write, but they are also afraid of it: hence they protect themselves by stereotyped requests (cf. page 194 Guilhermina, The course). Beginning with the first sessions, some time must be devoted to reading and writing but also attention given to recounted experience which — in the long run — triggers reflection and self-correction.

Most often the foreign workers who begin to attend evening courses have been living in France for a year, sometimes far longer, as if this period were essential for them to organise their life: their attempts to improve means of communication come afterwards. This involves remodelling the French they already use, either by reinforcing their knowledge, or by correcting their errors.

Self-correction. We distinguish two levels of 'spoken language': where the idea is to obtain the most spontaneous expression possible and to foster group relations; and at which it becomes possible to reformulate this collective speech by self-correction.

This procedure, which is also a pedagogical choice, fosters the individual's reflection on what he has said. Often such reflection will result in a different formulation, to get round the difficulty — proof, if need be, that the speaker is thinking of what he is doing, and is reacting in terms of his interlocutor.

The discussion can be 'free' or aided by a 'support', and the initiative can come either from the group leader, or from a foreigner, or even from the group as such.

---

1 The existence was noted of levels of stabilisation which at present appear to be impassable, in the case of certain foreigners who have been in France for 20 years and for whom further instruction is useless, everything else being equal.

Model session. We present a model session, as a guideline and not as a rule for the group leader. It enables both the group leader and the foreigners to rely on a given order, which spares them anxiety. In this way, a tested procedure can be transmitted to the new group leader with as few disadvantages as possible; as soon as the leader feels sure of himself, he no longer needs to follow it: he will arrange its elements in terms of the group reactions, for every group and every group leader is unique.

Stress should be laid on the need to follow the discussion, and hence the digressions proposed by the group, adopting an attitude of listening, though it should also be noted that to intervene in respect of form and not of content does not imply a lack of organisation during the session.[1]

The group leader/foreigner contract. This is an implied contract whose protagonist is the group leader. The fact that, in the course of the first 12 or 15 sessions, the size of the group sometimes diminishes before stabilising thereafter shows that the foreigners have only this inverted, hollow power: that of leaving. The objections that they may formulate concerning method are most often reinterpreted by the group leader as a stereotype on their part, associated with their image of the traditional school. They have to accept things as they are or go away.

There is means then of bringing back into play this excessive power that the teacher has by taking stock of the situation, frequently, with the foreigners, and acceding to their requests, however stereotyped, temperamental and anti-pedagogical they may seem.

There will then emerge a sort of hierarchy within the group, based on indices perceptible only if the group leader is willing not to force the foreigners to be 'students'. Life before migration, the status and the various roles which were theirs in their country of origin, modelled by a type of economy and of social relationships quite different from those of the country of production, enable the group to structure itself after migration also in terms of status and roles. The emigrant who speaks, and who seems closest to the French working class, was often already different from the others at the start. Thus the group (if one listens) emerges, in its own structure, sometimes quite opposed to the hierarchical structures typical, for example, of the French business firm.

The question of evaluation, initiation and social status quo. School is the locus of social initiation, of conformity, for both foreigners and the French; it answers a basic historical concern of industrial society, which is to reduce particularisms and 'unsociable' differences. It alone tends

---

1 Details of the teaching situation will be found in Allain-Dupré et al., 1977.

to have to assign to an individual his place in society.

The teaching offered by the society of production to the foreign worker may be considered in two ways: on the one hand, the teaching of a certain functional technique that improves his productivity; on the other hand, the teaching of an exclusive 'social status quo': the foreigner must adapt himself as he can to 'being different'. While the first type of instruction is expressed rather in the form of content, the second is expressed rather in the form of a 'pedagogy'. The traditional school space is a résumé and mould of the cultural universe of the society of production. An order prevails in it which, properly understood, implies an internalised passivity on the part of the student.

On the other hand, for our purposes, what is involved, more than a learning of the language, is an acquisition of speech. The foreign worker must be able to use daily, according to his own goals, the language of the country of production, and not merely be the possessor of a passive competence corresponding to a scale of linguistic conformity which would merely send him back to a supposed incapacity to produce current speech.

Nevertheless these two functions are closely intermingled in the industrial system; not because the social and the 'scientific' elite are necessarily one and the same, but because the school presents itself as the place where the transition from knowledge to power is (mythically) possible. School is ordinarily experienced as the locus of an individual or collective social ascent. We for our part advise teachers to adopt a different standpoint, reformulating what the foreigners say by reference to linguistic criteria, without judging the content.

The ability to listen to language is the fruit of a personal practical apprenticeship. First of all, it means that the group leader must withdraw to a certain extent; he must also succeed in situating himself in relation to his trainees by recognising the nature of the institutional power he exercises over them and taking into account the personal relations he maintains with them.

We suggest that the group leader adopt a position of 'analyst' which is indeed not a comfortable one. Deprived in the last resort of any theoretical certainty, he will be compelled to make a personal judgement whose degree of irrationality will be tempered only by sensitivity of his listening – or by the reaction of his public.

The role of the group leader. It is on these terms, however, that the group leader, withdrawing from his traditional role as a model, can enter into a true circuit of exchange, and that his speech, being no longer magisterial, will tend to become full, current, and specific.

By 'upgrading' the foreigner's speech, the group leader proposes to him that he should understand and reply, whereas he is usually obliged to repeat and obey. The group leader can only attempt to reduce the irrational part of his judgement by restricting his intervention with the group as much as possible, and by multiplying and refining his analytical points of view.

Discussion places the group leader in a dual position: he leads the spoken relations, and he takes these relations as learning material. Within this dual practice, his role is that of an 'introducer of change' with respect to only a fraction of such speech: its form, and not its content. It is certainly that here all the difficulties lie, and at the same time all the possibilities for evolution of the school institution, and consequently of the concept of school, both for adults and for children, nationals or immigrants.

In this type of leadership, the foreigners will ask, sooner or later, explicitly or not, whether they are expressing their thoughts in conformity with the French language. The leader's role thus gradually shifts from the censuring of ideas to a control of form, and it is only this control that the foreigners have come to seek, at least in so far as we can tell.

Language is a symbolic skill. Here finally is what is to us the crux of the matter and what accounts for the specificity of our entire approach, in both its linguistic and its sociological, anthropological aspects, and the *actions* which follow from it. Everyone learns in his family, spontaneously, from his earliest existence, to speak a language — that of his mother. Such learning is automatic, gradual, without any deliberate recourse by the adults surrounding the child to an instructional technique. That does not mean, however, that the learning is accomplished in a 'natural', 'biological' way. Each culture offers the child games, stories, songs and other activities which are part of the traditional collective memory and whose effect is to introduce the child to the social rules of communication, both verbal and non-verbal.

Little is known of the way in which a child adopts his mother's language, but it is certain that, even more than a mere ability to 'produce sentences' what is acquired is a *symbolic skill*, a certain way of perceiving time and space, an internalisation of the rules governing exchange and communication. It is this symbolic skill as a whole that will subsequently enable him to learn both foreign languages and techniques of graphic representation, including writing. It is this symbolic skill — enriched or atrophied, but omnipresent — that will continue to guide his innermost choices wherever in future he may find himself.

Teaching methods and training

Constraints emerging from the socio-linguistic circumstances of the training. We cannot deal with the whole socio-linguistic situation in the country of residence. We have singled out a few characteristics of the linguistic pressure exerted by the teachers on the group, which cannot, for lack of space, be quoted here. But we can at least indicate our theoretical approach to the systematisation of 'training' as such, and the findings of our analysis.

Having decided to observe the foreign women's expression with a view to reformulations of what they had already gleaned during their presence in the country of production, we accordingly gave preference to listening to their language and to the emergence of their plans. Hence the analysis was done from the foreign worker's viewpoint, or, more modestly, from what our team could grasp through the abundant and multiple speech of the foreign women with whom we were associated during the training cycle. Thus the 'exercises' counselled by findings of applied linguistics were completely subordinated to circumstantial speech. It was not possible to give them (surreptitious) precedence — quantitatively speaking, and with the best intentions in the world — over communication. Hence we respected our methodological choice: discussion.

Nevertheless, it is clear that our choice did not represent a course of action unaffected by the cultural constraints operating on all forms of teaching in the country of residence, whatever character it maybe sought to give them. The training is a proposed mould: however liberal it may seek to be, this mould refers to individual advancement, an individualistic philosophy; that is fundamentally in contrast to the traditional rural culture from which these women came. There seems to be no alternative; this is a school, where learning is institutional and formalised.

That being said, it must be qualified. The countries from which these women came are no longer marked, or are not marked, by an holistic[1] view of the world; they themselves, if only by their departure, withdrew from their native environment and from tradition. By their departure, they expressed a judgement on the state of transition and tension their own countries are experiencing between tradition and modernity, and they also expressed a judgement on their own families, neighbours, milieu and beliefs: they broke from them. One can therefore expect to find in the plans of these women who have left their closed environment: successful combinations of holism and individualism, and unresolved contradictions between holistic and indivi-

---

1 The terms 'holism' and 'holistic', which are repeatedly used in this study, express the idea that the whole is more than the sum of its parts and lay stress on the interdependence and cohesion of the members of a group, in contrast to 'individualism' and 'individualistic'. (Cf. also page 200).

dualistic values.[1]

Consequently, evaluation of the training cannot be monolithic. It will involve both an imposed model, one profoundly alien to certain aspects of their cultural system, and a model desired and received, chosen, under conditions which — even in their contradictions — henceforth incline towards the generalisation of individualistic values.

Thus the basic question that we endeavoured to answer relates to the actual experiences — successes or failures — of this transition from the traditional societies, with many features reminiscent of holistic societies, to individualistic society, with attention concentrated on the combinations that seem successful. Language bears the mark of this.

As the length of presence in France in the case of three of these women was more than ten years (and as Cecilia had already learned a bit of French in Portugal), the distinction between active practice and passive understanding of the language was quite marked.

Though the errors are ingrained (and practically *rebus sic stantibus* unchangeable in the case of Guilhermina and of Mrs B.S.), though they are susceptible of self-correction in the case of Cecilia and of Francisca, it will be seen that this is not the essential point. What emerged from the combined analysis of the practices of leading and teaching — once the content of their speech was made central to the training — was that no appreciable change in their performances was to be expected because the place in society assigned to these women did not require it of them (and because, ultimately, the customary practices in that place would not tolerate it).

The linearity of time. These remarks lead us to the questions relative to external and internal chronology. It does not appear that these women are inordinately concerned by the necessity for time schedules. They refuse to be caught up by the rhythm of obsessive work, and judge it negatively. However, they submit to the time schedules imposed and, as labourers do, attempt to alter them to their own advantage whenever possible (essentially, they attempt to create idle periods and to diminish attendance time).

They have not integrated a historical chronology, linked to dates, which implies a causal sequence: the references are always made to personal experience. Hence it is very difficult to have them situate

1 A word of explanation may be given on the meaning of the term 'closed environment' When considering the country as a whole, it may be wondered whether Moroccan Islamic culture was or was not holistic in the past; the same question in regard to Portugal, on the other hand, may be answered in the negative. But at the local level the situation is often very different: the ideologies of the élites and the history of ideas do not necessarily coincide with those of the comparatively closed local communities, where the population does not directly show the values that are given primacy at the national level. So far as local ethnography is concerned, the traditional local communities often display holistic features.

'objectively' the chronology of their lives: accounts are always in relation to a personal *before* and *after*. At the end of the training there does not appear to have been any change in their general attitude *vis-à-vis* the linear logic traversing the modern world and the country of production. Rather was there a superficial (and satisfactory, from the administrative, formal viewpoint) adaptation to it.

Results of the training. The training made no change in social status or pay. It reinforced among three of the women (Francisca, Guilhermina and Mrs B.S.) the feeling that they had not received enough of it. They now realise, more clearly than before, that they are marginal in comparison to the scholastic careers of natives, for their own led to no social advancement.

In the field of non-institutional social relations, the course opened up no new possibilities of contact with the French population. It made possible only (but that seems important to us) a better elucidation of the various levels of language spoken by natives. (Francisca and Guilhermina confirmed this during control discussions in 1977 by alluding also to reading and use of administrative forms.) Thus as a result of their training they gained some personal advantage, but nevertheless assumed no different role within the groups to which they belong. Those whom they frequent and their 'social spaces' remain the same as before their training. Though Guilhermina, Cecilia and Mrs B.S. continue to frequent only fellow-countrymen on a private, personal basis, Francisca, who was already the informal spokeswoman for collective demands before the training, continues in the same role (and balks at it, as in the past, saying that sometimes she refuses to go and discuss with the employer because she ought not to have to do it every time). Finally, the language training did not affect the social status already assigned to these women: they occupied and remain at an insignificant level in the scale of social consideration.

The social milieu in which these women move not admitting, in its exclusive logic, of any linguistic modification in the self-to-others relation on the one hand, and on the other hand authorising *only* an attempt at modification of the self-to-self linguistic relation, the problems really posed throughout the training cycle were: exploration of the semantic fields of French and their explanation; and sketching of a comparison with the semantic fields of the language of origin. But let us first analyse a pedagogic failure which may provide an explanation to the questions.

Guilhermina is not married but she would like to be; in the course of a conversation, Cecilia says that she talks about things 'often with my husband'; the teacher asks all the women to repeat this nice piece of phrasing; Guilhermina makes a muddle of the syntagma as she uses *com* (the Portuguese equivalent) in place of 'with', immediately afterwards commenting: 'I not have a husband! I talk by myself!'

It is thus evident that her mistake in the second language (with — *com*) involves a problem of psycho-linguistics and that the teacher ought to have taken this into account, since the exercise, with this particular semantic material, *could not be successful* in Guilhermina's case. It is also evident that Guilhermina can use a so-called popular level of language (*I not know* instead of *I do not know*) which is perfectly comprehensible and emerges forcefully when the emotional situation provides stimulus. The mistake in guidance made by the teacher thus provides evidence at the same time that psychology may *hamper* and *assist* the acquisition of the language. The selection of the semantic fields to be exploited consequently depends on the teacher's sensitivity. It will be the teacher's business, linguistically — with some quite different semantic material — to reformulate Guilhermina's *I not have* so as to arrive at the *I do not know* form.

Semantics. Semantic questions assumed very great importance, although they cannot be dealt with systematically in elucidating the relations between group leaders and foreigners and between foreigners among themselves, because in this field, there can obviously be no 'progression' in the scholastic sense of the term. For example, throughout the initial part of the group leading, the question of the *banlieue* (suburbs) was the subject. The idea was to impart to the three Portuguese women the meaning of the term with reference to both their lodgings in France and their lodgings in Portugal.

This procedure essentially involved projection of the socio-centric schemas of the group leaders and, reciprocally, socio-centric rejection by the foreigners. Not only that, but in both cases, and more clearly in the case of the foreigners than in that of the French, there was an interference of affectivity: *here* not being *there*.

What occurs then is that injection of the group leaders' terminology, their obstinacy in seeking to classify old and new zones of habitation, assumes — in addition to the affective colouring — comical aspects of misconception. Francisca wonders how to designate her Cape Verde 'village', lacking paved streets, surroundings, or suburbs — for it consists of neighbourhoods encircling small squares and one main square, while the surrounding housing is dispersed. For her part, Cecilia stoutly insists that the Parisian suburb where she lives *is* the country, for she can see wheat fields from her window and what is more, she considers it an advantage to live 'in the country', as all the real-estate advertising would have us believe. So saying, she uses *more recent* semantics than those of the group leaders who, hobbled by their pro-foreigner miserabilism, still implicitly think of the term *banlieue* in semantic values of workers and the poor. The result of these misappreciations is to be seen in the hypercorrection of Francisca who at one point says 'my village' and immediately, like a good student, corrects herself: 'My *banlieue*, as you call it'.

Finally, the fundamental question is eluded: to systematise on economic inferences series with economic inferences such as 'city, suburbs, municipal housing scheme, private house, furnished room, boarding house . . .' is mentally satisfying work (and within certain limits doubtless useful in terms of language learning); but two series of questions remain excluded. These are the apprehension of French space, at least that of the city, and retreating into 'foreign' space on French soil (cf. page 232).

Under these conditions, even a discriminating presentation of semantics reflects theoretical abstraction, *a priori* teaching in terms of 'supposed needs' (ideologically imposed in terms of schooling and of a uniform linguistic crucible); it does not reflect the foreigners' choices. We on the other hand set out to follow them in their discovery of France and French.

Comparison with the semantic field of the original languages: intelligent — instruit (educated). The question is very similar to that of the example already cited. As a result, it is difficult to circumscribe it well, for the training being done in French (a second language), the foreigners are not *explicitly* asked to sketch a comparison. The latter is subjacent, implicit, and it is hard for the group leader to elicit the facts, owing to his function of teaching French. Thus, to throw light on the pair *intelligent — instruit*, he would have to meet the foreigners individually, outside class, and speak to them in Portuguese, to gather material that would clarify how a complex use in the country of origin became a warped (*déphasé*) use in the second language.

In our case, while the pair *intelligent — instruit* is also known in France, in rural areas or among elderly persons, while the phenomenon of schooling may be considered similar, although asymmetrical, in the two countries, and while we may therefore suspect an analogy in connotation, we must not overlook a particular use of the term *intelligente* in Portuguese, which makes the matter more complex: in the *tourada* it is a matter of understanding and hence of evaluation of style in the combat between man and animal.

It then becomes clear that the way these women apply the *intelligent — instruit* pair in the training course involves semantics *external* to the school system. In connection with the *tourada*, one becomes *intelligent* (or understanding) by taking part, through experience, whereas the teaching received at school is abstract and theoretical. These women thus do not know what are the premises underlying the operation of the school, so that it is scarcely possible for them to learn anything there.

It will take more than 120 hours for the teachers to explain these

181

premises and make them understandable. And are they any better understood by the natives? What is the meaning of such expressions as 'this boy is good with his hands' and 'this boy is intellectually inclined' if not what we have just said? We know that it is this sort of division which determines whether the natives are enrolled in the technical branches of education or in the full length academic course.

The impossibility of overcoming this difficulty plays into the hands of the school, because it suggests those concerned are responsible for their shortcomings in regard to a uniform system of learning that relegates all others to the void of whatever is not institutionalised. So we have the triumph of the verb, and of a specific verb, that of schooling. These considerations introduce the questions relating to language levels.

Language levels, from the viewpoint of values. The question is not so much that of the use of various nuances in dealing with officials, fellow-workers or people considered as inferiors, although these skills are often *requested* by many foreigners (and by teachers).

In this group, it was necessary to fill in certain apparently inexplicable gaps, since they did not correspond to the image the group leaders had formed of the worker milieu (for example, it was necessary to explain the meaning of *pognon* − slang for *money* − though it was thought that these foreigners should have heard it used by their French colleagues. In actual fact these colleagues speak of *argent*, which lacks the pejorative nuance associated with the slang term), but the real question is entirely different.

What is the system in which are inserted these 'old-fashioned' terms in constant use, such as *vicieux, gentil, petites gens, riche*? The problem touches directly upon questions of semantics, naturally, but what of the generally moral colouring that constantly runs through this type of vocabulary and that by its frequency affects the language level?

In our work, excluding − or trying to exclude − any idea of judgement, we attempted to insert this terminology in the modernity − tradition contrast, for it appears to us to correspond to that type of question. The striking example is provided by Francisca's statement:

Changing one's country means changing one's flag

in which the ostensible modernity of the content is contradicted by the stylistic form of the aphorism, which is as traditional as can be (*ubi bene, ibi patria* is its equivalent in our culture).

How are these contradictory 'socio-cultural' elements reconciled in actual experience? That is what we attempt to show when we analyse actual experience to demonstrate the combination − and the interferences − between holistic and individualistic values. However, it would be advisable to devote more specifically historico-linguistic research to this question.

The junction between teaching and training and research: recognising the foreigners in training

To recognise that the teacher's intervention is a reformulation of what the foreigner (or the native) already knows; to recognise that language is 'a symbolic competence'; to make discussion the very basis of the didactic work, considering that the foreigners themselves are the authors of the course, implies of course that one winds up with semantics, but also implies comparison with the country of origin. Foreigners speak of their homeland constantly, for it is the fixed point from which their perception of the new country of residence and of production is organised.

The methods of this comparison, which is often a confrontation, are extremely varied; the conclusions can be very subtle. Within a training cycle, there are often as many opinions as people, so the comparison is not at all homogeneous; hence we also speak of confrontation.

This flow of assumed positions naturally constitutes a singularly rich source of information for the researchers, but there is no question of the teacher using it as such. Not only may he not have the training to do so (that is easily remedied), but he may consider that his work logically should not include a development in that direction. This is altogether legitimate, since the systematisation of such information transcends the primary purpose of the training, which is the guided learning of reformulations of what has been learned without guidance. Finally, though the teacher is not obliged to be a researcher, he is not excused from questioning himself on the references of the foreigners in training, because he must take them into account, on pain of didactic failure.

Concretely, without being a specialist, the teacher then pays attention to what is said *here* in respect of the comparison between there and here. But he retains only what relates to here, for those are his references. However, he does not impede the emergence of what is said in terms of *there*, but, as he is gradually thus informed by the foreigners, he retains it. In this way, he refines his perception of the complexity of what he hears, and he makes of it a cardinal point of his pedagogical relationship. Thus the teacher himself becomes one of the authors of the course, for he is — together with the foreigners — one of the analysts of its content. To put a training programme into practice, he needs to know who the foreigners are who reveal themselves in it as the days go by. While his task is different from that of the researchers (although it is desirable that he collaborate with them), his attitude *vis-à-vis* the facts is not different: he listens while acknowledging that symbolic universes other than his own exist.

The condition of a woman cleaner and the biographical elements which follow are accordingly at the junction between teaching and research: here the practice of the teacher ends, but here also begins the practice of the researcher. It is desirable, and sometimes one can manage to achieve it, for the same individuals to act on both sides of the junction, as in our case.

The condition of the woman cleaner is multiple, the training offered is uniform

Until quite recently, the condition of a 'domestic' was central for a Portuguese woman from the country or even from the poor neighbourhoods of the only two large cities of the country (Lisbon and Porto). To be a *criada de servir* was a possibility, a 'vocation' in the sense which that term had under the old regime, inscribed in the culture of the country.

The case of landowners living in the city, and bringing from the country the daughters of tenant farmers to be *criadas* is the very old model on which was — and is — moulded the present situation of domestic employment (1977), whatever the *milieu* of the employers of today. Traditionally, it provided not only food and lodging, but easier work than that in the fields, and a social rank higher than that of their contemporaries who stayed in the village, or in the insecurity of minor trades and of slums.

A similar situation used to exist in France, and it has not entirely disappeared, even though it subsists only as a relic of times past, which modern ideology generally considers as shameful (see Flandrin, 1975 and Guerrand, 1977). It was the experience of all Portuguese women born between 1940 and 1950, prevalent and apparently immutable, throughout Portugal at the very time when, in 1955 or 1960, already adults, they began to think of emigrating. We stress that this image was general; it was part of the culture, although it had been experienced by only some of the women, for not all of them had this lone prospect. What is more, this 'old regime' moral atmosphere is still (1977) current if not general in Portugal.

Thus, from the traditional viewpoint, it is understandable that many emigrant Portuguese women feel that there is nothing demeaning about employment as a *bonne*, as they continue to say.[1] They demand — and this is a successful combination of traditional and modern traits — that this *work* be properly paid and that they have some free time. Under those conditions, 'it's a job like any other', they say in essence.

Hence it is not surprising that the 130 women cleaners whom we met had practically all begun as full-time domestics living in. They were

---

1 Without using the jüridico-administrative expression 'employeé de maison' ('domestic').

badly paid — as they realised — but they nevertheless considered that such was part of their lot; at the same time they prized (in conformity with traditional values) the atmosphere, which *should have been* that of a family — seeking a set of reassuring rules that should not have been different from those *implicit* in their own country. The case is no different in traditional Italian society.[1]

De-qualification in the new country. Altogether different, naturally, is the situation of female immigrants who never were, actually or potentially, domestics in Portugal! They regard such work 'like the others' as quite demeaning, for (still in the perspective of traditional society) they go down in their own estimation.

Like the first group, they realise that, in France, this is one of the rare types of work available to them on arrival, hence they know that they must go through it to obtain (if they have arrived clandestinely — many of the 130 women in the reference and control groups had been in France for between 10 and 15 years) a work permit. But some of them also remember that, in their own country, they lived at home and never, or rarely, went to other people's houses.

The French transition. Let us consider, in a general way, the stages frequently followed by women from Spain and Portugal who realise they are, and call themselves, 'women cleaners', not being able to recognise themselves in the official categories of statistical tables, basing ourselves not only on the reference population, but also on contacts with the groups trained — within various frameworks — throughout some ten years of teaching.

Being a full-time domestic (*'bonne'*) is the initiation for the girl who has just arrived, does not know the language or customs, must adapt herself, for example, to different cooking (before learning how to do it so that she can aspire to a job with a 'family of quality'), a situation from which she suffers so much that she is reduced to begging for a *'comida portuguesa'* from other women friends. When the obstacles of language have been overcome (partially, but Lurdes, a woman cleaner, speaks better French than her husband, who works for Citroen) and a work permit obtained (or even without a permit if the woman is married, for she then works clandestinely), the full-time domestic servant becomes a cleaner on an hourly basis. If she is qualified for it, she later on chooses the finer sorts of work which she has already done in Portugal (ironing, mending or embroidering) and which immediately

---

1 *Senza Patente*, in which a Sardinian girl in Rome remains a maid for a long time without salary, before becoming a prostitute, See Gavina, 1976, because she is treated as a 'daughter' by the old woman who lodges and feeds her.

classify her as 'household staff' and enable her to frequent 'the rich', in other words, homes where she again finds urbane treatment (not always), the assurance of steady work, remuneration, etc., which are part of the 'traditional' conditions. This, plus an important change: the possibility of working when she wants to which enables her by turns to care for her own children, to take on a steady job and do cleaning on the side; and, above all, the possibility of changing employers; from the 'master' she has in fact slipped to the 'employer', with whom the relationship is essentially monetary and may, on occasion, remain cordial. Thus individualistic values and traditional values are combined, with preponderance given to the former.

However, this situation is unstable, the hourly wages are not very high; frequently there is no social security, for the employers do not declare the woman if she works only a few hours with them, much travel is involved, and (but how much influence does that exercise?) the profession lacks prestige. So there is the following trend towards steady employment as 'service personnel' in a business firm or an institution, or even a complete change of qualification.

(a) Full-time domestic service in the beginning (family)

(b) Domestic on an hourly basis (cleaning or finer work)

(c) Steady job + cleaning (main salary and supplementary income)

(d) Change of qualification

The transitions are not as linear as this implies. Case (b) essentially reflects women whose salary constitutes a supplement to the husband's and who have young children. Probably the time factor must also be added; they have not been long in France and have to compensate for the lack of steady employment by having a large number of contacts, working hard on jobs — no matter what may be asked of them — so as to meet the demands of employers to whom they have been introduced by friends who have already found better work.

Case (c) is typically that of women who have already *chosen* their employer, who put in a respectable number of hours with a single family, possibly even an entire day's work, and who supplement that with hours worked anywhere: offices, or other families. Where work as a concierge or custodian of a building is involved, the difference between the two should be noted: the latter works less than the former, unless he is a man, in which case the opposite is true. (One sometimes finds Yugoslavs.) At all events, there are more outside hours: chosen in the neighbourhood, not too far from the building, or sometimes even in it. Correlatively, the length of presence and ease of dealing are distinctly greater. They know French customs and how to deal with employers.

Still among case (c) one finds service personnel of cleaning enterprises, or those with steady jobs with institutions or factories, or service personnel who have wound up in the staff restaurant and who therefore remain in the sector, but belong to the higher ranks.

In case (d) one finds practically all the women of the Arpajon group. All of them had been domestics in one way or another, but they had then preferred factory work.

The new element in the experience of these women resulted from changing countries. This offers them the possibility of different strategies from those in Portugal (where evolution, when possible, is extremely slow). In France, the labour market for 'domestic help' is extremely mobile. Domestics are few in number and that entails first of all the possibility of living at home and playing the various employers against each other by threatening to leave. This is a new situation which the Portuguese women express well, naively saying that here the 'rich' greet their employees, whereas in Portugal, even when a domestic bows so low that 'she breaks her back in two', it frequently happens that the employer does not even deign to look at her.

However, this change in the relation, linked to an economic situation in which the woman may have more freedom than in the past, still remains an extremely subjective element: it is the way in which it is lived that gives it meaning; it has none in itself. Among the women at Arpajon, there were young and old at the factory — hence the old women had had the courage to start out in a completely new direction — whereas in the institutions of our own population we also find young and less young people who have not dared to make the break. That is because the foreigners must find among the nuns a sort of security that compensates for something; the trauma of migration, solitude, sterility, even though they are no longer 'maids' ('*bonnes*'). It is as though they had reached their level. Naturally, we must take into account those who are going to leave, and in whose case the courses contributed to their departure (to what degree?), but at all events it is clear that this analysis of the four stages of professional life revealed by the courses also brought to light a dual public: the one that endures the situation and the one that uses it as a springboard (for personal plans).

However, the training programmes (even those based on reformulation of the concrete speech of a given foreigner) basically reflect a uniform aim, a goal offered equally to all and sought after *for all*, with an image: 'a language to facilitate free movement'. In reality, the 'circulation' stops, disconnected from the programmes — and from the trainers — at the threshold of personal plans.

From this standpoint, one wonders why the employers pay for this training: Is it lack of analysis of the motivations of their personnel? — Is it an ideological belief in the benefits of further training to consolidate 'social peace' involving conscious or unconscious choices on the part of the employer? Purely theoretical calculations in terms of profitability? Prisoners of the ideology of internal promotion through effort? Means of controlling the 'good elements'?

In the role of both researcher and instructor, one is astounded by the constantly renewed observation that the employers are not interested in the matter, and that they control neither the ideological nor the functional aspects. To be sure, they will watch over the use of budgets, and they will select the training organisations conforming to their political preferences, but that is extremely superficial. The employees are 'doing' training. The function of the training is essentially symbolic and the control infinitely more subtle, for two fields of reference are in opposition: country of residence and country of origin, whose systems of values have nothing to do with one another (cf. pages 180 and 181, and Allain-Dupré et al., 1977 and Catani, 1973).

Biographical elements and personal themes. In the face of the complexity of the migratory situation and of the abstractness of the training proposed when even the employers do not define its reasons or its aims, we must elucidate the pertinent features of the foreigners' individual plans. Methodologically, that will make it possible to proceed with the analysis of sets of typical traits apprehended case by case and to extend them to other migratory situations.

We must, therefore, at the junction between teaching and research, describe the women's experience to distinguish the dichotomy: personal themes on the one hand, and group thematic variations on the other. The personal themes comprise the following items, firstly biographical details (family background, going abroad, work in the new country, marriage, children, housing, possibly health, linguistic or technical training, personal plans) and secondly individual thematic interests. These emerge from the analysis of the recordings made during the training cycle. They are, of course, individual but on many points they correspond (group themes). Since it is impossible to deal equally fully with all these items in the present context, reference will simply be made to some points in connection with Cecilia and Francisca whereas we shall deal at greater length with the information we have about Guilhermina and, to a lesser extent, Mrs B.S. We shall come back later to the themes (page 206) and expand on what is said here.

The plan is apparently quite clear,[1] for Cecilia wants naturalisation

---

1 The category 'plan', based implicitly on the relation of causality and of linear progression — understood in individualistic, modern terms — cannot be applied to Guilhermina or Mrs B.S. although it constitutes the underlying fabric of our description. Our research procedures impose a chronological order on us, but as these two women live their lives outside our frames of reference, they appear elusive when laid on the Procrustean bed of biography — the logical arrival-point of our modern construction — if we limit ourselves to purely descriptive instruments. Thus, while Cecilia and Francisca appear adapted to our cognitive scheme (it will be seen that this must be qualified), the file for Guilhermina ends not with her plans but with a tabular presentation of her thematic interests. Mrs B.S. for her part has no real plan either, so that her case resembles Guilhermina's.

and has applied for it. She considers that her work is a mere supplement to her husband's, and that the latter's choices are determinant for the family as a whole.

Similarly in 1975, Francisca applied for naturalisation, which was granted in 1976. She would like to be a switchboard operator, for she substitutes at the school, or a kindergarten teacher (and she was sharply told, in the French course, that such jobs are not for foreigners — the other women were quite clear in their formulation), or else she would like to be able to set up a dressmaking shop. During the discussion two years after completing the training, she mentioned the possibility of working at a hotel in charge of the cleaning of one floor. She would get that job through fellow-countrywomen. What is certain is that she does not leave the school (1977).

What does she want? Impossible to ascertain in detail, but the general drift is clear: if she asks for French nationality, it is because she doesn't want to retreat, and because it will enable her to duplicate juridically her work-life and her life of relations. She is building her material peace, in order to safeguard the image she has of herself, in order not to let herself down.

Guilhermina, biographical elements and a constellation of themes

Family of origin: Guilhermina was born in September 1919, in a family of 15 children, including 13 girls, in Lisbon. Two twins died in infancy, a sister died of typhoid fever while she was still a child and another sister committed suicide by throwing herself into the garden well. And these deaths occurred before the *'ferma'* was sold and Guilhermina left as a domestic. Thus, in 1975 she was 56 years of age and spoke constantly of her retirement. Her second brother died in 1976. Her father died in 1938, six months after Guilhermina left the family home to begin work. Her mother died in 1956, two months after Guilhermina arrived in Brazil.

Guilhermina emphasises that she is the only unmarried child and the only one to have gone far from home. One sister who has lived in 'the Portuguese Africas' is currently in South Africa with her children, 'though that is still a question of emigration', she says, 'it is nevertheless different'. Another sister was married in the UK, but is thought to have returned to Portugal, leaving a daughter, also married, in the UK. This niece, she thinks, plans to go to California.

In 1976, she quarrelled with one of her sisters living in Lisbon because the sister preferred friends whom she saw more often to her emigrant sister. While she regrets not being married as her sisters are and not having remained in Portugal as a mother and wife, and while she claims she wants to retire in Portugal because her family is there, Guilhermina hesitates to return and wonders whether she can become accustomed again to the old country. At the same time, she says she does not want to leave to her family the four-room apartment she bought through her migration.

School attendance: Guilhermina attended school when she was seven years old for a few months (maybe 3, 4 or 6); though the length of school attendance is not certain, the reason for its interruption is always the same, whatever the versions: the father had to work the land with his daughters' help; he needed many hands because he did market gardening.

Before leaving for Brazil in 1956, at the age of 37, Guilhermina thought she would need to know how to sign her name for such a long trip. She therefore attended evening classes, but to little avail.

So, Guilhermina says, the little she knows — reading Portuguese newspapers — she learned by herself; she says it was in reading a Brazilian newspaper that she saw the classified advertisement that led her to Paris. Her parents were illiterate.

Work in Portugal: Guilhermina began to work at 18 as a domestic servant. She does not say exactly how she found that job; she will only explain that she always served in good houses (those of judges, lawyers etc.) and that in such work she raised the children of a future prime minister of Portugal before leaving to keep house for a Frenchwoman who kept open house in both Paris and Lisbon, or serving as a sewing-maid for an ambassador's wife. She has maintained excellent relations with many of her former employers, so that she has left some of her luggage and personal belongings with one of them for 20 years, and meets another one on familiar terms to ask what she thinks of her retiring in Portugal.

Departure for Brazil and France — Work

Guilhermina left for Brazil with a co-worker who was a *maître d'hotel* and was leaving to join a sister who held out the promise of a good job in Rio, in 1956. She stayed there for seven years serving in the family of a president of the republic and working for several very wealthy foreign families. Her first employment was a disappointment (she lived far from town 'in the mountains' with nothing to eat, in total solitude surrounded by 'wild' monkeys and not in the least disturbed by a human presence). She says no more of the *maître d'hotel* whom she followed, and speaks of the families who live in the chic neighbourhoods of Rio.

During this period she had two accidents requiring hospitalisation, whose costs were assumed by her employers. She twice left one family to serve with another, returning once to the first and once to the second, the first departure following the accidental death of the head of the household, and the return following reopening of the house, which coincided with her release from the hospital.

This coming and going, both in Portugal and Brazil, frequenting of grand houses and quasi-symbiosis with a small circle of families who knew each other and hired the same domestics profoundly marked Guilhermina, though she never really managed to find her place in the system. Though she celebrated her birthday by dining with friends in a large restaurant on the Sugar Loaf, she was never happy in Brazil to the point of buying a house there and putting down roots, as had been suggested to her. She considers that country as wild, inhabited 'by dangerous people who at the least thing kill women who are alone, or rob them. She states clearly that she never considered staying there, but at the same time it constitutes the high point of her life, and has left her with a definite nostalgia.

> Alone at home, I was frightened. I had come down to the street in the morning and found a girl dead there, lying in the street, in front of the passerby! a black girl someone had killed . . . on the promenade! That's why I went to buy the newspaper. That's why I am in Paris.

> I saw that offer of a job, there was Princess de F.L. who was looking for someone who spoke Portuguese to come and speak Portuguese with her daughter. That was the reason.[1]

Guilhermina arrived in Paris in 1962 or 1963, stayed for two years with the princess as a governess for the child, but also as an extra helper when there were receptions (attended by the Queen Mother of England and General De Gaulle). She was in charge of the cloakroom and was given tips, sometimes in foreign currency. Moreover, she has a collection of foreign coins, which she brought back as tangible proof of her travels. Women friends give her other coins.

'The princess was so *mauvaise*! It was a good job, but she demanded too much work! I even called her every name under the sun . . . well, not really, but what did I say to her? That she treated people like slaves!' (1977, translated from the Portuguese. Italicised words spoken in French).

So, at the end of her two-year contract, Guilhermina refused the administrative regularisation that the princess offered her and had her pay her air fare to Brazil. On the stop-over in Lisbon, she consulted an astrologist (for the first and only time in her life, she says):

> He told me that even if I went to France without earning anything, it was still better than going to Brazil. There was a

---

1 In this book, to help the reader, we have reformulated Guilhermina's rather defective French, but the gain in clarity is unfortunately offset by the loss of linguistic information.

woman, a concierge, who lives next to the school (where I work) and I wrote to her to ask if she could find me a job. She asked the sisters and found me work right away, and I have been here for twelve years. I have been here for twelve years, and that is the end of my story.

She later added:

> For me *to change*, it is difficult *to change*. That is why I had many [difficulties] in my work, because *I do not like to change. I used to like to change*, but not now, now I am *old*, I am *old, I do not want to change* (1977).

Guilhermina is responsible for the children's classrooms, which she must clean and mop. She also serves in the school cafeteria.

She makes about 2,000 francs a month and pays 70,000 old francs in taxes each year (she always calculates in old francs), but she rounds out her salary by doing several hours of cleaning in private homes, in particular the home of an inspector of finance who is 'very exacting' but 'good' and who, it appears, does not declare her to the Industrial and Commercial Employment Association.[1] Before coming to the French courses, she also worked part-time for another employer, but she left, either to avoid fatigue and to think of herself, or because she did not get on with the employer.

She has worked for 14 years in France, but has contributed to social security for only some 12 years, because she was not declared while working for the princess.

Thus, she must work for three more years at the school before she is eligible for the minimum retirement pension (15 years as a contribution). She is quite familiar with her rights, but hopes to turn over her file to one of the group leaders of the training organisation, who would know how to maintain it better than she does.

Marriage: unmarried, she pointed out, on a trip to Portugal with the group leader, the houses where her 'sweethearts' had lived. During the courses, she would frequently joke with Mrs B.S., who told her that she could find her a husband. Guilhermina agreed and at the next session asks: 'Well, where is he?' At other times she said she did not want a husband who would allow himself to be kept. Her friend Cacilda reminded her that she still hoped to find a 'coronel', one of those rich Brazilians from the interior, the unchallenged master of farms, villages and entire regions, etc.

---

1 Guilhermina's retirement pension will therefore not be increased in respect of her earnings from this work as it would if she were properly declared.

Children: Guilhermina says she had thought of adopting a child, speaks of a young Maghrebian woman who had offered her hers, points out the difficulties she would have, but in the end concludes that she likes her rest too much for such an undertaking.

Housing in France: Guilhermina lived for several years in a house (belonging to the school where she works) under conditions which were not elucidated. Since 1973 she has been living on the third floor of a residential hotel which, at the time of the training courses, rented essentially to Portuguese; she felt at home there. In 1977 the hotel was deserted by the families she knew and the vacancies were occupied by Africans. She complains of this. Guilhermina protects her privacy and her television from inopportune and excessively prolonged visits; on the other hand, she likes to invite friends, often Cacilda and the latter's friend Henrique, a few sisters from the school and, less frequently, other acquaintances.

She pays some 500 or 600 francs per month, charges included, and complains both of being too hot because the central heating system operates at full blast and of the impossibility of turning it down or merely opening the window, because then she would not get her full share of what is covered by her charges, which she must pay at all events.

Housing in Portugal: in 1973 she bought an apartment in Odivelas at a cost of 40,000 French francs, to which 10,000 francs in costs must be added. One of her nephews, a builder, proposed it to her and is responsible for the finishing, painting, etc., which are in addition to the original cost. Guilhermina refused a long-term loan, and is proud of paying back the entire sum within three years. She is gradually furnishing the apartment with a small table, a *cristallière* (a sideboard with glass doors) for showing her plates and dishes. She is already hoping to change this furniture and is storing provisions, sugar in particular, which she brings back from France on each trip home.

This 'house' is extremely important to her. It would be easier to count the sessions when she doesn't speak of it than to enumerate all those when she compels the group leader and the other foreigners to listen on this subject, if she cannot manage to engage them in a discussion. As early as the second session, she spoke of the apartment, of retirement, and invited the group leader to visit her in Odivelas. However, the apartment, which is the symbol of her success and the justification for her trips, is also the visible sign of the approach of death and of the solitude of retirement that will precede it. Guilhermina wants to live in it, but she also wants to sell it:

> And then, one day, when I am older, *I sell my house*. I'm not going to leave it to the others! [With the money] I'm going

to buy a fine *coffin*. I'm going to buy the case first, I'm going, I'm going to buy the land ... there in the cemetery. I had an employer in Portugal and when he killed himself, before he killed himself, he bought the case, the urn ... the thing there, in the cemetery. But I don't want to kill myself. I want God to give me many more years to live ... But, I want ... to live! I'm not going to leave my house for my friends, for my family!

I am often alone here in Paris, and I think: 'Will I get used to it back there? To stay for a few months, yes; but to stay forever: I don't know!'.

Health: Guilhermina is rather stout, eats a lot and likes sweets. She has high blood pressure and poor circulation. Quite often, she suffers from bronchitis; muscular exertions are said to have 'put a bone out in her back', forcing her to bed for a long time. She has also had sciatica and injured her foot on a pilgrimage; the injury was very slow to heal, although she consulted both French and Portuguese doctors, as well as 'quack' healers. Her sight is not good, she has eyeglasses for presbyopia that she doesn't wear (out of vanity or shame).

The course: Guilhermina wants 'to learn everything well' and first to speak, but also to write: as early as the second session, she brought along a book, so that the image of the school she was attending should conform to tradition. Two years later she had not changed opinions: she says there is no one to encourage her, in the evening, to do her copying from her numerous French cookbooks. That means that, during class, she resigned herself to discussion leadership, but somewhere inside her the traditional image of school was not fulfilled. Did she make progress? Certainly in reading, but very little, or none at all, in writing.

At our last discussion, in 1977, two years after completion of the training cycle, she also repeated what she had said at the beginning sessions: 'When one is old, one doesn't learn' and in the same stride, 'to learn, much more time is needed than what we have'.

It seems clear that it is not learning *per se* that interests Guilhermina, but the fact of participating in an activity which, despite everything, proves that she is not the last (she reproaches her Algerian and Portuguese co-workers for not attending the courses) and — above all — that she is still *living*, because she has embarked on a new journey. What she wants to read are French cookbooks. 'Oh yes! that's why. That book there, there are lots of recipes and I keep (*guardo*) everything. So when I am in Portugal, I will go say to those *madames*: "Ha, I can do French cooking" '.

Table 4.1

A constellation of themes of Guilhermina

Marriage	Money and work	Death
adoption	food	health
solitude	travels	old age
	television	religion
	radio	pilgrimage
house	house	house
separation from	house as	house as
the paternal home	monument	cenotaph

Mrs B.S. and her plan: Mrs B.S.[1] does not speak of returning to Morocco: 'I live from day to day', she says, without specifying any plan.

The person of Mrs B.S. is of key importance in our study, being constantly at odds during the training: she was the negation of the institution, of its rituals, of its aims, and of the methodology adopted. For, however liberal it aims, the approach of *La parole de l'autre* is one of instruction, the key to which is reformulation. This is possible provided the discourse is, if not sensible, at least conscious that it must tend to have a meaning: that of learning (improving) the standard language of the country of production and residence.

None of this was true of Mrs B.S., who came to play with the hours of training as she played with her watches, constantly taking them out of her bag and putting them back in, pretending not to understand the discussions, not understanding them in fact for a while, and then letting fly a sharpened arrow indiscriminately at her interlocutor or at the theme of the discussion, de-structuring one or the other; or de-structuring herself.

Sociological discourse, even open to the diverse possibilities, had no hold — or rarely did — over her 'antics'. But that is not to say that they had no meaning. Quite the contrary! Mrs B.S. often provided us with a far more enlightening key to a *comparison of societies* than the three

1 We say 'vous' systematically to the foreigners for obvious reasons (and never say 'tu' to them until real reciprocal familiarity reigns). However, both they and we soon call each other by our given names. The case of Mrs B.S. is entirely different; she will always be entitled to special treatment: the reasons are complex, as will be seen, but they revolve around her deliberate *choice* of severance which we respected. We point out that this was not due to any disagreement; the group leader frequently invited Mrs B.S. to her home, for example.

other women from the politically Portuguese world — and she provides the material for the conclusion of this study.

Mrs B.S. is the irruption of a reality, structured according to other values, other acts, other choices, from a local environment still often holistic (although tending by great strides towards modern values) which obtrudes itself on the country of production and of residence by reflecting back its own image. It was Mrs B.S. the ethnologist, come from elsewhere, who was addressing herself to our system. And her experience (derisible in the eyes of our science) questions our science at the very roots of its epistemology, of its philosophical *raison d'etre*, and compels it to take the *comparative dimension* of itself: the ideology of modernity, and unmastered effects of that ideology.

It may be thought that this is already common knowledge; up till the present our civilisation has gone to other civilisations to study them with the leisure and the screen of distance, but Mrs B.S. was among us, and, with her, millions of immigrants who impose their differences, whatever the training programme one may offer them in the hope of resolving our internal contradictions and making them duplicates of ourselves.

What these four biographies reveal (as do the personal themes, as we shall see) is that it is impossible to trace the boundaries between the economic and symbolic reasons which prompted the departure of these four women. Everything is tied up in the family which is both a production and a reproduction unit, biologically as well as culturally, a unit of confrontation and conformity in its relations with the community of origin. In the case of Cecilia, her father's death led to the abandonment of her studies and to her departure, further prompted by the fact that her brother had already left. *But* her mother returned to Portugal, and offers the new couple the economic possibility of building a house: though she wants to be naturalised in France, her husband hesitates as to where to locate the home (see Catani and Mohamed, 1973, p. 171). Francisca for her part, not having a husband, goes off to Senegal, leaving her son in her mother's care; she will have her mother join her, and will become a French national. But she is certain her brothers and sisters will stay in Portugal. Thus it was not materially impossible to remain there. In Guilhermina's case her departure from home coincides with abandonment of the land by her family; her father's death can only precipitate its necessity. But she claims she is the only one to have left for good (and it is the researcher who must qualify this, adding that there were a few other emigrations to former colonies; nevertheless, it is clear that, remaining in the Portuguese 'world', those were not true departures). For her part, Mrs B.S. a soldier's widow, unable to love, or be loved by, her son, reduced by her widowhood to being the family servant if she conformed to tradition, preferred to leave, earn her living, waiting for a hypothetical military pension to come to her. But she has in her home country a social locus: if she leaves, it is because certain traditional symbolic values of her culture no longer mean anything to her, and because she has acquired other modern ones.

This is the heart of the matter: initially there are economic motives but the decision is affected also (in ways that vary from one empirical situation to another) by the de-structuring of the old symbolic system and the attendant appearance of other values. Tension produces the decision to leave. And the problem that these women (and emigrants in general) have to solve is not fundamentally economic,[1] though that factor is necessary, but rather of a symbolic nature. It consists of a change in the system of values wherein they would have to reconcile the idea itself of the possibility of a departure and the awareness that, in the former order of values, leaving was not even conceivable. That explains sufficiently why the linear and sectorial logic of the training programmes generally winds up in failure which cannot be dealt with in purely economic terms.

Comparative sociology

Ordering the cleavages through analysis

'Changing one's country means changing one's flag also', said Francisca, and the other women approved, or let it go unchallenged.

It was around this remark that our analysis was organised. Not that we had not, from the start, suspected this pivot between tradition and modernity which made the apparently most material references strange and unrecognisable; but Francisca gave it utterance. 'Everything has to be changed', said she in effect, taking as a formal token the symbol itself of the modern state, of the nation-state: the flag. But she poured this adherence to the values of modernity into the most traditional of moulds: the stylistic form of the proverb.

From the very first day the group in training was beset by tensions to which the teachers were unable to apply their Western causal logic, implying a linear explanatory model based solely on the principle of non-contradiction. Listening to the foreigners, it was impossible to reduce our perception of them to the point of regarding them simply as people progressing towards a cultural universe – the one in which we share – where the tensions, imbalances and contradictions of their *choices* would have been explained solely by the concept of transition

---

1 The question is too broad to be dealt with here, but (a) Guilhermina's mistake apropos of the Portuguese 'world' clearly shows that it was not a question of emigration in the modern sense of the term; (b) the case of Africans sent by older generations to earn money is a modern one, consequent on colonisation, but it also involves a mingling of values.

and transitional periods. These people were simultaneously balanced and unbalanced, both individually and as a group; they were in transition and in a state of permanence. They were within *their own* system of values where not only the linear logic of causality but also symbolic logic comes into play. Within these systems, levels have to be distinguished, choices ordered, and prime values reversed. This is an hierarchical logic (cf. Dumont, 1980).

Let us point out, to forestall the objection, that these cleavages far transcend the personal cases of these four women, and are not exceptional. Quite on the contrary, they are symptomatic of the problems posed by all foreigners in similar situations.

The work of observation in depth which we undertook (supported by like observations in similar groups) has a general significance, for it touches on the key situations which *all* first-generation foreigners encounter and to which they must find an answer. The training programmes should not hamper that.

Cleavages in directly observable facts. There are different sorts of cleavages. To begin with, cleavages were observed in the group: a man, who soon disappeared, was expelled by this female group, wherein only four 'students' — including three women — corresponded to the superabundance of women group leaders! He was no less qualified than Guilhermina or Mrs B.S. (who would join the group later) and so could have stayed. But he was a man, a Portuguese, and *perhaps* (we know nothing for sure about it, not having heard him say so) the constant 'chattering' was not for him. This was the first cleavage.

A second cleavage was represented by the degree of adherence to the institutional values of school: Francisca and Guilhermina, in different ways, believe in school, in its function of promotion: for them, we are still in the 19th century, with its values of personal advancement through effort, and the purest effort, the most consoling, is that of instruction.

But Cecilia embraces the values of the 20th century. To her, school is a means of promotion like any other, if one can manage to use it without tiring oneself too much, and without believing in it. She quite realises that, even with a diploma in her pocket, the road to social mobility will not open up for her: believing in the primacy of economics, she 'desanctifies' the institution of school and does not conceive that one could devote actual efforts to it, feel overwhelmed by it, or guilty about it.

In respect of this cleavage, Mrs B.S. is used for support: she sometimes arbitrates the discussions, plays with the material tokens of the situation, claims a status — that of pupil — without conforming to it, however. She does not know what to ask of the institution.

The third cleavage is between those who want to become French nationals and the one who clings to her own nationality. Francisca and Cecilia want to become French. Guilhermina asks Cecilia why her husband doesn't go back and settle in Portugal now that the dictatorship has fallen (25 April 1974). And when she learns that Cecilia doesn't want to have a house built in Portugal, but in France, she reproaches her for it.

In respect of this cleavage, Mrs B.S., who no longer has any particular place in Morocco, says nothing and spends her vacations in France, going to formerly fashionable summer resorts, and says that she has not been back to Morocco for eight years. She does not know how to situate herself *vis-à-vis* a definitive choice between the two countries, but she lives in one choice: that of her foreign enclave in the 14th district of Paris.

These cleavages are complex: though Guilhermina and Francisca are on the same side *vis-à-vis* school, they are on opposite sides regarding naturalisation. Though Cecilia opposes Francisca regarding school, she is on the same side in favouring France. And though Guilhermina looks down upon Mrs B.S. for having no place in Morocco, they are together in opposing Cecilia and Francisca, who favour integrating with the logic of the country of residence and who admit in a measure far larger than themselves the individuation of its political, administrative fields — abstraction of the relations formalised by institutions founded on the impersonality of modern individualism (Declaration of Human Rights).

Cleavage in values revealed in conversation. But to these initial cleavages, quasi-objective because related to the external (naturalisation — maintenance of nationality; values attributed to school), still other cleavages exist within the individuals themselves, and come to light in their conversation.

In this connection, Francisca's position is the most significant among those of the group, because it is the clearest: she exhibits individualistic values, and lives traditional, holistic values. It is in her that we find with the greatest clarity the combination or juxtaposition of the two types of values.

She represents two worlds:

1 That of her childhood and of the living body, the sea, the sun, the warm sand, the games with other children, work in common, the houses in a circle sheltering the open-air dance of the *entire* village, the set pieces in the holiday season (traditional cakes made only once a year), the friendly relations within the group, and the social groups clearly defined by their rank in the society as a whole. (The interval at Dakar is of the same type: the people are kind to each other, help each other.)

2 That of emigration to France, where all is work, overtime, solitude, pecuniary relationships, difficulty of material perception and comprehension in relations mediated by abstraction ('To work is to die', she says).

Her choice of naturalisation, of the French language for her son Alex, of schooling for her two children (which she says is far better than in her country of origin) is the apparent negation of the difference between the two worlds through the channel of a definitive choice. It is true that her choice is 'rational' (for 'here the government really helps parents; it's not the way it is there'), but it is partial.

Francisca takes great care of herself, she does no overtime, she goes dancing only when the following day is a holiday so she can rest; on Sundays, she stretches out on the lawns of the Trocadero with her fellow countrywomen; she goes off with them to visit her brothers and the Cape Verde Islands immigrant colony, in Amsterdam. And while school is the means of promotion (if not for her, at least for her children, who are their mother's pride and whom she would never have consented to abandon), she also says that A. Cabral was killed by one of his schoolmates, in whom he confided; that is a crowning horror in treachery, in ambivalence. If his schoolmates killed him, the horror is in the seesaw play between the holistic values of age class and the individualistic value of schoolmates.

It is not surprising that Francisca expresses the change by a proverb: she combines, or juxtaposes, two types of values. And preponderance of one sort over the other is dictated by circumstances; there is no linear logic, but a symbolic, hierarchical logic, in her actions. Her way of answering the linear logic ideologically imposed by our modern civilisation is to separate her French professional experience from her Cape Verdian experience. The guiding line is that of her childhood values which, however, she gave up trying to explain clearly in the training cycle. It is only when the pressure of affect or the repeated accounts of actions impose them that she alludes to them. In that, she is the perfect example of all the values that continue to run, under the surface, through all successful migration.

Tradition-modernity, holism-individualism. These cleavages, contradictory because manifold, need to be ordered, if not explained. For that we shall use the two major ordering categories offered us by the comparative sociology of Dumont (1977).

The West (however one seeks to define it) is a civilisation of an individualistic type which found its theoretical apogee in the *Declaration of Human Rights* (although of course this is only the formal expression of older ideas and was far from being actually achieved).

In this civilisation characterised by values of liberty and equality, every man is philosophically considered as representing the very essence of humanity, irreplaceable, unique and at the same time universal. The ultimate aim of an individualistic society is this free and equal man. Hence change is established as a value.

Altogether different are the holistic societies (India, China, etc. where one sees that the West is a reality in itself when compared to other civilisations, the best example being India). In this society, the needs of the individual (his happiness) are subordinated to the values of society; it is the social community, and not the individual, which has a reality. In this type of societies, what is privileged is order, conformity of the groups and their members to the overall social purpose. The social values are, fundamentally, hierarchy and subordination (which is not submission, but adherence to ultimate values). Society is not defined by equality, but by rank. The ultimate values are religious (or at all events philosophical), and they form a system providing an explanation of the world in which man is in the world, and not confronting it. Hence the stability.

In an individualistic society, a distinction must be made between 'the empirical agent of speech, thought and will, indivisible sample of mankind (which I call for analytical clarity the particular man, and which is found in all societies or cultures); and the independent, autonomous and thus (essentially) non social moral being, as found primarily in our modern (common-sense) ideology of man and society' (Dumont, 1965).

This man, both moral and empirical, is essentially oriented towards things, substances, the contract in determinate time and on determinate subjects. Thus he values material wealth precisely because it harmonises logically with the values of liberty and equality, since it implies only loose connections with individuals.

On the other hand, in a holistic society, though an empirical man (who suffers, enjoys, attaches himself to substances, etc.) must be recognised, an independent and autonomous moral being cannot be recognised. Rather one recognises in it the member of a community whose social destiny and function are established in advance in the framework of ultimate values. A member of a community exists only in terms of the community.

The result is that, in conformity with the values of hierarchy and rank, the privileged relations are those which connect individuals. Substance is not privileged, but rather the respective situation of groups and consequently of members. Thus, the concept of wealth in itself as a value' is unknown (whereas empirically of course it is perfectly situated), and the question is above all one of privileged relations between men in relation to material acts (e.g. the multiple rights to land, which is the place wherein groups are rooted). The encompassing values that give coherence to the whole are religious (or philosophical), and the juridical, political, economic fields have no autonomy, for they are only elements subordinated to ultimate ends. Thus, even in the 'empirical' case of revolt, peasant uprisings, what must be restored are the ultimate values, and the principle of cohesion is, in most cases, religious: the case of India is exemplary.

Let us stress that these distinctive features (holism-individualism; equality, liberty-hierarchy; relation to individuals-relation to things) are not linear oppositions on the same plane. Were that so, we would still reason within a single frame of reference − our own − opposing the collective to the individual. Such is not the case. It is a question of two systems, two representations of the essence of man, which exclude each other, which have no logical connection, and which accordingly can only be compared on the basis of the most frequent type of civilisation, the least exceptional, the holistic type.

It follows, then, that this fundamental difference prohibits any nostalgic utopia of a retreat towards a holistic Western society. Even if such a society had existed in the West − in however imperfect a manner, as in the France of the old regime, for example (cf. A. de Tocqueville) − it must be noted that Christianity, from the outset, gives rise to an altogether different situation placing importance on the moral individual.

But to pose these differences is not everything. It must also be seen that every society includes, alongside fundamental holistic or individualistic features, traces of the other series of features. This is necessarily so, methodologically speaking, for otherwise comparison would be impossible; indeed, it must be postulated that all societies contain the same 'elements' or 'factors', it being understood that the 'elements' may appear in each case (to a greater or lesser degree of importance). Thus they will be in each case either S (substantive) or a (adjective), and hence are profoundly altered by their position.

This latter condition naturally deprives the elements of all reality save for the reservation that $S + a$ = constant. This amounts to saying that one must always find in a society what corresponds residually (as a) to what another society differentiates, articulates and emphasises (as S).

(Adaptation of Dumont, 1980, p. 296, note 118^d.)

This defines the limit for the present research. These foreign women come from traditional (strongly holistic) societies and face a fully individualistic society. More precisely: the holistic societies of origin differ from each other, either because in the case of Cecilia and Guilhermina, although the same country (Portugal) is involved, the age, local community of origin and past experience make of these two women, from the start, two individuals dissimilarly related to their groups of origin; or because in the case of Francisca, the Cape Verde

Islands represent a society in itself, by reason both of its insularity and of the colonial and racial situation; or yet because in the case of Mrs B.S. the society is that of rural Islamic Morocco.

These traditional societies are far from homogeneous: they combine and juxtapose holistic and individualistic features, if only through their colonisation on the one hand and the monetisation of relations on the other. It follows that none of these women can represent uniformly holistic or uniformly individualistic values. Hence it is not possible to oppose tradition and modernity by substantiating them. Not only do they carry with them the combination or juxtaposition of features peculiar to their groups of origin, but they must face and resolve combinations and juxtapositions peculiar to the new country of residence and production, as well as changes within their own country.

Thus it is obvious why one finds these multiple cleavages. What we shall attempt to do is show that the cleavages can first be reduced comparatively: to the presence of traditional holistic features; and thereafter to the combination (successful) or juxtaposition (unstable and contradictory) of holistic and individualistic features which are superordinated or subordinated in the new country, according to circumstances.

The advantage of using these two elements of comparison is that it respects the complexity of reality – its 'multiplexity' – without rigidifying in a uniform (and socio-centric, Western) scale alternated movements in which holistic and individualistic values predominate for a time under different circumstances. That enables us to bring to light, as far as possible, the delicate mechanisms of synthesis employed by these women in order to live out their situation as immigrants, which includes the dimension of ambition, but not exclusively, for it also includes the presence of rank.

Finally, note that when we indicate that the personal and social strategies reveal a hierarchisation of values as a procedure in making choices in respect of given actions, we emphasise the logical necessity of the presence of hierarchy in society and in any human group. The real issue in this analysis does not lie in the impossible holistic definitions of country of origin, but in the alleged co-existence of contradictory levels of experience in these women; the women in fact organise them hierarchically.

When one speaks of hierarchy in the usual sense one has in mind the military hierarchy, linear and solely descending. Such is not the case in hierarchical logic, which is not based on submission, but on agreement in respect of ultimate aims, and in which the primacy of relations between men produces reciprocity and the symbolic necessity for the presence of other groups according to the ranks assigned. However, the subordination or superordination of ranks varies according to circumstances, in an *explicit* manner. Subordination and superordination are based on agreement and interdependence in respect of ultimate ends, which both de-structure hierarchical relations and make them necessary by reconciling the opposites at the same time.

It should also be mentioned that, in our society, the logical necessity of hierarchy, which nevertheless exists in everyday life, is misconceived and reduced simply to a chain of command, because our cardinal values are liberty and equality and thus rule out the subordination of the part to the whole in society. In consequence, it is difficult to present the hidden and therefore pernicious presence of hierarchical logic in an individualistic society in explicit terms because that would presuppose careful consideration, case by case, of whatever has to be distinguished (to be subordinated or superordinated) by reference to a *social* whole recognised as being superior and therefore the source of order.

More visible in the case of foreigners, but present also in the native population, this de-structuring — and the multiple aspects it assumes — is then generally felt as a relegation apart, non-participation in social life, and hence condemned as abnormal behaviour, as a false consciousness: one thus fails to see that it exists, determines choices, and constitutes a system.

It is the contemporaneous existence, itself hierarchised, of two systems that our conclusions will illustrate: the traditional system explicitly (albeit diversely) lived through by the four women (and many immigrants), and the modern negation of the system, peculiar to the new country, which nevertheless imposes its implicit hierarchy, scaled down and concealed.

The ethnography of biographical elements. It may be objected that the transition from the empirical individual (his psychology) to his quality as a member of a community (his sociology) is difficult. Though in our procedure the question is resolved logically because the empirical individual is moulded by society and even his individual choices can be analysed as acts within a given cultural framework, the fact remains that we are dealing with immigrants cut off from their countries of origin, and that we listen to them in an individualistic framework (the course) which cannot but influence them.

Guilhermina spoke of both husband and marriage. The theme of the husband (of man in general and of solitude) is obviously her own theme, the one in which her choices, however culturally determined they may be, are her own and belong in the final analysis to her own chronicle, quite different in that respect from the chronicles of Francisca and Cecilia. However, when she speaks of marriage being broached at a dance, of the proper clothes, of the games and the ceremony, when she highlights the respective status of the man and the woman in this regard, when she defines what a good husband is, contrasting him with a bad one, when she compares the cultural customs of men in Brazil, Portugal and France and the other women second her, values emerge which are not peculiar to her. This illustrates our procedure and why we speak of cultural features. It follows that: beyond the personal empirical input (which undoubtedly colours the situation) there appear values, complex and contradictory, which relate to the total ideological functioning of the group and of the population to which it belongs: we then have a set of cultural features.

In this work, the characteristics of the transition from the empirical personal to the social are hence twofold:

1 Emergence of speech in terms of values (whose forms may be more or less clearly normative or preferential, as in the case of wedding clothes; or again very often comparative, as in the case of the 'good husband' in whom are combined characteristics garnered from different countries) — *features of a culture*;

2 the reply by the interlocutors, confirming that the speech thus attains to general significance even if (and sometimes especially if) the discussion is contradictory — *set of features, several cultures*.

In reality, the system of social values, especially in the case of migration, is never exhibited in a coherent ensemble of propositions as it would be in a religious or philosophical text. On the contrary, it is fragmentary and contradictory because allusively recalled apropos of actual experience. However, since the one speaking wishes to lend coherence to this actual experience (to justify or explain the choices being spoken of at the moment), the ambivalence of the social norm is thus exploited to the said end, to rationalise the empirical facts.

It is only by comparison both internal (speech of the individual) and external (the replies of the interlocutors) that the personal and social strategies tracing the moving contours (non-univalent and yet logical) of the hierarchisation of values as a procedure in making choices in respect of given actions are revealed to the researcher (provided that the available material comprises a sufficient number of occurrences or is spread over time).

Hence one cannot afford to omit a fine and detailed analysis of personal choices (even though in the present report it will not be completely set forth) if one seeks to apprehend social values in their application to daily life.

This observation introduces the second series of reasons justifying the presence of biographical elements: the sociological richness of the group.

In the Portuguese field, we have the representatives of two sets of typical features, transcending the individual case, of migration: the immigrants whose ambitions constantly tend towards the country of origin, however long their stay (Guilhermina); and the immigrants whose ambitions tend towards the country of production and residence (Cecilia).

The case of Francisca is significant of the difficulties that must be resolved once the orientation is towards the new country. She demonstrates the real complexity of the choice.

In this perspective, Mrs B.S. combines the typical features of immigrants for whom it is impossible to orient their ambitions towards the new country, because — for reasons different or even opposed *inter se*, if they are examined case by case — the natives refuse to recognise them as equals and they themselves do not ask to be so recognised.

Themes

Themes and values. The following is a more detailed discussion of what was outlined on page 188. Determined by both material constraints and the aspirations of the individuals, the migratory experience will be organised in space/time terms around the plan for life.

1 *Spatial axis*: the plan may tend towards the 'country of origin' pole or the 'country of residence' pole, or yet oscillate between the two;

2 *Temporal axis*: the plan evolves through time.

The here/there relations (past-present-future) result from the confrontation between two systems of values with which the individual is faced and in which he makes choices (voluntary, by hierarchising what is possible and impossible, desirable and undesirable). Account being taken of the characteristics of the country of origin and those of the country of residence, these two systems are ordered around tradition on the one hand and modernity on the other. It is from this permanent interaction of oscillations, ambivalences, conflicts, renunciations, rejections or adherences that the plan will be formulated. It will adapt itself in terms both of the subject's internal dynamism and of external dynamic factors. We shall attempt to apprehend and order the women's speech by addressing ourselves to their own themes.

Cecilia, who says 'I am ambitious' will enable us to grasp the dynamics of change and of integration. Francisca, who says 'I am nothing', will enable us to see how integration is in fact organised, and the price that must be paid to achieve it. As for Guilhermina, the same coherent presentation is impossible; either one must refer to the biographical elements and observe the mere succession of facts; or else, if we wish to grasp the interconnection of choices, we must perceive her in her desire for travel.

Neither can Mrs B.S. be placed within the framework of this modern conceptualisation, not only because, as a Moroccan, she is marginal in comparison to the other women, moulded by Western culture, but because she never recognised herself in their speech. At the level of personal themes we thus have nothing to say of her, for that would require a different study; we can only publish a text, to indicate that she exists. But it is she who, in coming from elsewhere and observed by us from the outside, will provide us, through her radically foreign practice, with the bases of our conclusion. The outsider is absorbed by ourselves but also enlightens us about ourselves in our effort to distinguish between the universal and the particular without renouncing either.

Personal themes

CECILIA: 'I am ambitious'.

The individual experience of Cecilia is to be situated in the global context of Portuguese emigration and in the more specific framework of female Portuguese emigration (Rocha-Trinade, 1973).

The historical circumstances (migratory currents already well established, an initial Portuguese immigration having occurred at the time of the 1914 War and the present flow having assumed very important dimensions since 1965) introduce among the possible choices open to the individual (limited choices) the 'possibility' of emigrating, it is part of the 'landscape' of customs, and can orient the life plan.

Her decision to emigrate followed upon the loss of her employment in Porto. Hence there was an economic necessity, but that was not the sole determining factor. The choice is bound up with a project of mobility which itself is linked to the social function of the family and the place which Cecilia occupies in it. The children are a generation in ascending mobility, compared to the parents.

Her brother and sister, both married, emigrated; her father died. The family no longer has a social locus in Portugal. The result of this set of factors is that departure is imposed on Cecilia. She is then 20 years of age and unmarried. By emigrating, she hopes for both personal and professional fulfilment. The departure is no adventure, for it is organised by the family: she is accompanied by her mother, and her brother will receive her and find her work.

(a) Professional fulfilment. She first works in dressmaking, later in a printing firm and at the time of training had been employed for a year as cook's helper and cleaning woman. Thus we are far removed from the initial project ('I was quite sure that in France I could be a secretary'). Work as a domestic is to her a real come-down, for which she consoles herself by thinking of the extra income that can be made from it.

In addition to her salaried work, she does cleaning on the side at an office located in the building where she lives. She is paid for an hour and a half but manages to finish in half an hour. Through this activity, she calculates that she thus manages to reduce her actual rent from 700 to 400 francs. When the other women remark that her rent is high, she points out that 400 francs is all it actually costs her.

She would like not to have to work. That wish is related both to failure of her initial plan and also to the function she performs and the social status corresponding to it: 'Occupations that are looked down on are like us, women cleaners, dustbins too . . . '.

Cecilia is dissatisfied with the situation she occupies. She feels a certain bitterness and at the same time is developing a certain combativity in regard to exploitation. She knows her rights and demands that they be respected, she wants to know about unions and claims that wages should be higher in her sector. She specifies that French nationals and immigrants should be paid at the same rates.

Cecilia's dissatisfaction only increases in the course of the year and she considers leaving her job during the vacation period, for she emphasises the experience she has of factory work.

The training cycle, in her opinion, will not lead to access to a more qualified occupation (the ideal job being the one she lost in Portugal, where she was employed as a secretary in an office). She does not believe in promotion through instruction. She feels doubly excluded because of her situation as a woman and as a foreigner.

Thus it is through the professional success of her husband that Cecilia seeks to fulfil her aspirations: 'My husband, he has a good position. He has a qualification. And then his boss, no not the boss, because he is his own boss, the trimmers don't have a boss, well there is one who is the boss of the others, well he likes my husband'.

Cecilia is flattered by these good relations; for example, the boss was invited to their marriage and she invites him to their home. Moreover, her husband is the union representative of Force Ouvrière, after having been a member of the Confédération Générale de Travail:[1] Cecilia speaks of this change in terms of promotion, of a voluntary choice.

But the relations to bosses are ambiguous: she condemns practices of favouritism by the nuns who employ her, whereas her husband is favoured in the same manner by his boss. Thus in the wedding photographs that she shows to the group she indicates: My husband's 'master' ['maître'], the one who taught him to work as a trimmer.

This is naturally to be viewed as the prolongation of traditional relationships (the term 'maître' indicates this) in which interpersonal

1 Cf. footnote on page 170.

relationships largely transcend the professional framework and have a strong affective and status colouring. Thus the juxtaposition is obvious at the level of values, and at the level of material facts the synthesis appears impossible: 'He likes his boss, but his boss can sack him just like the others'. This, strictly speaking, would be unthinkable in a traditional social structure.

Unable to achieve her professional aspirations, Cecilia wants to see her husband provide for the family's economic position and status. She considers her own work not as a value (which would place her totally on the side of modern society and its individualistic values) but as an economic necessity (which makes her individualism a juxtaposition of traditional and modern features, the latter more accentuated than the former).

(b) Personal fulfilment. Single on arrival, she married in the country of production. She quickly met a Frenchman who wanted to marry her: 'But I didn't marry a Frenchman because my brother wouldn't let me marry a Frenchman'.

The relation with a native thus constituted to the brother a transgression, and as the older brother substituted for the father, Cecilia acquiesced. Though that is 'coherent' in relation to the brother's values (and in general to male and female functions in the society of origin), it goes without saying that it destroyed something in Cecilia's migratory project, related to ascendant mobility and the image of France, 'better' than Portugal: 'If it were now, I wouldn't let my brother tell me what to do. I have my rights, I know that now. But before, I was living in his house, he found me work . . . '.

She then met a Portuguese at a dance, they had sexual relations, which constitutes, in the particular case concerned, another transgression and must be redressed. Virginity had not been safeguarded, but Cecilia wanted to make it appear that it had been by getting an abortion. She does not succeed in doing so and is married when three months pregnant.

Is it so certain that 'were it now' she would act against her brother's order? The discrepancy between her speech and her choices could not be more present than in Cecilia's account.

The marriage ceremony was performed in France by a Portuguese priest; Cecilia had sent wedding announcements to Portugal that mentioned only the ceremony at the town hall, and that provoked a scandal. The adoption of French behaviour was bound to disturb the traditional order, however de-structured it might be by migration. Reputation was necessary, with supporting evidence.

She entrusts her child to her stepmother's care: though that is traditional behaviour in France, it is modified by a new relation to money. Cecilia pays her 270 francs a month for looking after the child who, at two years of age, has still not been baptised. They can't decide whether to have it done in France or in Portugal. On the whole, Cecilia has broken with tradition (which she constantly transgresses, so that the values no longer form a coherent system). But, incapable of assuming, of interiorising, this break, she submits, or tries to sidetrack issues. In the final analysis, it is through her children and the education she will give them that the break will be consummated: 'Some day, my son, he will want to marry a French girl. I'll let him. Black or white, I don't care . . . My mother, she didn't say how one should do, so like that [I got pregnant]. Well, when I have a daughter I will do like this: I will show her the words, and tell her there is this and that, you are starting out'.

This attitude obviously brings to mind that of Francisca faced with her elder son's wish to marry a French girl. But here again, it is open to question whether speech would not be given the lie or modified by the facts. Cecilia, in the group, most often brings up questions of sexuality, with a complacence (betrayals, homosexualities, bestiality etc.) that probably indicates that she is ill at ease: has she only learned 'words', or has she interiorised them? It is only in the second case that she will know how to use them.

There is a constant tension, and interference, between tradition and modernity. Cecilia tends towards the values of French society, but tradition always warps her choices.

(c) Relations of the couple. Changes intervene also in practices within the domestic space: the husband helps with household chores and takes care of the child. These changes in values also intervene in leisure pursuits. The two spouses share their evenings within the home, looking at television, or they go out together.

Social life, the external world, are no longer the man's exclusive province: Cecilia imposes herself on it. By going out with her husband in Paris, Cecilia realises in a way the old dream of Portuguese wives: to control the husband. The traditional separate roles are blurred and the wife 'possesses' the husband more completely. The price paid for this tête-à-tête is twofold: since their marriage, they no longer go dancing, they go out less and especially in quite a different way, for they go to see friends. In the second place, they are obliged to talk to each other, whereas they have little to say, cut off as they are from the village context and thrown back to their situation of producers constantly comparing themselves to others.

Cecilia sometimes falls asleep in front of the television set, whereas she and her husband have commissioned the derisible 'planetary village' to talk in their stead. Cecilia clings to her son, she is not stirred or deeply moved except for him, for she is alone, and that quite plainly is not enough to give density to living.

Social life outside the home essentially involves fellow countrymen, but in family groups. These are Sunday family outings with numerous children and with friends. They go to the woods, by car, to grill sardines or chickens, and picnic.

They are then outside that urban — and symbolic! — space where foreign odours are criticised by the customs (not solely dietary) of the natives whereas naturally the Portuguese themselves are upset by the odours given off by the natives' kitchens (Catani, 1976a).

Holidays are family affairs, and Christmas Eve is celebrated Portuguese-style. A trip to Portugal is awaited before observing their own friends' rites of passage, etc.

Contacts with the French are chiefly confined to the place of work, and relations with neighbours are rather bad. The French seem to be racists, jealous, envious of the success of immigrants. As long as an immigrant has nothing, is wretched, he is tolerated, but as soon as he has something, he is envied and reproached for it.

This situation is not to Cecilia's liking, and she says: 'I don't like France because of the racism there is in France'.

(d) Cecilia and her immigrant fellow countrymen. Outside the family circle, Cecilia expresses an attitude of rejection towards Portuguese who allow themselves to be exploited or submit to employers who buy their submission. She is also very critical of Portuguese who, in turn, exploit their fellow countrymen.

She has no sympathy for those who live 'badly' in France, in slums, saving on heat or food. In her opinion, sending money back home is no excuse for such living conditions: these are *choices* in life, but Cecilia rejects this way of life — community network or slum — whose non-consumerism is entirely oriented towards investment in the country of origin. She opts for individualism and no longer conceives of long-term choices (except, possibly, for the sake of the children) but rather those of the era of credit, opposed to hoarding and payment in cash.

In political matters, she criticises the conservative behaviour patterns that these traditional practices of economy induce: the immigrants fear for their savings and their 'house', they are afraid the communists may get in at the next Portuguese election (1975).

However, Cecilia's attitude *vis-à-vis* the communists is far from univalent, and it is not because she has confidence (as many emigrants have) in the Armed Forces Movement that she will go vote at the consulate in the first free election in Portugal to ensure the victory of a political choice of the kind such as she would like, combining order and progress. What is clear, however, is that she is breaking away from the old bond of relations, even though she is still beset by the difficulty of defining a modern position in which the political factor would enjoy full autonomy.

There is in her a strong desire to set herself apart from her fellow countrymen, but she does not place all the blame on them for their behaviour. She attributes responsibility for that to the governments of the country of origin.

When she speaks of migrants of other foreign extraction, she sees them as radically different (the Tunisian brother-in-law; Mrs B.S.; the neighbour married to an Italian, etc.) and this difference as an obstacle, is a source of reassurance to Cecilia with respect to her marriage to a Portuguese, she who had hoped to marry a Frenchman.

(e) Cecilia and France. For Cecilia, emigration is a break, both in respect of the country of origin and of the community of emigrants: correlatively, it is a question of an individualistic affirmation expressed through her mode of housing, her economic practices, etc. But from the prospective of economic status she falls back on family assistance, and in that respect her recourse to her cousin is fully as marked as Guilhermina's resorting to a nephew for the building of her house.

Interiorising in this way 'bourgeois' aspirations and models apropos of the house 'in the country' when she speaks to other members of the group, she means to inform them of what she considers as her difference, but is she so far from retreating to a life similar to that of her childhood? For whom is she speaking: for the other women, for herself as an adult, or for herself as a child?

The home, in which aspirations are realised and the life plan materialises, undergoes the fluctuations of that plan: 'Because [for] my husband, it's Portugal. That's the way it is. We are thinking of buying a small plot there and building, then afterwards leaving ... '.

Colour television, a car, household appliances, etc. − Cecilia is a consumer conforming to the model of the society of residence, which naturally then integrates her with the system of classes. All Cecilia's activity in consumer matters is henceforth imbued with the spirit of calculation and the economic and social individualism that is bound up with it.

She tends towards the possession, the purchase of material goods, which are distinctive features of success both in the country of production and, when a trip is made, in the country of origin.

All her behaviour aims at conforming to the values of the country where she resides; with her it becomes an ironclad system to which everything is subordinated. When she says she is paying her mother-in-law for looking after her son, there is a general outcry in the group: love is not paid for, especially not in *those terms*. To reimburse, to share expenses is one thing; 'to pay', and to use the term, is something else.

Naturalisation is the ultimate means to equality of rights, and at the same time its guarantee. It is complete adherence to the system of values of the society of residence and a determination to melt into it through identity and thus achieve nationality.

However, though Cecilia, for her part, chose naturalisation, her husband is unsettled by the political changes in Portugal. A defaulter from military service, having lived in Portugal only until he was twelve years old, he never expected to be able to set foot there again, but on 25 April 1974 his project became subject to reconsideration.

The plans of Cecilia, the wife, depend on those of Jorge, who is both husband and son; but those plans themselves depend on external events. They oscillate between France and Portugal: attitudes to both countries are ambiguous. At times France is esteemed, at times hated, because foreigners are exploited there, looked down on, and because even '40 years of presence' will not enable Cecilia to get back her job, or rather, her *identity*; which sounds, here, like *difference*.

But the same is true of Portugal: at times a condemned country that one had to leave through the fault of those governing it; at times the beloved land, because it is said that only in the country of one's birth can one find happiness.

Thus the house dreamed of, the house that will crystallise the project, floats between here and there: 'if one day, I remain in France . . . '; but also 'we are thinking of buying a small plot back there . . . ', though these oscillations reflect more the hesitations of the husband than those of Cecilia herself. When she curses France, it is the expression of her bitterness towards this country which she chose and which rejects her — but it was here that her son was born and that she would like to remain. Caught in the mesh of this individualistic society, she aspires only to integrate with it; as her fulfilment lies in that integration, Cecilia has made of her personal happiness an end in itself. Western individualism is irreversible.

The circle is complete, as opposed to Francisca's case. To be sure, the colour of her skin renders this dissolving of herself impossible for the Cape Verdian, and that factor is not the least important. But the image of itself that Cecilia holds up to the country of production should cause concern by its absolute lack of strong, cohesive social values. And yet it is the extreme individualistic image, and it is to be thought that many politicians and technocrats regard it as the very image of the 'good' citizen — a very short-sighted and biased view in our opinion.

FRANCISCA: 'I am nothing'.

Alex, born in France, marked the point of no return in respect of Cape Verde. When Francisca was able to take him back at the age of three, when he entered the 'école maternelle', she decided to send for her elder son, then three years later her mother, and in 1975 her naturalisation was under way.

Why that decision, despite all the trauma from the conflict between two systems of values? To Guilhermina, she replied that immigration, to her, was not a question of having adventures, but the result of a bad economic situation in Cape Verde: 'You don't understand anything. You know, if there were work, we wouldn't have to leave home! As for me, I'm in France to earn a living!'

Although that is extremely true, it is also, in part, a rationalisation: she still feels like a foreigner, and despite her efforts, the values that made her life there or in Senegal she still seeks to find here, in a struggle that makes her foreign, voluntarily so, in the country of production and residence: 'Me — I'm neither Portuguese, nor Cape Verdian, nor French. I am nothing'.

The admission is terrible, and there is no economic solution to such a situation. Yet all life, here, for Francisca, revolves around that admission, around the defence against 'nothingness' through reunion of the family, her children, her mother, the trips to Amsterdam to see her brothers, the Cape Verdian ball, the Cape Verdian holidays, etc.

There is constant duality in her speech: on one hand, the speech of reality, of the values openly exhibited, revealing her knowledge of the country of residence; on the other, that of her actions. The disparity is obvious. If one is subjected to 'spite', then it must be expiated: concerning a dismissal from employment, here is what Francisca had to say: 'If the employer fires him for no reason, he will pay dearly . . .. Something will fall on his head, and he will drop dead. He will pay in any case, he doesn't sleep'.

Francisca's life is ordered around these ambivalences: there is a certain formal assimilation of the institutions that may be useful for her advancement but there is also a deep belief in a moral world wherein a 'good' act corresponds to every 'bad' act. It would be an endless undertaking to list all Francisca's uses of moral terminology: a *good* government is one that looks after the *poor people*; she speaks also of the *goodness* of General Spinola, who she thinks put an end to the wars and the killing; the French racists are *egoists*, but one still finds *good* French people who say that the immigrants are *nice*.

Thus Francisca eludes our system of values, as moreover she has retreated from her own, which remains of capital importance to her.

GUILHERMINA: space and the fantasies of travel

As early as the second session, Guilhermina flaunts her travels, which she thinks will raise her in the esteem of others: 'I came from Brazil. Then I stayed at the Hotel Moderne, in the Place de la République, for five days. To visit France, I came for a while to have a look'.

Thus the entire situation is described: what counts is to see Paris, a trip made to get to know a place in the touristic sense, over and above the difficulties and failures of the real journey – one of displacement – there is the fantasy of the visit.

The difference is striking with the other Portuguese members of the group, who mention only the countries of the migratory route: Portugal, Spain, France; with them, we return to the usual world of migration, where what counts is the move towards the goal, even if to get there one suddenly switches from donkey to plane, without any travel by train, hence skipping the routes of the national networks, leaping from home soil to international flights.

Guilhermina has no reality save in travelling; it is *elsewhere* that enhances *now* and gives it order.

MRS B.S.: 'He doesn't come to see me; I don't go to see him'.

'What about your son?' asks Cecilia, once when the discussion touched upon 'sending money'.

> He doesn't come to see me. Ah yes, I'm the one in charge after all. When I telephoned, he doesn't want to answer me . . . He doesn't want to come, I won't go. It's my brother [my brother-in-law] who eggs him on. The land, my brother-in-law he's in charge, but it's not his. And I don't want to leave [things] to my husband's brother, who sells everything. It's my son's father who did it, to his son! I have sheep, camels, I'm not going to give them to my brother [-in-law]! It's my husband's brother who attends to it. Because he has only his brother; so he puts him in the papers, because he didn't want to work for nothing. So part for him and the rest for my son.
>
> I lived there after my husband died, but my son wouldn't stay at home. Always at the cemetery. I couldn't stand it. He was too spoiled.
>
> One day [when he was a child and my husband was still alive] a teacher who did that [she grasps her arm] then: 'You know, the teacher hit me!' So [the father] he went to see the teacher, [who said] 'I didn't strike him, I took him like this so he would see the blackboard'. [The father said] 'Ah, no! You must not strike my son!' He had never gone to school, never.
>
> [Another day] I made cakes all afternoon. But when he came home, everything was for the kid! [I protest, the father tells me] 'Leave him alone'. I can't say anything.
>
> One day I struck him with an Arab shoe [a *babouche*], I struck him in his little balls, and we had company. [The father] he didn't say anything to me. He telephoned to the ambulance, to the hospital. Well then, he didn't hit me, but

he said to me, 'If my son he dead, you are going to die with him'. And then my father, my brother, everybody came to beat me, struck me; my mother. Three at me. I was two weeks in bed, without eating, without anything at all.

So, I can't touch him any more. I get irritated [but] he's my son! Okay, other people's children [you can't touch them], but he's my son, but he is too spoiled. It's his father: everything given, everything out, the bread in the oven, the cakes, the meat . . . my son [that day] left nothing for me. Everything, everything [given, with his father's approval].

But, now, he's with my brother [-in-law], he's quite calm, he can't do as he likes. Because when his father died, he wouldn't eat. Always at the cemetery. I could always run after him. At the cemetery. He played marbles, and wouldn't eat. I called my brother [-in-law], he eats; but later it started up again. So I telephoned to my brother [-in-law]; 'Come down, I can't control him'. He comes down to Rabat and he eats and we move. So that was it, he stayed on like that with my brother [-in-law]. Oh, I couldn't stand any more! He does well in his studies. I can't say anything. He did stenography, yes. But my brother [-in-law] sets him against me, and he doesn't want to come.

'How long since you've been down there?' Cecilia asks again.
'Eight years'.
'Well!'
'You know why? When I go down, I go to my elder brother's. But the women are all jealous: three days with one, three days with the other . . . but the elder brother comes. He says: "I'm the one who gives the orders! Come here". The others, they're crying here, crying there. I said: "With your squabbling that this makes, I come to rest (and I can't), I'm not coming any more" '.
'You no house?' asks Guilhermina, following her *idée fixe*.
'Oh, no house down there! I can tell you that. No house. The farm, yes, but no house. The husband had military housing'.
'But the farm will be your son's when your brother-in-law dies?' asks Cecilia.
'Why? My son may sell it, but I don't want him to. What for? You work in life when you have kids (it's for them you buy a house). Do you think when I get too old I'm going to stay here? There are two rooms of mine, down there. There are six rooms, there are. It's all on one floor, but . . . it's a country house. But my brother, he has five floors. He was a lieutenant in the French army. He did everything, Italy and all. Yes. He has four daughters and a son'.

It is not surprising that, within the context of research on training programmes, the life and future of Guilhermina and Mrs B.S. cannot be understood, whereas they can be in respect of Cecilia and Francisca. The latter two organise their lives in relation to the country of production; the other two (one with no child, the other having lost hers) are merely sojourning there. It is usually agreed then that the evaluator should turn the matter over to other specialists, more qualified than he to account for this rejection of promotion, this failure of the development model proposed by the training programme. In fact, the analysis needs to be taken further: we have already identified points relating to personal aspects and shall now examine the elements that the group offers for a better understanding of these people. An essential feature of traditional civilisations will be brought out: the relation between individuals, in which hierarchy is clearly manifested. That trait is replaced in modern civilisation by the relation to things: it will be seen how the use of television (and, by degrees, of the various media of information) serve to bring out the persistence of traditional values in relation to 'politics' and its actors. The four individual cases illustrate a general situation.

Group themes: ambiguity of the relation to things, and persistence — to varying degrees — of the relation to individuals[1]

(a)   Television, the radio and information. 'Newspapers are the token of the facing of reality', says the group leaders' manual. The intention was to stress the importance of information and to make of it a means of instruction oriented towards the external, so that the course should not be autarkic. This attitude is coherent with the modern ideology that makes the politics a category in itself; but how does that fit in with the practices of the four women from the group observed?

Of world news through television and the radio, Guilhermina, for example, retains everything and nothing. *Everything* because she knows what is going on; *nothing* because she relates the news to her immediate universe when possible; otherwise she distorts it and reduces it to a fantasy.

Regarding a case of the seizure of an aircraft by bandits, she mixes Palestinians and Japanese, saying that the two countries are close: thus she systematises in space what is only ideological collusion between armed groups.

In respect of the rivalry between Mitterrand and Giscard d'Estaing during the French presidential campaign, she asserts that the left is unfavourable to immigrants. If Mitterrand should be elected, foreigners would have to go home. The misconception is obvious, but the other women also fear the same.

---

1   A more detailed, and especially more exhaustive, study of these very numerous themes would be of the greatest interest, given the wealth of available material.

On the other hand, when the group leader sought her opinion in respect of the presidential elections in Portugal, she became relatively eloquent, but very soon slid from the French-language broadcasts to which the group leader referred to the almost confidential broadcasts done in Portuguese very early in the morning by the French radio. The reason was that very interesting things were said at that time of day about retirement. And Guilhermina added an extremely significant fact: 'There are also some for the Algerians' (of these interesting broadcasts). Thus it is the immigrant—emigrant category that comes first.

The case is exactly the same with Francisca. Though her remarks relative to aircraft hijackings were less incoherent as compared to our categories of space, she also thinks that a victory by the left in the presidential elections would entail great risks for foreigners. Though she thus appears to understand better the representation of the world underlying news items, she relates some of them solely to her own situation. Do the French do otherwise? Doubtless not; but that is less apparent, for the foreigners move in a dual sphere, as opposed to the natives, who have only one.

Apparently, in contrast to the first two women, Cecilia exalts television as the means per excellence of status information: through it one learns how to do, to be, to consume, etc. But it is precisely for that reason that she rejoins the others in her lack of interest in information and her political fears. She often falls asleep looking at television, not from physical fatigue but from boredom. Furthermore, she never looks at television unless her husband is there.

The television scans the daily scene, but does not penetrate the values: it is part of the things both inevitable and obligatory. Through it one expects to be reminded of when to declare taxes or to hear what the journalist says to think of an explosion that Guilhermina heard during the night near where she lives. A criminal assault or a joke? The evening news broadcast on television will say.

In reality, television places these women, who till then had been active participants, in the role of spectator. It dispossesses them, making them spectators of themselves.

The following example shows very clearly how general this attitude is becoming, for it relates to the reference population, involving about a hundred people. The foreign women had watched an 'ethnographical' programme on Portugal showing the old way of growing, gathering, retting, beating and spinning flax. So far as the producers and French viewers were concerned, the interest of this programme lay in its exoticism, whereas for the cleaning women from Portugal it represented a dramatisation of something with which they had all been familiar in their childhood and in which some of them had taken part until they left the country.

At this level, the lack of comprehension is great, not to say absolute.

Torn as they are between the necessity of adhering to modern values and the necessity of finding some coherence in their approach, they attempt to attenuate the disparities between two worlds from which they must choose. It is no accident if Guilhermina, though hoping to return to Portugal, counts on going back as a cook specialising in French dishes and working on commission: it is not possible to return to the rank she held on leaving. The purchase of a house (an apartment, in reality) is not enough to guarantee the change in social status, because now (in her fantasy) everybody has a house. There must be some more visible token of the change, or, more precisely, a system of differential tokens.

Thus, even rejection of *a* spectator status, adoption of the role of spectator of oneself, or even the complete acceptance of spectator status — all still lead back to the basic question: one receives only what can be understood in terms of consolidation of the image of oneself, at the cost of making what appear, in the eyes of an observer belonging to other social groups, to be misconceptions.

As usual, proof of the absurdity of this situation is provided by Mrs B.S. Not having a television set, she is invited by her neighbours on the same landing or on the floor above. But she either soon leaves or distorts the programme by starting a great flow of words. She is *afraid* of television. She does not accept the spectacle.

On the other hand, she listens to the radio all the time, though she is no better informed for doing so.

The fact is that, once the television set has been purchased (as a status symbol) use of it is dictated not by the need for information but merely by the symbolic categories of entertainment. The function of information is assumed by other channels, all centred on personal experience. Though one has heard a matter spoken of, it will be evaluated elsewhere, among fellow-countrymen, if it is of concern to the spectator.

Otherwise, one reinterprets according to the old values whatever information is offered by television or the other media.

(b) Politics as a category in itself (modern), and as a symbol (traditional). 'I know nothing about politics', say the four women, while at the same time declaring that independence for the former Portuguese colonies is a bad thing, because it will impoverish the mother country, and everybody — Africans and Portuguese alike — will suffer from it; or while stating that those who take hostages or hijack planes should be executed; or while misinterpreting the intentions of the left, etc.

It is not a question of an ordinary lack of understanding, but of something much more profound: a relation to politics quite different from the one we know.

Based on a newspaper headline ('Seven political assassinations in

Paris'), the discussion immediately lapses into the 'I know nothing about politics' reaction. When the group leader insists, Guilhermina gives the first twist to the discussion: if it must concern politics, she will speak of the election of the President of the Portuguese republic, which she has heard about on the French radio. For the time being, the other three women merely listen to her.

In accordance with her habitual oral mode of information, Guilhermina puts aside the printed form provided by the group leader (thus abandoning as it were the training cycle) and launches into what she heard over the radio in the morning (in the evenings, naturally, she watches television). She already considers it a great concession to consent to speak of politics, any politics, thus indicating that the whole field is undifferentiated so far as she is concerned. But after announcing that there are to be elections in her country, she immediately moves on to questions of retirement: the point is, she had heard both matters spoken of during the same broadcast, but only the second one interested her. Mrs B.S. avails herself of the opportunity to intervene in the discussion and to recall for the nth time her own personal affairs (the retirement of her husband, the army veteran).

Called on again by the group leader, Guilhermina is led back to speak of the presidential candidates. The question was: 'Do you know them?' which, in our system, is to be understood as: 'Have you heard about them?'. But Guilhermina understands something quite different: 'Do you know them personally?' The situation becomes comical and points up the cultural and sociological gap. Of course she knows at least one of them! Hasn't she been a servant in the best houses? He was: 'The [present] minister of the "foreign corps". I have worked in the house of him, I know [shall know] if he is going to be president'.

Yes, Guilhermina knows one candidate personally, she knows him in the flesh. And the group leader is completely thrown, together with all the implications of the country of production and its abstractions.

But we must go beyond this. Guilhermina is not alluding to physical knowledge when she adds, 'I know [shall know] if he is going to be president'. The fact is, Guilhermina is moving in another sphere, that of symbolic politics, not in the sphere of representative government.[1] It is of little importance that she has physically served in a family of politicians.

The question is not the vote; it is not in that sense that she is alienated. She will not vote at the consulate despite the fact that she knows one candidate and that a French priest came to the parish where she goes each Sunday to preach from the pulpit the moral obligation to

---

1 Are things really different in this respect in France, save perhaps among extremely limited groups of intellectuals? Has the charismatic function of the leader really disappeared? We think not.

vote. Naturally, if she wanted to vote, Guilhermina would vote 'well'. But Guilhermina doesn't vote (any more than Francisca does — being still a Portuguese national at the time — or Cecilia).

Guilhermina is alienated because she is constantly confronted by her own foreign body: separated from the country that constitutes her sole intelligible reference (I will know if he is to be elected) — a country which, owing to this separation, is not as interesting as are the broadcasts that speak of retirement. To Guilhermina, politics (or the political category) is a question of hierarchy and rank, questions which touch closely upon the sacred — and moral — character of authority.[1] The reference is made over and above the vote and, while knowing that one will know the results, one is prevented from participating in it because one is not bodily confronted by it. One is confronted by it only in spectator terms.

The same is true of the other women of the group, even of Cecilia, though in different ways.

Presence of hierarchy

A long series of quotations culminating, once it has been organised according to traditional and modern traits, and the notion of individual and group member, in a striking explanation of what was advanced earlier in respect of the clientele relationship is here omitted.

At the level of the empirical individual, all divergences, all confrontations, all personal strategies are permissible, but at the level of what hierarchy and its ranks represent, things change completely. It is not, as one might imagine, sentimentality that makes Guilhermina *and* Francisca admire the tears of G. Marchais at the funeral of J. Duclos,[2] but, over and beyond the egalitarian protests of the one and the terror of communists of the other, the fact is that in this funeral ceremony there is the echo of what Mrs B.S. says apropos of Moroccan royalty: importance of descent.

This burial of the 'head' of the communists corresponds, far more profoundly than the succession of the presidents of the French Republic, no longer to be seen in television newscasts, to one of the constants of holistic values: continuity.

Likewise, the mythification of President Giscard d'Estaing's being invited to dine in the homes of people living in modest circumstances

---

1 The remarks made by the foreign women have had to be omitted: the subjects discussed were the assassination of President Kennedy, the mortal danger to which any prominent politician is exposed, and the sacred aspects of the funeral ceremonies for great political leaders. News was very much to the fore in this context but the interpretations that went with it referred to parameters which were not 'modern'.

2 Marchais being the new, and Duclos the former, Secretary of the French Communist Party.

oscillates between distortion of the information, telescoping of acts both by the President or the opposition (holding them up to ridicule), and pure and simple culinary discussions. The discussion in fact represents, beyond what one would say to the President if he came 'to my house', a symbolic exchange in which *this president* does things that the others do not. It is a reference to the charismatic power of the king who can cure scrofula, who doesn't change anything but who slakes an unquenched thirst for reciprocity by his 'kindness' in noticing the existence of 'the poor' — who may, like Guilhermina, have 'bought' their money in Brazil by visiting for an evening as the messenger of order and stability, those whom he comforts in their condition, for he recognises them for an instant as superior to himself, since he subordinates his food to theirs, since he sits at their table, enthroning them, this once, as providers. (This provides a good example of hierarchical logic.)

Whence the vibrant yet muted appeal to the possible charisma of Mitterrand, described as a 'poor' man who should, who could, take sides with the poor, take Giscard's place without changing the necessity for order, but turning it around, according to the model of all millenarian thought, drawing new sources for the present from the wellsprings of the past.

And these sources naturally relate by their most intimate fibres to the danger of ritual assassination to which all heads of state — in 'open cars' — are exposed. It may be necessary to kill Spinola, through whom destabilisation of Portugal is believed to have started but it is also certain that when great leaders die, lesser leaders take their place. Who is this lesser leader? He may be Pompidou's son, who speaks seven languages, or Marchais, or the heir to the Moroccan throne — no matter. What emerges here is the search for sacred authority, with its risks of death and triumph; it is that authority which Giscard restores — at least as interpreted by these women — with his dinners at citizens' homes and his invitations to Black African garbage collectors. Or more precisely which Giscard exhumes, for the necessity of hierarchy, organised for ultimate ends, has never ceased to haunt these four women, and also the natives of the country of production.

It is striking to note in these four women four different degrees of adherence to traditional values in relation to the charismatic function of the custodian of authority (not at all confused by them with power) (see Dumont, 1977).

Without challenging the sacred royal Moroccan authority, because she alludes only to the direct descent of the present sovereign, whereas historically the thing is much more complex (Jamous, 1977), Mrs B.S. constantly indicates that the fundamental trait of the authority is religious power, all-encompassing, which assigns to each his place in the order of the relationship to men and the earth. Significantly, the group leader sums up: 'For her, the king is God on earth!' Mocking the others and the French, Mrs B.S. leaves them to struggle on with their degraded forms of symbolic royal authority: 'In our country . . .', adds she, and that to her is enough to establish the gap, whereas on the empirical plane she rails as much against old traditions as against current excesses.

On the Western scale, Guilhermina is at the extreme limit of a residual holism, or nearly so. Nothing any longer connects her with a royal authority, whose characteristics she would probably not be able to sketch, save in monetary terms, despite having served in the home of a princess who received the Queen Mother of England. Personal wealth, always present and brought to mind, is what has de-structured her initiatives through irruption of the empirical, painfully experienced, in an hierarchic system which she feebly tries to justify through questions of inheritance. Francisca can then easily give her a pat answer: in the scale of possessions, too much is too much, says she in essence.

The reference of Guilhermina is the church, the priest: it is from the continuity of religion-in-the-world that she derives her glimmers of intelligence, of instruction, of subordination, her feeling of belonging to a 'condition' and the modesty of her personal aspirations. But the church has long since prepared the advent of individualism and the justification for an autonomous economic field extremely tenuously subjected to ultimate values. The holistic model that the church can offer Guilhermina is greatly de-structured (Dumont 1965).

Francisca has completely abandoned the religious model, if she ever had it, and never speaks of it. Her traditional values revolve around kindness, morality, dignity.

In this discussion, and throughout the cycle, she was passionate in the defence of her rights according to the models *adapted* to the country of production. But though half of her interventions tend to counterbalance whatever in her opinion is too traditional in Guilhermina's observations when she speaks, Francisca for her own part reverts to the traditional relationship between rich and poor encompassed in the same values. It is a question of working, at the risk of a fit of hysterics, to protect the poor. That, from her point of view, is what justifies the presidential dinners. As always, Francisca chooses to separate carefully exhibited values (modern) and real values (traditional); pushed to the wall, in her life and her personal aspirations, she holds on firmly to the values of her upbringing. It was no mere chance that, with her low salary, two children and poor lodgings, she took her mother from her brother-in-law's house, where she had more room and freedom of movement, because her sister's husband didn't treat his mother-in-law properly.

Offhand, Cecilia appears totally opposed to the traditional values: she constantly takes the opposite view to what Guilhermina says (and generally takes no notice at all of what Mrs B.S. says); if the President visited her, she would serve him dinner in a mess-tin, and would complain; such talk is that of any French worker (until the thing occurs). And yet it is she, after having reduced everything to monetary terms, who will ask whether Mrs Pompidou has a child — the child who ought to be the dead President's heir, no longer mentioned on the television — and will accuse Giscard d'Estaing of 'filling his pockets': though the image of authority is contested in accordance with the modern, individualistic practices of the country of production, the *remains* of another relation to the total individual show up in the *non sequitur* concerning the son of a politician, in the overly simple (and quite widespread) image of a president using his office to make prices rise and fill his pockets, in the exclamation 'too bad' when she finds out that the priests, according to what Francisca says, cannot do anything to stop communism.

In a word, Cecilia is the perfect example, with only a few differences, of that public opinion which the President addresses, wherein, over and above exhibited egalitarian values, the remnants of a hierarchical situation no longer able to achieve coherence still have currency.

Thus while Cecilia reflects what adherence to the individualistic values of the country of production has made of her, she returns the question to the teachers of this country and, through them, to the country itself: how are holistic elements combined or juxtaposed, how do they affect one another, once they are no longer upheld by a system, or its fabric, when nothing is left of them but remnants?

In the case of the four women observed, the beginning of an answer may be found in their reactions to racism.

The theme of racism is that of a hierarchical situation that it is impossible for the two parties involved to observe

If one listens to Guilhermina and Francisca on the subject of racism, what one finds is anecdotes of the familiar, hurtful slights, rendered quasi-'ordinary' by the spiteful clichés heard hundreds of times. The fact is that these two women are not very 'visibly' foreign, for they rarely cross the paths of the French and, especially, they do not compel recognition by the natives.

Though Guilhermina had a heated argument with a bakery woman to whom she finally said, 'If there were no foreigners, you wouldn't have anyone to sell your bread to', and though she ceased buying from her and insults her — *in pectore* — every time she passes the shop; though Francisca relates no anecdotes of that sort, but both women report racist remarks by one employer or another, the fact is that throughout the entire training cycle they never spoke on this theme in profoundly emotional terms. Neither enters into competition with the natives, and does not even consider any comparison: one because she lives obsessed by her dream of her 'house', and the other because she knows she is of a different colour and leads a parallel life alongside the natives, but with Cape Verdians.

Not that the classic insults ('*I* am French — and I'm better than you; if you're not happy, go back to your own country'; etc.) are any different from what Mrs B.S. hears. The phenomenon and the language are the same. But the commonness of the situation is such that three of these women give no details because, for different reasons that happen to coincide here, they are not counting on integration into France, despite the fact that Francisca requested naturalisation.

The case of Cecilia and her husband is entirely different. They live, by and large, as the natives do, take part in the consumerism of their environment and give rise through their use of money to a sort of 'sporadic' racism, no longer of the general type, directed at them personally.

When Cecilia recounts the jealousies roused by the purchase of their car, it was Francisca who, as usual, blazed up and recalled the individualistic values ideologically prevailing in France ('people come here to work', 'nobody gives you a car, you buy it'), but it is clear that she is not affected by that situation for, actively resigned to her difference, all she asks and at the same time demands is to be left in peace. It was no accident if she refused to do extra cleaning on the side.

Moreover, Francisca continues: 'the world belongs to everybody; they didn't make France!' The first affirmation might seem egalitarian and modern, but the second is a correction and reveals the true holistic nature of the thing. If nobody made anything, that means in the final analysis that its established existence is organised under the eye of God. So then it is not a question of a 'right' over the world in the sense in which we might understand it but of a 'right' in the world as part of a totality which transcends us and over which we cannot hold sway because it is not of our making.

Quite different is the individualistic reasoning of the citizen of a modern nation who considers that it, like himself, is master of its fate. Men and men alone have made the nation. It follows that, though in the individualistic universalism of the Declaration of Human Rights everyone should be allowed to go wherever he chooses, the fact of being the citizen of a nation correlatively creates rights, including that of expelling those who are not native-born.

In their constant efforts at comparison with the French, Cecilia and her husband imperil the distinctive external features of the rightful-citizen species (whose characteristics are, in turn, to have a finer car than the immigrant, to be able to consider him as the national of a country that has no roads and, more generally speaking, is not 'civilised', 'developed', etc.), for Cecilia and her husband *are* developing, and gradually they are taking over the distinctive features which the individualistic modern citizen would implicitly like to keep for himself.

When this citizen finds himself stripped of his visible trappings (car, tie, lodgings etc.) which distinguish him from the rabble, and no longer feels protected by the assurance of an extrinsic superiority owed to his own 'development', it is *then* that racism comes into being.

'Your husband wants to be naturalised? Why, he can't even read and write!' To which Cecilia replies in essence that she herself, and not only her husband, speak better than the 'Breton' insulting her.

Since material individualistic equality is established, an *ad personam* comparison emerges, and in the case of Cecilia is compounded by equality in the power and pertinence of the insult ('Breton'); the equality is not merely extrinsic, but also intrinsic, ideologically established. The two women fight on equal terms and with the same weapons, for Cecilia also knows how to use hurtful words.

The difference between the two women, which nevertheless exists, can no longer be demonstrated in any way, neither materially nor in speech; there is no means of hierarchising, and separating, what consequently cannot be given a name. It is no longer possible to fall back on more or less complex traits which of themselves would indicate belonging to distinct groups, thus sparing any need for opposition between empirical individuals.

So nothing is left but personal insult, involving effects of language, which rapidly progress from snide attacks to physical violence, if, as in the case of Cecilia, the language and its refinements have been sufficiently mastered. In the play of language, it is the very essence of man one faces, of the individual in the modern sense that one seeks to reach. One ends by giving a different *nature* (an impalpable and shifting difference, elusive and hence always renascent, impermeable to reason) to what it is impossible to keep distinctive as regards *culture* or specific cultural traits.

That is why the other three women are not affected in the same way as Cecilia, and also why Cecilia has henceforth adopted a system of individualistic references, whatever contingent solutions she may find to her wish (which is traditional) to remain at home and leave everything to her husband.

It is not enough, therefore, to speak of the reverse racism of foreigners (many examples of which were provided by the four women), or, on a more general plane, of the racism said to be developing – and developing in fact – in the formerly colonised countries. The matter has much deeper roots than explanations in terms of alienation, i.e. of ignorance, suggest. That is true, even though Francisca and Cecilia themselves use this explanation when they seek to find a difference in behaviour between educated and uneducated Frenchmen, between the 'little people' and 'the rich'.[1]

1 Francisca's remark about 'Algerians who kill in cold blood' would be worth further analysis. There are within migratory flows attitudes of discrimination reflected in the speech of the four women. That is an example of one of the themes which ought to be broached if it were possible to continue to analyse this material.

The root of the matter is the social shock between a diffuse hier-archical logic that nevertheless persists and dares not speak its name, and the 'foreign wave' that imposes itself precisely by playing on the contradiction between exhibited values and social realities. Foreigners make a breach, supported by the corollary of the two cardinal values, liberty and equality, saying 'my money is as good as yours', and there-by impose themselves. Although that is 'ideologically correct', those of the natives who are in *daily* contact with them — education or wealth as such is not involved — and whose social status does not distinguish them from the foreigners, cannot help feeling 'somewhere' (unable to name it but living it with shame and hence with greater ferocity) the attack on their essence of men riveted to the relationship to things. The scourge comes into being because social hierarchy, nevertheless necess-ary, is at variance with equality which, at the level of things, resolves into identity.

What would be necessary is to manage to keep the two things sepa-rate: equality of rights is not identity of destinies; difference in identi-ties does not exclude equality. The means of reconciling tradition and modernity — the conflict between which is generally described in the wrong terms — are to be found here.

Francisca and Guilhermina, and Mrs B.S. also, do not seek formal equality; they partake but little of that trait of modern individualism: egalitarianism. Above all, each of them living a personal life still imbued with traditional values, they claim their difference and reject identity.[1]

Quite different is the case of Cecilia, probably symptomatic of a short-term development, for the cardinal relationship is now to things and no longer to people, the first being the essential element in the decision to emigrate.

Departure as abandonment of a system of relationships, and the necessity for individualisation

As a general rule, one emigrates when one is no longer integrated with the social system of the country of origin, when one is already an 'internal emigrant' because one no longer rightfully belongs to the old symbolic system.

That this symbolic system was destroyed by colonisation, or main-tained for a while, artificially, by a dictatorship (in earlier times Italy, yesterday Spain and Portugal, even today Turkey) does not negate the proposition. Prolonged ethnographic observation, collecting the foreign-er's speech so as to grasp his system of values, adequately reveal that

---

1 The sources of this analysis of the genesis of racism are to be found in the work by Dumont (1980). We assume full responsibility for application of the demonstration to the present case.

the question does not lie in generalised introduction of the monetary equivalent in itself, at a precise date, nor in the introduction of the salary-labour pair as the standard for the reality of production: the question lies in the transition from tradition to modernity (signified by autonomisation of the money-labour pair), which alters the entire system of values, or initially unsettles it. It is the de-structuring of the old symbolic system, replaced partially and with difficulty but irreversibly, by the system of production in and of itself, individualistic, that must be considered.

Hence it must be seen that those who leave, and who belong to what we call the 'first generation' that must adapt itself, are those whose status within the symbolic system of the country of origin is already impaired. Therefore, in that perspective, there is hardly any more true 'first generation' of migrants today, although, at the level of the empirical individual, departure confronts each migrant with problems that he must solve as if he were the first to leave, even when, as in the case of so many Portuguese and of an even greater number of Algerians, the emigrant's own father has already gone through the experience (see Ath-Messaoud and Gillette, 1976; and Sayad, 1975 and 1977).

Obviously, these departures occur either because people are forced into them by circumstances or because they are desired (our analysis is not a plea for a return to an immutably traditional past). The question posed by these departures, however, is the following: how and when is the symbolic requirement all migrants carry in them transformed? What of the holistic *and* individualistic values, still existing, but which each society distributes differently, predominance in the country of production being given to the second, beyond all question?

Guilhermina and Mrs B.S., who previously could not be placed within the framework of our modern conceptualisation, provide answers here. Not affected by a 'project' within the framework of the new country of production and residence, they are relieved of the necessities of combining or juxtaposing the two systems of values in order to concretise, here, a choice clearly assumed, although difficult, of the new individualistic values. They show, without mediating factors, the shock (and it is painful) between de-structured holistic values and individualistic values constantly curbed, not accepted, rejected through the attempt not to surrender anything, aside from the long years of presence, whereas these individualistic values exist in them, for they have emigrated.

It is in these two women that all the tensions that every immigrant must cope with — facing up to lack and absence — are revealed in two different series of features. Lack and absence of relationships (holistic), lack of identity, absence of identity (individualistic interiorisation).

To demonstrate this, we start with Guilhermina's story which, from whatever angle it is approached, is constantly marked by deprivation: abandonment of the soil, the death of her father, the departure for Brazil and the impossibility of settling there. Everything sooner or later (from one session to the next) boils down to a lack of what should have made her happy.

Her speech always begins in altogether realistic terms, but from her childhood of poverty to her present health, less good than in the past, from the pilgrimages to her 'house' which she perceives as a cenotaph, reasons slowly develop which combine to make Francisca say that Guilhermina is like a child. She lives an eternal present, a life never lived, in which everything meets and remains apparent, never bringing satisfaction.

'What would the other Portuguese say if they knew that, at 55 years of age, I was still going to school?', she asks, calling the group leader to witness. But it is not of what they would say, these members of her family, all of them married and most of them never having considered emigrating, that Guilhermina is afraid. What she fears is this sudden confrontation with passing time, reminding her that she is no longer a child of school age. Thus, when she speaks of her training course with a nun at the school, the sister, her patience exhausted, omits what at bottom she is thinking when she says, 'It's not a matter of intelligence, you must learn': she skipped the second real term: 'it's a question of will' — for such is the ideology of the school. But, even in eluding the issue thus, she touches on the root of the problem: Guilhermina does not want to know that time is passing; she wants, like the child she was (now that she lives near a school, whereas in her childhood she stresses that schools were rare), to continue to copy, purely and simply, from a textbook: 'That is something I really like'. On another occasion, she says:

> I went on a pilgrimage to Lisieux, where a woman stepped on my foot and injured it. Prayers and faith healers did no more for it than the Portuguese or French doctors. Even when a man in my family went and fetched a leading specialist, so that I had the best care there was, they weren't able to cure me.
>
> In reality, I got well by myself and, the whole time, I was thinking of my house: I am going to die in a foreign country and I won't even have lived in my house!

What is the logic of this speech? Certainly not that of causality. What injury is involved? — the one to her foot which took so long to heal because of the general state of her health; that of migration, which from country to pilgrimage has her wander over a geography of lack; or, deeper down, that of her solitude as a woman compelled (who compels herself) to chastity, whereas Portuguese men in the street call out to her?

'Within five years, I am leaving for Portugal, if I'm still alive, if the good Lord so wills. I say it's not worth staying in France any longer. I have bought my house in Portugal'. This was at the third session of the training cycle.

Right away, the house is related to retirement *and* to death by a link which is that of the need to speak of it on every occasion. (And, in the beginning, the group leaders did not understand this.) However, one can follow here a *crescendo* as the cycle proceeds: from clear, simple and material, univalent 'things', the story leads to a paroxysm of relationships in which reality disappears (did it ever exist?) in favour of the symbolic. It will take almost three months for Guilhermina to feel sufficiently assured, within the group and in regard to the group leader, to tell everything (or almost everything, for does one ever tell it all?).

Her house is near a cemetery, where will-o'-the-wisps are seen; her house was paid for within three years, whereas her nephew had offered her credit for fifteen; someone who, like her, had bought a house had committed suicide, not having been able to keep up the payments, whereas she, an old woman, still had the strength to pay within three years. What is she speaking of: death, the cemetery, the flat, or life? That is still not enough. There is a saint, a virgin, who lived and died in the house where she was born, who never went out and whom crowds of pilgrims honour. Guilhermina opens her house to her friends Cacilda and Henrique (who ask her to leave it to them in her will), opens it also to fellow-workers (the Algerian woman who does not want to learn to read), and to the teachers. Guilhermina also saw at the *Foire de Trône* in Paris an enormous woman who stays in her house (her caravan) all the time. She weighs more than 200 kilograms, and is there with her father and mother: her father draws aside the curtain when it is time for the show, and her mother sells the tickets for admission, and souvenir photos. *Who* is the saint to whom Guilhermina vowed to pilgrimage as soon as she could finish paying off her house; *who* is the monstrous and fascinating girl? And what does this collusion of the house with horror, saintliness, immobility and virginity signify: perpetual life, thanks to the refusal to leave home? The saint changes clothes with each ceremony; she has an entire wardrobe so that the mummified body should always look pretty; the freak at the *Foire du Trône* has her mother and her father to watch over her. Guilhermina refuses to leave her house to her nephews, even if they promise to see that she wants for nothing when she is old. She wants to live in it for a while, then sell it and rent another one: *to stay at home is to die*.

Guilhermina has worked all her life to have that house; she says she would not have been able to have it had she continued as a servant in Lisbon. But now that she has it, this house with no garden, no flowers, no chickens, no children (as Cecilia points out) — whereas her sisters have all of these — this house of her retirement is the house of death. Though traditional society showed her the encompassing image of the saint, thus safeguarding the two orders (that of values and that of empiricism), individualistic society sends back to her her own image in the unfortunate girl at the *Foire du Trône* in the purely monetary connection between her and her potential collateral heirs, in the uselessness of a retirement in which money (the relationship to things) has been superordinated to the fruit of her womb (the relationship to people). She wanders from country to country, pilgrimage to pilgrimage, and proposes to sell her house both in order to ward off death by renting another one and at the same time — *escarnio*, oh, bitter irony — to buy the cemetery plot and the coffin.

Guilhermina, like Mohamed, is at the frontier area between two worlds, juxtaposing, but not managing to achieve a synthesis of, traditional and (Catani and Mohamed, 1973) modern values. Guilhermina is caught in the trap of the ideologically economic migration, the very symbol of her people, at the deepest level of the choices of existence, though, fortunately, the tensions are not as dramatic in all cases.

Let us forestall a possible objection. Guilhermina is not 'crazy'; she manages her affairs perfectly well and takes her pleasure exactly as she dictates to her world in this country, which she chose because she found nothing good about Brazil. Furthermore, Guilhermina could not but have left Portugal, as that country long since lacks ultimate aims sufficiently powerful to stem modern ideology. If her story is so loaded with the symbolic, that is due solely to her personal chronicle, not to some reason that might set her apart from the other emigrants. The other women recognise themselves in her themes and model their attitudes on hers. The fact that Guilhermina lives with particular intensity the contradiction between the values apropos of travel, the home, death, etc. is but the echo of (or the occasion for) the reflection of the others. Thus the objection must be reduced to its true dimension: that of the surprise that teachers of French as a foreign language (or others who are *intelligent*) may feel at seeing emerge, in a place normally devoted to institutionalised speech, a speech corresponding to another logic. It is a speech that insists, which is not solely concerned with psychological analysis — and which might even be liable to de-structure it! — but which says how things are, for *all the members of the group*.

All the immigrants are at the frontier area between two worlds, juxtaposing old and modern values; caught in the snare of a migration where resolving tensions forces them to leave the community, to compromise with the values of their upbringing, and seek other ultimate ends that set them on the way to individualisation.

The transition is not effected in a linear manner: depending on the levels of consideration of the facts, symbolic elements of one system or the other are superordinated. Fellow-countrymen, moreover, will often form an element of reference that will make it possible, case by case, to reach a determination apropos of the old values. But though recovering them may represent a haven of peace — the possibility of a combination of the two systems (hence altogether different from a mere juxta-position, as of course from outright opposition) — it is clear that the country of production and residence leads, through its own logic, to the constitution of the individual as a moral being via the new relationship to things that it imposes.

This relationship is affected in a special, though not unique, way by the 'habitation' factor, traversed by a multitude of relationships that condense the tensions between traditional and modern values. In this regard, the other women parallel Guilhermina, and it will be seen that the theme of the 'house' belongs to the thematic group, the 'constella-tion', of each.

Four houses in the background, or the primacy of relationship?

The relationship to the 'house' is the most meaningful of all those involved. The recurrent theme in all conversations, fundamentally emphasised by the country of production and residence, insistently reiterated by all the group leaders, all like to consider it as something positive and unshakeable. To Cecilia, it meant confirmation of the success of her integration; to Guilhermina, confirmation of the success of her return. Even Francisca, who had been waiting for three years for the social worker to find her a council flat and still mentioned it at the control discussion, regards it as a positive value; so does Mrs B.S., who insists on the size of her household, its reputation, the richness of her son's house, even though she is not going back to the country.

For these four women, this theme is that of renunciation of the rela-tionship, something which they cannot bring themselves to do.

Cecilia does not know where to buy her country house, whether in Portugal or France, and the *summum bonum* of French individualistic values — the secondary residence — no longer involves a mere functional choice, but a rending decision.

Francisca still lives (1977) in her two servant rooms which are not even adjoining, have no shower or any place to install a washing machine, and lodges her mother there too.

Guilhermina, within the construction of all that has already been said, wonders as if in passing: 'Will I be able *to live a whole year at a stretch in Portugal*?'

Thus above and beyond the aspects which the thing may assume case by case and which are innumerable, is limned the relationship to the symbolic place, where one remains, sleeps, whence one leaves and whither one returns, oneself and one's family.

In the eyes of the teacher and of the researcher — not to mention those of the administrators! — these lodgings exemplify many contradictions; it would be easy to yield to horrified consideration of the physical deprivation, to proclaim migration an intolerable scandal, to engulf oneself in the vortex of measures to be taken or avoided: discourse apropos of foreigners, which — from our viewpoint — is necessary for the mastery of the empirical facts. But does it look the same to the foreigners?

It is Mrs B.S. who provides the basis of a reply that opens up another field than that of the ambiguity of the *house*, by saying that foreigners are essentially elsewhere (where neither the teacher nor the sociologist can reach them, nor the statistician do anything more than circumscribe them intellectually). For her, the 'house' is a place where the hierarchy is reversed.

'Ah', she says to Guilhermina, 'if only you had told me you were looking for a room! I rented one a few days ago! I am the one who does the renting, I choose the tenants, there where I am'.

She 'rules' both the new tenants, whom she chooses, and the proprietor, on whom she imposes her protégés. Having once been burnt, he lets her do as she likes, for when he tried selecting tenants on his own he made a mistake and rented to some young indigents who staved in a door upon leaving. 'I had warned him!', says she in triumph.

So Mrs B.S. rules her small world and, from the Black who is a Muslim to the owner of the buildings, bends them all to her own values ('I've been there the longest') and dictates their behaviour, taking charge both of the Africans' problems with their love affairs, and of the management of their business.

The building, a 'locality' even smaller than the street, lost in the neighbourhood, is an enclave on which the encompassing values may impinge (Mrs B.S. *works* and *has a right* to training courses), but where they are suddenly out of place, at variance. There, they are only necessary alibis: necessary to the individualistic society and to the foreign woman for feigning to speak to each other, feigning to have something in common. But once across the threshold of the building, the real question is represented by the rooms to be rented (and that is accomplished without any need to hang out a sign for passers-by, for the concierge and Mrs B.S. work in unison). The real question is in Mrs B.S.' refusal to pay an increase in her rent; she manages that because the proprietor needs her.

From her territorial enclave, Mrs B.S. (like all these women, like all emigrants who in time have become immigrants and like all natives) builds herself a world which, at the empirical level, is enough for her. At school, she scolds the pupils, her co-workers, and even the headmaster! They all find that she is right to do so at this boys' school, for thus she is respected and liked, as the headmaster confirms. Likewise, outside, Mrs B.S. lives with other foreigners, her Algerian friend who cohabits with a Tunisian Jewess, for example; like Guilhermina, she clings to quite strange, and quite real, friendships: those of exiles, who *act* holistically, within their enclaves surrounded by the individualism of the country of residence. There is a change of level and a reversal of prime values.

What is apparent here is the ambivalence of the 'habitation' factor — the environment — which assumes the value in our analysis of a recapitulation of all we have learned. Within this space, to different degrees and according to quite dissimilar superficial conditions, relationships are developed which, seen from the native standpoint where we place ourselves, never entirely agree with the system of individualistic values which form the frame of reference for the training programmes.

The latter are in any case (even when they seek to prompt the foreigner's speech, and succeed in doing so) organised as a system of social initiation (Catani, 1973b, p. 330) which the immigrant must achieve alone, through his own strengths, his own suffering, his own choices in terms of interiorisation of the new values.

But after having listened to them, what is to be 'taught' such women who live within a tiny circuit of relationships perfectly tuned but profoundly fragile? One can reformulate their speech, and above all accept it as the group leader and the research team did, but it is certain that the question is not situated at the level of empirical individuals. These women have no need for a modified speech: we are far from a purely functional — and poor, because reduced to the requirements of work and survival — second language, or even from the hypothesis of a language that could be improved. But such is the statistical reality of migration, not that of mythical 'new arrivals' individualised *ex officio* (as if they came from a country and to a country where the juxtapositions of values do not create islands of differences) by training programmes whose clearest function is to circumscribe and 'tame' the foreigner's speech, in terms of the imaginings of the 'host' country.

To be sure, foreigners must be helped to learn the new language; but, though totally inadequate training programmes exist which ought to be abolished (those which are restricted to instructing the foreigner, without allowing his speech to emerge), on the other hand no absolutely adequate programmes exist.[1]

1 Though it is true that Mrs Col. (a Serbian), who came to France in the hope of having her son treated for blindness, cannot manage to read the administrative forms and in that respect requires training, it is equally true that this woman, school-trained in her own language, has had her son treated in the German Federal Republic, in Italy and in Spain, travelling from Paris through Europe for eight years. A woman cleaner with a business firm, paid the minimum statutory wage, though she has not succeeded in having her son's eyesight restored, she has managed to have him trained as a piano tuner, to find him employment and independent lodgings. Though a language training course is imperative, there ought also to be considered as imperative a very detailed, sociological study of the splendid success of her project as a mother.

If it is admitted that teachers cannot consider the immigrants as a 'blank page' and, therefore, programmes with rigidly pre-established progressions solely in terms of linguistic criteria are excluded, and if it is granted that the immigrants' speech has to be reformulated, then it is clear that there is scarcely any alternative to making the formulation of the new values in the second language linguistically more 'economical' for the immigrants.

Analysis of the 'habitation' factor, oscillating between the relationship to the 'house' as an economic asset and that to the 'lodgings' (centre of symbolic relationships characterised by the old values), shows that this interiorisation process which the training programmes should facilitate is far from easy, even though, apparently, this thematic aid to reformulation in the foreign language is everywhere accepted, and even emphasised, and would thus seem to offer extensive teaching possibilities.

From this standpoint, it is clear that even the generalisation of training programmes led by foreigners for foreigners could not escape the necessity of a tension between modernity and tradition that will have to be resolved whatever the approach. Indeed, it is the very status of teacher that places the teacher in a modern individualistic position (since the curriculum is instinct with that individualism).

Though there are difficulties of relationship in the psycho-sociological sense, unmastered language registers, misapprehensions of the reality of the 'students', these very real problems are not at the same level as that, epistemologically foremost, relating to the modern frame of reference that conditions the training-programme idea itself.

Tens or hundreds of thousands of foreign workers, and their families, have lived out in the past, and are living out, their future projects (successes and failures) in the *real* system of the country of production and residence. They are not primarily confronted by problems of training, linguistic or other, but by situations of existence over which the training programmes have no hold.

The fragility of this universe withdrawn and in reserve *vis-à-vis* the modern ideological milieu is evident to the teacher, the sociologist, the statistician. It is at the mercy of any economic and political change, or even of any administrative squeeze under any régime or government whatever. But (and this is our conclusion) it is clear that this aspect of things lies totally beyond the realm of education. Therefore there is no need to remind the reader that, in 1978, the economic recession brought to the forefront *not* the objective needs of the economy, but the fantasy of foreign *competition*, irrespective of any training.

Consequences for the training programmes

This is precisely where the contradiction lies: the effects of the training programme are by their own logic part of the individualistic system of the relationship to things. Their function is to have the foreigners accept this essential feature of modernity. However, it is found that this relationship (far over and above the short period of time allowed for the training and the exact place where it is conducted) is at variance, to a greater or lesser degree, with the original system of symbolic references, the more so as one finds the multiform re-emergence, case by case, of hierarchical relationships wherein the immigrant, subordinated (and with what violence!) as a general rule, becomes superordinated in such and such a sector of the relationship to people, whatever, moreover, his linguistic or technical capabilities.

If certain training programmes can better elucidate these problems (and, we repeat, accompany the immigrants in *their own* resolution of tension by explicitly offering them discussion and comparison), it must be understood that we are in the frontier area between the ordered world of qualified *and* native wage-earners on the one hand and, on the other, the world of those whom these same wage-earners call, on the basis of individualistic values, 'marginals'. It is well to remember that a not inconsiderable percentage of the 'marginals' is also composed of natives, and that the real but concealed presence of hierarchy within the modern world itself, its logical necessity, is revealed in it.[1]

To presume, over and above comparison during the sessions, to *influence* this 'multiplex' situation through training programmes, of whatever length, is a pure voluntaristic illusion, born of the individualism that fails to recognise the totality and interdependence of the social body, which are in logical contrast with it.

From this there ensues an involuntary but disastrous consequence: the training programmes *in this situation* are but a diversionary tactic, a means of having the foreigners interiorise the individualisation of failure, the emergence of an individualistic and unhappy moral consciousness; thus there is a logical need for a hierarchy of choice among individuals, though explicit statement of the principle is not ventured; it is even denied by the individualistic assertion of the possibility of social mobility via the training programmes.

For these 'new Individuals', this amounts to submission, not subordination, in the guise of individual accession to freedom.

---

1 In the case of France, one speaks of those 'excluded' or of a 'Fourth World', and it is alleged that they represent some 10 per cent of the population. Parallels are found in the phenomenon of poverty in the USA, and in the proposals here and there in the Western world of a 'negative income tax' intended to re-integrate these populations with the circuit of the relationship to things.

Bibliography

Allain-Dupré, B., Catani, M., Desgoutte, Doneux, J.L., *La parole de l'autre: les travailleurs étrangers et le français*, Classiques Hachette, Paris, 1977 (Collection 'Pédagogies pour notre temps').

Arondo, M., *Moi la bonne*, Paris, Stock 2, 1974.

Ath-Messaoud, M. and Gillette, A., *L'immigration algérienne en France*, Editions Entente, Paris, 1976.

Bloch, M., *Les rois thaumaturges*, Editions A. Colin, Paris, 1960.

Catani, M., *Apprentis: 4 heures à l'école et 36 à la production*, Cerf, Paris, 1973a, (Collection 'Attention école).

Catani, M., *L'alphabétisation des travailleurs étrangers: une relation dominant-dominé*, Tema Formation, Paris, 1973b.

Catani, M. and Mohamed, M., *Journal de Mohamed*, Stock 2, Paris, 1973.

Catani, M., 'Jardins comparés: nos choux — vos poireaux', in *Traverses*, no. 5-6, *Jardins contre nature*, Editions de Minuit, Paris, 1976.

Catani, M., 'Tatouage, maquillage: signe ou symbole', in *Traverses*, no. 7, *Maquiller*, Editions de Minuit, Paris, 1976.

Catani, M., 'Ici la viande n'est pas bonne', in *Traverses*, no. 8, *Les bêtes*, Editions de Minuit, Paris, 1976.

Catani, M., Carton, M., *Guide to the analysis and evaluation, from the social and cultural point of view, of training programmes for migrant workers and their families*, Reports/Studio, Green Series MIW.I, Division for the Study of Development, Unesco, Paris, 1977.

Dumont, L., *Homo Hierarchicus: The caste system and its implications*, completed and revised edition, University of Chicago Press, 1980.

Dumont, L., 'The Modern Conception of the Individual', *Contribution to Indian Sociology*, VIII October 1965.

Dumont, L., *From Maudeville to Marx; the genesis and triumph of economic ideologie* (Homo Aequalis 1), University of Chicago Press, 1977.

Dumont, L., 'The Anthropological Community and the ideology' in *Social Change Informations*, Vol. VX VIII, no. 6, 1979, pp. 785-817.

Flandrin, J.L., *Amours paysannes*, Collection 'Archives' no. 57. Gallimard-Juillard, Paris, 1975.

Gavina, C., *Senza patente, una prostituta romana racconta il mondo*, Collection 'Tascabili Bompiani', no. 14, Bompiani, Milan, 1976.

Guerrand, R.H., 'Les promiscuités de l'Ancien Régime', in Chabot, P., *Jean et Yvonne domestiques en 1900*, Tema, Paris, 1977.

IRFED, *Esquisse d'une méthodologie interculturelle pour la formation des enseignants et des opérateurs sociaux intervenant dans le milieu des travailleurs migrants*, Rapport établi dans le cadre de 'Travaux préparatoires aux interventions du Fonds Social Europeén', Paris, 1975.

Jamous, R., *Honneur et baraka*, Thesis for the Doctorate 3rd cycle, Paris, EHESS, 1977 (polycopié).

Rocha Trindade, M.B., *Immigrés Portugais*, Lisbon, Instituto Superior de Ciências Sociais e Politica Ultramarina, 1973.

Sayad, A., 'El Ghorba', in *Actes de la Recherche en sciences sociales*, no. 2, Editions de Minuit, Paris, 1975.
Sayad, A., 'Les trois âges de la migration algérienne', in *Actes de la Recherche en sciences sociales*, no. 15, Editions de Minuit, Paris, 1977.

Unesco, Division for the Study of Development, *Guide to the analysis and evaluation, from the social and cultural point of view, of training programmes for migrant workers and their families*, Reports and Studies, Green Series, no. MIW 1, Paris, 1977.

Additional reading

Icart, F., *Rapport à l'Assemblée Nationale* (no. 2685) on the social costs of immigration, *Journal Officiel*, Paris, 1976.

Lepors, A., *Immigration et développement économique et social* (Etudes RCB), Documentation Française, Paris, 1977.

These two studies provide all the information currently available on the foreign presence in France; the second publication is remarkable for its attempts to simulate the effects of an increase or decrease in the foreign presence in relation to the French economy.

Furthermore, the Ministère du Travail et de la Participation, Direction de la Population et des Migrations, Mission de Recherche et Documentation publishes 'Comptes rendus, synthèses de travaux sur le fait migratoire', which are forwarded on request.

Regarding the training of foreign workers, see the collection of periodicals *Migrants-Formation*, published by the Centre National de Documentation Pédagogique, Ministère de l'Education Nationale (91, rue Gabriel Péri, 92120 Montrouge). In particular for the training within firms, nos 17-18.

Within the context of our own critical analysis of the phenomenon of the foreign presence, the present study constitutes a continuation and application of: *Critiques à propos des cours d'alphabétisation* (Catani, M. 1973); *Recueils de données ethnographiques et sociographiques* (Catani, M. 1973); *Propositions sociologiques, linguistiques, pédagogiques et didactiques* (Catani, M. 1973) which naturally determine the Unesco 'Guide' and the present study.

5 Joint theoretical and methodological commentary

MAURIZIO CATANI , NORBERT DITTMAR
AND CAROLYN SWETLAND

Although characterised by dissimilar scientific approaches, the three preceding studies reveal a definite convergence in their analysis of the conditions of second-language learning, from a sociological and anthropoligical as well as linguistic standpoint.[1] The present commentary, jointly prepared by the three research directors, seeks to stress these convergences.

The populations observed are made up of adult foreign workers of both sexes, but observations are also made concerning the children of migrant workers. The linguistic situations observed in the three countries first call for reflection on the effects of guided learning (training courses) and unguided on-the-job learning, which is by far the most frequent and probably the most effective hitherto. Hence a considerable portion of the analyses is devoted to defining the inter-relations between the actual situation (learning on the job) and the largely hypothetical situation (generalisation of specific methodologies of instruction).

This observation, valid for the three countries usually considered so different in respect of language, as sources of migratory flows and as

1 The three studies correspond, though only partially, to the Research Reports of the Division for the Study of Development, Green Series, no. MIW 1, Unesco, Paris. They are not the synthesised summary of as many research reports, bearing the same titles, which can be read *in extenso* in the Green Series.

regards their numerical size, prompts the three authors to formulate the hypothesis that the observations and proposals of these studies are also applicable to the other Western European countries of immigration, independently of the specifically national ideologies which each of these industrial countries habitually advances in order to differentiate itself from the others. The authors consider that the substance, and quite often the form, of the difficulties, not only linguistic, but also social, that foreign workers encounter are common to them all whatever the country of residence.

We may note also that the countries of origin constitute the background of the comparison, even if they are not analysed specifically and in detail, although for purposes of demonstration a few pertinent factors may be mentioned. It should be emphasised that from the scientific standpoint, subsequent studies should explicitly include detailed comparative aspects, even though it has not been possible to provide them in the present case.

The migratory situation

We must point out that we mean by 'migratory situation' much more than by the term 'migration' alone. Indeed, that word covers historically too many circumstances for it to be used without ambiguity. The case of Norway will sufficiently illustrate how difficult it is to distinguish within a brief time-span between situations of conquest, of colonisation, and of populating.

What we affirm is that though each of the three countries has, in the past, had diverse forms of migration, resulting in a population situation induced by quite dissimilar political relationships, World War II and the postwar period modified the traditional definitions of the migratory situation in Western Europe:

1 Traditional flows have changed in composition, and migration no longer appears irreversible to them, whereas it has been felt to be so in the past.

2 New sectors of activity distribute the migratory flows differently; foreign workers are more 'visible' than in the past.

3 The economy of industrialised countries can no longer do without the foreign presence, which has become structural; that is a known fact, although it is not always stated with sufficient clarity in political circles.

On the one hand, the new migratory flows are increasingly linked to the vicissitudes of the international economic situation and, on the other, the individuals composing them wish — as a general rule, but without really being able to manage it — to return to their country of origin after an interval which they would like to be a short period of transition. As such a plan in most cases cannot be realised, the stresses between individual desires and collective possibilities are exacerbated.

Whatever the case, individually, of the success or failure of migration, there are fewer 'good' immigrants, i.e. fewer foreign workers disposed to melt into the mass of natives, or at least willing to be ignored by them. On the whole, the migratory flows are now composed of foreign workers who demand to return home with a certain social status, a feeling of their dignity besides the savings deemed adequate for realising their plans. Rarely obtaining satisfaction, they seek and settle into a back-and-forth situation between the two countries that voluntarily maintains them in a state of critical availability.

The appeal made by the countries of production (employment) to migratory flows which have become increasingly more culturally and economically remote, has no other objective than this rapid increase in the economic and status demands of the former 'good' immigrants.

The economic and symbolic domination exercised by the industrial countries in relation to the underemployment in the insufficiently industrialised and culturally dominated countries maintains their power of attraction, even though the juridical, economic, social and symbolic situation of foreign workers in them is detestable. This asymmetrical dialectic between centre and periphery exempts the industrialised countries from planning necessary investments commensurate with actual needs, once the flows of potential migrants are maintained through the attraction such countries exercise.

Migratory flow management policies

Although there are minor differences in the laws and regulations of the three countries, the same economic and ideological logic underlies the actual management of migratory flows: it springs from the structural need for the presence of foreign workers. Although details of the various laws differ, both police and administrative practices as well as the choice of factors to be controlled are the same. Whether it is a question of a clandestine or ill-controlled presence (as was long the case in France), or a question, as in the German Federal Republic, of an apparently better-controlled and restricted immigration; whether there are, as in Norway, official categories of immigrants duplicated by other forms equally official but lacking the right to the same classification (foreign workers in the merchant marine or the petroleum industry), nothing alters the fact that the foreign presence is initially desired by the economic and ideological power. Thereafter, it will be disciplined by the administrative decisions of police courts.

Expulsion is the typical police-court measure in these circumstances. It is of course possible in all three countries to appeal through legal proceedings, but that is most often difficult and unavailing: not being native-born logically implies the possibility of expulsion, and from this basic discrimination stem all the special laws and the even more restrictive police practices. Thus, the provisions restricting the geographic and professional mobility of foreign workers vary, but in all three countries the final result is the same.

The worker's place of residence and his lodgings are controlled, whether by the state or the employer matters little; or else he is left to the so-called laws of the private real-estate market which fosters the development of 'ghettos' or shantytowns invariably kept under surveillance by the police, who find in them an excellent means of localising potentially dangerous populations.

The various categories of residence and work permits, apparently differing widely in the three countries, all correspond to the same basic logic: the economic and statutory protection of natives. Finally, although the Universal Declaration of Human Rights[1] recognises the right of family members to be united, the legislation for acceding to public housing is so complicated and inflexible in the three countries that it ends in a vicious circle: to be eligible for public housing, the family must already be present in the new country, yet it has no right to be there unless already assured of lodgings. The result is that the foreign head of a family is almost absolutely obliged either to break the law or resort to the free real-estate market in seeking sub-standard accommodation which the natives, naturally, would not accept. It has already been noted that the overall result among the countries of production is a decrease in the total amount of social investments; it must further be pointed out here that, though the difficulties are more acute in the case of foreign workers, the situation of a large proportion of the native workers in the three countries obeys the same logic.

What fundamentally differentiates foreign from native workers is their lack of the right to vote, though they are compelled to pay the same taxes as natives. This is a clear manifestation of the actual existence of a statutory hierarchy exceeding mere economic domination. In the perspective of modern egalitarian values, there is no more urgent political task than that of proposing a philosophically satisfactory solution to the internal logical contradiction between the universalist affirmation of Human Rights on the one hand and their particularist denial on the other. When the principle of nationality is at variance with the declarations of principle, practice subordinates non-natives to natives.

---

1 Adopted on 10 December 1948 by the United Nations General Assembly.

Hence it little matters that, on the surface, Norway and the German Federal Republic refuse to consider themselves as countries of immigration, whereas France frequently alludes to its traditional role as a land of asylum open not only to political exiles, but to migrants of all sorts. In practice, all the countries devise different laws, jurisdictions and practices whose end result is a distinct discrimination between natives and non-natives.

Training policy

The dominating-dominated relation between the countries of production and their immigrant populations is apparent not only in its structural economic aspects, but also in its ideological, and ultimately symbolic aspects. Training of the foreign worker and his family offers the most classic form of this ideological domination. The basic characteristics of this training, despite minor details in the three countries, are the following:

1 An official rhetoric consisting of statements of a variable number of intentions, accompanied by an enormous lag in achievements.

2 Even the few 'showcases' that go by the name of training programmes are all based on classic institutional models faithfully reproducing the cognitive models of the countries of production. Furthermore, there is a refusal to recognise other institutional, and especially cognitive models. No allowance is made conceptually or institutionally for any but the scientific models of the industrialised countries.

As a result, approximately 90 per cent of the adult immigrant populations never attend a training course in the language of the country of production. In Germany, statistically, one immigrant will have this possibility every 400 years. In Norway, when he enters training, he is obliged to do so alongside diplomats, businessmen, etc., since courses specifically designed for immigrants are almost non-existent. In France, not only is the relation between foreign adult workers' potential needs and the courses actually given very unfavourable to them, but the spirit of lifelong education laws is thwarted, for the foreigners will be involved in learning the language, whereas their native colleagues (through the funds automatically deducted from everyone's earnings) can start technical training immediately.

In the case of the few foreigners who attend courses, the morpho-syntactical and semantic teaching system is derived from the culture of the country of production, and hence is virtually incomprehensible to a great portion of the immigrant population. As for the others without any training course, it is at their work that they learn haphazardly and informally a bizarre mixture of codes which the studies describe in detail but which socially nearly always brand them as 'linguistic inferiors'.

If we posit initially the theory that the language of the country of production is required for potential social mobility in the new country or for professional training, and if we grant that one or the other, or both, are required for the country of origin in case of return, it can be said that the lack of an adapted training policy perpetuates not only the exploitation of the immigrant in the country of production, but also that of the countries of origin, for their nationals are no longer being trained. Only one model of development, based on industrial scientific models, is dangled before them, no account being taken of their own conceptual universe.

Aside from the naive and obviously blameworthy ethnocentrism of such scarce training, there is a fundamental socio-centrism which not only exaggerates the ideological and symbolic disparity, but feeds on it in order to maintain, in addition to a conceptual primacy of the scientific models of industrialised countries, a single means of access to such conceptualisation through its educational forms.

Research reports

Aims of the studies

Our preceding three studies have roughly three main purposes:

1 They seek to document the processes of second-language learning by foreign workers of different origins in three countries of production.

2 They attempt through various methods of analysis — in which the structural frame of reference is nevertheless the same — to recognise the linguistic, socio-cultural and ethnic factors that foster or hinder learning, both in language-training courses and in the daily situations where unguided learning occurs.

3 The results of the observations relating to 'learners' careers' (guided and unguided situations) are subjected to a pedagogic, socio-political and ultimately ethical evaluation with a view to drawing conclusions that will make better language training possible. The consensus that emerges is the importance of tackling the problem from the standpoint of the social and cultural interests defined by the immigrants themselves.

The three teams approached these questions differently. The French team neglects them and the Norwegian team criticises the customary formal and institutional training in the courses for immigrants. They consider that such courses inevitably lead to failure unless the social and cultural differences between instructors and students are taken into account. It does not suffice to recognise the immigrants' actual experience, but rather it must be taken as the starting point for any training. The latter will then be based on reformulation of their experience. The essential, though not sole, result of this is that 'face-to-face' relations are the essential pedagogical choice for such a type of training. We emphasise this because audio-visual methods for immigrants can be considered as ineffectual since based on presuppositions unsuited to such populations. The success of second-language learning is further analysed by the West German team from the standpoint of success in transferring achievements to situations in the social context. Stress is placed on the linguistic characteristics constituting a restricted verbal repertory that will be both a reflection of the semantic requirements in everyday conversation and evidence that the conditions of social environment, contacts and future planning, etc., essentially determine the level attained in both guided and unguided learning. The three studies are complementary. The French and Norwegian studies explain the aspects of failure and the necessity for language training within an institutional framework (once maximum account has been taken of the preceding period of unguided learning), whereas the West German study explores the linguistic conditions for a satisfactory transfer to everyday social communication.

Methodology

Methodology is here taken in the sense of analytical data; theoretical approach; methods of description; levels of analysis; conduct of the research.

Data

The three studies are concerned with verbal learning. Hence, their entire argumentation is based on verbal statements that are explained by pragmatic, social, cultural, and other situations. The verbal data are transcribed and used differently by the three teams. Obviously, if the aim is a detailed analysis of the morpho-syntax of the immigrants' speech (as in the German study), one must start with a 'closer' phonetic transcription. On the other hand, if the aim is an ethnographic analysis of the discourse as a whole, it suffices to start with a semantic realisation of the content which is spelled in a standard way for the dual purpose of merely reformulating incorrect performances and of interpreting and studying the semantic fields (French study). The Norwegian study falls between these two approaches, transcription of the data serving for both a linguistic and an ethnographic analysis.

A functional differentiation can also be applied to the extra-linguistic data (social, cultural, etc.). Depending upon whether an analysis is based on a qualitative or quantitative model, the methods of description will be adapted to that chief function of the study. Thus the German team classifies the social data obtained in a guided conversation into categories, which presupposes a quantitative and correlative description. Processing of the extra-linguistic data by the French and Norwegian teams differs fundamentally from that procedure. Social and cultural manifestations are classified and interpreted according to the methodology of an ethnographic monograph.

While there is a common point in these studies based on specific linguistic and social data, yet there are two differences, albeit superficial ones: the sampling in the Norwegian and German studies is larger than in the French study; recordings of the linguistic data in the German study were made in the immigrant workers' social milieu itself, whereas the French study chiefly involves recordings made during second-language courses. In the Norwegian case, varied sources were used to document language use both during courses and in different social situations.

Theoretical approach

The theoretical approach bears essentially on two aspects of the analysis, i.e. description and explanation of the linguistic and extra-linguistic data. Without going into a detailed discussion of the studies, it will be noted immediately that the German study is more confined to linguistic fields, whereas the French study is oriented toward comparative sociology and the educational sciences. The Norwegian study, comprising both aspects, is linguistic and ethnographic, quantitative and qualitative. But, without denying the differences, one observes that there is also a common socio-linguistic trait.

As regards the approaches in general, a distinction must at all events be made between the substantially different starting-points of the French and West German studies. The French study starts with the fact that social and linguistic data so overlap at all times that they form a process of mutual interaction. The process can then be described by a pragmatic and interpretative analysis which does not separate these two aspects of the analysis. Such separation was made for purely analytical purposes in the German study. The basis of that study can be considered as structuralist. The two sets of data can be related only if each set in itself is analysed separately. We call this approach 'correlative'. The other approach, although considering itself structural, goes beyond this aim, ending with a symbolic and anthropological systematisation, and can be considered as functional and interpretative. The correlative view is both quantitative and static and is thus opposed to the other, which could be considered as qualitative and dynamic. Once again, it must be stressed that these two approaches are complementary. The Norwegian study comprises a quantitative analysis of the linguistic data and a qualitative analysis of the data of social interaction. For details concerning the theoretical approaches, we refer the reader to the reports themselves (*Reports/Studies* of the Division for the Study of Development, Green Series, no. MIW.1, Unesco, Paris).

Methods of description

The different theoretical approaches produce different methods of description. The 'grammar of varieties' and the 'correlative' approach require advance representation, segmentation, classification, correlating on several planes of analysis and of correlation (West German case). What is essential for processing the data is definition of the sampling and quantitative differentiation, but it must be emphasised that this process is possible only for the fields of grammar. Beyond that, in the semantic and pragmatic fields, as shown especially in the French study, a qualitative description is necessary which, in future, should lead to the anthropological description of the system. Ideally, the occurrence ought, at each renewal, to be interpreted in its immediate context and in the symbolic system to which it belongs. Without discussing these various techniques of systematising, we draw the reader's attention to the fact that, in the first case, the descriptive models are derived from an explicit system model, whereas in the second case the model involved is flexible and 'open'.

As concerns the levels of analysis, the German study is restricted to grammar, especially syntax, but also analyses phonological, morphological and semantic features. The French study consists of a description of the semantic fields, occasionally using the techniques of comparative sociology and linguistic reformulation. The Norwegian study comprises the two levels of morpho-syntax and ethno-linguistic comparison.

Practical consequences of the three studies

The three studies can be examined from two points of view: linguistic and pedagogical. On reading them, one may also feel, depending upon which aspect is stressed, that what is gained in linguistic formalisation is lost in dynamic pedagogy — and vice versa.

However, one of the practical applications that follows from a reading of these three studies is the obvious possibility of combining the linguistic and pedagogical aspects in the light of the common sociological analysis. While the French study stresses pedagogy, and in that context[1] the linguist is asked to legitimise scientifically what long teaching experience has shown to be effective, and though in the French study the linguist is therefore subordinated to the practitioner, it is clear that in the West German study the emphasis is placed on the necessity for the instructor to adhere to the linguist's minimal scientific requirements, lest he prevents himself from accomplishing his mission.

Convergence of the German linguistic work (which, from the French viewpoint can be defined as *a priori*) with the altogether comparable results of the French linguistic work (which, from the German viewpoint, can be defined as *a posteriori*) augurs the discovery of an extremely fruitful line of research/action adapted to the situation of foreign workers.

Indeed, from the standpoint of research/action, the functional schema is outlined, even though not yet fully realised, in the Norwegian study. The research/action team is not only balanced in its composition, but is also composed of instructor-researchers belonging to the same migratory flow as the foreign workers being trained. Hence it is of little consequence that from a linguistic standpoint these studies momentarily lack the West German or French systematisation. What should be emphasised as a positive result of the Unesco research in Europe is that effective instruction lies in the confluence of the West German and French requirements, once the implementing team is composed as is the Norwegian one.

To summarise, the instruction cannot be effective unless it begins with the foreigners' experience, however ill-formulated, in the second language. The essential pedagogical device — but not the only one — is reformulation; to be effective, such reformulation must satisfy three criteria:

1 Respect the original culture in order to understand it linguistically.

2 Find where the difficulties lie in terms of the target language and of the mother-tongue (West German studies).

3 Find where the difficulties peculiar to a given group lie in relation to output thresholds (*'seuils de sortie'*) in terms of a communication fraught with the symbolic need 'for a perpetual expression of language, which is a locus of a set of occurrences (*déroulements*), repetitions and combinations that perpetually renews and enlarges its field of application.[2]

1 B. Allain-Dupré, M. Catani, Desgoutte and J.L. Doneux, *La parole de l'autre: les travailleurs et les francais*, Classiques Hachette, Paris, 1977 (collection 'Pédagogies pour notre temps').

2 *La parole de l'autre, op. cit.*

The reformulation then is based not only on what the foreign workers say, but also on what the linguist can say of the reasons for the result.

Hence, to be effective, training requires instructors who, as the methodological requirements of the Norwegian team show, are capable of teaching and of formalising their teaching practice, while distinguishing the scientific levels that compose their work as a whole.

Once again, the situation of foreign workers is no different, save in intensity and urgency, from that of part of the native populations. If the instruction is to be other than a passive — and unsuccessful — apprenticeship, teachers must be thoroughly trained, both those working with natives and those working with foreigners.

But that affirmation of principle and the remarks preceding it should not obscure the fact that the clarity and coherence of the results obtained by placing the three studies in perspective indicate that *any* individual teacher can benefit from reading them. Even without being part of a research/action team, he can now ascertain how and in what direction to evaluate and modify his own teaching practice.

Prospects for a training policy

One thing is evident. The three teams, each working independently of the others, using different methodologies and studying dissimilar immigrant populations in three Western European countries displaying great quantitative differences in population, culture and language, reached the same conclusion: the foreign worker, whether in Germany, Norway or France, has no actual possibility of mastering through institutional channels the language of the country where he works and resides. Moreover, the logic of the rare training courses offered him serves only to camouflage the empiric reality of a negation of his very presence.

The profusion of details found in the three studies allows no reason to assume that the migratory situation would be any different in the other countries employing immigrant labour in Western Europe. Can one therefore hope for a meaningful training policy for the ten to twelve million foreign workers who are helping to strengthen and develop the European economy?

Although studies posing the problem in its full scope are rare, they are nevertheless possible (we are here giving proof of this). The question lies then not in the lack of scientific and methodological indications, for they exist or can be rapidly provided, but in the political determination to change them from their role as an alibi or 'showcase' into socially meaningful achievements.

251

PART II

6 Introduction: research on a 'lost generation' — educating women migrants in industrialised countries
MICHEL ORIOL

In the social sciences, the initial aim of a research project often bears little relation to what comes out of it. Initially, the purpose, more or less explicit, is to gather data which will facilitate the running of institutions, and will allow objectives to be better and more accurately defined. In the long run, this regulatory function is brought into question because the social need formulated *ab initio* is seen to be less and less relevant. Even if the investigators reject a purely ideological function, they point out to the institution that it is not actually doing what it believes it is, and that the problems it wishes to resolve are beyond its scope. This persistent contradiction between official investigations and their outcome is a characteristic feature of the field of study covering training and education. If the aim is to analyse processes, instead of a discourse on methodology one gets a theoretical study of socialisation and acculturation. If one speaks of effects, one ends up, not by evaluating educational action, but rather by viewing it as part of a whole network of causal factors and manifestations which makes it virtually impossible to consider it in isolation.

Our research team and our partners experienced this inevitable drift when attempting a comparison, on an international scale, of the conditions and types of education dispensed to women migrants, particularly to illiterate women. It is not that the necessary information simply has not been collected but that it could be if the need for it was pointed out sufficiently strongly. To begin with, we shall have to consider the real meaning of this non-availability of information, whether it is not the reflection of a crisis confronting our 'blueprints for society' and extending in every direction far beyond strictly pedagogical matters.

If the record of failures and successes is inconclusive, we feel that this is because criteria are lacking or are contradictory, which amounts to the same thing. Pakistanis in Norway, Greeks in Australia, Turks in Germany: these women only resemble each other in respect of negative aspects — isolation, insecurity, instability — which, rather than reflecting inability and incompetence, express the quandary of the 'host' societies with regard to them. In the maze of uncharted paths, how can they be led with assurance and resolution along the right path to progress?

Doubt does not justify passivity. If education *per se* fails to provide solutions, it is still worthwhile to be aware of the conditions likely to contribute to effective training. The few examples that can be brought to mind tend to show that essentially the women must be persuaded to speak for themselves, on the basis of their almost universal status of 'specialists in primary relations'. But, no one can prejudge what they will then be ready to say or to associate themselves with. A threefold alienation — economic, cultural and sexual — characterises the situation of women (Hoffman-Novotny, 1978). Prevalent theories deal with these three aspects separately and generally do not intermingle, either in theory or in practice, trade unionism, anti-racism and feminism. The immigrant to whom these distinctions mean nothing will perhaps some day have a lot to teach us.[1] The three studies presented hereafter touch on the various aspects of this interrelated alienation.

Situation without prospects

The gathering of information about measures taken to teach immigrant women to read and write and to provide them with further education was doubtless no easy matter, owing to the relative rarity of actions of this type. But what is far more striking is that they have been so little institutionalised. Either, as in Germany, there is no public or private body which centralises and co-ordinates information on this subject. Or else, as in Switzerland, there are only local initiatives. Or again, as in France, while benefiting from public recognition and encouragement,

---

1 Before dealing specifically with the problems raised by the different accounts assembled here, we wish to stress that, since international communication has proceeded in an increasingly difficult context since 1973, most of the contributors gathered their data and drafted their reports in unfavourable conditions. This should be taken into account in view of certain gaps in information or unevennesses in drafting, and the absence of papers from countries whose contribution would have been sizeable: Belgium, the Netherlands, the UK.

the experimental measures that have been taken are on no more firm a basis, being at the mercy of government policy changes. (One need only observe the gap between the 1971 law, which assigned twofold priority to the education of immigrant women – related to their sex and their origin – and the recent administrative memorandum which bars women from joining their husbands or fathers on the job market, thus practically denying them any access to rationally directed training). Sweden is apparently an exception, but though it possesses a legislative and institutional apparatus unrivalled for the means it proposes and the objectives which it sets, the fact remains that here too there are no field surveys able to shed light on the actual use made of this apparatus. The available evidence seems to suggest that while the effort to take into account the needs of immigrants is remarkable and exemplary, it remains marred by ambiguities. For the adult migrants, the pressure of economic conditions is so strong that the arsenal of laws on education is liable to lose some of its effectiveness. Without even mentioning segregation, if women migrants are at a relative disadvantage in regard to access to the job market,[1] they are not likely to take Swedish culture to their hearts. It is important in particular to know whether the institutionalisation of cultural pluralism, of which Sweden offers a brave example, fully enables the women to choose a path devoid of alienating contradictions. This is a concern, too, in other countries.

'Betwixt and between', repeats Ayse Kudat, speaking of Turkish exiles in Germany. Let us make no mistake: the question here is not one of a role of mediator or intercessor, enabling the family group to place itself comfortably between two poles, but one of simultaneous reference to two incompatible value systems. The Algerian woman described by Camille Lacoste-Dujardin (1977) watches so closely over the education of her children that, despite her attention, her eldest son can very quickly be emancipated from the family in true Western fashion. She can be said to succeed in losing him, or to lose him by success. 'Some loss in gains', to quote Kudat once more.

Generation lost between two cultures

In 1820 or again in 1920, bourgeois intellectuals, faced with breaks in the history of civilisations, felt strongly that life was irreversibly deprived of all meaning, pending the emergence of new value systems. The

---

1   Hilde Smith, 1978 shows that this also applies to immigrant girls, both with respect to the risk of unemployment and the relationship between job status and level of qualifications.

woman migrant feels this break just as strongly, but she lacks the language and the words to write a book about it.

Language handicaps, added to sexual handicaps, destine her for jobs for which there is no competition. Her work is only made bearable by projection, on behalf of her children. This doubtless explains the astonishing statistics which show that second-generation immigrant girls surpass Swedish girls, even in linguistic tests.[1] For her, however, working life is too impoverished to supply the means of restructuring her personal values.

Thus we can easily see why she abandons her job, to return and/or to marry. But return to what? Henceforth, she has other needs, other aspirations, other desires. She finds herself in a situation which is neither the extended family nor the working class. How can she be trained for this ambiguity?

Ayse Kudat discusses returning Turkish women whose working experience in Germany paradoxically imparts to them *petit bourgeois* aspirations and conduct, and who return to find themselves in a blind alley.

Sossie Andizian and Jocelyne Streiff recount the meandering of a North African woman between two models, haplessly bounced back and forth between them.

Mirjana Morokvasic shows that persistent recourse to abortion and reluctance to use contraceptives is an indication, among Yugoslav women, of continued underlying dependence on the male partner, even when outward behaviour — sexual freedom, rejection of family tutelage — seems to point to 'feminist' leanings.[2]

This last example provides ample food for thought and discussion. On the one hand, it raises questions concerning the meaning of official equality between the sexes in Yugoslavia. Is the 'emancipation' model there radically different from those created by struggles against sexual inequality in capitalist countries? Are the pertinent distinctions here those between religious traditions or political regimes?

But it must also be noted that the women often regard abortion, in contrast to contraception, as 'natural'. What is the origin of this? Rapid, controlled 'modernisation'? Traditional recourse to abortion-inducing remedies? Or resistance to the idea of one's own body being reduced to the status of an object by the chemical drugs? If, as Mirjana Morokvasic

---

1 It would also be useful to know the breakdown of this second generation by cultural origin. It is doubtless mainly Finnish.

2 It is none the less worth mentioning that Yugoslav women living in Sweden are an exception, in the sense that they avoid repeated abortions. Information and education are thus not devoid of influence, as Hilde Smith 1978 suggests, when a climate of exchange is vigorously stimulated.

points out, 'Information is not enough', this is because the way in which perception of self and of the environment is organised on the cognitive plane and raises major obstacles to any new approach. The reaction of North African immigrant women to the use of contraceptives is an even more striking throwback to the historical dimensions of culture, in terms of ritual and taboo. Lost between two cultures, the female immigrants of this generation summon up all the force of their innermost cultural heritage to defend themselves against deeply anxiety-provoking situations. It would be useless to attempt to unmask these 'prejudices' with the magic wand of liberating ideologies.

When will the time come to speak out?

Any really serious educational project begins then by admitting cultural realities, namely, not only acknowledging the right to express them, but also recognising their positive significance. Sweden again represents among receiving countries a positive example in this direction.

> Can we always be so sure, in the collision of cultures which we see every day in Rinkeby, that it is our own culture which should dominate? Perhaps we should make an effort to learn something and not just teach. Do not several of the immigrant nations have a considerably more humane outlook on life than the Swedish society offers today, at any rate in the family and among relations? I am thinking of the contact between different generations, between the healthy and the sick, the weak and the strong. Is not their ability to enjoy the simple pleasures of life something for us to regain? Perhaps in fact we should consider whether that which we have, without doubt, won by means of increased freedom and openness of example in sex education should be supplemented with something of the respect for fundamental values which is hidden in their apparently primitive and unmodern fear in these matters (Smith, 1978).

This statement, made by the Principal of Rinkeby School in Stockholm, proves yet again the seriousness with which Swedish society tries to acknowledge the right to be different. But, as everyone knows, Sweden has not been spared from racialism, and there will be some to fear that this humanism is not reflected in practice, particularly when it involves the right to be a foreign woman living among the working classes.

The Swedish experiment nevertheless provides an initial answer to these doubts, even if the verdict of history is still undecided (and it may turn out to be a model pattern for assimilation into an exceptionally liberal industrial society). Let us simply mention the great popularity which greets foreign films televised at weekends, which are primarily aimed at the immigrant audience.

What this example shows is the priority that attaches to introducing an anthropological awareness into the state apparatus. It is first up to the dominant society to exorcise its racist and sexist demons. By limiting the training of administrators to law and economics and that of social workers to psychology which is often ethnocentric, one induces in them a sort of blindness to specificity. Leviathan in 1978 is not only cold: he is blind and deaf, so his particular barbarity towards women is not surprising. While it is true that language and literacy training for women migrants constitutes a major objective of research and initiative, there is an even more pressing need to teach a large number of social workers the languages of the foreign communities with which they are in contact. This is the most direct means of acknowledging not only the dignity of the immigrants' culture, but also the validity of what it has to say.

This point was confirmed by experiments that we conducted, against strong bureaucratic resistance, in south-eastern France. To North Africans, the sharp distinction made by the state apparatus between social work and educational work is totally meaningless. Bilingualism, encouraged — or tolerated — in schools today, is essential when the significance of marriage, birth and children is being discussed. To be able to talk together is undoubtedly the one educational recommendation we can make without too much risk of belittling the specificity of any culture.[1]

In most social groups, the woman is socialised in such a way that her extreme competence in the direct management of interpersonal relationships contrasts with her inability to participate in the control of formalised institutions. This is a serious handicap in dealing with companies, social services and municipal facilities. But it can be overcome by reliance on her most solid cultural asset, her vigilance and mastery in direct interpersonal strategies, which make her, within the community, a flexible and efficient bond, as shown for example by the descriptions of Sossie Andizian and Jocelyne Streiff.

Education and training must be organised flexibly enough to get away from tedious school rituals and draw life from natural groupings, whether pre-existent or formed under their influence.

---

1 As suggested by Jocelyne Streiff, it would none the less be wise to inquire into the factors which make learning really 'functional', in terms of both social goal and technical objectives. It is unfortunate that the debate on methods, which gradually intensified as the World Functional Literacy Programme got under way, has today lost some of its impetus.

This is certainly not a cure for all ills. Women migrants cannot escape the fundamental contradiction which prevents women from speaking out, namely the fact of being educated to live and to deal, in relationships, with the facets that the dominant logic hides away in institutions.

The result is fragmentary knowledge, leading with difficulty to the mobilisation of total identity: the employer masks the company and class relationships; the husband hides hierarchical family structures; diplomatic and consular relations mask neo-imperialist cultural and economic domination.

There is nevertheless perhaps more reason for patience than for pessimism. Gramsci showed us that a group can only constitute a political totality through the ideology of the 'organic intellectual'. Some second-generation women immigrants are sufficiently well advanced to assume this unprecedented role, when the opportune moment arrives.

Bibliography

Andizian, S. and Streiff, J., 'Transpositions et réinterpretations du rôle féminin traditionnel en situation d'immigration', paper prepared for the Symposium on Migrant Workers, Heidelberg, 1978.

Ayse, K., 'Personal, familial and societal impacts of Turkish Women's immigration to Europe', paper prepared for Unesco, 1978.

Hoffman-Novotny, H.J., 'Sociological aspects of the situation of migrant women', paper prepared for the Symposium on Migrant Workers, Heidelberg, 1978.

Lacoste-Dujardin, C., *Dialogue de femmes en ethnologie*, Maspero, Paris, 1977.

Morokvasic, M., 'Limitations of births among Yugoslav women migrants in France, the Federal Republic of Germany and Sweden', paper prepared for Unesco, 1978.

Smith, H., 'Living conditions of French migrants in Sweden', paper prepared for Unesco, 1978.

7 Limitation of births among Yugoslav women migrants in France, the Federal Republic of Germany and Sweden

MIRJANA MOROKVASIC*

Long before modern methods of contraception were developed and made available to the general public, people had found that they were able to control their reproductive capacity and still have a normal sex life. This realisation was heightened with the development of the most up-to-date techniques, putting women on the road to emancipation and equality between the sexes.

We have chosen the term *limitation* of births for our title out of a number of possible terms: family planning, birth prevention, control or regulation. The term limitation seems to be the most appropriate in regard to the Yugoslav women who are the object of this study, for 'prevention' and 'planning', particularly, suggest a preconceived plan or design as to reproduction. And although Yugoslav women have very definite ideas about the number of children they wish to have, and by and large manage to keep their fertility to something near the desired rate, they do not usually choose the means of achieving their end, and more often than not wait until there is only one way out of an unwanted pregnancy — abortion. It is not until they have had one or two abortions that women begin to think in terms of contraception.

Our primary object in this chapter is to describe the attitudes and behaviour of Yugoslav women as regards birth control. We shall refer to a variety of sources, but the body of our work has been based on the initial findings of our current study on Yugoslav women in France, the

* My research on this topic was terminated in 1977, and my thinking has developed further, so that my interpretations on the basis of new data would now be expressed with more caution. For that I owe very much to Kate Young — who perhaps does not know it — and I would like to express here my sincere thanks to her.

Federal Republic of Germany and Sweden.[1] This is an empirical study aimed at analysing the changes brought about by situations of conflict that result from being a migrant. The analysis covers both working and private life.

The problem of birth control is only one of the subjects dealt with in our study. We have put forward the hypothesis that behaviour patterns and any changes in such patterns are alike determined both by the original socio-cultural background of immigrants and by the impact of their new environment.

Finally, we shall make a number of proposals with a view to informing and educating Yugoslav migrant couples on sexuality and family planning.

The desire to limit the number of births is in itself a refusal or rejection of 'natural' reproduction. There are a number of different cultural or individual reactions to the methods employed. Some are readily accepted, for they are considered 'natural', while others are often rejected as interfering with a woman's physiology. Thus abstinence and coitus interruptus ('my husband is careful') are regarded as 'natural', whereas contraception is unnatural. Curiously enough, although abortion implies external intervention, it is thought of by Yugoslav women as a more natural method than contraception. In this sense, natural is tantamount to 'healthy'.

In many countries, the limitation of births depends on the *status* of women. In some societies, the criterion of a woman's status is the number of children she has produced; the more children she has, the higher her status, whereas an infertile woman is rejected by the community. Thus, there is a connection with socio-economic level; in places where a man's wealth is gauged by the number of hands working on his land, a greater premium will clearly be put on fertile women (World Population Conference, Bucharest, 1974).

In addition, the country's legislative and judicial system can either facilitate family planning by giving women guidance on which course to adopt, or prohibit any form of contraception other than methods considered as natural. There are thus a great many psychological and social pressures that come into play when a couple — or more often, a woman — decides to take measures to curb fertility.

In this particular field, as in any other sphere of life, the difficulties and problems are more acute for immigrant women than for the women of the country itself. The former frequently have to comply with conflicting demands made upon them by virtue of their present and past status. There is also the language problem, which makes it more difficult for them to have access to information and communicate their needs. Even when they are familiar with the language, it does not

1 The study is completed and is available in the form of a mimeographed report (Morokvasic, M. 1980).

264

necessarily mean that the problem of communication (with the doctor or local social worker) is solved.

Most of these women have had some experience of cohabitation, and therefore of various means of birth control (or at least an attitude towards them) before leaving home. What happens when they have to pit their own customs — often those of a small village or region — against those prevailing in their new social environment? To what extent do they submit to these new influences? And which ones? To what extent do they remain true to the original patterns?

The scarcity of studies on birth control among immigrants is part of the overall lack of research on female immigrants (Morokvasic, 1974). Until fairly recently, it was assumed that migration concerned men and men only, with the result that the problems discussed had to do with the sexual deprivation of men on their own; the loneliness of men with no female companionship. Family planning is not thought of as a male problem, and still less as a problem concerning men on their own. It would seem as though it was not until the *legitimate* wives arrived (or were 'discovered' on the spot) that the subject of family planning among immigrants could begin to be discussed.

Yugoslav women seem to be the most emancipated, resourceful and independent of all female migrants. As they nearly all work and earn their living, they acquire a reputable status and are respected by those around them, including their husbands. However, their potential economic independence does not necessarily remove the burden of a collective consciousness, and the more intimate their personal experience is, the more submissive they are to men. At the same time they are also perfectly aware of the fact that there is no law compelling them to have an unwanted child. For them, the right to have an abortion is a fundamental right, and they take as much advantage of it as they did in their home country.

But abortion is no way for a woman to control pregnancy. They have no means of control over what leads up to abortion. They have no control over their bodies; many of them know nothing about their bodies nor about the way they function. The decision as to whether or not they will conceive rests initially with the man. The responsibility, suffering and shame of having an abortion are borne by the woman. The question may be raised why this awareness is not aroused sooner; why do they wait to be confronted with a dilemma; abortion or keeping the unwanted child?

The original socio-cultural background

Unlike societies in which a woman's status depends on her capacity to procreate, in Yugoslavia the criterion of a woman's worth is her capacity to work. Some remote areas are exceptions to this rule, but they are not areas affected by emigration. The fact of working outside the home has an influence on fertility (Breznik, 1971). There are many families who do not want more than one child. This outlook can be attributed to several factors:

1 It may be the consequence of extreme poverty, a situation 'in which even the extra hands would not make much difference', as is the case in Portugal (Ferro, 1975, p. 36).

2 It results from a desire for a certain quality of living for oneself and one's child.

3 It may signify evidence of a realisation by women of the meaning of their traditional role.

4 It may also be evidence of new parent-child relationships.

Yugoslav women emigrate from comparatively developed areas of the country, in which the birth rate is very low. The birth rate is in fact dropping steadily in Yugoslavia. In 1950 it (number of live births per 1,000) was 30.3. By 1970 it had fallen to 17.8 for the whole of Yugoslavia. Of the regions with the highest female emigration rate, Vojvedina (where 42 per cent of emigrants are women) has a birth rate of 13.0; Serbia (where 32 per cent of the total migrant population are women), 14.8; Croatia, the republic which has the highest emigration rate, a third of which is female, has a birth rate of 13.9.

Kosovo, the least developed region of Yugoslavia, has a high birth rate: 36.5. The women hardly ever emigrate from Kosovo. There are only 4 per cent of women among all the migrants from this region and we may assume that they are not a very representative segment of the local female population.

The aforementioned regions are also the most developed areas of Yugoslavia (together with Slovenia, which is more highly developed but has only a small percentage of emigrants). The proportion of women employed, and their levels of education and skills, are higher there than in areas from which there is no female emigration. We know as well that, generally speaking, the higher the standard of living, the higher is the level of education among women, the greater their participation in socio-occupational life and the sharper the decline in the birth rate.

The situation in Yugoslavia is by no means surprising, or different from the situation observed elsewhere. But it is important to bring out these facts in the context of migration as a whole. They show simply that these women are already accustomed to keeping their reproduction under control, with the help of the law.

As we shall see in the next section, abortion is a major method of limiting family size. In her 1939 survey, Ehrlich (1971) mentions abortion as a common practice, especially in Serbia and parts of

Croatia, where there is, however, also a trend towards the prevention of pregnancy. The American anthropologist, Halpern (1967) also reports recourse to abortion as a deliberate means of birth control in his study of the village of Orasac in Serbia.

The legislative framework and practice in Yugoslavia

The socialist countries have all been through periods in which very liberal attitudes to abortion were adopted, and also more restrictive periods (Gardun, 1971; Blayo, 1970). Before the Second World War, abortion was a criminal offence in Yugoslavia (with some exceptions). In terms of the new law of 1952, it is still an offence, but the woman herself is not liable to any penalty. Abortion is permissible only under certain conditions:

1 If rape or incest has occurred;

2 if the pregnant woman is handicapped or a minor;

3 if the life of the woman is in danger; or

4 if there is a risk that the child would be born with serious abnormalities. Social and material conditions are taken into consideration in exceptional cases.

In February 1960, these 'social conditions' were admitted as additional grounds for abortion, and Yugoslavia became one of the countries in which abortion was *de facto* liberalised. From that year, the number of clandestine abortions decreased, but the ratio between the number of legal abortions and the number of births rose sharply (Blayo, 1970; Breznik, 1972). Breznik's study is the most thorough document we have on fertility and related problems in Yugoslavia. It shows how the rate of births, legal abortions and 'incomplete' abortions[1] has evolved over the period 1949 to 1970 in Yugoslavia. It reveals a sharp decline in the birth rate, a rise in the number of abortions and a decrease in the number of 'incomplete' abortions.

The birth-abortion ratio fell from 15 births to every abortion in 1949 to 0.89 births to every abortion in 1960. In that year, there were 139,000 abortions. The number went up to 215,063 in 1963 and 276,249 in 1967, when the ratio reached 0.68:1. The only republic in which there has been a slight drop in the number of abortions is Slovenia. It was also the only republic in which the number of births exceeded the number of abortions in 1967 by two to one. The republic of Serbia alone — which is where two-thirds of our interviewees originally came from — accounts for half the total number of abortions

1 An 'incomplete' abortion is when the woman or another person induces a haemorrhage as though it were a miscarriage. The woman is then taken to hospital.

practised in the country. There are twice as many terminations of pregnancy as births in this republic (0.43 births to every abortion). These figures apply only to official abortions performed in hospitals, clinics and dispensaries, and do not include illegal abortions for which by definition an accurate estimate cannot be made.

In 1969, alarmed at the large number of abortions which had become virtually the only means of birth control, the Federal Assembly on 25 April adopted a resolution on family planning (*Zena Danas* no. 264, 1969; Tomsic, 1973; Vida, 1975). This ruling formulates family planning policy in Yugoslavia, stressing the right of parents to decide on the size and spacing of their family. At the same time, the federal law on termination of pregnancy was adopted, providing, over and above the conditions already stipulated in previous legislation, for specific individual circumstances as 'indications' for legal abortion. Simultaneously, the law provided for greater contraceptive freedom. As a result, it is henceforth more difficult to refuse to perform abortions on women belonging to certain social categories, particularly young and/or unmarried women seeking abortion.

Stampar (1971) explains that the 1960 law was chiefly designed to put an end to illegal abortions, which had become widespread, and thereby to check mortality and the complications arising from clandestine abortions. However, abortion became the usual means of birth control in the 1960s. At the same time, there was little recourse to contraceptive information. The author, who restricts his study to Croatia, claims that in 1969 there were twice as many legal abortions on record as first visits to contraception advisory centres (35,644 and 17,908 respectively). In 1970, the pill was used by only 30,000 women in Croatia (which has a population of 5½ million).

A survey of 2,788 women (Kozina, 1975) who had sought advice at the contraception guidance centre in Zagreb shows the types of question asked, the applicants' circumstances and their past history. It was found that from the beginning of 1968 to 1974, most of the women coming to the centre were married, and had had a number of abortions. After 1969, and especially in 1970 and 1971, they were younger, often unmarried, and there were even schoolgirls aged 15 to 19 who had never experienced sexual intercourse but wanted to take contraceptives and seek advice. In 1973, the women would often come with their partners and there were even men on their own. In the author's view, the mass media, the press, radio and television, had had a major role in determining what category of person would come to the centre and in bringing it increasingly close to the 'ideal': young women who had never had sexual intercourse or unwanted pregnancies.

It emerges from the foregoing observations that abortion has become a habit with Yugoslav women, whereas contraception has only recently begun to make any headway.

Impact of migration on the personal and family life of the couple

It is reasonable to believe that the migration process has considerable influence on the psychosexual equilibrium of the couple and on family life in general. One of the few Yugoslav studies in which the link between migration and sexuality is discussed is the research undertaken by the anthropologist Ehrlich (1971). It is based on a wide-ranging survey of 'informants' in 300 Yugoslav villages. The data were collected in 1939 and provide extremely useful insights into the prewar period, just before the great changes brought about by the Second World War and the revolution.

There were regions (Macedonia) in which women remained absolutely faithful to their husbands, waiting years for their return home. In other areas, half (or more) of the women had extramarital relations while their husbands were away. These were regions from which there is now the highest rate of emigration – Bosnia, Croatia and Serbia.

The Muslims of Bosnia and Macedonia adhered to very strict moral standards. According to the author, other attitudes have, however, been observed, especially in Bosnia (p. 288): 'According to the Islamic religion, a wife must not be left all alone for years'. Thus, women are allowed to re-marry after their husbands have been away for one or two years. In the rural areas, people generally approve of the wives' behaviour and disapprove of the husbands who have deserted them. In other regions where emigration is prevalent, the fact that a woman may have sexual relations with other men is considered normal by both her and her immediate environment. 'The peasants think it is normal for a woman to want a man. She does it out of necessity and not for pleasure'. 'Why did I ever get married . . . to be alone? How do I know what *he* is up to?'

It is important to bear in mind these regional discrepancies 40 years ago when it comes to discussing the effect of migration on the life of the couple today. Women then were not all alike, invariably submissive, sad and resigned.

Furthermore, a sex life is often openly regarded as indispensable, just as necessary for a woman as for a man. Seen in the present context of migration, the problem of the influence of migration can be approached in a variety of ways depending on the different 'actors' involved.

Some immigration policies have tended to discourage family immigration. The Federal Republic of Germany is an example. It has been clearly specified that the country needs workers, not families (the implication being 'no dependents'). Sweden and, to a certain extent, France, to take only the countries concerned by this study, have encouraged family immigration for demographic reasons. However, it should be pointed out that Yugoslav migrants are perhaps the least affected by the contingencies of government policy on family immigration. In Germany, France and Sweden, the pattern of Yugoslav immigration is the same. Immigrants are working people, either alone or couples, with few or no children (0.5 children per couple in France). Yugoslav women enter the country as workers, either alone or married, and sometimes make use of family connections, where such connections exist, to gain entry as 'wives' and work illegally.

For a long time migration was thought to concern men only, with the women being there only as companions, or not being there at all. In this perspective, loneliness, the true companion of all migrants, the want of a partner, and sexual deprivation were apparently a male problem only. Those concerned were young men who would come to European countries to work and whose fundamental human needs could not be satisfied, or others who had left their families behind and who felt even more desperately alone. The reverse side of this image was the wife at home, a 'grass widow', Penelope awaiting her Ulysses.

As for the solitude of women migrants, who are fewer in number and less conspicuous, it is mainly their solitude as housewives that has been remarked upon, and this is in keeping with the image of the housewife in our Western societies, with a few extra cultural ingredients.

But — and this has been a mistake — no attention has been paid to the solitary position of immigrant women on their own. They are young unmarried persons living in hostels, or young and not so young women who have left their husbands behind and gone abroad. It is true that there are fewer of them, and in the case of some nationalities, none at all. What is more, they do not fall into our stereotyped vision of 'wives of immigrants', and we refuse to believe they exist. Yet 10 per cent of immigrant married women in Germany are alone, their husbands having stayed behind. This is the figure for 1972/1973 and corresponds to 20,000 Yugoslav women without their husbands in Germany.

It should be emphasised, however, that these women who have emigrated on their own — a minority, of course — have done so out of economic necessity and not because the socio-cultural framework defining the woman's status and role sanctioned their behaviour as a matter of course. Thus the women who emigrate alone not only have loneliness to contend with but also a sense of shame and guilt with regard to their traditional background. At the same time, however, they feel safe from the scrutiny of their families and seek temporary or permanent outlets for their solitude, just as men do, except that they, the women, usually feel guilty about their behaviour.

Unmarried women behave according to two distinct, concurrent sets of values prevailing in Yugoslavia. On the one hand, there are the new socialist values in terms of which a woman has the same rights as a man, she being an equal partner in both social and private life. For many women, it amounts to a remote consciousness of 'what might be, if . . .'. Subconsciously, this attitude takes the form of a rejection of the double standard in sexual morality: 'Why is it that he can and I can't?' This rejection can only materialise in another country, away from the second, 'traditional' set of values whereby the man is thought of as being older and therefore more worthy of respect, superior, a set of values which imposes the double standard in sexuality: what is permissible for men in matters of sex is not permissible for women. Single women thus enter into relationships with men, live with them because they feel it is only normal and that they have as much right to a sex life and to sexual pleasure (they speak about it quite freely) as men. But then their emancipated behaviour is promptly counteracted by the second set of values with which they are still profoundly imbued, and they see this relationship as a lasting, stable union ultimately leading to marriage, and believe all the promises made by the men they live with.

The men's attitude to the emancipation of their female compatriots is not one of equality with their partner, but the loss of a sense of responsibility towards her. Worse still, it often leads to a form of contempt: 'they are all whores'. The result is something of a disaster. The couple live together for a number of years, with the woman becoming involved emotionally and financially and consciously assuming the role of a wife, accepting the man's authority. He will become responsible for their combined savings and dominate their sexual relationship.

The man's expectations are of a totally different nature: a woman is an object of pleasure and he takes advantage of this, both sexually and financially. He leaves home when he wants to. She cannot lodge a formal complaint, and cannot prove that all her savings have vanished. The onus of solving the problem of any pregnancies or children that may ensue from this relationship rests with her and her alone (de Trenc, 1973).

The number of children born out of wedlock amounts to 30 per cent of all children born to Yugoslav mothers in Germany (Morokvasic, 1976). Although one should be cautious[1] about interpreting the rate of extramarital (or 'illegitimate') births, this figure is alarming for many of the children are abandoned or given for adoption, and there have been cases of infanticide.

Married women on their own who abide by the rules of traditional morality live in women's hostels or share lodgings with another woman, go to work and never go out. Others find that difficult, and adopt the attitude that 'a woman must have a man'. Since their husbands are unfaithful to them in Yugoslavia, they can do the same. These relation-

---

1 For Swedish women in certain age groups, children born out of wedlock are practically the rule, but marriage does not have the same significance for them as it has for Yugoslav women, who are still imbued with traditional moral standards (Fiedler, 1955).

ships are temporary and unstable, at least to begin with. They can, of course, develop in different ways, as the Yugoslav psychiatrist de Trenc has pointed out: some women have their first satisfactory sexual relationship abroad, and begin to be critical and more exacting *vis-à-vis* their husbands at home. He quotes one woman as saying: 'I realised for the first time when I went to bed with him [the husband] again, how he had humiliated and taken advantage of me all these years of marriage' (de Trenc, 1973).

Unlike single women, married women are not, therefore, looking for a lasting relationship — not because they feel they are being more 'faithful' to their husbands by changing partners than by keeping the same one, but simply because traditional morality does not enter into the super-ego at the same level. They have not their virginity to lose and do not feel compelled by the fear of 'what people might say', making them cling to the first man they meet. Situations of this kind often end up in divorce, but as long as they last they are the source of distressing conflicts. I have met women who took their daughters, at the age of puberty, with them. The girl and the couple shared the same room. In situations such as these, cases of the child being raped by the 'stepfather' are not infrequent, but are never mentioned in an effort to hide the 'daughter's shame and misery'. As for birth 'control', it is always the man's responsibility to 'be (or not be) careful'. But it is the woman who suffers the consequences.

The situation is quite different according to whether the people concerned are married couples living together abroad or individuals living alone. Where the former are concerned, migration can be a source of conflict stemming from the greater independence of the working woman. However, for Yugoslavs, the main problems have to do with jealousy, the husband or wife meeting someone else, or unwanted pregnancies. According to de Trenc (1973), the return home of Yugoslavs on holiday coincides with an upswing in the number of requests for termination of pregnancy.

As we shall see later, Yugoslav women on the whole have little inclination to have children. Furthermore, they have been able to avail themselves of a means to avoid unwanted births legally for some years, and this means has been used so widely that it has become 'normal' and 'natural'. It is only when they go abroad that the whole problem of actually planning a family arises. The Yugoslav woman who leaves home to work abroad, thus contributing to the migratory process together with her husband, undoubtedly prefers not to have to stop work because of an unwanted pregnancy.

It is therefore reasonable to assume that most of the women in our sample survey, all of whom are of child-bearing age, are affected by birth control.

Legislation in countries receiving immigrants

Family planning legislation varies greatly from country to country. It may concern access to information, methods of birth control, sex education, the use of contraceptives and access to abortion (or intentional termination of pregnancy).

The transmitting of information can be compulsory, tolerated or prohibited. The response to it is reflected directly in the attitude towards contraceptives. Information on and use of contraceptives in some cases precedes abortion legislation and in others coincides with or comes after it. The purpose of this legislation may also vary, being determined by already existing practices and by overall attitudes towards the rights of men and women. In some instances, the liberalisation of abortion has been prompted by anti-natalist policies (Tunisia); in others it has been associated with measures to prevent the birth rate from falling (e.g. Hungary). Abortion legislation may also have precise short-term objectives, such as to curb the growing number of clandestine abortions and their consequences when the practice is already widespread.

Having confined our study in the preceding section to the country of origin and to the women of that country who are the subject of our research, we shall now discuss the situation in the three countries in which our survey was conducted, namely France, Sweden and the Federal Republic of Germany.

In France, information on, and the import and sale of, contraceptives was legalised in 1967. The decrees concerning the application of the law did not take full effect for several years, with the result that even at the Bucharest World Conference in 1974, France was referred to as one of the countries in which the sale of contraceptives was authorised, but all anti-natalist propaganda and information pertaining thereto was prohibited (see World Population Conference, 1974). On 4 December of the same year, a new law provided for the reimbursement by social security of contraceptives and laboratory analyses connected with contraception.

In France today, according to the newspaper *Le Monde* of 9 November 1977, 47 per cent of women of child-bearing age (aged 18-50) use some method of contraception, 25 per cent employing oral contraceptives, 17 per cent local contraception and 5 per cent an intra-uterine device. It appears that the use of the pill is still on the increase but that the rate is dropping steadily. The 'Veil Law' on voluntary termination of pregnancy is provisional and is to be revised in 1980 in the light of five years' experience.[1] It provides for a social consultation, the woman being given two days in which to think it over before a decision is taken. Termination of pregnancy is legal for women 'in distress' only up to the tenth week of pregnancy. What can be said, halfway through the

1 The Veil Law was confirmed in 1980.

law's trial period (*Le Monde*, 16, 17, 18, 19 November 1977), is that it is applied very inconsistently, that its opponents have not given up the battle, and that abortions are still performed illegally, despite the apparent protection of the law. Women 'in distress', panic-stricken and pressed for time, will accept anything. Whatever happens, when they do not obtain permission to have a legal abortion, they still find some other way of having it done. The figures speak for themselves. According to the Ministry of Health, 132,500 abortions were performed in France in 1976, whereas the most optimistic estimates for the time when it was still illegal put the annual figure at 350,000 (clandestine abortions).

Yugoslav women have had to fit into structures which are as yet incomplete and not always properly equipped to receive them. There are 30,000 of these women concentrated in the Paris area, which is negligible compared with the number of Portuguese women, of whom there are ten times as many. Some hospitals and dispensaries have full-time interpreters (unless they hold French diplomas, which is rare, foreigners cannot be members of the French medical corps). Some provision is also made for immigrants in certain mother and infant care centres and the Red Cross. But these experiments have failed for want of adequate information. We shall come back to this subject later.

Sweden is a case apart in respect of its legislation: information and services must be provided on request. Since 1946 it has been compulsory for chemists to sell contraceptives to any person wishing to buy them. Sex education became part of school curricula as early as the 1940s and was made compulsory in 1956. There have been motherhood information and care centres in Sweden for over 30 years.

Thus on becoming a recipient country for immigrants, Sweden, with its family assimilation policy, was already geared to receive immigrant women from Finland, Yugoslavia or Greece within an already existing framework originally devised for Swedish women. All it required was for it to be adapted to migrants' needs. One of the heads of the R.F.S.U.[1] claimed in 1976: 'There is no longer any problem with the Swedes. We now work only with teenagers and immigrants, especially Turkish, women'. Brochures in the various languages spoken by immigrants are distributed to couples. Social workers often try to approach the men first, in situations where it is difficult to gain access to the women.

As regards abortion, from as early as 1938 it was authorised by law on certain medical and ethical grounds: when the life of the mother

1 Riksförbundet för Sexuell Upplysing (Association for Sex Education) founded in 1933 by Elise Ottensen-Jensen, 17th out of a Norwegian family of 18 children. Its guiding principle: each child should be welcome and wanted.

and/or child was in danger, in the event of foetal malformation and in cases of rape or incest. The law passed in 1963 provided for a further category; when there was a health hazard for the foetus injured during pregnancy, i.e. a medical-social clause further liberalising abortion up to the twentieth week of pregnancy.

Sweden has been able to avoid fully legalising abortion because of its contraceptive information policy. The problem of a sharply declining birth rate was partly resolved by immigration, but also by introducing a series of measures similar to those taken in Hungary, such as 7 months' paid maternity leave (raised to one year in 1978) and the possibility of part-time work for a year or two. All women are entitled to it without exception, e.g. whether they hold jobs with security of tenure or not. An interesting point is that this leave of absence can be taken either by the mother or by the father, and the number of fathers taking leave on this account has risen from 1 to 6 per cent over the past few years. All fathers are entitled to it, without having to apply for permission from their employers, as is the case in France.

Yugoslav women in Sweden have been given information in their own language by social workers or doctors, many of whom are Yugoslavs practising in Sweden. Some Yugoslav women have themselves taken the initiative of disseminating information; with the financial aid of the Stockholm municipal authorities, the women from the Yugoslav Club organised a series of lectures on the problems of contraception and birth, assisted by a young Yugoslav gynaecologist practising in Sweden.

In Germany, abortion and birth control legislation was extremely strict until very recently. It was not until a century, or to be precise 99 years, after the 1871 law that the Social Democrats and Liberals took the first steps towards amending paragraph 218 on termination of pregnancy. After a great deal of discussion (Becker, 1972), parliamentary debate and rejection of proposed texts, and amendments to the first bill (1974-1975), the new law only finally became effective on 21 June 1976. Termination of pregnancy is now authorised on certain grounds: if the life or health of the pregnant woman is in danger; if there is a likelihood of abnormality in the child; if the pregnant woman is in serious danger. The pregnancy can only be terminated after consultation with a social worker and a physician, and the latter is not authorised to perform the abortion himself.

Thus a woman wanting to terminate a pregnancy must first consult with her social worker and with her doctor, who will decide whether she comes under one of the categories provided for by the law. The social worker gives advice on public aid available to pregnant women, mothers and children. The doctor must explain all the risks involved for the mother if she terminates her pregnancy. The abortion cannot be performed until three days after the expectant mother has seen the social worker and doctor. Consultations are free of charge and the operation is reimbursed by the 'Krankenkasse' (Health Insurance). If all these conditions are not met (with a few exceptions provided for by the law), both the person performing the operation and the woman are liable to a penalty in terms of the law.

Yugoslav women can also obtain information and help from Yugoslav gynaecologists and social workers. A survey of Yugoslav social workers in Germany has shown that they are frequently consulted by persons seeking advice on the problems encountered in married life, and contraception.

Limitation of births among Yugoslavs living abroad

The following section is based chiefly, although not entirely, on the replies to the survey we conducted in 1976 among 258 Yugoslav migrant women: 64 for Sweden (Stockholm), 97 for Germany (Aachen, Frankfurt), 97 for France (Paris). The questionnaires included questions on the respondents' work and private life, particularly birth control.

We shall first describe the survey sample in order to place the replies in their proper context and enable us to interpret them correctly. We worked on the assumption that birth control practice, whether contraception or abortion (there are so few cases of definitive sterilisation that we shall not consider this alternative), is keyed, at the individual level, to the desired family size and to information on contraception and the woman's fecundity cycle. External factors — such as legislation or the socio-cultural context, discussed above — will only be referred to in order to throw light on or interpret certain facts or findings of the survey.

Who are the women who emigrate?

When Yugoslav women emigrate, work becomes even more important to them than in their home country. We have discussed this elsewhere (Morokvasic, 1976). Once again let us stress the extent of Yugoslav migration, which is motivated by the search for employment and is a decisive factor in family limitation.

The total number of Yugoslav women varies greatly from one country to another: approximately 250,000 in Germany, 30,000 in France and 20,000 in Sweden, amounting to between 30 and 40 per cent of the total number of 'temporary Yugoslav immigrants' in these countries. The proportion of working women varies according to one's sources of information and from one country to another, but it may be said that at least two-thirds of these women work, and at least half of the working women are married. In France they account

276

for barely 2 per cent of all female immigrants, whereas the proportion of Yugoslavs among the working female population is 5 per cent. In the Federal Republic of Germany, the proportion of Yugoslavs in the total female immigrant population is 17.2 per cent, as against 22 per cent of the working female population. These proportions are the exact reverse for Turkish women. These figures show that employment is a crucial factor in Yugoslav female migration. The feature which sets Yugoslav women apart from most immigrants of other nationalities is work, and a certain attitude towards it.

Most foreign women, both in France and in Germany, have their first experience of a gainful occupation when they migrate. They come from countries or regions in which women are as yet largely unaffected by recent industrialisation. They come from poor rural areas where women do indeed work very hard but are not paid for it. In countries such as these where there is already a high level of unemployment among men, it has not been difficult to keep up the traditional pattern whereby women were not expected to work outside the home. But with emigration, a range of completely new opportunities has progressively opened up, economic necessity has forced traditional taboos into the background and Spanish, Portuguese or Turkish women have begun to earn a living. Thus with both spouses working, migrants aim to double their earnings, save more quickly and be able to return home more rapidly. At certain periods it has been easier for women to find jobs, with the result that they would leave first, ahead of their husbands. We have heard of cases of rushed marriages amongst Yugoslavs and Turks because of migration. However, for many of these women, work in a foreign country is thought of as a temporary necessity, and migration is simply a convenient way of obtaining it.

The situation is different for Yugoslav women. At first sight the difference is not very noticeable, for most of them have never had a salaried job before leaving home either. According to the 1971 census in Yugoslavia, only 30 out of every 100 migrants had had a salaried job before leaving home. This percentage does not, however, include those who had, for example, done seasonal work but failed to mention it to the investigators. More important still, this percentage does not reveal the large numbers of women who, despite having wanted and looked for work in Yugoslavia, had never found any there. Long before they emigrate, Yugoslav women cherish the idea that women, too, should carry on with their studies as long as they can, and should work. And this attitude is shared even by those for whom the chances of its ever materialising are extremely remote. They are prepared to assume, and do assume, the contradictions and conflicts arising out of the double standard imposed upon them by Yugoslav society: the traditional or ancient pattern, sometimes rehabilitated and brought up to date by a consumer society, and the pattern of the working woman, man's equal, which has been transmitted by socialist ideology and has been firmly established there since the war.

However, many women have been unable to find jobs on the Yugoslav labour market. The 1965 economic reform hit women particularly hard, and unemployment was proportionally higher for women than for men. Migration thus afforded a similar outlet for Yugoslav women as for the men; they emigrated as members of the labour force.

The study

We opted for a 'selective' sample corresponding as closely as possible to a cross-section of the Yugoslav population in the three countries. We shall now outline some of the characteristics of the sample which have a significant bearing on this study.

With respect to place of birth, a slightly larger proportion of women from a rural background are to be found in France than in Germany or Sweden. Furthermore, their original place of residence was found to be different from their place of birth in two-thirds of Yugoslav immigrants to Sweden, whereas the two coincided in nearly half the immigrants to France. Among Yugoslavs in the Federal Republic of Germany, they coincided in 54 per cent of the sample and differed in 46 per cent. Thus, there had been considerable geographical mobility experience among Yugoslav women prior to their emigration to northern or western Europe. Thus, they would appear to be more inclined to go abroad, and to accept and adjust to an urban way of life and to urban values.

The majority of Yugoslav women in France and Sweden are Orthodox, and in Germany, Roman Catholic. We find the highest proportion of women claiming to have no religion in France. These proportions are comparable with those of the larger Yugoslav population in each country, except for Sweden, where our sample is representative of the population of Stockholm. As is the case for religion, there is a majority of Serbs in Sweden and especially in France, and a majority of Croats in the Federal Republic of Germany. Furthermore, more than half of those who declare themselves to be 'Yugoslav' with no mention of their original nationality are to be found in France. Out of eight Muslims interviewed, one lives in France and the other seven in Germany.

Table 7.1 shows the marital status of the 258 women in our sample. The overall breakdown for the sample indicates that there are 176 married women, 5 of whom are separated from their husbands because the latter are in Yugoslavia or elsewhere; 14 are cohabiting with a man in a free union, 38 unmarried women are living on their own, and 29 are divorced. Thus, we have 72 persons (38 + 29 + 5) claiming to live on their own and the rest living with a man who may or may not be their husband. The proportion of single persons is 10 per cent in

Table 7.1

Marital status of respondents
in sample (per cent)

Married	68·2
Divorced	11·2
Unmarried, single	14·7
Unmarried, but cohabiting	5·4
No information	*
	(258)

* Less than 1 per cent

Table 7.2

Family size (number of children) by country

Number of children	Country			All countries
	France	FRG	Sweden	
0	17·5%	25·7%	15·6%	20·2%
1	16·4%	39·1%	32·8%	29·1%
2	42·4%	28·8%	39·0%	36·4%
3 or more	16·5%	6·2%	10·9%	11·2%
No answer	7·2%	0·0%	1·5%	3·1%
Total	(97)	(97)	(64)	(258)

Note: Percentages may not total 100.0 because of rounding results to nearest tenth.

France, 15 per cent in the Federal Republic of Germany and 6 per cent in Sweden.

Actual and desired number of children

Table 7.2 shows the actual number of children born to the 258 respondents in France, Germany and Sweden. In Germany there are the greatest number of Yugoslav women who are childless or have one child. Sweden, and even more so France, have larger proportions of women who have two children.

279

The women were asked to state how many children they wished to have, regardless of how many they already had. The results are shown in Table 7.3. Most of the respondents were in favour of two children. Those with one or no children 'swell the ranks' of the two and three-child category. A larger family seemed unrealistic.

Table 7.3

Desired family size (number of children) by country

Desired number children	Country			All countries
	France	FRG	Sweden	
0	0·0%	0·0%	3·1%	0·8%
1	11·3%	11·3%	10·9%	11·2%
2	53·6%	78·3%	64·0%	65·5%
3 or more	31·9%	8·2%	18·8%	19·8%
No answer	3·0%	2·0%	3·1%	2·7%
Total	(97)	(97)	(67)	(258)

The proportion of women wanting only one child is the same in the three countries. The differences arise in the two- or three-child categories. The largest number of Yugoslav women wanting only two children is to be found in Germany, followed by Sweden, while France is well in the lead as regards those who would like a third child. A possible explanation for the more Malthusian attitude of women in the Federal Republic of Germany might be their background; the north of Yugoslavia — Croatia and Vojvodina, from which immigrants to Germany come — has had the lowest fertility rate in the whole of Yugoslavia.

Thus, the tendency to restrict births existed prior to migration; migration only served to intensify the trend, with women seeking a more rational life style consistent with their occupational activity. It is to be expected that these women would be more alert to contraception and be less inclined to let themselves be drawn into a situation to which the only solution is recourse to abortion. The circumstances prevailing in the host country also have some influence. We have seen for example that legislation in Germany was extremely harsh up until 1976, and in France, the Veil Law was adopted in 1975.

When we compare actual family size with desired family size (see Table 7.4), we can identify the women who are content with the number of children they have at present, and those for whom the ideal figure is higher or lower. Three-quarters of the women with one child

280

want another and 8 per cent would like two more; the remaining 17.5 per cent are content with one child. Most women (75 per cent) with two children are satisfied with what they have, 6 per cent would have preferred one less, and 10 per cent one more; only two would like two more. Most (11) of the 16 women with three children are satisfied, one would like one more, and the others would have preferred one less. There were only nine women with four children; four are satisfied and the others would have preferred one less. Of the women with no children, 60 per cent want two, 20 per cent one and 11 per cent three.

Table 7.4

Desired family size by actual family size (number of children)

Desired family size	0	1	2	3	4 or more	No ans.	Total
0	0	1	0	0	1	0	2
1	10	13	6	0	0	0	29
2	32	54	71	3	3	6	169
3	6	6	10	11	3	2	38
4 or more	3	0	3	1	6	0	13
No ans.	1	1	4	1	0	0	7
Total	52	75	94	16	13	8	258

It appears that the ideal is two children, and that there is good correlation between the actual and desired family size among women with two or three children. If their behaviour is rational (assuming all other things equal), women who are satisfied with the actual number of children they have and those who would rather have had one less presumably pay greater attention to contraception. And conversely, it is to be expected that those who are willing to have more children would take a negative attitude towards contraception. Thus of the 258 interviewees (discounting those who did not reply), at least 116 may be thought to exercise some care over contraception, while 127 are theoretically not concerned. This assumption would be valid only if the number of children women wanted applied to the immediate future — which is not necessarily the case. Having made no inquiries on the subject, we cannot reply to these questions.

What people know about birth control

The proportion of women who do not know 'when a woman can fall pregnant' or 'when she cannot' is extremely high: one-third. France has the highest proportion of inaccurate answers and Germany the greatest number of 'correct' replies. The sort of reply that we regarded as incorrect were replies such as 'when the man and the woman reach orgasm at the same time', or 'when the woman's pleasure or desire is very intense, she cannot fall pregnant'. Replies were considered correct when they showed that the woman was familiar with the mechanism of ovulation.

As regards contraception, the smallest proportion of women who knew nothing about it was to be found in Sweden. The most frequently mentioned male contraceptive was the condom, sterilisation being mentioned by only three women in Sweden. It was in France that women were least conversant with female contraceptives, although in absolute terms the number of women who knew nothing about them was very small (eight in France, two in Germany and two in Sweden). Most of the women living in Sweden are more conversant with a broader range of contraceptives than those living in Germany or France who know about the pill and little else, and never explicitly mention sterilisation.

The highest proportion of women who knew nothing before leaving Yugoslavia is to be found among Yugoslav immigrants in Germany. For those living in Sweden, access to information before leaving home had been obtained through formal channels — the doctor and the media — whereas for those living in Germany and France it had been acquired 'through women friends'. This is particularly enlightening on the category of women emigrating to Sweden.

As was to be expected, the rate of information is proportional to the level of education. It does not, however, vary according to age. The dissemination of information also depends on whether the women come from a rural or an urban background. Among those from an urban, or semi-urban background, there are far fewer women who were totally ignorant before leaving the country.

In practice: 'contraception' and abortion

We have assumed that the minimum number of women likely to be interested in contraception is 116 of the 258. In practice, the number of women actually using contraceptives is 97. But if we assume that those wanting children wish to plan their families, the number of women theoretically concerned by contraception should be higher, and the figure of 97 is not a true estimate of the actual needs.

Sweden has the smallest number of 'non-users'; in France and Germany the number is the same. The most frequently used method is the pill. The coil is used in Sweden, but not in Germany, and there are only three women with one in France. The diaphragm is not mentioned in Sweden, unlike France and Germany. We have ascribed these differences to the different means of access to information in the three countries, Sweden being a case apart.

What do women do when they do not want any more children but refuse to employ contraceptives? The majority say 'Muz me cuva' (my husband is careful). This group is equivalent in number to those using contraceptives, namely 98. This means that half of all the women who feel the need to control their reproduction have recourse to effective methods, while the other half delegate that responsibility to their partners. There are as many of the latter group in France as in Germany (39 and 40 respectively) and fewer in Sweden (19), i.e. expressed as a percentage: 40 per cent, 41 percent and 29 per cent.

Abortion is explicitly given as a method of contraception by a few persons in France. There is a far greater proportion of women who have had abortions than those using contraceptives (we are speaking in absolute terms; in some cases they may be the same women). Out of 258 women, 146 (or 56 per cent) have had abortions. About two-thirds of them have had one or two abortions, and the others more than three and sometimes even more than six. This rate is extremely high, far higher than Ferro's findings (1975). The proportion of women who have had an abortion is highest in Sweden, but they have rarely had more than two. More than half of the Yugoslav women in France have had abortions, but half of these have each had more than three. Half of those interviewed in Germany have had abortions, but in most cases not more than one or two. These differences may be ascribed to a combination of factors that have partly to do with the different origin of migrants and partly with the context in which they now live.

Swedish legislation can feasibly be regarded as having been a 'facilitating' factor in the number of abortions performed; on the other hand, the local context has also led to an increased awareness as regards contraception, enabling women to avoid having frequent recourse to abortion.

In the Federal Republic of Germany, the stringent laws had the effect of keeping abortion in check. In France, the laws were liberalised slightly earlier. But since Yugoslavs were concentrated around Paris, they were able to organise networks in which clandestine abortionists operated. A sizeable proportion of women would also go back to Yugoslavia for an abortion. This has become common practice, especially in France and Germany.

Table 7.5 shows the abortion experiences of women in our sample — how many had abortions and where. Sweden has the highest rate of abortions performed by a member of the medical profession, and France the lowest — more than a quarter of the women there having recourse to unqualified persons. At first sight, the practice followed by Yugoslav women migrants may not appear to pose a problem. More than a third of the women in our sample practice contraception, which

Table 7.5

Number of women having abortions in Yugoslavia, and away from
Yugoslavia, by present place of domicile

Place of abortion	Place of domicile			
	France	FRG	Sweden	Total
Yugoslavia	36	33	13	82
Elsewhere	7	8	14	29
Yugoslavia and elsewhere	16	5	13	34
Total	59	46	40	145
As a % of respondents in that country	60·8%	47·4%	62·5%	56·2%

is almost as high as the level of contraceptive practice in France, for example. But there is more cause for alarm when we realise that while a third of the women wish to restrict their families, they make no attempt to find an effective means of doing so. The result is an extremely large number of abortions: 146 women have had 367 abortions. The same woman have had 234 children.

Although we are not entitled to speak here in terms of a representative sample, these figures do call for reflection. On average, for every three pregnancies, Yugoslav women give birth to one child. We have already pointed out the extent to which the behaviour of women migrants is influenced by their motives for migrating. They want to work as much as possible and will therefore avoid, or try to terminate, unwanted pregnancies whenever they possibly can.

It is essential for all women to enjoy the full freedom to have children only when they want them. But when there is nothing in their country's tradition to prevent birth control, and when their social status is not linked to the production of children (and in fact it is higher when their progeny is less numerous), why do they choose the method they can least afford psychologically, physically and financially? Even when it is performed in the best possible conditions, an abortion leaves a scar. In fact, most of the abortions performed on Yugoslav women are done by ill-qualified persons with no medical supervision. As we have seen, many of the women will go back to Yugoslavia to have an abortion, where it is authorised. But migrants cannot afford to waste time on doctor's visits, and even less to wait their turn in hospitals.

To have access to an abortionist who is prepared to operate over a weekend, they have to pay out large sums of money to a succession of go-betweens in the city networks. After an expedition of this kind, they often have to be admitted to hospital on their return to the country in which they work, for to add to the insalubrious conditions of the operation, they are suffering from a lack of rest and from their journey.

Why, then, do they not try to avoid abortion? Before replying to this question, let us try to understand them.

Attitudes towards contraception and abortion

Women's resistance to contraceptives has various root causes. The use of contraceptives may have been prohibited, by tradition even, or by law, and women accept these taboos and refuse contraceptive methods. Even when no social pressure is brought to bear on them, individual resistance is still very strong. Generally speaking, providing information on its own will not suffice to lift these taboos for they are deeply ingrained and are attached to traditional social values which might be disrupted without them.

Family planning may be regarded as a positive source of strength for a couple, for it will emancipate the woman and enable her to play a more positive role in society, and at the same time promise equality, love and mutual responsibility in producing, caring for and bringing up their children. It may result in a decline of patriarchal authority. In places where patriarchal mentalities remain deeply rooted, men are still fiercely antagonistic towards the knowledge and use of contraceptives by their wives. This outlook is usually linked to the double standard in sexual matters which condones considerable sexual freedom for the man both before and after marriage but requires absolute fidelity on the part of the woman. It would appear that men believe that if women use contraceptives they will no longer be faithful to them sexually. In fact, the implicit postulate is that family planning would make women more independent, especially if it gives them a greater chance of acquiring further rights (World Population Conference, 1974, document E/CN.66/575/Add. 1, p. 47).

In our study, the explicit reticence of men is mentioned by one quarter of our respondents. Moreover, the women adopt the men's attitude as though it were their own: 'If I take the pill, I shall be too free'. Women are afraid of becoming 'like men', and 'sleeping around'. For some women who have had no fulfilment out of married life, intercourse is 'his business', and they regard it as an ordeal — 'my duty as a wife'. Frequent intercourse is a phobia with these women: 'If I take the pill, he will want to do it every day!' A number of Yugoslav women stress the unnatural, unhealthy aspect of contraception, particularly the pill. This type of argument was also given frequently by the Portuguese women interviewed by Ferro (1975). Abortion is considered more normal and natural, as we shall see later. 'I have heard that the pill is not good for you, and you have unhealthy children' or 'you cannot have any more children'. 'My husband has told me that women lose all desire, so if I take the pill he will think there is someone else!' All told, the best method is the 'natural' method. 'My husband doesn't drink, he can be careful, it is healthier'. 'It is my husband's duty to "look after" me' (be careful).

As a preventive measure, some women also have recourse to the douche: the use of vinegar is mentioned most frequently. As for the condom, the only male contraceptive, it is very rarely used. Men and women are unanimous: 'it's not the same, I don't like it'. Men only use it if they have sexual intercourse with several women, for fear of contracting some disease.

Yugoslav women regard abortion as 'natural'. In Yugoslavia it has been and still is the most widely used 'method of contraception' (de Trenc, 1973). It is thought to be 'normal' for women to have had one or two abortions. The older women who have had several are there as an example for the young. 'I have had ten, one is nothing'. They take a sort of pride in the number of abortions they have had, although this pride is only to be found amongst women, and abortion is stigmatised in the rest of society, and has always been done secretly. 'Everyone knows about it, but no one talks about it' (Ehrlich, 1971). When it was still illegal in France, the women who had to go back to Yugoslavia for an abortion were careful not to let people in the village see them. Everyone would have known that if a woman came back by herself halfway through the year, it was because she had come for an abortion. Abortion is also considered 'natural' by the Portuguese women interviewed by Ferro (1975), although the number of women who had had a 'desmancho' in her sample survey was infinitely smaller.

In Yugoslavia the principle of limitation of births goes back a long time, especially in the regions most affected by emigration today — Croatia, Serbia and the non-Muslim parts of Bosnia. It has been widely practised there, and from being statistically normal it has become, simply 'normal'. The reasons given by Ehrlich in her prewar study are chiefly economic. But it is interesting to note that the differences between Serbia and the other parts of the country were apparent even then. In Serbia, the sole means of birth control was by having frequent abortions. In Croatia, where Catholicism had a stronger influence than the Orthodox religion in Serbia, 'preventive' methods were also used. Thus for many Yugoslav women migrants, abortion was part of a woman's life, and their sisters, mothers and grandmothers had all had abortions. Postwar legislation helped to place abortions under medical supervision and cut down the number of clandestine operations. Abortions, and especially clandestine abortions, are thus a matter of course with Yugoslav women. They are not put out by all the suffering and pain involved. 'It is normal for a woman to suffer'. 'I can stand it, what do you think I am?' Since abortions became legal in France, the women wanting to terminate a pregnancy under the new law have been unwilling to have an anaesthetic. This attitude is part of their fierce hostility towards medicines — which take away the natural feeling of things — but also reflects a certain wish for self-punishment.

The number of abortions some women have had is scarcely credible. Twenty of the women we interviewed had had more than five, but cases of 20 or 30 are not unknown: an example was a woman who at 41 had just had her first child — it was her eighteenth pregnancy, and she had had seventeen abortions before that.[1]

In most cases, after a number of abortions, the women lose count and are unable to give the exact number. These figures should not be taken too literally, for there is often some confusion between an actual abortion and some form of intervention the minute a woman's period is overdue. Ferro (1975) has observed the same thing with Portuguese women.

One woman in France told us, for instance, that she has had an abortion 'every three months, and had only been to the doctor's three times'. Others believe in various other remedies: 'drinking vinegar', 'washing oneself with vinegar' or 'douching oneself with very hot water', 'drinking red wine mixed with yeast' or 'red wine mixed with herbs'.

When asked outright what they felt to be the best method of birth control, most Yugoslav women say 'the pill or some other contraceptive'. Only eight women thought that abortion was better 'because it is better for you'. Clearly even women who are not in favour of contraception feel it is preferable to abortion. A small number of them prefer to rely on the hazardous method of withdrawal and therefore on their partner.

Conclusion

In migrating, these Yugoslavian women have tended to bring with them the customs and beliefs about sex and contraception that are character-istic of their home country, and as we have seen, these beliefs and customs generate some problems — or, at least, our somewhat different perspective would lead us to label them as problems. And, these prob-lems are obviously compounded by living in an alien society.

It appears at first sight that Yugoslav women are reasonably well informed about contraception. However, this information is often 'supplemented' by a variety of preconceived ideas, fantasies and beliefs, with the result that it is still inadequate. Moreover, Yugoslavs often

---

1 Information supplied by the St Antoine Hospital.

know little about the human body and its workings and therefore have little control over it.

Yugoslav women, and couples, therefore need to be informed, as do immigrants from other countries living in Western Europe (and indeed the indigenous populations). But the information supplied to Yugoslav women must necessarily be different (or be presented differently) from that given to Turks, Spaniards or any others. All immigrants have their own history, their own customs. Unlike some of the other migrants, Yugoslavs have had years of experience of family limitation and liberal abortion laws. Any information overlooking this fact is bound to be inadequate.

In the final analysis, the content of the information to be conveyed will have no effect whatsoever unless the informer meets certain requirements:

1 he/she must speak the language of the migrant;

2 he/she must be familiar with and understand the immigrant's background;

3 he/she must inspire confidence by his/her status, medical and administrative knowledge, etc.

The ideal solution would be for medical personnel and social workers to be of the same origin as the migrants. Yugoslavs themselves provide evidence to support this by consulting Yugoslav doctors whenever they can. In France, where there are no Yugoslav practitioners, Yugoslav women have sought out doctors of vaguely Slavic origin (established Polish or Russian immigrants).

Whatever the Yugoslavs' own situation may be, the information they should be given regarding contraception, and the way in which it is to be communicated and made effective, should proceed from the same basic principle that should be applied to all migrants — a knowledge and understanding of their culture, before commencing the process of informing them. Unless this principle is borne in mind, information can never claim to have a truly educational role.

Bibliography

Becker, C., *Problem 218*, Fischer Taschenbuch, Frankfurt am Main, 1972.

Breznik, D., Mojic, A., Rasevic, M. and Rancic, M., *Fertilitet stanovnistva u Jugoslavji*, Social Science Institute, Belgrade, 1972.

— Conseil supérieur de l'information sexuelle, de la regulation des naissances et de l'education familiale (Council for sex information, birth control and family planning), *Bulletin*, no. 4, 15 July 1977 (p. 26).

- Circulaire no. 813 du 3 avril 1974 relative aux centres de planification ou d'éducation familiale (*Circular*, no. 813, 3 April 1974, on family planning and education centres).

Ehrlich, V., *Jugoslavenska porodiva u Transformaciji*, Liber, Zagreb, 1971.

Ferro, J., *Limitation des naissances et intégration socio-culturelle*, Thèse de doctorat, Université Catholique de Loubain, 1975.

Gardun, Y., 'Komparativna analiza pobačaja u nerim pravnim sistemima', *Žena*, no. 6, 1971, pp. 43-56.

Halpern, J., *A Serbian Village*, Harper Books, New York, 1967.

Kožina, Z., 'Pntovi komunikacije pri upucivanju zena u savjeto-valiste za kontracepciju', *Žena*, no. 4, 1975, pp. 49-53.

- Loi no. 75-17 du 17 janvier 1975, relative à l'interruption volontaire de la grossesse (Law no. 75-17 of 17 January 1975 on voluntary termination of pregnancy).

Medawar, J. and Pyke, D., *Family Planning*, Penguin Books, Harmondsworth, 1971.
Morokvasic, M., 'Les femmes immigrées yougoslaves en France et en R.F.A.', *Hommes et Migrations*, 15 November 1976.
- 'Les femmes immigrées au travail', paper presented at the European symposium on migration, Louvain-la-Neuve, 1974.
- *Yugoslav women in France, Federal Republic of Germany and Sweden*, Paris, Centre National de la Recherché Scientifique, no. 642, 1980 (mimeo).

- *Reforma porodicnog zakonodavstva, Rad, Beograd, 1971* (translation: Reform of family legislation) pamphlet, published by the Federal Statistical Office, Belgrade, 1971.
- *Rezolucija oplaniranjn porodice (10.04.69) i realisunjn za prekid trudnoce* (translation: Resolution concerning family planning (19.04.69)), *Zena danas*, no. 264, 1969.

Stampar, D., 'Neki aspekti planiranja obitelji; demografska politika u S.R. Krvatsko', *Žena*, no. 5, 1971.
- 'Problemi planiranja obitelji u zena na privremenom radu u inostranston', Conference on Yugoslav women migrants, Zagreb, 6 November 1973, roneo.
- 'Study on the interrelationship of the status of women and family

planning', World Population Conference, Bucharest, 19-30 August 1974.

Tomsic, V., 'The status of women and family planning in Yugoslavia', *Faits et tendances*, no. 10, 1973, pp. 57-80.
de Trenc, P., 'Utjecaj ekonomiske migracije na odnose medju spolo-vima, brak i planiranje porodice', Conference on Yugoslav women migrants, Zagreb, 6 November 1973 (roneo).

8 Personal, familial and societal impacts of Turkish women's migration to Europe
AYSE KUDAT *

This chapter analyses the impact of international migration of Turkish women from the individual, the familial and the societal perspectives. The main emphasis is on working women. The analysis is based upon over five years of participant observation, several large-scale surveys, intensive case materials collected from both women abroad and from returnees, other available statistics, and many valuable studies undertaken by outstanding scholars.

During the last two decades women from the Mediterranean countries have become a significant economic factor in the developed European labour markets. In the Federal Republic of Germany where there is the highest concentration of Turks — the topic of this chapter — women constitute over a quarter of all migrant workers; Turkish women outnumber those from other nationalities. As there is also sectoral concentration, the share of women in the migrant population varies from region to region, reaching, as was the case in West Berlin, over 40 per cent of all foreign employees.

There are cultural differences in the impact that migration has on the migrating women, on their families and on society. Yet, in many respects the observed differences in outcomes are more a matter of degree than of kind.

* This study was written with the assistance of Seval Gürel.

Facts and trends

The Turkish migration into Western Germany has undergone four substantial phases. In the first phase, migrant workers were composed primarily of married men who left their wives behind upon migration. In the second phase, spouses were allowed to join under specified conditions. In the third phase, priorities were attached to female labour, boosting both the incentives for spouses' reunion and the migration of women alone. In the last phase, which currently prevails, recruitment has been stopped and significant numbers have returned home.

Our studies for West Berlin, as well as available statistics for other regions and countries, point to a number of differences between Turkish migrant women and men; women have lower levels of education, tend to originate from urban areas and have much less previous work experience. Further, migrant women hold the least skilled jobs, earn less than their male counterparts and consequently save and remit less; their stay abroad tends to be shorter.

However, in many ways, they are better off than the female population that remains in Turkey: migrant working women are much better educated than average Turkish females. A higher percentage of them are single and, relative to the Turkish female population, fewer had been employed previously in the agricultural sector. About a fifth of the migrant women in West Berlin had previous employment experiences in industry or in service occupations — a rate higher than that for women in Turkey. A significant fact, then, is that the majority of migrant women (about 80 per cent) worked for wages for the first time in their lives after they had migrated.

According to our West Berlin surveys, 40 per cent of the married working women migrated first, thereafter followed by their husbands. In another 13 per cent of the cases they were working alone while their husbands were back at home. (The respective percentages were 58 and 15 for male workers.) Considering that 14 per cent of all working women were single and that they also migrated alone, over half of all women have shown an initiative and independence — behaviour that is somewhat at variance with Turkish values concerning the role of women. Although the Turkish society has accepted and approved of the working of women outside the home in times of utter necessity, it is only under the constant supervision of the family.

In one-fifth of the cases abroad the married women were the sole providers for their families because their husbands were not employed. Another 8 per cent of these women had husbands working in Turkey but earning much less than what they earn abroad. Considering the temporary unemployment of their husbands abroad, or the level of their income, it is not misleading to state that nearly half of all migrant women are the main providers of their household. To this number must be added the single women who also provide for their parents and siblings with their remittances.

The position of women in Turkey

The status and problems of Turkish women are not significantly different from those of women in other capitalist countries. As a result of the widening gap between public and private, household and factory, productive and reproductive spheres, women have become peripheral to the social and economic organisation; they are socially underprivileged and subordinated — a highly exploited source of cheap reserve labour.

With the development of feudalism, property rights crystallised in favour of men. Capitalism added to the existing inequalities between men and women. 'Reforms' adopted during the Ataturk era did not bring major changes in the status of women, since many of them were not put into practice while others were arbitrarily forced upon the system with little chance of acceptance. For instance, women were given equal right to vote. Yet, in practice, the majority were illiterate, uneducated, uninformed and unexposed to the relevant media. Society still expected them to do as their husbands or fathers told them; even when they went to the polls, for all practical purposes it was these men who voted for them. Even today, the majority of women living in rural areas, small towns and backward cities have little interest or involvement in politics and do not depart from the path of the men in their families in their voting patterns.

It is an illusion to believe that housework is the major preoccupation of women. In the agricultural sector, where over half of the working population is found, women's labour matches that of men's, according to official statistics. Moreover, there is an increasing need for the wage labour of women and children. In southern Turkey, as many as 200,000 women and children are seasonally brought to work in cotton fields. Thus, even in the traditional areas of women's unpaid work, wage labour is becoming increasingly visible. The productive labour of women in agriculture does not get translated into social acknowledgement; working women of the urban areas also submit to their men (leaving emancipatory reservations for the bourgeois sector). Inherent in the logic of capitalism is the exploitation of the labour of women. Capitalism critically needs women to reproduce the labour force. While serving the reproductive needs, women are also engaged in domestic labour, which earns no wage for them or their families. That their reproductive and domestic labours earn no income becomes, then, a basis for exploiting women outside the home when they enter the industrial sector of society. Such a pattern exists in underdeveloped countries such as Turkey; it is perpetuated among women when they migrate to northern Europe.

Main features of women's migration experience

Migration presents the Turkish woman with a totally unfamiliar experience, an experience that differs from her previous life in a variety of ways. What is perhaps even more important is the fact that this happens in an abrupt fashion. The novelties are imposed on her without any prior or proper introduction, without allowing any adequate preparation on her part. Therefore what such a transplanted person can absorb from the stream of events surrounding her is quite limited. Apparently, however, she manages to learn enough to enable her to survive, get along with others and do her job.

However, of the skills she succeeds in acquiring and the personal changes she accomplishes, only some will be retained and carried back home as a permanent acquisition. Even the gains from employment experience won't be lasting. For instance, the skills she learns at work will not remain with her for long since her status as a working woman will, in the majority of cases, terminate upon her return home, leaving no opportunity for them to be exercised.

Of the newly formed attitudes and the accompanying changes in her perspectives and world view, a considerable portion will not have a chance for survival either. Since many such subjective attributes go along with objective conditions, when similar conditions are not found back home, these attributes will become irrelevant. Even simple changes, such as those in consumer habits, can and do become reversed; original behaviour and attitudes will reappear.

Upon return, not only will some of the personal changes cease to be supported by outside circumstances, but others will be actively opposed by the people in her immediate surroundings. She will be coming back to her kin group and she will be subjected to their influence more now than was the case when she was abroad.

This will then start a process of adaptation in the reverse direction. In order to function comfortably and minimise friction with her environment in a traditionally-oriented kin-group network and the respective socio-cultural circumstances, she must now unlearn or suppress her newly-acquired habits and behaviour — those which are regarded as deviant by the others around her — and she must reactivate the former, more acceptable ones. The net result of this process of change — forward and backward — can perhaps be described as 'some loss in gains'. Since, even if all the changes that occur in her do not last, not all that has been gained will be lost either; part of it continuing its existence in some latent form even when not openly expressed.

For example, the obstinate struggle on the part of a migrant working woman to possess some security in terms of assets and property, and her unrelenting claim to have a say in decision-making matters of her family, would be unheard of in the case of the traditional woman.

Other changes, however, will probably persist only in a latent form, waiting to find a proper occasion for expression. The internalised values associated with women's participation in paid work will probably be recast into some new shape, to be expressed, for instance, in the form of educational and occupational aspirations for her daughters.

With this general framework in mind, let us now look more systematically into the details of the main components of women's migration experience.

Multi-faceted abruptness

The outstanding feature which characterises the phenomenon of migration of Turkish women to European labour markets can be referred to as the multi-faceted abruptness of their experience abroad. Changes in a variety of dimensions in their lives occur at unexpected speed. What normally develops in a slow dialectical thesis/antithesis relationship emerges almost simultaneously in the same cluster and takes effect abruptly. For many women, the trip to Europe is the first trip they have ever made out of their familiar community. For those women migrating alone, it is the very first time they are unchaperoned. The anxiety they must feel is probably unmatched by anything that has happened before — the fears associated with not being led along, not being able to understand what is said and done, not knowing where the place of work is and how to get there. The feelings of frustration, subjugation and humiliation must be as oppressive as the foreign environment itself.

For the majority, wage work itself is the new experience; however, for about a quarter of these women, it is not employment that constitutes the newness of the experience, but the nature of it. That one works in shifts, sometimes at midnight, sometimes at a great distance from home, that the employer is usually not to be seen, are all part of this new fact of life. As estrangement is inevitable in a work setting where little is comprehensible, only the wages earned have significance; it is this fact that is channelled into the consciousness of these women.

They live unaware of and uninterested in what is being produced, to what end or for whom. Whatever it is, it must be 'better' than that which is made in their own country. As many say, 'If you take something with you to Turkey during your "urlaub" you need say nothing but that you bought it in Germany and you can sell it for ten times its price here; because this is an advanced country in need of labour and we are here for that'.

Discontinuity

It is discontinuity in both the productive and the reproductive functions of a migrant woman's life abroad that underlies her peculiar experiences. She is most unlikely to be employed again upon return to Turkey. Her participation in social production is translated into asset accumulation: a handful grabbed in a gold rush in which hundreds of thousands join. Once this is achieved she is reluctant to continue working, and even if she may be willing, she can rarely find a suitable job.

Paralleling the tentativeness of her productive role is the temporary nature of the changes in her reproductive role. The labour she contributes towards the creation and maintenance of the family's manpower potential, the care of the husband, parents, and children, the maintenance of the household, preparation of food, and the choice of appropriate consumption patterns are all temporarily altered. During the period of migration, the migrant woman refrains from part of her reproductive 'duties'. Some or all children are left behind, sometimes her husband, parents and in-laws are left behind, housework is made more practical and easy, and measures are sought against procreative activities.

The primacy of women's responsibility in reproduction has three aspects worthy of mention *vis-à-vis* the migrant woman. The reduced amount of labour performed for reproduction is offset by the adjustment difficulties the women go through in their new environment. For instance, by leaving some of her children behind, she has less physical work to perform than she would have had with all her children with her; at the same time she has less direct interaction with those children who have accompanied her and is much less of a support to them in their growing and learning processes than she would have been at home. Second, the attenuation of her reproductive performance is likely to continue upon return because the children will be older, her house will be better equipped with labour-saving devices, and her increased wealth will enable her to purchase partly or wholly prepared consumer items that further save on her labour. This reduction in her reproductive labour will probably persist despite the discontinuity of her work outside the home. Third, during her stay abroad, her relationship with persons to whom she bears reproductive responsibilities often takes on a monetary dimension. Since her new experience is defined as 'making money' rather than as 'working' she can readily substitute monetary obligations on her part for the reproductive functions she has left behind. Rather than fulfilling the traditional obligations as mother and wife, she partly abandons them and contributes money to the family — the maternal role being replaced by an economic role. The consequence of all this is her estrangement from her children and family, as well as from the social relations, of which they are a part. Even more prominent than her own estrangement, is the estrangement of her children. As millions of persons are subjected to these estrangements — no matter how temporary — it is important to consider what effects this will have on society.

Easing up of social controls

A number of *de facto* changes in the family tend to alleviate the traditional social control mechanisms and create the ground for new home-based social relations:

1 Maternal links no longer dominate the network of household relations, and social norms which favour such links lose their strength.

2 There is fluctuation in household membership.

3 Co-residency emerges. Cases of co-residency between unrelated members and even between persons of the opposite sex find acceptance.

Women migrating jointly with their husbands, or following them later, will probably not be freed from kin controls to the same extent as women migrating alone will be. However, the potential conflicts that result from the new financial power of the working woman *vis-à-vis* her husband will lead her to seek alternatives to the expected strict submission to his authority.

The physical separation of the migrant woman from her familiar social milieu releases her from the social control mechanisms and participation modes integral to her previous daily life. She is cut off from the extended family and their daily rituals, expectations, and interactions. There remains only the conjugal pair and that only in a few cases. The migrant family milieu is eventually supplemented by diverse interactions between the migrant and other individual workers who are experiencing the same loosening of norms and social controls. New reference groups are formed. The Turkish woman, for whom the family has always been of sole importance in dictating her daily life, discovers hitherto unknown social alternatives. Her stay in women's boarding houses, her move into jointly rented flats and foreign neighbourhoods, the ease and informality of the manner in which she and her family form new friendships and partnerships are events with powerful psychic effects.

Personal and familial outcomes of women's migration

The migrant woman goes through a complex educational/socialisation process during her stay abroad. Some elements of this process are more easily observable than others; she gains a skill, no matter how low; she learns a foreign language, no matter how little; she learns the culture patterns of her new environment – no matter how incomplete. Other aspects of this learning process, on the other hand, are more latent; she

297

gains a new perspective in her familial and social relations and she has a different image of herself.

The fact that a woman supplies an important source of family income and the accompanying *de facto* changes in her family and social milieu are reflected in the raised status and power within the family, and in some cases, in the shifts in the division of labour. In cases where the woman is the sole provider, there emerges a relationship that is deviant, unrealistic and unstable, one which presents a potential threat to male authority. In this situation the burden of the wife reaches superhuman dimensions, for she not only remains the breadwinner of the family, but she also has to see that her husband does not really feel that this is so. This unrealistic and unstable relation seems to be associated with a high divorce rate.

Even when women are not the sole providers but contribute only part of the family income, they change most visibly in that they insist on participating in the decision making concerning property acquisition and income allocation. Many feel they should make such decisions on their own, at least as regards the money that they earn, while others demand assurances in the form of the joint registration of all property acquired. These are the major areas of dispute among the spouses. In addition, there are cases where women working abroad fail to remit because of disagreement with their husbands' or fathers' mode of investment. In other cases, their new-found capacity to earn an independent income justifies a sense of personal worth and, when encouraged by the extraordinary availability of enticing material goods, an excessive purchasing of personal belongings.

Not trusting their husbands' mode of income allocation, women request that their employers have their earnings deposited in an account separate from those of their husbands. The latters' authority is shaken; they lose control of spending, savings and investments. For any investment they plan to make, the women's consent is needed. The adjustment of both men and women to this change in the balance of power is not always easy or smooth. Men sometimes resist this change and women sometimes tend to assume too many other 'liberties'. Whatever the outcome of these conflicts, most women, sooner or later, feel rightly entitled to the control of their savings and to a tangible economic security after years of hard work in a stressful environment.

In the emerging division of labour, fathers come to assume the major child-caring roles when mothers are sole providers and in other cases share the household duties with their wives much more than before. From the viewpoint of the children, the image of 'mother' also changes. While a mother's absence from the household for a duration of several years would normally have been intolerable, migrant women improve their relative status at home and receive greater appreciation from their children. However, this is neutralised by the exposure of children to the

German culture and through the greater ability they gain by language acquisition. Bilingual children, even at young ages, help solve many family problems by establishing contact between the parents and the larger society. This elevates their status in the family and diminishes the 'respectability' of the parents in their eyes.

Whatever their relative status within the family, the educational aspirations of the migrant women do indeed change in comparison with those of the male migrants. In a postal survey we conducted in late 1975, the emerging pattern of reasons given for a continued stay in Germany rested heavily on the educational standing of the children; those with children in German schools expressed a desire to stay longer to allow for the completion of schooling. Those with children still at the early levels of their schooling and showing no visible achievement, stated a desire to go back soon and/or send back the children. Women differ from men, however, with respect to the level of educational aspirations for their children, particularly for their daughters. More than males, they aspire to occupational or professional education for their children without distinguishing between sons and daughters — such distinctions being made in Turkey, however. (Unfortunately — though this can in no way be directly attributable to the choice of parents — most children do not get a chance to attend an occupational or a professional school, and among those attending, there are hardly any girls.)

One important impact of the external migration of women needs to be emphasised. Despite societal reactions against their mobility, women actually search for jobs on their own and they go to work under financial conditions that are not too pressing; they do so not out of necessity but more as a response to an opportunity for rapid improvement of the family's economic position. This has helped redefine the position of women. A parallel change has occurred with respect to internal migration which, until recently, was a male-led movement. Today families tend to migrate jointly to the cities, especially to the metropolitan areas, wives finding informal employment in the service sector as domestic aids, for instance, and serving as a financial buffer until their husbands arrange for jobs — a process that might take anywhere from several months to several years. It thus no longer constitutes an 'embarrassment' for a husband to let his wife work; nor is it looked down upon as a sign of her readiness for 'prostitution'. These are the inevitable consequences of the fall in real income and the growth of increasing relative poverty, all operating to transform the relevant social norms as the need arises.

Illustrative case studies

The following section presents some different cases to serve as an illustration of the background experiences of different types of women, showing the ways in which they have been affected, and the degree to which they have internalised patterns of behaviour and thought to which they have been exposed.

Sevim

When she left for Munich at the age of 24, Sevim had worked as a government employee for six years. Among the four sisters in her family, only Sevim attended the secondary school and succeeded in graduating from there. Sevim thinks that no one influenced her decision to go to Germany, that she herself came to that decision after drawing her own conclusions from the information she had gathered and from what she had heard around her. She was young and single then. As she had a job, and a salary sufficient to support herself, she did not feel a need to get married, nor did she like anybody enough to marry.

Sevim worked at the Siemens factory in Munich and lived in a 'heim' with other Turkish women workers. At first she thought that many Turkish women were acting rather strangely, as though they were just released from their chains, trying to enjoy life fully, in fact to enjoy being at a safe distance from the iron claw of the social pressures back home. In the evenings young Turkish men with cars would be waiting in front of the dormitories and try to persuade women to go out with them. Sevim, too, began keeping company with a young Turkish man. After some time when Sevim rented and moved into a small apartment, he frequented the place, and eventually they started living together. They lived together for six years, something that would be absolutely impossible in Turkey.

Sevim had no German friends and she only visited the neighbouring Turkish women. Meanwhile she changed her job and worked as a cleaner in offices and schools, which she found easier, better paid and not to her distaste any more. She found it quite an accomplishment on her part that the label of the job no longer mattered to her.

Since her return to Turkey after marrying her boyfriend and giving birth to a child, Sevim leads a quiet life. She does not want to work; her views on premarital relations have changed a lot after her own experiences in this respect.

Ayse

Ayse went to school for three years, then left to take care of her young brothers and sisters. She worked for some time as a cleaning woman, with her mother who was also a cleaner. It was she who got the initial information and idea about going to Germany. Her husband, who was a janitor, agreed to go there for a short time to earn enough money to buy a house in Turkey. This would, they thought, lessen the burden of paying rent for the rest of their lives.

However, they had two small children and their care would be a problem. Her mother refused to take care of them saying' 'Why should you leave your country, and go and work for the atheists? Is it fair to separate children from their parents?' In spite of all her mother's objections, Ayse had made up her mind. Ayse applied immediately but was astonished to be told that the couple would not be able to go together; priority was given to women. She was sent to Germany in two weeks, experiencing a trauma-like separation. She knew nothing about Germany except what appeared in newspapers and what she had learned through hearsay. The moment she stepped into the train, she had an uncontrollable urge to turn around and go straight back home, thinking 'what a crazy thing I am doing'; and she felt an overwhelming sense of loneliness. At the Munich railway station all the women workers arriving in Germany were placed in groups and driven to the places to which they were assigned for work. She understood nothing of what was happening; she could only move to the place pointed at when her name was called. As one of a group of six, Ayse was assigned to work in a hospital and was placed in a room for two. 'In Turkey, it was formally arranged that we would work in a laundry, but in Germany they put us to work in a kitchen. We didn't think to inquire about the change. Not much would have changed even if we had'.

She didn't know whether she was being paid overtime or not. She had no complaints about not getting some more time off; she did not really care much for time off as she never knew what to do with the time on those days.

Soon after arriving, Ayse discovered that it was impossible to bring her husband to Germany. She wrote to him twice a week and asked him to try to find other means of coming there. By this time her husband had already resigned from his job and was taking care of the children. He was annoyed about the situation and started to complain saying that he was ill, that either he must go to Germany, or Ayse should return home.

Ayse sent her husband 600 marks a month, after retaining 100 for herself, in order to put an end to his complaints. She had no idea how he was using the money and never thought of asking him about it. On her days off, Ayse would take a walk with her roommate, watch TV or write letters. She made no attempt to get to know the environment in which she was living.

A total of 10 months had passed before Ayse, with gifts and presents for her children, took the train and returned to Turkey. Her homesickness coupled with her husband's complaints were unbearable. As she left her employment during annual leave and without letting her employers know that she was leaving on a permanent basis, she was not entitled to any benefits.

After the excitement of seeing her husband and children again subsided, Ayse regretted her return. Problems arose as her husband had not been able to save any of the money she had sent from Germany, so once again she took on her old cleaning job.

Hatice

Hatice is 30 years of age and was born in Turgutlu, a town in the province of Izmir from where she departed. She finished primary school and at 16 started earning money by sewing for pay. Having been treated badly by her father and brother, she filed an application with the Turkish State Employment and Placement Centre to get a job abroad. She felt the first signs of nostalgia and regret for the decision when, with her mother, she came to Istanbul to take the train for Germany. But she wouldn't give up. What would the neighbours say about her giving up the plans? She recalls the people in Turkey shouting to the people in the train 'here goes the caravan of prostitutes'. On their arrival in Munich, a big group of people, mostly Turks, were there to see the newcomers. What she experienced between the time of making the decision to come and her arrival in Munich was no less unpleasant and unbearable than what she had been running away from. She observed a tense atmosphere among the Turkish workers in the same work place. Her first payment was not much. She noticed that people were being paid different wages even though they were doing the same work. She tried to learn how to keep track of her money. Hatice thinks that German people and the employers are quite nice as long as you work continuously without even putting up your head for a second. But once you get sick or want to have some days off, they turn out to be tough and rough people. Foreign workers were not allowed to take advantage of the rights the natives were enjoying. Whatever the natives would do would be overlooked, but once the foreign worker attempted to do the same, German employers would get tough.

She thinks men in general do not behave well towards women. She has never known a couple in Berlin who like and respect each other. She did not think of getting married. All she expected was that her parents would arrange something for her future with the money that she had sent so far.

Hatice is now married to a man whom she had met in Turkey in 1973 at the time of her visit home to ask her father to purchase a piece of land. She managed to carry through the whole process of marriage within 15 days and brought him to Berlin. Soon after he was able to

302

find a job. Now they work together and plan for the future although most of the plans are being decided by the husband. Hatice does not complain about the new life. 'In the past I worked for my brother and father. Now I am working for my husband. Before I had my own work, now I am working for others. There is not much difference between these alternatives; I am bound to remain as the second person in line. Women should work and help the financial matters of the household. And the husband in turn should be helpful to the wife on housework', she comments.

They are saving money for her husband's plans (he plans to run a supermarket) and they also want to buy their own house. Hatice hopes to have her seamstress — or tailoring — shop in Turkey. But the major emphasis is on her husband's work.

Nezihe

Nezihe, a brunette with a tired and wrinkled face, is 33 years old; she was born and grew up in Adana. Her father was a junk dealer and her family was rather poor. She could attend primary school for only three years and then had to drop out in order to look after her three siblings at home. She was 17 when she got married. Her husband first started to earn money by working in an auto repair shop and eventually got a job in a factory. He also kept talking about the people going to Germany and coming back with brand new cars. It was obvious to Nezihe that her husband was rather envious of those people and thus she too began to entertain the idea of going to Germany. She disclosed her intentions to her husband who showed no sign of objection. Since it was easier for women to get a job abroad, Nezihe was the first to come to Germany. Six months later her husband joined her.

Although he joined her in Berlin only six months ago, he is now back in Adana, their home town in Turkey. He did not want to work in Berlin even though the firm wanted him. He has no job in Turkey. As Nezihe sees it, he is irresponsible towards his children and wife. Nezihe took control of their money; she thinks her husband is likely to spend it all on alcohol. Her major concern is to save some money.

During her second year of work in Germany, Nezihe was able to buy a flat in Turkey and save some in the bank for the dowry of her daughter. Nezihe is planning to buy another house for their own use and still another to rent. These are being planned and executed by Nezihe. Her husband has little part in it.

She admits that in the past her husband did bring home some of his earnings, but that was not enough; it could buy only their daily bread. As Nezihe sees it, men cannot think of better situations anyhow; they think that only the food for their wives and children should be paid for and the rest of their earnings should be spent for their own entertainment. They don't think about the future: 'Who is going to be responsible for the future of their daughters?'

He is in Turkey and makes attempts to get a divorce. In spite of all these uneasy relations between them, Nezihe does not want to divorce him. She believes that her husband may come again to work in Germany and earn some money. If he comes, she won't let him remain unemployed; the 1,000 marks she earns is not enough to maintain them and for carrying out her plans.

Societal impact of women's migration

It is of critical importance to place the replications of migrant women's experiences in a societal perspective. As we have seen, individual women attempt to achieve 'emancipation' or 'liberation'. However, these attempts do not necessarily generate social change. Whatever 'liberation' does occur is restricted to the personal relations of each woman, reflecting itself in her 'ability' to make independent decisions concerning clothing, shopping and similar activities pertaining to the use of earnings. Clearly, so long as migrant women do not transmit their consciousness to the working women at home, so long as when returning they leave behind in Germany whatever consciousness they have gained, so long as they cognitively separate the work-related consciousness from a societal one, and so long as the social structure appears to have prepared the necessary conditions for their 'upward mobility' or 'class mobility' from a proletarian to a bourgeois status, then a positive transformation of their experience abroad is unlikely.

Moreover, little in the way of political consciousness develops among migrant women. The insecurity of their work and, more importantly, of their existence in a hostile environment limits the emergence of a political awareness. That they have no previous work experience adds to this. Their inability to communicate in the language of the 'host' country and the social humiliation they are subjected to reduces the strength of a possible urge towards organising themselves into any kind of effective union.

They fail to identify the humiliation, which they face at work and which they face in their everyday life, with their existence as 'women'. Their work is interpreted merely as 'contributing' to family income; this blurs the contribution of their experiences to the creation of new values. Thus, migrant women do not find their experience abroad, particularly that pertaining to their role in the production process, relevant for the future. The transmission of such experiences into a proletarian movement at home is further hindered by the lack of opportunities for employment in Turkey.

The individual bourgeois aspirations surrounding the emigration of

304

women and their desire to be freed from the social pressures ruling their lives work against the translation of the migrant work experience into an effective proletarian movement. Thus, neither the structure of experiences shaping women's departure from Turkey, nor those confronting them abroad, nor the conditions awaiting them upon return lead to the formation of a proletarian class consciousness and a consciousness of being proletarian women. Furthermore, there are no avenues for the transmission of even a rudimentary degree of awareness to the Turkish society as a whole.

Those married male returnees who have succeeded in accumulating enough assets to materialise their aspirations, living off rent or off the income of a business they have established, find it 'unnecessary' for their wives to work. These women aspire to belong to the bourgeois class, yet they share little of the bourgeois culture, way of thought, sentiment or behaviour. Their new place can best be described by the phrase 'betwixt and between'. Thus, although women of their economic status and European exposure living in cities often participate in different kinds of voluntary organisations, taking sometimes important roles in women's branches of different political parties, the migrant women returnees will neither be readily accepted by the bourgeois parties and organisations, nor have the cultural readiness to express interest in such involvement. The returnees interact with those in the class from which they originated. They achieve their escalation to the 'upper class' only on the subjective level, by feeling 'much better off than before', or rather, better off than their relatives and other acquaintances.

Even though the migrant woman who has returned has moved many steps ahead on a personal basis, her achievement does not immediately translate itself to the societal level. The fact that she can free herself from the restrictions imposed on her by family structure and setting also points to a fertile ground for her societal participation. That is, if she can work alone, shop or travel alone, she can also vote and voice her opinion alone, form such opinions or become a member of a political organisation. For the returning migrant woman, however, the society has little readiness for the utilisation of her potential.

9 Transpositions and reinterpretations of the traditional female role in an immigration situation

SOSSIE ANDIZIAN AND JOCELYNE STREIFF

The study of female migration occupies a minor space in the literature referring to the sociological analysis of migratory phenomena. Women most often appear within the 'family' category. They are labelled 'problem people', for they are seen as people whose 'inactivity' aggravates the problems of 'adaptation' experienced by the family group. The discussion largely centres on their 'alienation', the 'cleavages' which arise between them and other members of the family, and their 'lack of understanding' of the industrial world in which they live.

The picture which Minces (1973) paints of the situation is highly significant from this standpoint:

> She [the immigrant woman] does not speak the language of the host country; and she can usually neither read nor write and, since she does not work, she has no personal resources. Above all, she has no real possibility of relating to the industrial world in which she lives. Feeling herself surrounded by hostility, she will often live in an even more restricted social milieu than in her country of origin, possibly only meeting other women, her neighbours, usually of a similar age and from the same socio-cultural level (p. 433).

For Michel (1973) on the contrary, these characteristics mark the women out as an 'innovative' group. The author suggests that as they form one of the groups 'most restricted by the family tradition', Algerian women are, for this very reason, the most inclined to 'adopt the values and behaviour patterns of the average French family'.

In all these examples, women are studied as forming a special migrant category, which, according to the authors, has varying degrees of success, in comparison with other groups, in effecting the transition from the system of values inherent in traditional societies to a system of modern values, clearly presented, whatever the customary precautions taken in that respect, as emancipating values.

The methodology indicated by this type of approach is the questionnaire or personal interview, which tries to place the subject at a specific level of adaptation to the modernisation process, modernity being regarded as conformity to the average behaviour patterns of the majority.

This type of approach, however, fails to reveal the complex modes of interaction which develop between community groups and the dominant society. Our hypothesis is that the communities built up in the 'host' country by virtue of contiguity give the immigrants a chance to recreate transposed or reinterpreted characteristic role patterns of their native cultures. The ways in which these communities come to perceive and interpret the differing status of their members undergo changes which, far from reflecting a smooth progression from the traditional to the modern, embody all the possible types of reaction of the dominated to the dominator: borrowing, reinterpretation, emulation, rejection.

This hypothesis led us to select as especially suitable subjects for research groups created on the basis of residence conditions in the host country. With this in view, we attempted to determine the nature of the changes that affect family relationships, as applied to immigrants, focusing our attention on two questions:

1 How do the living conditions within the host society alter the functional roles of women in the community?

2 What consequences do these transformations have for the process by which the young girl finds her place in society?

Constitution and function of female groups

Our investigations of North African families gathered together on dwelling sites jointly allocated to them (transit areas, run-down urban zones) lead us to believe that analysis of the domestic female role is central to an understanding of the internal cohesion of immigrant communities.

The fact that women are essential to the group's identity is not, as often claimed, because they are guarantors of the traditional order, but rather because their uninterrupted presence in the living area enables them to establish a complex network of relationships which ensure the greater part of social control within the community, in ways closely similar to those described by Vasse (1964) regarding women's gatherings in Algerian society.

> Within, everything is said that is withheld outside. Intrigues are related, deepened and unravelled, opinions are given, more or less explicit agreements take shape, and these compacts then serve as instruments of leverage and power, to which the outside world and men will inevitably have to pay full heed.

This unique position places the women's group in a position to assume control over the 'cleavages' arising between the symbolic representations at the core of the group's cultural identity and the practices engendered by conditions governing life in the host society. The lack of older women (mothers-in-law and mothers), who represent 'paternal power within the society of women' in North African society, results in the disappearance of all those attributes which determine the status of power within the women's group. Social control based on status conferred by age and family hierarchy is replaced by joint control shared between the women of the same generation, in which the custodians of power must demonstrate that they can behave according to traditional roles as well as show a capacity for 'resourcefulness' in the host society.

Social control is implemented through a network of relationships associated with female roles (visits to expectant and nursing mothers, looking after children, kitchen chores, etc.), and it is exercised to its fullest extent when the men are absent. At night and on weekends the women return to the confined world of the home and the exterior becomes the men's domain. It is only on special occasions (celebrations, weddings) that these relationships emerge into the open. At these high points of social interchange, the choice of the suitor, the negotiations between families, the organisation of the celebration and the selection of the guests provide the women with opportunities to make alliances, to provoke disputes and to exercise their influence.

Reinforcement of the maternal role

Contrary to other categories of migrant women, for whom immigration means a chance to attain wage-earner status, the arrival in France of a North African woman deprives her (inasmuch as she had the opportunity at home) of any possibility of outside work, for a series of reasons: amongst these are the inability to entrust infants to the care of other children in the family, language difficulties, and the growing resistance shown by her husband, alarmed by the danger represented by the example of French women.

This situation, combined with the man's prolonged absences (often protracted by the distance between home and work), results in the women taking a stronger hold over the domestic sphere and over the children's education. Thus the woman is called upon to assume the main share of responsibility for the education of her children and also to be answerable to the group for their behaviour. However, she is poorly equipped to perform this role and she is forced to make up for the unchallenged authority of the head of the family, and the power conferred on him by his status, by means of sanctions based on rigid taboos or by recourse to an authority outside the community — as when a mother whose daughter's honour is impugned tries to defend it by producing a certificate of virginity.

The socialisation of the young girl

Thus the education of the young female immigrant is largely in the hands of the women's group, which punishes 'deviant' behaviour in order to preserve the community's integrity.

The mother is held responsible for the 'bad behaviour' of her daughters, and it is she who bears the brunt of the group's disapproval. One of the young girls from the neighbourhood in which we worked returned to live with her parents after six months of marriage, and, as a result, her mother was banned from the 'company of women'.

Transgressions are tolerated as long as they do not compromise family honour or that of the community as a whole. We attended the wedding of a young Moroccan girl which was celebrated with the utmost respect for ritual. As the display of the bloodstained bed sheet (proof of the young girl's virginity) excited the indignation of a young woman living in another neighbourhood, one of the women in the community (apparently among the most 'emancipated') tried to explain why the rite was 'indispensable' in this particular case: 'A. often went out with boys, and many bad things have been said about her, so today it is necessary to show everyone that she is innocent, and to stop their tongues wagging'.

All the young girl's education is oriented towards marriage. Thus although the mothers' aspirations regarding the schooling of daughters are as high as for sons, everything they do actually tends to hinder it: they often enlist their aid with household chores, looking after the children and making applications to the social services.

Similarly, in spite of positive attitudes towards the idea of the girls working, they raise obstacles to this whenever the work threatens to hinder marriage. This is stressed by an article in the Algerian daily paper El-Moujahid:

> . . . Everyone is fully aware that one of the main concerns of the heads of migrant families is to safeguard their children

from all influences arising from the foreign milieu within which they are momentarily forced to live. These influences are responsible for all of the worries which bedevil many parents when their children reach a certain age, above all, for daughters . . .

Actually, it is in areas related to the children's education that the pressures of the host society are brought to bear most forcibly, because this touches on matters of the most fundamental symbolic significance.

From childbirth (and already during pregnancy) the mother is subjected to a series of constraints and inducements by the social services, aimed at imposing on her a number of educational practices, and to imbue her with a forward-looking mentality far removed from traditional attitudes towards maternity.

Furthermore, school attendance, by interiorising certain roles in children, and by the type of representation that it arouses amongst parents, fundamentally questions the status of the child within the family. It is not surprising that the most bitter disputes within the community are almost always concerned with the children's education, and especially that of the girls.

The women's vigilance concerning the young female immigrants' education can be interpreted as a reaction against the host society's policy of assimilation, which offers no opportunity for social integration other than through a process of marginalisation. In order to accomplish the 'adaptation' of young migrants, the host society uses practices that tend to 'deculturate' them by destroying all the characteristics of the socio-cultural system of origin, which are seen in a purely negative light, as elements of resistance.

Consequently, the young immigrant girl's search for identity involves very complex processes, which are often experienced as 'tragic moments' in her life.

The identity of the North African girl: a dynamic concept

Caught between many cultural affiliations, the young immigrant girl is faced with a difficult choice between models which clash more often than not. Valabrègue (1973) describes the situation of young Algerian girls in France which illustrates their state of 'continual inner conflict':

It is not easy to be 16 years old in France when one belongs to a family of migrant workers. Which model is one to identify with? A backward mother? A French classmate whose freedom one envies? For young Moslems, this poses a serious and often painful problem.

The clearest example of 'intercultural conflict' is the refusal to accept an 'arranged' marriage (marriage to a man chosen by the parents, perhaps a cousin or another immigrant from the same ethnic group); this conflict can even lead to suicide. Valabrègue notes the high number of suicide attempts made by young immigrant Algerian girls.

Thus 'choice' situations unavoidably tend to result in conflicts between the young immigrant girl and her social group. These conflicts, which are the manifestation of interaction between different cultural models, must be seen as phases in the personal development of the young North African girl. Her identity is built up in a dynamic way inasmuch as she is in an almost permanent state of adjusting her behaviour to the set of norms and patterns imposed on her both by her own social group and by the host society. This implies 'partial' identification with certain models of the host society and the 'momentary' or 'irreversible' negation of certain potential internal identities. Thus one can observe behaviour patterns comparable to those noted by Bourdieu and Sayad (1964) amongst the 'uprooted' Algerian peasants:

> The behaviour models and the economic ethos imported by colonization coexist in each subject with the models and the ethos passed down by ancestral tradition. It follows that behaviour, attitudes and opinions appear as fragments of an unknown language, incomprehensible both to those who only know the cultural language of tradition and to those who only refer to the cultural language of colonization. Sometimes the words of the traditional language are strung together using modern syntax; sometimes the opposite occurs, and sometimes what we get is a surface veneer resulting from a combination of the two.

We observed this type of behaviour exemplified in a young Moroccan girl of 20, in one of the neighbourhoods in which we worked. We shall try to retrace a part of her 'experience of being a young immigrant girl' while trying to grasp the significance of her behaviour, which both social workers and local inhabitants find inconsistent.

A., who came to France at the age of 10, received the characteristic schooling of immigrant children: transition classes and practical classes until the age of 16, following which the authorities advised her to enter working life. After refusing to marry the cousin to whom she had been destined from birth, she took a training course to become a hostess and started to look for a job. She came up against problems of unemployment and segregation, and was eventually forced to remain at home, like most of the other elder daughters in the community, much sought after by their mothers for performing domestic chores. She spent a great deal of her time at home, together with the other women, at the same time trying to develop relationships outside the community.

She was reportedly seen 'with boys in cafés'. Two years later, 'to everyone's surprise', A. agreed to marry a Moroccan immigrant 20 years her senior, introduced to her by her neighbours. The whole community took part in the wedding ceremony, organised and run by the group of women who saw to it that there was strict observation of all ritual practices.

Her French friends talk of 'resignation' and of a 'forced return' to native cultural models.

However, within the first weeks of her marriage A. found difficulty in assuming her role of the traditional wife, especially when it came to confinement within the household area. Refusing to recreate the family pattern so familiar to herself, she refused to have a child until the couple's financial situation improved. Under increasing pressure from her husband to conform with the role of the traditional wife, A. obtained a divorce and rejoined her family. According to the latest information, she is now living with her parents and is looking for a job.

Confronted with such a situation, there is a great temptation to see nothing more than 'conflicts of models' or 'disorganised behaviour patterns'. It is impossible to grasp the significance of such behaviour unless one analyses the different ways in which the subject is symbolically acting out the alternatives open to him and the meaning he ascribes to them. This is what we propose to do using this case study, which reveals the general conditions governing the strategies employed by young girls in order to cope with 'cultural difference' situations, as well as the potential modes of 'evolution' available to them.

Schooling and work

School attendance gives young North African girls a chance to discern the limits imposed on them by their socio-cultural affiliation. At best they can gain access to one of the shorter technical training courses, but even here it is the 'softer options' which are allocated to them, e.g. the clothing industry. This is not dictated exclusively by their aptitudes but also corresponds to the parents' desire to resist any training which is liable to 'Westernise' them.

However, whether steered towards one of the shorter technical training courses or towards entering working life immediately, the young girls themselves are keen to start work as soon as possible, as a means to 'acquire a degree of independence'. On the one hand, this enables them to escape from the pressures of the family milieu and a more or less forced marriage, while on the other it provides them with opportunities for social integration which they would otherwise have difficulty in finding.

The objective conditions governing the socio-occupational integration of young immigrant girls are not very encouraging. Their poor qualifications and their socio-cultural affiliation relegate them to the same level as their parents, placing them within the most under-privileged occupational categories.

Spared the same financial burdens as their fathers and brothers, they are even less 'motivated' by work, in which they not only fail to discover the advantages they hope for, but also find that working conditions (an unrewarding job, long working hours far from home, etc.) are a real burden and deprive them of the independence they enjoyed during the day spent at home. They have to leave home just when it becomes female territory, and the lack of 'warm relations' at their place of work causes them to idealise the relational life of their native group and to take 'refuge' within it. As opposed to their 'dread' of the outside world which rejects them in various ways, the 'hospit-able' family or community allows them to rediscover their identity.

Marriage

The 'failure' of her work experience thus led A. to seek integration within her native milieu, where she was 'taken in hand' by the women's group. She participated in their relational life and was 'initiated' into the secret, predominantly sexual conversations (it is well known that in North African societies, sexuality is the main topic of conversation at the women's gatherings).

Her participation in the women's group gave her the opportunity to discover what Lacoste-Dujardin (1977) has noted among Kabyle women, 'a degree of independence from men and a strong sense of solidarity' as well as 'the warm female sympathy, deriving from a certain kind of complicity which is specific to intimacy among women'.

This whole atmosphere prepared her for her future role as a North African woman, a role that was to be 'consecrated' by marriage. Thus she gradually accepted the prospect of a traditional marriage, a pre-requisite for her permanent introduction into the world which would henceforth be her own. She submitted to all the regulations decreed by the women's group, deriving support from the young girls of the neigh-bourhood gathered around her. 'From tomorrow I will be part of the women's group', she proudly confided to us, alluding to a step which stirs up admiration and also a certain apprehension among the young girls. Not only did her marriage permit her to attain a woman's status, but it was also a factor of social advancement. She left the neighbour-hood, which was always poorly regarded by its inhabitants, to live in a flat in town.

However, although this new way of life gave her a certain indepen-dence, it tended to separate her from the community, depriving her of the company and support of the women. Consequently, she spent the entire day among the family in which she occupied a privileged position as a 'married woman'. She was often seen at the gatherings of the women in the community, making cakes. However, her continued presence in the neighbourhood started becoming the topic of conversation within the women's group. Was she fulfilling her role as a wife properly? Moreover, since she publicly announced her intention to put off having her first child, rumours began to circulate that the couple were having problems. These doubts were confirmed by her husband, who complained about her to the people who had introduced her to him. He reproached her for neglecting her household duties, for refusing to have their first child, and for always being away from home. By her behaviour, A. fundamentally compromised the traditional role of the head of the family, and sullied the image of masculine virility in a society where to have a large number of descendants is a point of honour.

Because of increasingly frequent quarrels with her husband, A. decided to obtain a divorce and subsequently returned to the family milieu. The fact that she had taken the initiative was seen as yet another insult by the husband, especially since her family seemed to accept this return without much reluctance.

Finding a job, an act seen formerly as a mythical way to 'freedom' now became a necessity. A. knew perfectly well that her marriage had irreversibly changed her status within the family. Henceforth her presence would only be tolerated if she could support herself. Apart from modifying family relationships, her return also totally altered the pattern of alliances within the women's groups.

Ever since rumours started spreading about the couple's difficulties, the women of the community gathered around her mother to decide with her what should be done. The person who had served as the go-between held a central position in these discussions. It was she who would bear the blame if the marriage broke up.

When the break became imminent, she took the husband's side and continually pressed the mother to prevent her daughter from taking such a step. Not only did the divorce take place, but A.'s parents also agreed to take her back. The insult was exacerbated by the mother taking her daughter's side. This implied that her daughter had a 'bad husband', namely that he was a 'bad choice'. From this time onwards, the go-between arranged to have A.'s mother ostracised, posing as the upholder of flouted moral values.

After this, the only women who maintained relations with A.'s mother were those who themselves had been more or less rejected due to the 'weakness' shown in their daughters' upbringing.

The young girls' attitudes were more ambivalent. They were forbidden to associate with A. On the whole, however, they approved of her behaviour. 'She was right to get a divorce, she could not live with a man she was forced to marry'. A further difficulty in ascertaining the effects of A.'s return on the young girls stems from the fact that they do not make up a formal 'mobilised' group.

Beset by conflict situations in which she is required to cope with the contradictions and ambivalence stemming from the interaction between community groups and the dominant society, the young North African immigrant girl is thus able to work out a new behaviour pattern which will tend to modify the definition of roles within the family and the group.

The strategies developed by the young immigrant girls as a reaction to the dominant economic and social conditions will be determining factors in mapping out new courses of action in the future, courses which may vary from one group to another.

Bibliography

Bourdieu, P. and Sayad, A., *Le Déracinement, la crise de l'agriculture traditionnelle en Algérie*, éditions de Minuit, 1964, p. 163.

Lacoste-Dujardin, C., *Dialogue de femmes en ethnologie*, Maspero, Paris, 1977.

Michel, A., 'Groupes novateurs et valeurs familiales des immigrés algériens', *Cahiers Internationaux de Sociologie*, vol. IV, 1973, pp. 321-338.
Minces, J., *Les travailleurs étrangers en France*, éditions du Seuil, 1973.

Valabrègue, C., *L'homme déraciné*, Mercure France, 1973.
Vasse, D., 'La femme algérienne', *Travaux et jours*, April 1964, pp. 85-102.

Epilogue: living in two cultures — some sociological considerations
DEAN HARPER

The migration of peoples both within and between nations has occurred throughout history; today the widespread movement of people, in circumstances sometimes dramatic, continues. Political and economic forces of the late 1970s and early 1980s have thrust upon the world's attention the plight of political and economic refugees. And as long as scholarly activity has been conducted, some of it has been devoted, in one way or another, to the investigation and analysis of migratory movements. The present volume, then, represents a contribution to the understanding of these phenomena.

What does sociology as a discipline bring to bear on a fuller understanding of the migration process? In the study of social phenomena, one sociological approach is to focus on social positions or statuses people occupy. These positions are age-related (e.g. adolescent, adult, retired and the like), sexual (i.e. male or female), occupational (e.g. soldier, cleric, teacher, doctor, farmer), religious (e.g. Catholic, Jew), political (e.g. Socialist, Communist), affiliational (e.g. Rotarian), ethnic or national (e.g. Black, White, Italian, Spanish), class (lower class, middle class) and so on. The relevance is that people's behaviour (actions, opinions, beliefs) are partly determined by the positions they occupy and these positions are usually unequal in terms of the wealth, power and prestige associated with them. In our discussions, the important positions are immigrant and non-immigrant. The latter will be referred to as citizen, i.e. as a member of society with membership being legally defined. Though I use the term 'citizen', I do not use it in a laudatory sense — as if citizenship were somehow anointed by sociologists as conveying superiority. However, it is obvious that members of a society see themselves as superior to non-members or immigrants.

The situation of migrants

Land masses of the world are carved into civic entities — neighbourhoods, cities, provinces, nations — and the world's population is categorised according to area of residence. Thus, individuals have a regional identity, which takes on the characteristics of a social position. For example, individuals are known as Parisians or Sicilians or Swedes, and so on. These regional identities are important because many individuals' social ties are within some geographic locale, and although there is considerable migration, many individuals still think of themselves as members of a particular civic and geographic entity.

One such geographical area, i.e. the nation, has other facets of importance. One of these is that each nation devises rules about the movement of peoples — rules governing movement both within the nation, and to and from that nation. Migrating peoples are characterised in terms of their purpose of migration, and the ease or difficulty of migration is determined partially by the intended purpose of the move. In general, in most nations it is easier, both psychologically and in respect to the prescriptive and proscriptive rules, for citizens to migrate within the nation than from that nation to another, though in some countries both forms of migration seem to be equally difficult.

The point of this brief excursus is that if it were not for these rules which regulate migration, 'immigrant' and 'alien' would be meaningless terms. It should be stressed too that these rules are embedded in cultural differences that are even more complex than identifiable rules. These rules reflect the attitudes and feelings of nationals and explicate too the material dichotomy between 'citizen' and 'migrant'.

The migrant's place in industrial society

It should be clear that, in general, migrants occupy the lowest social positions in industrial societies. They receive or earn few rewards of authority, wealth and prestige, and in migrating they acquire additional handicaps that worsen their situation even more. These are the handicaps stemming from being alien — not knowing the language or the customs of the country of employment. Because of this, they are usually relegated to occupations that require minimal skills, i.e. service occupations, such as being janitors, agricultural jobs, unskilled factory work. In these occupations, they have little power to command more than a minimum wage. Migrating from rural areas, they are disinclined, both by habit and by personality, to pursue their interests collectively.

Thus, in the competition for scarce resources, the migrant is not very successful.

Where the immigrant is seen as a threat, the citizen will invoke and emphasise the 'citizen-immigrant' distinction as grounds for most or all of the wealth going to citizens. There exists an implicit belief that the wealth of the group should be divided *only* among members of the group, and immigrants are outsiders; since wealth is partly vested in land, which is (or in the minds of citizens, ought to be) owned only by citizens, the immigrant may even be denied access to ownership of land. 'They should be sent back to their home country' is a belief held by many citizens, and implemented in the policies of many governments.

At the same time, immigrants are welcomed because they will do the menial labour that citizens will not do. Alternatively, employees of that menial labour are unwilling or unable to pay wages that will attract citizens to do it: hence, such employers pressure their governments to allow workers to migrate from countries with surplus labour — workers willing to work for the low wages. Confounded with this is the situation of an expanding economy, where the labour supply is not sufficient even to meet some of the more attractive and less menial tasks, and in this case there will also be pressures to allow immigrants into the country. But, if the economy undergoes a recession, and thereby employment opportunities become limited, there will be pressure to deport the immigrants. 'Citizens should have priority in respect to employment', will be the claim.

The individual who is an immigrant, if he or she is to compete successfully with citizens, will try to leave his or her immigrant position. This may mean becoming assimilated, i.e. learning the language and customs of the host society sufficiently well; and being formally and legally declared a citizen. This may be relatively more or less difficult. The difficulty will, in part, depend on the skills and talents possessed by the immigrant.

Consequences of migration

What consequences does migration have for migrants, for members of the country of employment, and for the country of origin?

Consequences for migrants

Psychically, the experience of migrating is probably both exciting and stressful. The means by which the migrant travels may be fraught with danger and possible death; such was the case for Jews fleeing Germany, Vietnamese fleeing Vietnam when the American military departed, for

Europeans travelling to the New World in the 19th century, for Africans travelling as slaves to the New World in the 17th and 18th centuries, as well as for many others. Once in their new land, the stresses change. These result from the need to find housing and work, and to adapt to a new cultural and physical setting. The migrant finds himself having to cope with the problems of 'living in two cultures'.

Over the long run, one possible effect on the migrant is that he acquires new ways of speaking and acting. And, of course, the younger the migrant the greater the socialisation that occurs, and perhaps the easier it is. There is some suggestive and impressionistic evidence that young migrants may become more strongly motivated to achieve and in fact achieve more than either older migrants or natives. That this could be so, may ironically stem from their dual cultural background. They are forced to adapt to a new culture before they are fully assimilated to their old one; this may leave them better able both to see how success can be achieved in the new society and to achieve it. They are not constrained by a single cultural standard, but find that partial commitment to one cultural milieu helps free them from the other, and they are able to see possibilities that the native cannot. Further they realise their disadvantage, which motivates them to work harder. At the same time, migrants may be even better prepared than comparable segments of the native population to succeed by virtue of the particular strength of their social and ethnic backgrounds. For example, a recent study of school performance of 2,300 school leavers in five multi-racial secondary schools in England, and coming from more or less the same depressed physical, social and cultural environment, shows that West Indian girls and boys achieved better results on the whole than English boys and girls, and that the latter obtained the poorest average results in the critical subjects of English language, mathematics and science. The author explains such success among West Indians in terms of the influence of the strength of the social and cultural forms characterising the country of origin and in the positive role of their ethnicity.[1] Such results certainly run counter to the 'popular wisdom' and even some tenuous social science theories, which take for granted the underachievement and intellectual inferiority of blacks.

Consequences for the country of employment

Many citizens will believe that immigrants pose an economic and cultural threat. They are seen as taking away the jobs held by citizens

---

1 G. Driver, 'How West Indians do better at school (especially the girls)', *New Society*, 17 January 1980.

and they are seen as bringing new customs, which may supersede or alter their own; each perception may be partially correct. For example, following the US Civil War, many freed blacks were able to work in skilled trades, such as carpentry, in southern cities. However, Irish immigrants of the 1890s slowly took over many of these skilled and semi-skilled occupations, and blacks lost their access to these jobs. The concentration of political refugees in Miami, Florida is a contemporary example of the displacement of blacks and a threat to their position. But the immediate threat to employment is felt only by those at the bottom levels of the host society because, for the most part, immigrants enter the occupational structure only at those levels.

In respect to changes in culture and customs, it is clear that with any sizeable immigration there will be some changes in the existing culture. Probably the first, and by no means the least, effect is that new foods and diets are introduced. Some immigrants will set up ethnic restaurants — perhaps at first for their compatriots — but some of these will soon attract citizens, and the more successful may in time cater only to citizens. And, as immigrants expand geographically, so also will ethnic restaurants, until at some point the ethnic foods will lose their ethnic character and become a part of the diet of citizens, and will be found in grocery stores and fast food restaurants. In addition to foods, the immigrants may introduce a few new words and terms to the native language, and perhaps some styles of clothing will also be taken over by members of the country of employment.

Another consequence of immigration is that many of the menial jobs are done and done at minimal cost to citizens. This allows them to live in greater luxury, free of the demands of the more onerous tasks. Thus, the status quo is preserved to an extent, and short-run harmony is maintained.

Some of these things also occur, and perhaps at a faster rate, during wartime, when alien soldiers reside in the nation, either as allies or as occupying enemy soldiers. In this there is a period of temporary and forced immigration; the immigrant is a military person, and may occupy a superordinate position relative to the citizen, or at least does not occupy a subordinate position as does the typical immigrant.

Consequences for the society of origin

Three distinct consequences for the society of origin can be discerned. In the first place immigration may relieve population pressure. Second, to the extent that immigrants send money to relatives remaining in their native country, immigration may have favourable effects on the balance of payments of the society of origin and certainly contributes something to the wealth of individual members, if not to society as a whole. Third, and to the extent that immigrants return periodically to their native society (as with Yugoslavs, Italians and Spaniards who move back and forth between Southern and Northern Europe), the customs of the native society may become modified by those of the country of employment. Returning immigrants bring new ideas, ways of thinking, dress and the like.

The migrant as a social problem

At the same time that migrants are used and exploited by many citizens of the country to which they have migrated, and are feared or rejected by other citizens, there is also a small number of people who see the presence of the migrants as a social problem — that is, a problem in that they need aid and support in finding a place in and assimilating to the country of employment, which they now take as their own, if even for only a short time. The aid and support is direct aid in the form of educational programmes and various social services (e.g. securing or providing housing) for migrants; and indirect aid in the form of trying to alter the ways in which the surrounding society treats the immigrant.

In any industrial society there is disagreement and conflict (which is one essential feature of social problems) among citizens around the issue of immigration and immigrants. Presumably, the governmental policy reflects the wishes and ideas of a majority of its citizens. But unless the immigrant is completely *persona non grata*, there will be both public and private efforts to help the migrant adjust to his or her new environment.

The problematic issues (some of which are not articulated by the citizens of the host society) include the following:

1 To what degree should immigrants give up (or be forced to give up) the customs of their native country and take on the ways of the country of employment?

2 Should special programmes be devised for migrants, or should they adapt and assimilate to the host society in whatever 'natural' and haphazard way that occurs?

3 If special programmes should be devised, what kind?

4 How can the programmes be implemented most effectively and efficiently?

5 What role should immigrants have in the design and implementation of such programmes?

6 To what degree should immigrants or their offspring be accorded special, and perhaps preferential, treatment — as a remedy for early prejudicial treatment?

Citizens and immigrants will disagree in their answers to these questions. For example, some individuals will believe that immigrants should be allowed to retain their language and customs even though they are in an alien society; these individuals may further believe that members of the country of employment should learn, to some degree, the language of the immigrants. Modern industrial society is viewed as heterogeneous and diverse, with room for different ways of living. Other citizens will not accept this; they believe that the immigrant should assimilate completely and become like the citizen. Many immigrants will also share this view.

And opposing answers will be given to the other questions above. Some individuals, for example, will try to promote special programmes for migrants, and others will say that no special programmes are needed: the immigrant should make his way on his own. In a society such as the USA, which has had multiple waves of immigration, citizens will justify this latter viewpoint by citing the experience of their ancestors who were immigrants and did not have special programmes; but such justification is really not justification and additionally may reflect a faulty memory.

Case studies

The reader may see the chapters in this volume as quite diverse, and wonder why they are joined together in the same volume. We believe that the fact that both sets are concerned with migrant workers is sufficient justification for joining them together.

In these chapters, one can see either explicitly or implicitly a concern with two basic questions:

1. How do immigrants cope with the society of employment which to them is also an alien society?

2. How does the society of employment respond to and treat immigrants, who are seen as aliens?

Citizens of any society have the problem of feeding, clothing and housing themselves, which demands that they perform some useful activity — that each has some kind of a livelihood. Immigrants also have this problem, but they must solve it in the context of being limited in their knowledge of the social rules, one important set of rules being that of how to use the language and communicate with others. Over the long run, immigrants cope by doing work that citizens do not want to do (and their willingness to do this is the basis for whatever welcome and acceptance they receive) and by slowly assimilating, i.e. learning the social rules. The country of employment responds by attempting to ignore the immigrants. When citizens recognise their presence, it is frequently with the demand: 'Assimilate, and become like us, or return to your homeland'. And, if immigrants have some identifiable physical feature, such as dark skin colour or epicanthus (eye fold), citizens will shorten their demand to only the second half of the above paraphrase, because, in the minds of citizens, assimilation means to 'look like us'.

But, of course, matters are far more complex than the above would indicate; much more could be said that modifies and elaborates the relation between immigrant and citizen, as superficially articulated in the preceding paragraph. The chapters of this volume attempt to fill in the details, and provide a richer and more complete answer to the two questions stated above.

Rather than considering the chapters serially, I would like to point out some of the themes and major issues that are highlighted.

Economic dispossession

As we stated earlier, immigrants and migrant workers occupy the lowest social positions in the host society. As such, they receive the fewest rewards. They may be denied rights and privileges that the citizen receives as an unquestioned matter of course. While today's migrant worker may not be enslaved, as was one sizeable segment of immigrants to the New World, the immigrants of today have few resources that can be used to confront the vicissitudes of life — and some of those vicissitudes are unique to immigrant status.

If immigrants are dispossessed, women and children are doubly so, because to be a woman or child is to occupy a subordinate status in the donor society (as in the country of employment, also). Thus the dispossession that comes from being an immigrant is compounded by the additional dispossession of being female. This theme is clearly evident in the three chapters on female immigrants.

The integrity of immigrant culture

A second theme is the obvious notion that immigrants bring with them the culture of their homelands and this is a powerful force affecting their adaptation to their new environment; in particular, it affects the attempts to provide them language training. These themes are implicit, if not explicit, in each of the chapters, but they are articulated in a particularly insightful manner in the chapter on the situation of Turkish women by Kudat (Chapter 8).

Lack of success in language training programmes

In reading the four chapters on language training the reader gains the impression that the diverse language training programmes have been less than successful. The idea is particularly pronounced in the chapter by Swetland and her assistants, but it is seen in the chapter by Dittmar and his colleagues (that in Germany, language training 'in the aggregate, amounts to very little' and 'practices like those in Sweden should be instituted in the FRG') and is elliptically evident in the chapter by Catani and his co-workers. Cicourel discusses the factors in the failure of bilingual education programmes in the USA. In this we see the social scientist functioning as critic of society, saying, in effect, to the society being observed: 'You are not doing what you think you are doing'.

These, then, are three major themes that emerge from these chapters; other ideas of less prominence (e.g. the degree to which immigrants learn a second language is dependent on the amount of contact they have with natives; training projects reflect the needs of teachers more than the needs of the students and the like) will be evident, but the reader may derive these to his own convenience. It is necessary to state that research on the situation of migrant workers is extremely difficult and evaluation research of language training programmes for migrants is even more difficult. That realisation, I believe, will make us appreciate the efforts of these diverse social scientists and will lead us to again commend Unesco for its continued work in trying to improve the lot of the world's people — many of whom are migrants or refugees.